Irish Nationalists in America

Irish Nationalists in America

The Politics of Exile, 1798–1998

DAVID BRUNDAGE

OXFORD
UNIVERSITY PRESS

OXFORD

UNIVERSITY PRESS

Oxford University Press is a department of the University of Oxford. It furthers
the University's objective of excellence in research, scholarship, and education
by publishing worldwide. Oxford is a registered trade mark of Oxford University
Press in the UK and certain other countries.

Published in the United States of America by Oxford University Press
198 Madison Avenue, New York, NY 10016, United States of America.

© Oxford University Press 2016

Library of Congress Cataloging-in-Publication Data
Names: Brundage, David Thomas, 1951–
Title: Irish nationalists in America : the politics of exile, 1798–1998 /
David Brundage.
Description: Oxford : Oxford University Press, 2016. | Includes
bibliographical references and index.
Identifiers: LCCN 2015037327 | ISBN 978-0-19-533177-6 (hardback : acid-free paper)
Subjects: LCSH: Irish—United States—History. |
Nationalists—Ireland—History. | Exiles—United States—History. |
Political activists—United States—History. | Irish—United
States—Politics and government. | Irish Americans—United
States—Politics and government. | Ireland—Relations—United States. |
United States—Relations—Ireland.
Classification: LCC E184.I6 B88 2016 | DDC 327.73041709/034—dc 3 LC record available at
http://lccn.loc.gov/2015037327

1 3 5 7 9 8 6 4 2
Printed by Sheridan, USA

Earlier versions of material in this book appeared as "Matilda Tone in America: Exile, Gender, and Memory
in the Making of Irish Republican Nationalism," *New Hibernia Review* 14, no. 1 (Spring 2010): 96–111,
© The University of St. Thomas, and "'In Time of Peace, Prepare for War': Key Themes in the Social Thought
of the New York's Irish Nationalists, 1890–1916," *The New York Irish*. Ed. Ronald H. Bayor and Timothy J.
Meagher. pp. 321–334. © 1996 The Johns Hopkins University Press. Reprinted with permission of Johns
Hopkins University Press.

CONTENTS

ACKNOWLEDGMENTS

This book has been many years in the making and it is a pleasure to finally acknowledge the friends, colleagues, and fellow researchers who have helped me along the way. My deepest thanks go to Kerby Miller and Kevin Kenny. Both scholars have been enthusiastic supporters of this project from the beginning and both have been wonderfully generous with their time and their insights. It goes without saying that neither of them should be held responsible for any errors of fact or interpretation in the pages that follow.

Many other people have provided me with help at various points, providing leads, sharing ideas, or commenting on parts of the research that I have presented at scholarly conferences. For this invaluable help, I am grateful to Eric Arensen, James Barrett, Ronald Bayor, Francis Carroll, Marion Casey, Kathleen Conzen, Francis Devine, Jay Dolan, David Doyle, Joe Doyle, Catherine Egan, David Emmons, Terrence Fitzmorris, Joshua Freeman, Tom Garvin, Luke Gibbons, Robert Grace, James Gregory, Ronald Grele, Rick Halpern, Brian Hanley, Tom Hayden, Dirk Hoerder, Ely Janis, Aki Kalliomäki, Patricia Kelleher, Laura Kelley, Alison Kibler, Bruce Levine, Niamh Lynch, James McCloskey, Elizabeth McKillen, April Masten, Timothy Meagher, Theresa Moriarty, José Moya, Angela Murphy, Gary Nash, Miriam Nyhan, Sean Prendiville, James Rogers, Dorothee Schneider, Moira Tierney, Robin Whitaker, David Wilson, and Howard Winant.

Archivists and librarians have assisted me at every turn. I would especially like to thank the able staffs of the National Library of Ireland and of the McHenry Library at the University of California, Santa Cruz. My work received support from an Irish Research Fund Award from the Irish American Cultural Institute and a Summer Stipend from the National Endowment for the Humanities, as well as from a number of grants from UCSC's Social Sciences Division and its Academic Senate Committee on Research.

It has been a true pleasure to work with Susan Ferber at Oxford University Press. Every page of this book has been improved by her insightful comments and detailed suggestions. I would also like to thank production manager Maya Bringe and copy editor Patterson Lamb for their expert help in transforming the manuscript into this book. The final work also benefited immensely from the astute and thorough comments provided by two anonymous readers for the press.

Finally, I would like to thank Susan Stuart and Jonah Stuart Brundage, both of whom lived with this book for longer than they would have liked. In what seems like a thousand conversations over the years, Susan and Jonah helped me think through and clarify many of the ideas in this work and both of them read drafts of the manuscript at various stages of completion. Most of all, I want to thank them for their support and for their love.

Irish Nationalists in America

Introduction

Exile is the nursery of nationality.

—Lord Acton (1862)

On October 8, 1996, a small gathering organized by the Irish-American Labor Coalition took place in Brooklyn's Green-Wood Cemetery to honor a long-dead Irish nationalist named Matilda Tone. Several dozen people looked on as Mary Robinson, president of the Republic of Ireland, unveiled a painstakingly restored headstone marking Tone's grave and eulogized her for her efforts to lead Ireland toward a "nonsectarian, democratic and inclusive politics." Referring to the dedication of statues of the former American first lady Eleanor Roosevelt and the jazz singer Ella Fitzgerald several days earlier, the Irish president observed that it was "a good week for women in New York City." But who was this woman that Robinson and the others celebrated?[1]

Matilda Tone had lived a hard life, one scarred by exile and loss. Born in Dublin in 1769, she was not yet thirty when her husband, the United Irishman Theobald Wolfe Tone, committed suicide in a Dublin prison on the eve of his execution for treason in 1798. She was widowed again when her second husband, Thomas Wilson, died in 1824. She lost all three of her children to tuberculosis. Matilda Tone herself lived to the age of eighty. But it was a life of exile, first in the United States, then in France, finally in America again. "Here I am for thirty years in this country and I have never had an easy hour, longing after my native land," she told a visitor from Ireland in 1849, two weeks before her death.[2]

Matilda Tone never wielded a firearm nor harangued a crowd, and, as a woman living in the eighteenth and nineteenth centuries, she was never even able to cast a ballot. Yet she made an absolutely essential contribution to the cause of Irish nationalism. She used her energy, intellect, and imagination in a determined struggle to keep the cause of Irish republican nationalism alive in the wake of its disastrous defeat in the bloody rebellion of 1798. Her painstaking efforts to gather, preserve, and edit her first husband's papers culminated in the 1826 publication of a massive two-volume work entitled *Life of Theobald*

Wolfe Tone. And it was from the pages of these volumes—poignant, witty, and possessing what one modern critic calls "the radiant quality of a romantic art-work"—that Wolfe Tone emerged as the profoundly compelling hero, martyr, and symbol he became to subsequent generations of Irish nationalists in Ireland, the United States, and throughout the Irish diaspora. Though the precise meaning and value of his republican ideals and convictions would be matters of debate for decades to come, the central place of his life and beliefs in the Irish nationalist tradition had been assured.[3]

A practice of selectively quoting from Wolfe Tone's writings over the years has allowed Irish figures as varied as Catholic nationalists, nonsectarian liberals, mainstream politicians, and activists of the socialist and communist left to claim him as one of their own. By the late twentieth century, however, it was the republican movement in Northern Ireland that most forcefully claimed his mantle and cultivated his memory. Sinn Féin and the Provisional Irish Republican Army began celebrating the anniversary of Tone's birth in the 1970s, and at a 1980 commemoration at his gravesite in Bodenstown, County Kildare, the Sinn Féin leader Gerry Adams first acknowledged his organization's "failure to develop revolutionary politics and to build a strong political alternative to so-called constitutional politics." Sinn Féin's subsequent embrace of electoral politics, furthered by the 1981 Hunger Strike, eventually paved the way for the Northern Irish peace process. When Adams visited New York in September 1997, on the eve of the all-party talks that would lead to the 1998 Good Friday peace agreement, Matilda Tone's influence and that of her husband hovered over the trip. The enthusiastic crowd that attended Adams's Roseland Ballroom appearance, for example, was treated to "feisty rebel songs" performed by a popular Irish folk music group called the Wolfe Tones.[4]

This book provides a history of Irish nationalists in the United States from the 1790s to the 1990s, from the era of Wolfe Tone to that of Gerry Adams. As the labors of Matilda Tone demonstrate, the Irish in America had an enormous impact on the course of nationalism back in Ireland. The influence of Irish immigrants and Irish Americans has been consequential, especially on republican and so-called physical force nationalists, who looked time and again to what they sometimes called "our greater Ireland" for support. The oath-bound Fenian Brotherhood, for example, which sought Irish independence from Britain through force of arms, was founded nearly simultaneously in Dublin and New York in 1858–59 and quickly gathered a following among the Famine migrants to North America so large that the one-time Fenian and land reformer Michael Davitt would salute the American Irish as "the avenging wolfhound of Irish nationalism." Half a century later, Irish American republicans were among those who took part in the planning of the 1916 Dublin Easter Rising and, in the subsequent five years, built a mass movement in the United States that raised millions of dollars in support of Irish independence. Fifty years later, in the deadly conflict that convulsed Northern Ireland from the late 1960s to the late 1990s, what the Belfast-born journalist Jack Holland memorably called "the American connection" provided a steady stream of guns and money to the IRA.[5]

Moderate and so-called constitutional nationalists in Ireland long benefited from an American connection of their own. The towering barrister and politician Daniel O'Connell, for example, who vehemently opposed both republicanism and the resort to physical force, developed an extensive network of American associations in the 1840s as an integral part of his campaign to repeal the Act of Union that bound Britain and Ireland together in a single political unit. The charismatic parliamentary leader Charles Stewart Parnell captivated audiences throughout the United States, including a historic session of the US House of Representatives, during his 1880 speaking tour to build support for the related aim of Irish Home Rule. Parnell's political successor, John Redmond, relied so heavily on Irish American financial support in the early twentieth century that his opponents called him the "Dollar Dictator." More recently, Northern Ireland's constitutional nationalist John Hume helped orchestrate moderate Irish American political pressure on President Bill Clinton that shaped the critical role his administration played in the Northern Irish peace process.[6]

Irish nationalists also exerted considerable influence on political and social developments in the United States, a second theme of this study. Exiled members of the United Irishmen, for example, became central figures in Thomas Jefferson's Republican Party in the early nineteenth century, and thousands of Fenians later served with valor and distinction as Union army soldiers and officers during the American Civil War. American supporters of Michael Davitt's Irish Land League put a distinctive stamp on labor and political reform movements in the Gilded Age, while Irish American nationalists played a key role in pressing the United States Senate to reject membership in the League of Nations after World War I. In more recent times, supporters of Irish nationalism played an important part in what some have called the "roots" phenomenon, the ethnic revival that was a major feature of the American cultural landscape in the 1970s and 1980s. Thus, while a history of Irish American nationalism reveals a great deal about Ireland, it also sheds considerable light on the history of the United States.

Finally, this work contributes to an understanding of what some contemporary social scientists have called "long-distance" or "diaspora" nationalism, the phenomenon of nationalist activity and enthusiasm among far-flung groups of emigrants, exiles, or refugees. Groups as diverse as Haitians in New York, Slovenians in Australia, and Tamils in Norway have organized nationalist movements in recent years, using email, the Internet, cell phones, and electronic money transfers to achieve political objectives in homelands sometimes literally on the other side of the world. In the present era, when some 217 million people worldwide live outside the countries of their birth and when nationalism remains a powerful political force, long-distance nationalism demands attention. While sometimes drawing inspiration from Lord Acton's proposition, offered more than 150 years ago, that "exile is the nursery of nationality," many commentators regard this phenomenon as essentially a product of contemporary trends, such as globalization, multiculturalism, the emergence of new communication technologies, and the spread of transnational human rights ideologies. This book underscores that, at least in the Irish case, long-distance nationalism is as old as nationalism itself.[7]

Nationalism may be old, but it has been far from unchanging. One of the main objectives of this study is to delineate the continuities and discontinuities in the history of Irish American nationalism. Naturally, the nationalist impulse responded to changing social and political conditions in Ireland and the United States, but other important alterations occurred as well. Over the course of two centuries, for example, the balance of power between constitutional and physical force nationalists in America fluctuated dramatically, with one or the other usually attaining dominance for significant periods of time. At a deeper level, the animating ideas and concerns of Irish nationalists on both sides of the Atlantic shifted, in one era inspired by the republican and secular ideals of the American and French revolutions, at others permeated with a deeply Catholic sensibility, and at yet others influenced by agrarian or working-class demands for land, labor rights, and a political voice for the poor. At certain moments, Irish nationalists dramatically expanded their social and political vision, linking their struggle to causes such as the abolition of slavery, women's rights, and freedom for British colonial subjects in India and Africa, while at others they narrowed their outlook, consciously avoiding or rejecting such "extraneous" concerns and connections. In some periods, Irish nationalism's base of support in the United States shrank to a small cadre of diehard activists, while in others it erupted as a genuine mass movement, drawing to its ranks not only large numbers of Irish Americans but also significant numbers of non-Irish men and women. Such non-Irish supporters, however, could occupy vastly different social locations, from Robert Tyler, the pro-slavery son of a sitting president who became a leader of O'Connell's American repeal network in the 1840s, to Marcus Garvey, the Jamaican-born African American nationalist who was an enthusiastic supporter of Irish republicanism in the 1910s and 1920s. Meanwhile, continuous improvements in the technologies of communication and transportation over these 200 years profoundly affected the geographic reach of the movement, forging increasingly tighter links between Irish nationalists in Ireland, America, and other locales as the world became steadily "smaller" over the decades.

Yet for all the vicissitudes that the following pages chronicle, there remained at least one constant. In America, as in Ireland itself, nationalism was never the unmediated expression of some kind of primordial Irish identity based on common language, religion, custom, or territory—though it certainly drew on all of these elements. It was, rather, throughout its history an ongoing work of political imagination and discursive invention. The point is exemplified by Matilda Tone's sustained and successful efforts to construct her husband as a potent symbol of Irish republicanism, but this example is one of many. Another is the effectiveness with which the Young Ireland writer and political exile, John Mitchel, developed and communicated a powerful (if historically inaccurate) interpretation of the Great Famine as an act of deliberate British genocide against the Irish people. This book's attention to such cases is not intended to minimize the destructive impact of British rule in Ireland but rather to underscore that its harshness alone did not automatically bring forth movements to challenge that rule. These challenges required the intervention of generations of activists, journalists, politicians, intellectuals, and artists, whose ideological labor this book details. Rather than providing ammunition for a critique of nationalism, in the manner of what in Ireland is often called "historical revisionism," their story empirically substantiates the single most important insight advanced by recent theorists of the phenomenon: its manufactured, invented, or, to use Benedict Anderson's signature term, "imagined" character.[8]

This book is the first comprehensive history of Irish American nationalism, tracking it from its beginnings in the early American republic to the later stages of the Northern Irish peace process in the 1990s. Numerous scholarly articles, essays, and monographs have analyzed specific aspects or periods of Irish nationalism's history in the United States, and the topic figures prominently in works on the Irish immigrant experience. Other works also take a diasporic perspective, notably Kerby Miller's masterly *Emigrants and Exiles*, which presents Irish American nationalism as the prime expression of a powerful sense of exile among Irish immigrants to America. Deeply homesick, predisposed to see all emigration as involuntary, and resistant to the culture of individualism and materialism they encountered in America, Irish migrants experienced very high levels of alienation, leading to a strong Irish American commitment to homeland nationalism during the nineteenth and early twentieth centuries.[9]

The most influential study of the phenomenon, Thomas Brown's *Irish-American Nationalism*, published in 1966, explained it not as the expression of a diasporic culture but as a manifestation of almost the exact opposite: a powerful hunger on the part of Irish immigrants and their descendants for social acceptance, respectability, and upward mobility. Less a response to Britain's domination of Ireland than to their own bitter experiences with poverty and prejudice in the United States, the enthusiasm of Irish Americans for Ireland's struggle for political independence represented an effort to elevate their own status in the United States, for they believed that Americans would only grant them the respect they craved if their homeland was free.[10]

While the insights of these scholars have informed the present work in many ways, the overall emphasis of this book is different. Echoing research on contemporary long-distance nationalism, *Irish Nationalists in America* will show that Irish American nationalism was pioneered in the 1790s and then repeatedly rejuvenated as late as the 1970s and 1980s, by actual (not metaphorical) political exiles who, much like Matilda Tone, "never had an easy hour," longing after their native land. Although their abiding sense of displacement, alienation, and loss was nothing less than a tragedy for such men and women, it breathed life into the Irish nationalist project as a whole.[11]

This work draws on a wide range of newspapers, memoirs, and political documents from different eras as well as on archival sources in the United States and Ireland. To extend its scope beyond Ireland and the United States, for both a comparative and transnational approach, it also draws on a large body of published research. Because Irish nationalism took root throughout the Irish diaspora, there are brief comparative discussions of Irish nationalist activity in Britain as well as the colonies or former colonies of the British Empire, particularly Canada and Australia, where the Irish settled. Even more central is a transnational perspective: Irish nationalism was, throughout its history, an almost textbook example of a transnational phenomenon, one involving the movement of people and the exchange of ideas, information, money, and—on some occasions—arms and ammunition between Ireland and a global network of Irish settlements, the most important of which was the United States. Such transnational exchanges and connections are central to this book's analysis.[12]

Like diasporic political movements in other times and places, Irish nationalism in America encompassed at least three analytically distinct groups of people: leaders, including the movement's founders; rank-and-file activists, the "militant minority" without whom the movement could not have functioned; and members of the larger imagined community (especially the Irish American ethnic community) that leaders and activists regarded as potential supporters. Although this book endeavors to give each of these groups its due, any history of Irish nationalism should begin with its founders. The most important of these was Theobald Wolfe Tone, who also happened to be one of the first Irish political exiles to make his way to American shores. Tone's life thus provides the logical starting point.[13]

Subsequent chapters take the story chronologically from Tone's death in 1798 to the 1998 Good Friday Agreement, which, by bringing the bitter conflict in Northern Ireland to a kind of resolution, provides an equally logical endpoint. Irish nationalism in America over the course of these 200 years was a complex phenomenon, sometimes displaying the "nonsectarian, democratic and inclusive politics" that characterized the outlook of Matilda Tone and sometimes presenting a much narrower face, shaped by the larger structures of social inequality in Ireland and the United States. Regardless of the generation in question, Irish nationalists have proven time and again that exile, forced or voluntary, temporary or permanent, is the "nursery of nationality," just as Acton observed.

The Transatlantic Odyssey
of Theobald Wolfe Tone

Wolfe Tone hated America. The man generally acknowledged as the founder of Irish republican nationalism resided as a political exile in the new American republic from August to December 1795. Throughout these five months, spent mainly in Philadelphia and the New Jersey countryside, Tone filled his journals and letters with expressions of distaste for the sweltering Pennsylvania summer and Philadelphia's high cost of living, "three times as dear as at Paris, or even London." He also developed "a most unqualified dislike" for the American people. He ridiculed the "boorish ignorance" of New Jersey's farmers and castigated the residents of Philadelphia as "a churlish, unsocial race, totally absorbed in making money." Tone's greatest fear in these months was that his adored young daughter, Maria, would grow up to be the wife of an American. "I could better bear to see her dead," he wrote.[1]

Nonetheless, America had a significant influence on Tone. His experience of exile deepened his sense of his own Irish national identity while sharpening his republican ideals in the forge of America's bitter partisan conflict. In both his involvement in the tumult of American politics and his intense feelings of displacement and alienation, Tone's experiences prefigured those of many future Irish nationalists in the United States. Equally important, the evolution of his outlook during the longer period from 1789 to 1798 prefigured the critical fault lines of race, class, and gender that would mark Irish American nationalism as a whole over the next 200 years.

The Making of a Nationalist

Theobald Wolfe Tone was born in 1763, the eldest son of a middle-class and moderately prosperous Dublin coachbuilder. Though his mother had been a Catholic, she converted to Protestantism in 1771, and her son was raised in the established Anglican Church, the Church of Ireland. A bright if somewhat lazy student, Tone won admission to Dublin's elite Trinity College and by the time of his graduation in 1786, he had read widely, made many influential friends, and emerged as a leading figure in the College Historical Society, a prestigious debating club that groomed its members for inclusion in Ireland's political elite. By this time he had also eloped with the sixteen-year-old Martha Witherington, whom he rechristened "Matilda" after the character in a popular historical tragedy of the day. Following the birth of their daughter, Maria, he left his family and set off for London to study law. But Tone found legal study a bore and spent most of his time attending plays, concocting a plan for a British military colony in the South Pacific, and engaging in what he called "adventures with the fair sex." Although he returned to Dublin and his family in 1789 to begin a legal practice, he "soon got sick and weary of the law" and turned his attention instead to politics. Joining Dublin's new Whig Club and cultivating the connections he had made at Trinity, Tone was by 1790 setting his sights on a seat in the Irish Parliament. "I now looked upon myself as a sort of political character," he later wrote, "and began to suppose that the House of Commons, and not the Bar, was to be the scene of my future exertions."[2]

The Irish Parliament of Tone's day both reflected and reinforced the country's deep social inequalities. A small Anglican landed upper class, just then beginning to be called the Protestant Ascendancy, exercised political power both through the House of Lords, made up of hereditary peers and bishops of the Church of Ireland, and the House of Commons, a large majority of whose 300 members were selected in the country's boroughs, where irregular and highly restricted franchises gave local political patrons a great deal of power. As was true throughout Europe and in all but one of the states of the US republic, women were excluded entirely from the right to vote. So too were propertyless men, since even in the counties, where the franchise was uniform, voters were required to hold property worth at least forty shillings. And, finally, so too were all adherents of the Catholic faith, representing about 70 percent of Ireland's 4 million people. Men who were Presbyterian (a dissenting religious faith practiced by about 13 percent of the population, concentrated overwhelmingly in the northern province of Ulster) often met the property qualification for voting but not the greater one for holding office. All of this effectively made both houses of the Irish Parliament the voice of the Ascendancy. Not only Catholics, but also northern Presbyterians of middling wealth, deeply resented these political restrictions and the latter group, in particular, formed a key constituency for reform.[3]

The law disenfranchising Ireland's Catholics had been enacted in 1727, one of a body of parliamentary statutes known as the penal code that also prevented them from carrying arms, buying land or inheriting land from Protestants, and practicing the professions, except medicine. At various times in the eighteenth century, their church and clergy had been proscribed as well, though the over-riding purpose of the penal laws was less the destruction of the Catholic faith than the weakening of Catholic Ireland's political and military capacity—a matter of great concern to Protestants even after the decisive victory of William of Orange's forces over those of Catholic-supported James II in 1690–91. Some of the laws had been enforced only intermittently and reform measures passed in 1774, 1778, and 1782 had weakened the penal code as a whole. By the early 1790s, what contemporaries called the "Catholic question" meant mainly the efforts of propertied Catholic men to regain the vote and take up seats in the Irish Parliament.[4]

Another important characteristic of this Parliament had long been what many in Ireland regarded as its humiliating subordination to the British government. A sequence of dramatic events, beginning with the American Revolution, began to alter this state of affairs. With the sudden departure of thousands of British troops from Ireland to fight the Americans and subsequent declarations of war from France and Spain, a part-time and independent military force called the Volunteers sprang up to defend the island against the threat of French invasion. Overwhelmingly middle class and Protestant, the Volunteers grew rapidly, numbering as many as 80,000 at their peak in 1782. Nearly every week of Tone's first year at Trinity, Dublin's streets and squares reverberated with the sounds of the Volunteers' parades, reviews, and musket salutes, intensifying a romantic attraction to military pursuits that the young man had evinced since boyhood. The Volunteer movement also took on a wider political importance when it provided extra-parliamentary support for the political program of the so-called Patriots, led by Henry Flood and Henry Grattan.[5]

Grattan, a commanding parliamentary orator much admired by Tone and his fellow members of the College Historical Society, personified the newly assertive movement for a greater measure of Irish political autonomy. Capitalizing on both Britain's preoccupation with the American war and the barely veiled threat of thousands of armed Volunteers marching in the streets, he mustered the Patriot forces in Parliament to fight for a significant expansion of Irish commercial and political rights. Under the circumstances, Britain had little choice but to give in. In what Patriot leaders would call the "Revolution of 1782," the government repealed the humiliating Declaratory Act of 1720, which had given the British Parliament the power to legislate for Ireland "in all cases whatsoever," and amended Poynings's Law (originally enacted in 1494), which had prohibited the Irish Parliament from initiating legislation on its own. Ireland was no longer a colony, Grattan thundered on the eve of victory, but a nation, "manifesting ourself to the world in every simple instance of glory."[6]

Nonetheless, as Tone would later decry, other forms of British domination, only slightly more subtle, continued to exist. Despite the new arrangements, the king of England remained by law the king of Ireland and his lord lieutenant, or viceroy, was the country's chief executive. Operating out of Dublin Castle, just a few hundred yards west of the Parliament, the lord lieutenant and his various secretaries and under-secretaries constituted the political administration of Ireland as a branch of the British government. "Managing" the ostensibly independent Irish Parliament with the help of a trio of talented, ambitious, and relentlessly pro-British Members of Parliament (MPs) known as the "three Jacks" (John Foster, John Fitzgibbon, and John Beresford) was one of this administration's main tasks, giving rise to the cry of "bribery and corruption" among political reformers.[7]

These reformers, determined to realize what they saw as the unfulfilled promise of 1782, began a new campaign to extend Irish autonomy and democratize the Irish Parliament. Rebuilding the alliance of Patriots in Parliament and Volunteers in the streets, they called for more frequent parliamentary elections, an increase in the number of MPs, an end to "rotten boroughs" (election districts so small that they could be dominated by a single large patron or districts with no electors at all), and an extension of the franchise. Unlike its forerunner, the campaign of 1783–85 ended in total defeat, in large part because most of the reformers drew back sharply at the prospect of extending political rights to Catholics. As one Dublin reformer put it, the Catholic question was "the rock we have split on." Tone himself would later remark that the reformers were bound to fail: by refusing to fight for the enfranchisement of Catholics they had "planned an edifice of freedom on a foundation of monopoly."[8]

What revived and simultaneously transformed the reform movement was the growth of a powerfully felt nationalist sentiment among many people in Ireland, an intensified belief in the primacy of the "nation" as a community of people with the right to have that community reflected in particular political arrangements, specifically a much greater degree of political autonomy from Britain. While such nationalist sentiments had some historic roots in Ireland, the most important catalyst for their full emergence in the modern era was the French Revolution, especially the dramatic series of events that transpired in the summer of 1789. The creation of the National Assembly to replace the old "estates" of nobles and clergy in June, the fall of the Bastille in July, and the National Assembly's promulgation of the Declaration of the Rights of Man and the Citizen in August—all breathlessly reported in Irish newspapers—provided a powerful stimulus to nationalism in Ireland. Many in Ireland watched transfixed as revolutionaries sought to liberate the French people from the intertwined tyrannies of monarchy and aristocracy, replacing these with what they regarded as the more legitimate authority of the nation. "The principle of all sovereignty rests essentially in the nation," asserted the third article of the Declaration of the

Rights of Man. "No body and no individual may exercise authority which does not emanate expressly from the nation."[9]

It was in this highly charged milieu that the young Wolfe Tone began his metamorphosis from failed lawyer and aspiring Whig politician to dedicated propagandist for a nonsectarian Irish nationalism. In his pamphlet, *Spanish War!* published in the summer of 1790, he began inching toward a view that would come to define Irish republican nationalism for the next two centuries, that Ireland needed to fully separate from England. Tone's pamphlet was prompted by the looming threat of war between Britain and Spain over access to the Pacific Coast of North America and the Irish Parliament's rush to provide funds for a possible British war effort. Though the Irish Whigs regarded themselves as a parliamentary opposition on many issues, when it came to defending the British Empire, they were very much a loyal opposition. As their leader, Henry Grattan, proclaimed, Ireland would "rise or fall with Great Britain."[10]

Wolfe Tone disagreed. He began *Spanish War!* by posing the question of "whether the Parliament and people of Ireland be, of right, bound to support a war, declared by the King of Great Britain, on motives and interests purely British." His answer—which he realized might well "appear extraordinary" to many—was that Ireland was not so bound, that it had a constitutional and moral right to remain neutral, and that its own national interests dictated that it should do so. Tone argued his position with biting sarcasm, heaping scorn on stock phrases such as "the good of the empire." The pamphlet constituted a frontal assault on the assumptions of the compromise of 1782, because the monarchy that Ireland and Britain still shared implied a shared foreign policy. Tone not only called for an Irish foreign policy built on Irish national interests, but for an Irish army and navy, an Irish flag, and even Irish colonies. He pleaded with the Irish Parliament to take a stand, "fixing the rank of your country among the nations of the earth."[11]

The publication of *Spanish War!* immediately ended Tone's career with the Whigs, with one parliamentary leader fuming that "if the author of that work is serious, he ought to be hanged." But Tone's separatist sentiments only grew stronger over the next few years. In a letter to a Dublin newspaper in July 1793, he pronounced that he could only support Ireland's connection with England if "a speedy and effectual check be given to the continuance of existing abuses and corruption." If that did not occur, and he thought the prospect highly unlikely, he "would hold it a sacred duty to endeavour by all possible means to break it." Tone was even more forceful in his private correspondence. "My unalterable opinion is that the Bane of Irish prosperity in [*sic*] the influence of England," he wrote to his friend, Thomas Russell, in July 1791. "I believe that influence will ever be exerted while the connexion between the Countries continues." Separation from England, Tone concluded, stating a view that would become an article of faith for Irish republican nationalists for the next two centuries, "would be a *regeneration* for this Country."[12]

Russell, whom Tone had first met in the Irish House of Commons gallery while watching the parliamentary debate on war with Spain, concurred. Born the son of a British army officer in County Cork in 1767, Russell had followed his father into the army, serving in India in the mid-1780s. He and Tone became fast friends and spent much of the summer of 1790 at the Tones' house in the Dublin seaside suburb of Irishtown, dining, walking, and discussing politics. "Russell and I were inseparable," Tone later recalled, "and, as our discussions were mostly political and our sentiments agreed exactly, we extended our views, and fortified each other in the opinions to the propagation and establishment of which we have ever since been devoted." These "happy days" came to an end in late August, when Russell was assigned to the 64th infantry regiment, then stationed in the northern town of Belfast.[13]

A growing commercial center of about 18,000 mostly Presbyterian inhabitants, Belfast was rapidly becoming Ireland's leading center of radical politics. Russell threw himself into the political whirlwind immediately. The French Revolution deeply inspired the town's radicals, who began celebrating Bastille Day in 1790. Tom Paine's spirited defense of the revolution, *Rights of Man*, took Ireland by storm the following year, going through seven editions and selling over 40,000 copies, twice as many as in England. Paine's earthy language and rich imagery, his impassioned attack on monarchy and other forms of despotism, and his clear explanation of the philosophy of natural rights accounted for much of the pamphlet's appeal. But resonating even more powerfully in Ireland was his stirring and open-ended conclusion: "From what we now see, nothing of reform in the political world ought to be held improbable," Paine wrote. "It is an age of Revolutions, in which every thing may be looked for." Nowhere was this message embraced more enthusiastically than Belfast, where lengthy extracts from the pamphlet were printed in the *Belfast News Letter*. As Tone observed in October 1791, in Belfast "Paine's book [is] the koran."[14]

In the same year, Belfast's radicals welcomed another political writer, Olaudah Equiano, a leading figure in the British movement to abolish the slave trade. Born in the 1740s, most likely in what is today Nigeria, Equiano had been kidnapped as a boy, sold into slavery, and subsequently transported across the Atlantic to the Americas. Sold in Virginia to a British naval officer, Equiano soon found himself working as a slave in England and as a navigator on a ship in the Caribbean. He learned to read and write, converted to Christianity, and by 1766 had saved enough money to purchase his freedom. Moving to England, he eventually found his way into the growing British anti-slavery movement and in 1789 published *The Interesting Narrative of the Life of Olaudah Equiano or Gustavus Vassa, the African,* a riveting autobiography that delivered a powerful political message against slavery. In May 1791, Equiano traveled to Ireland to arrange publication of a new edition of the book and spent the following eight months promoting it throughout the country. Nearly seventy Irish men and women subscribed to the new edition, and he eventually sold some 1,900 copies of his book in Ireland. "I found the people extremely hospitable," Equiano later recalled, "particularly in Belfast." Samuel Neilson, the son of a Presbyterian minister who was perhaps the most radical activist in the town—Tone would later nickname him "the Jacobin"—served as Equiano's patron during his stay. Other leading Belfast radicals, such as the watchmaker Thomas McCabe, who had successfully fought to keep the slave trade out of the Belfast port in the 1780s, and Thomas Digges, an American Catholic residing in Ireland, also provided support. By 1792, Belfast was becoming one of the leading anti-slavery centers in the Atlantic world, with radicals taking up the anti-slavery movement's nonconsumption of sugar and rum campaign and highlighting anti-slavery banners in their Bastille Day parade.[15]

Despite the flowering of this multidimensional political radicalism in Belfast, controversy over the "Catholic question" continued to stymie the movement for parliamentary reform, just as it had in the 1780s. Frustrated at this state of affairs, Thomas Russell wrote to Tone, asking him to propose some resolutions for discussion at a Volunteer demonstration in Belfast on Bastille Day 1791. Tone was happy to oblige and sent three, summarizing them in his diary as follows: "First that English influence in Ireland was the great grievance of the Country, 2d That the most effectual &c., &c., way to oppose it was by a reform in P[ar]l[iamen]t, & 3d that no reform could be just or efficacious which did not include the Catholics." When notified that, "contrary to all justice and expediency," the third resolution had been dropped, Tone angrily determined to become, as he put it, "a red hot Catholic." Just two weeks later, he published *An Argument on Behalf of the Catholics of Ireland*, one of the most significant and explosive documents in Irish political history.[16]

"To subvert the tyranny of our execrable government, to break the connection with England, the never-failing source of all our political evils, and to assert the independence of my country—these were my objects," Tone later recalled, summarizing his thinking as he sat down to write the pamphlet. "To unite the whole people of Ireland, to abolish the memory of all past dissensions, and to substitute the common name of Irishman in the place of the denominations of Protestant, Catholic and Dissenter—these were my means." Tone had concluded that Ireland's two great plagues, British domination and Irish sectarianism, were thoroughly intertwined. In a forthright style that owed much to Paine, he set out to convey this conclusion to as wide an audience as possible, and especially to his fellow Protestants.[17]

"I am a Protestant of the Church of Ireland as by law established," Tone began. "I am therefore, no further interested in the event than as a mere lover of justice, and a steady detester of tyranny, whether exercised by one man or one million." But he took strong issue with those among his fellow Irish Protestants who believed that Catholics were not "prepared for liberty." Not only were they so prepared, he argued, but there could be no liberty for anyone until "Irishmen of all denominations" united against those who ruled them and fought together for parliamentary reform. Echoing passages in *Spanish War!* Tone lamented that Ireland was "without pride or power, or name; without ambassadors, army or navy," but his nationalist sentiments went far beyond this. "The misfortune of Ireland is that we have *no National Government*," he proclaimed, but only "a Government derived from another country, whose interest, so far from being the same with that of the people, directly crosses it at right angles." Rather than producing an independent government, the settlement of 1782 had only "enabled Irishmen to sell at a higher price their honour, their integrity and the interests of their country," and—even worse—it "left three fourths of our countrymen slaves as it found them."[18]

In a pamphlet of just sixteen pages, Tone used the terms "slaves," "slavery," or "bondage" nearly a dozen times to describe the position of Ireland's Catholic population. "We prate and babble, and write books, and publish them, filled with sentiments of freedom and abhorrence of tyranny and lofty praises of *the Rights of Man!*" he wrote in one of the *Argument*'s angriest passages. "Yet we are content to hold three millions of our fellow creatures and fellow subjects in degradation and infamy and contempt, or, to sum up all in one word, in *slavery!*"[19]

By itself, Tone's choice of words was hardly noteworthy: the slavery metaphor had become commonplace in political writing throughout the eighteenth-century Atlantic world. Grattan and other Patriots used the metaphor frequently, claiming rhetorically that Albion had enslaved Hibernia, that trade regulations were commercial bondage, and that opposing politicians were slaves to corruption. Paine had used the term in *Rights of Man*, describing the storming of the Bastille as a contest of "freedom or slavery." The metaphor had been nearly ubiquitous during the American Revolution, even by the Revolution's leaders, many of whom were in fact large slaveholders. Paine had caught that contradiction incisively in 1775, when he had asked how Americans could "complain so loudly of attempts to enslave them while they hold so many hundreds of thousands in slavery."[20]

It was different for Tone. Like his friend Thomas Russell, who wrote impassioned essays against the enslavement of Africans and refused to eat or drink anything containing sugar, he strongly opposed the ownership and trade of human beings. It is certain that he knew Equiano's *Interesting Narrative* and probable that he came to know Equiano himself in Belfast in October 1791. To be sure, his evocation of the "slavery" of Ireland's Catholics remained a metaphor, not an assertion that their conditions were the same as those experienced by Africans in the Middle Passage or on the plantations of the New World. But, in Tone's hands, the metaphor became an expression of a commonality of interest and feeling between Irish Catholics (or Irishmen in general) and Africans. It revealed nascent Irish nationalism at its most expansive and made the *Argument* an important text in an Atlantic world that seemed to some to be literally churning with revolution.[21]

Tone's passages on economic inequality within Ireland, however, exposed a much more narrow and class-bound perspective. Responding to Protestant fears that once enfranchised, Catholics would simply take over the Irish Parliament, he argued that such a scenario was unrealistic in light of "the great disproportion of property, or in other words, power, in favour of the Protestants." Tone had absolutely no intention of challenging either this economic "disproportion," or the property qualification for voting that transformed "property" into "power." He even argued that Ireland should consider raising the property qualification for the vote from forty shillings to ten pounds, for Catholics and Protestants alike. "Thus will you at one stroke purge yourselves of the gross and feculent mass which contaminates the Protestant interest, and restore their natural and just weight to the sound and respectable part of the Catholic community."[22]

This was not simply an argument of expedience. In the early 1790s, Tone shared many of the fears and prejudices of Ireland's urban middle class. He showed little sympathy for the poor and regarded the Defenders, the agrarian protest movement of impoverished Catholic peasants spreading throughout rural Ulster, as "misguided and ignorant rabble." Hints of a different point of view did sometimes appear in his writings of these years. In pamphlets addressed to the weavers of Dublin's Liberties district in 1792 and 1793, Tone exhibited a more generous attitude toward the urban poor and their daily struggles to make ends meet. The poor, he wrote, were "a shrewd knowing people, who see a thing very quick." The *Argument,* on the other hand, was filled with condescending references to the political "ignorance" of the peasantry. Tone spoke for his class, even though he understood this class to include Catholics as well as Protestants.[23]

More accurately, he spoke for the men of his class, for Tone did not include women as potential actors in the political world he hoped to open to (propertied) Catholic men. This was typical of the period's republican writers in America, Britain, and France, as well as in Ireland, who drew a rigid line between men and women and excluded the latter from the body politic. A year after the *Argument* appeared, the British radical Mary Wollstonecraft launched a scathing attack on this way of thinking in *A Vindication of the Rights of Woman.* In Belfast, Martha McTier urged her fellow Irish reformers to read Wollstonecraft, as "*she too conspires to make an important change,*" and Thomas Russell was one of those who did, filling his personal journals with thoughts on the nature of sexual difference and speculating that "women in public offices" might well be "as clever as men." Tone, however, never reconsidered his refusal to admit women to the public realm.[24]

In the view of Tone and most republican writers, women lacked the quality of rational intellect that was essential for citizens and voters. This view was implicit in what was, rhetorically speaking, one of the most effective passages of the *Argument*, in which Tone implored his Protestant readers to put aside past fears and prejudices about Catholics. "Let us, for God's sake, shake off the old woman, the tales of our nurses, the terrors of our grandams [*sic*], from our hearts; let us put away childish fears, look our situation in the face like men," he wrote. "Let us speak to this ghastly spectre of our distempered imagination, the genius of Irish Catholicity! We shall find it vanish away like other phantoms of the brain, distempered by fear." Tone associated "woman" here with childish fears, tales, and phantoms; and "men" with the opposite—enlightened rational thought. A few paragraphs later, he introduced an imaginary character—"an old Protestant lady"—who disagreed with his argument and expressed irrational doubts and fears that the author could then quickly put to rest. If Tone's use of the slavery metaphor displayed nascent Irish nationalism at its most expansive, these representations of women, and the deeper political privileging of men, displayed it at its most closed and narrow. Propertied Catholic men might be "prepared for liberty," Tone believed, but women—rich or poor, Catholic or Protestant—were not.[25]

As a piece of political propaganda, the pamphlet's success was unqualified. *An Argument on Behalf of the Catholics of Ireland* sold 6,000 copies in 1791 and another 10,000 in 1792, making it, if not quite the *Rights of Man*, a definite bestseller. Catholics—or at least those "sound and respectable" Catholics whom Tone was concerned with—embraced it as the best presentation of their case to date. "A better pamphlet on that or any other subject I never read," wrote Dr. Hugh MacDermot to a fellow Catholic reform leader in November 1791. "It should become the manual of every person who is worthy of being an Irishman." But even more important, it influenced Presbyterian radicals in just the way Tone had hoped. By knitting together the cause of parliamentary reform with that of Catholic enfranchisement, the *Argument* struck a hard blow against their sectarian feelings that blocked the development of the Irish political reform movement.[26]

The pamphlet also made Tone himself a leading light among radicals, ensuring that he would be invited to participate in the founding of a new reform organization in Belfast. He readily accepted the invitation and in October 1791 arrived in the northern town to help establish what would be the Belfast Society of United Irishmen. Amid dining, sightseeing, and, as he noted in his diary, "a great deal of general politics *and wine*," Tone quickly became the dominant figure among the thirty-six founders of the new organization. He not only proposed the name "United Irishmen," but he also wrote the three resolutions, more radical versions of those he had written for the Volunteers back in July, which served as its ideological foundation. Among these was the resolution, passed unanimously, that "no reform is practicable, efficacious, or just, which shall not include *Irishmen* of every religious persuasion."[27]

Presbyterian and Anglican distrust of Catholics, of course, did not simply disappear overnight. But Tone had cause for optimism in early November, when he returned to Dublin to take part, along with the veteran reformers Dr. William Drennan and James Napper Tandy, in the founding of the Dublin Society of United Irishmen to advance the causes of parliamentary reform and Catholic emancipation. The initial membership of both societies was overwhelmingly middle class, with well-known Presbyterian merchants and manufacturers dominating the Belfast organization and the Dublin society attracting prominent Catholic and Protestant lawyers, physicians, merchants, textile manufacturers, and even a smattering of gentry. Though complaining bitterly about Britain's corruption of Ireland's institutions, the organization issued no call for national independence and even a year after its founding, Edmund Burke, the famed Irish critic of the French Revolution and republicanism, could characterize its views as "rational, manly, and proper." In light of Ireland's history of Catholic disenfranchisement, political corruption, and violent religious conflict, however, the range and depth of the United Irishmen's radicalism—even in their early years—was remarkable. "We have thought little about our ancestors—much about our posterity," the Dublin society proclaimed in a December 1791 circular. "Are we forever to walk like beasts of prey over fields which these ancestors stained with blood?"[28]

Tone would never play the critical role in the Dublin organization that he had in Belfast and with a family to support and little interest in practicing law, he was also seeking out avenues of employment. Naturally he jumped at the opportunity in July 1792 to become assistant secretary of the Catholic Committee, at the generous salary of 200 pounds a year. Formed in 1760, the Catholic Committee sought to give formal representation to the Catholic community of Ireland, but until the 1790s, it was extremely cautious in its outlook and mostly inactive. Beginning in 1791, however, under the new leadership of two wealthy Dublin merchants, John Keogh and Edward Byrne, the Catholic Committee grew more assertive, leading to an exodus of conservatives from its ranks, while creating a new set of worries for the British government. Tone threw himself into the work of the committee, traveling around the country to organize the election of delegates to a Catholic Convention in Dublin in December 1792. At this convention, the committee broke decisively with its past moderation, petitioning for "the total abolition of all distinctions" among Ireland's people. Responding to the perceived threat of Catholic militancy and its potential alliance with the new United Irishmen, as well as the looming certainty of war with France, the British government moved quickly to open up negotiations with the committee. Tone played an important role in these negotiations, which led to the passage of a Catholic Relief Act in 1793. Although the act granted the vote to proper-tied Catholic men, it did not permit them to hold seats in the Irish Parliament. Tone denounced this "radical defect of the bill" as "the last relic of interested bigotry" and urged opposition to it. But his was a minority voice. The Catholic Committee not only accepted the compromise but also dissolved itself as a body, confident in its eventual success. Tone was out of a job.[29]

Even while immersed in his work for the Catholic Committee, Tone had maintained his involvement with the United Irishmen by penning a number of articles for their newspaper, the *Northern Star*, which Samuel Neilson began publishing in Belfast twice weekly in January 1792. The *Northern Star* played an indispensable part in the society's early growth, soon reaching a circulation of between 4,000 and 5,000, larger than any other Irish newspaper of the era. The paper was international in its coverage, giving considerable attention to political developments in America, France, and Britain, and editorializing on a wide range of social and political issues, including the international slave trade, which it denounced, and Wollstonecraft's *Vindication of the Rights of Woman*, which it praised. Publishing a cheap edition of Paine's *Rights of Man*, compilations of Locke and Voltaire, and several iterations of a popular collection of poems and ballads called *Paddy's Resource*, the *Northern Star* exemplified the United Irishmen's efforts to use the printed word to spread their ideals among "mechanics, petty shop-keepers and farmers," who, in the view of Thomas Addis Emmet, an emerging leader in the organization, "wanted a practical engine, by which the power and exertions of men like themselves, might be most effectually combined and employed." The society, Emmet later recalled, worked tirelessly "to embrace the lower orders, and in fact make every man a politician."[30]

The reform program that the United Irishmen drew up in early 1793 reflected this deeply democratic perspective. Tone participated in the formulation of this plan, but it went well beyond his own 1791 *Argument*, with its defense of property qualifications for the franchise. The society now demanded the right to vote for all adult men in Ireland. There remained significant disagreements within the organization on this point, as well as over how far to go in address-ing the conditions of the Irish poor. "By Liberty we never understood unlim-ited freedom," explained William Drennan in December 1792, "nor by Equality the leveling of property, or the destruction of subordination." But other United Irishmen, especially in Ulster, held more radical views. The Belfast manufac-turer Henry Joy McCracken, Armagh's firebrand Catholic priest James Coigly, and a Presbyterian linen weaver from County Antrim named James Hope all supported aggressive measures to relieve the economic plight of the poor. So did Thomas Russell, who believed by 1793 that "property must be alter'd [sic] in some measure" if political reform were to be meaningful, remarking in his journal that "he who knew the recesses of the heart loved not the rich." Though most United Irishmen did not share such views, in an era when even those who considered themselves advanced reformers feared that universal manhood suffrage would inevitably lead to rule by "the mob," advocating this measure alone put the United Irishmen on the far left of the Irish political spectrum.[31]

Even as the society was hammering out its reform plan, the outbreak of war between Britain and France dramatically altered the political terrain. Stunned by France's rapid transition from constitutional to democratic revolution, the creation of a French republic, and the execution of Louis XVI in January 1793, the British government declared war on France in February. It also began a crackdown on radicals in both England and Ireland that left democratic reformers reeling. In England, the plebian democratic London Corresponding Society was outlawed, Paine's *Rights of Man* was banned, and what the government labeled "Jacobin" meetings were prohibited. In Ireland, the government suppressed the Volunteers, dealing a huge blow to United Irishmen who had hoped to rebuild the alliance of reformers and Volunteers that had led to the concessions of 1782, and formed a new Irish militia more fully controlled by Dublin Castle. It also outlawed extra-parliamentary conventions, another blow to the United Irishmen who were already laying plans for a series of nationwide reform conventions. Finally, the government went after reform publications, the *Northern Star* in particular. By the summer of 1794, no fewer than eight United Irishmen (including such key figures as William Drennan, Hamilton Rowan, and Napper Tandy) were facing trial for seditious writing. "Their great aim," observed Drennan, "is to get rid of us by prosecution, persecution, or the terror of it." While Drennan was eventually acquitted, others were convicted or ended up fleeing Ireland to avoid imprisonment.[32]

Tone was not arrested, but Lord Chancellor John Fitzgibbon personally denounced him, citing his "separatist" 1791 letter to Russell. This development, on top of the problems facing the political reform movement and his own financial difficulties, led Tone as early as July 1793 to consider emigration. William Todd Jones, a friend and fellow reformer from County Armagh then living in Pennsylvania, offered to introduce him to a wealthy acquaintance who was "possessed of large tracts of territory, and requires settlers." But Tone turned down the offer. When he set sail from Ireland two years later, it was as a political exile, not an ordinary emigrant.[33]

As the war progressed, the governments of both Britain and France began to look on the United Irishmen—still enthralled by the French Revolution despite the Terror of 1793–94—as a potential fifth column. In 1794, with repression growing and hopes of parliamentary reform fading fast, some of them responded enthusiastically when the Reverend William Jackson, an Irish-born agent of the French government, approached them to gauge the degree of support in Ireland for a possible French invasion. Tone went so far as to prepare a memorandum on French military aid. In April 1794, however, the Irish government arrested Jackson, convicting him of treason the following year. The Jackson affair gave the government a pretext to suppress the United Irishmen entirely, and in May 1794, police raided a meeting of the Dublin society and confiscated its papers.

While governmental repression was a serious blow to the organization, it also helped radicalize it, driving away moderates like Drennan and allowing more militant leaders to fill the vacuum. By the end of 1794, radicals like Tone, Russell, and Neilson were exerting increasing influence within the society, working to transform it into a revolutionary movement seeking full independence from Britain and military assistance from France. Political events in early 1795 furthered this trend. When Earl Fitzwilliam, a moderate Whig genuinely committed to Catholic emancipation, became Ireland's viceroy in January, many hoped that repression would come to an end and that Britain itself would begin to reform the corrupt political practices of the Ascendancy. Hope turned to dismay barely six weeks later when Prime Minister William Pitt abruptly recalled Fitzwilliam and replaced him with Lord Camden, a well-known hardliner who opposed admitting Catholics to the Irish Parliament. This dramatic reversal further strengthened the hand of those who called for completely reorganizing the United Irishmen. On May 10, 1795, representatives from seventy-two United Irish societies around the country formally adopted a new structure originally pioneered by a small group of Belfast radicals. Previously open clubs were replaced with secret cells of seven to thirty-five members, each organized along military lines. The Society of United Irishmen had transformed itself from a constitutional reform movement into a secret, oath-bound organization actively preparing for revolution.[34]

While this transformation was taking place, Tone himself was preparing to leave the country. Although officials harbored strong suspicions about his involvement with French agent William Jackson, they did not have the evidence to guarantee a conviction. When Tone, working through a former Trinity acquaintance, offered to make a statement about his part in the affair and then go into voluntary exile, the government readily agreed. In early June 1795, Tone and a group of his friends, including Russell, Neilson, and McCracken, climbed to McArt's Fort on the summit of Cave Hill overlooking Belfast. Here they "took a solemn obligation," as Tone later put it, "never to desist in our efforts until we had subverted the authority of England over our country and asserted her independence." On June 13, Tone and his family sailed for America.[35]

Political Exile

The Tones landed at Wilmington, Delaware, on August 1, 1795, and made their way to Philadelphia, then the nation's capital. The United Irishman Hamilton Rowan, also implicated in the Jackson affair, was already there, having settled in America following a tumultuous time in France under Robespierre's Committee of Public Safety. After discussions with Rowan, Tone decided to approach the French minister to the United States, Pierre Auguste Adet, with a proposal for a French invasion of Ireland. Adet turned him down, however, and Tone began to reconcile himself to a life of permanent exile in the United States. He bought a farm near Princeton, New Jersey, and wrote to Russell asking him to purchase seed for him.

Yet the prospect of spending the rest of his life in America was abhorrent to him. Tone regarded the American government, which arguably owed its very existence to French military support during its revolution, as both ungrateful and reactionary in refusing to support revolutionary France in its war with Great Britain. Though treaties signed in 1778 clearly committed the United States to a French alliance, President George Washington abrogated these in 1793 when he declared American neutrality in the war. Tone appreciated that many ordinary Americans still sympathized with the French, but Washington's Federalist administration did not, a fact that became obvious when the terms of the Jay Treaty—which made the American republic Britain's commercial ally in the war—were made public on the eve of Tone's arrival in Philadelphia.

Domestic social and political trends in the United States also deeply troubled him. Though Tone may have harbored fears and prejudices toward the Irish poor, his deepest hatreds focused on the aristocratic pretensions and political corruption of the Protestant Ascendancy. Tone saw the growing merchant classes of the great seaports of Philadelphia and New York, with their opulent homes and carriages and their servants dressed in imported livery, as eerily reminiscent of the Ascendancy. "What is it to me whether it is an aristocracy of merchants or of peers, elective or hereditary?" he wrote to Russell in September 1795. "It is still an aristocracy, incompatible with the existence of genuine liberty." And in America, just as in Ireland, "property" rapidly became "power." Tone condemned President Washington not only for refusing to side with revolutionary France, but also for pursuing domestic economic policies that undermined true republicanism in order "to bring in more dollars to the chests of the Mercantile Peerage of America."[36]

In expressing such views, Tone indicated his deep affinity with the hopes and fears of many American republicans, who, like Thomas Jefferson, regarded the political battles of the 1790s as nothing less than "contests of principle between the advocates of republican and those of kingly government." Local popular organizations calling themselves Democratic-Republican societies had emerged in America as early as 1792 in reaction to the British-influenced financial programs of Washington's treasury secretary, Alexander Hamilton, and they grew rapidly after war broke out between Britain and France the following year. Adamantly pro-French and propounding a transatlantic democratic vision influenced partly by the United Irishmen themselves, these societies garnered adherents across the social spectrum with their efforts to fight what they saw as the monarchical and pro-British tendencies of Washington's Federalist administration. It was the Jay Treaty, however, that brought the political conflict to a head. Audience members stoned Hamilton when he attempted to defend the treaty at a mass meeting in New York and Wilmington's citizens voted to oppose it at a town meeting just four days after Tone's arrival there. When Tone reached Philadelphia, the Democratic Society of Pennsylvania, the largest of the Democratic-Republican societies, had organized the most active opposition to the treaty and Washington's policies as a whole.[37]

Tone immediately found his way into Philadelphia's republican circles, becoming an avid reader of their newspapers, especially Benjamin Franklin Bache's *Aurora*, and developing a friendship with Pennsylvania's passionately anti-British governor, Thomas Miflin. He expressed sympathy with James Monroe, the American ambassador to France who was increasingly sidelined by the Washington administration because of his republican and pro-French views. He also expressed strong support for the Republican political opposition forming around Jefferson and James Madison. "In America, a representative government . . . has been carried by the two upper Estates, manifestly against the sense of the great majority of the People," he wrote to Russell, echoing the heated rhetoric of the Jeffersonian Republicans and deliberately (if imprecisely) using European terms to refer to the presidency and the Federalist-dominated Senate. "This, if I wanted anything to confirm in me my political creed, would completely furnish it." Thus Tone's intense engagement with American politics served to greatly strengthen both his fears of monarchical and aristocratic reaction and his deep commitment to republicanism as an international, or at least transatlantic, ideology. "These are the things that make men Republicans," he wrote, after cataloguing a long list of both Irish and American ills, "and this will be yet, with God's help, the system of Ireland and of Europe."[38]

At the same time, in ways that prefigured the experience of many later emigrants and exiles from Ireland, Tone's time in America, marked by a deep sense of displacement and longing, intensified his embrace of a specifically Irish national identity and of Irish nationalism. As an exile, he could never be at home, nor feel himself to be a "real" American. It was only in the United States, in fact, that

Tone realized just how "Irish" he was. This realization, more than anything else, accounted for what he called his "gloomy frame of mind" while there. "I bless God I am no American," he wrote to Russell. "I have but one country . . . and wherever fortune may drive me, I shall never consi[der] myself for an instant released from my natural allegiance to her."[39]

It was this commitment that led Tone to approach Adet one last time. This time the French minister welcomed the plan for a military invasion of Ireland and persuaded Tone to go to Paris to personally lobby the government, even offering him money to cover his expenses. Traveling with an American passport issued under the name of James Smith, Tone sailed on January 1, 1796, reaching France a month later. On February 15, he called on Ambassador Monroe, who received him "very politely." The two discussed "the state of the public mind in America," particularly the conflict over the Jay Treaty, which both men bitterly opposed, along with what Tone called the "manifest bias" of the Federalists generally in favor of Britain.[40]

Tone then immediately set to work on his mission to persuade the French government to launch a military invasion of Ireland, which, he argued, was "indispensably necessary as a *point de ralliement*" for a popular rising against British rule. Having ended the Terror, deposed the Jacobins, and executed their leader, Maximilien Robespierre, in July 1794, France was now governed by the Directory, a five-man executive body that had come to power at the end of 1795. The Directors were determined to win victory in their war with Britain and were thus more than willing to entertain Tone's proposal for an invasion of Ireland. Though they rejected his request for a force of 20,000 French soldiers, changing it initially to a mere 2,000, they did appoint General Lazare Hoche as commander of the proposed expedition. Tone was gratified, for Hoche was a rising and ambitious young general, as well as a known and enthusiastic supporter of an Irish invasion.[41]

The Road to Rebellion

Over the course of his time in America and France, Tone continued to follow events in Ireland, particularly the growth of the now-secret and revolutionary Society of United Irishmen. A key factor in its growth, especially in Ulster, was the remarkable alliance it forged with the predominantly Catholic and clandestine Defenders, the emergence of which was one of the most important developments of the 1790s. The Defenders had first surfaced in 1784 in Armagh, a rapidly commercializing Ulster county about equally divided between Presbyterians, Anglicans, and Catholics where sectarian conflict had long been rife, with the immediate aims of defending Catholics against Protestant attacks, fighting excessive rents, and opposing the tithes demanded by the Anglican Church. Unlike earlier Irish rural secret societies, the Defenders had larger political objectives almost from the start, seeking nothing less than the complete destruction of the Ascendancy and its Anglican church and the reversal of the land confiscations that had accompanied the plantation of Ireland in the seventeenth century. They "swear the whole country to be true to the Irish nation," wrote a worried viceroy to the prime minister in 1793. "They have been frequently heard to declare that the king was not the catholic king—they look upon or talk of the English settlers as not of their nation." The fact that, in the words of another observer, "the lower orders in the North are of a military turn, capable of being immediately formed into excellent soldiers," added to the government's concerns.[42]

Though Ulster remained the heartland of the Defenders, by the mid-1790s they had spread far beyond Armagh, constituting a significant presence in as many as fourteen counties and reaching beyond tenant farmers and agricultural laborers to include canal workers, schoolmasters, blacksmiths, and, in Dublin, weavers and tradesmen of the Liberties manufacturing district in their ranks. As they grew, they also showed signs of moving away from a purely defensive outlook toward a broader political stance. At least some Defenders began to view Protestant loyalists, rather than Protestants per se, as their enemy and, like the United Irishmen, began to see revolutionary France as a model, inspiration, and potential ally. By 1794, according to one anxious observer, rural lower-class Catholics "talked of the famous system of liberty and equality in the most extravagant manner." The society's most popular oath bound those who took it to work "to dethrone all Kings, and plant the Tree of Liberty in our Irish land— whilst the French Defenders will uphold the cause, and the Irish Defenders will pull down the British laws." The prospect of agrarian unrest linking up with French republicanism naturally frightened the authorities, who responded with brutal acts of repression, such as the trial and execution of a popular County Meath schoolmaster, Lawrence O'Connor, for Defender activities in the summer of 1795. On the orders of Lord Lieutenant Camden himself, O'Connor's body was disemboweled and quartered and his head placed on an iron spike over the jail, which Camden believed would have "a great effect on the people."[43]

Even more significant than the Defender agitation alone was the alliance that the organization gradually fashioned with the United Irishmen. As United Irishmen reached out to Catholic peasants and as the Defenders moved toward something resembling republicanism, the possibilities seemed limitless. In Ulster, the Presbyterian radical Samuel Neilson joined forces with the Catholic linen merchants Luke and Charles Teeling to develop a plan for the complete merger of the two organizations. Though that never occurred, by mid-1796 many Ulster radicals were taking United Irish and Defender oaths simultaneously.

In the later words of James Hope, the Presbyterian weaver who played an important role in this emerging alliance, Defenders and United Irishmen became
"sworn brothers" and it was mainly through their partnership with the Defenders
that the United Irishmen became a fully national, rather than just a regional,
Ulster-based movement.[44]

Determined to spread this underground alliance to the capital itself, United
Irish leaders in Ulster dispatched Hope to Dublin in the summer of 1796, where
he strove with considerable success "to disseminate our views among the working classes." Radical and pro-French plebian clubs in the city, as well as the local
Defenders, who claimed to have four thousand members in Dublin, responded
enthusiastically to the proposal for a secret United Irish society in the capital
that would begin making serious preparations for a revolution. By the fall of
1796, the organization was also beginning to grow in south Leinster counties
like Wexford and in the southern-most province of Munster, appealing especially to younger artisans, farmers, teachers, and clerks.[45]

In response, the government began to step up its policy of repression. In late
1795, Lord Carhampton, the commander of the Irish military, had commenced
what came to be known as the dragooning of Connacht. His forces burned
houses, tortured many suspected Defenders, and arrested hundreds of others,
summarily impressing them into the Royal Navy. In early 1796, the government
passed the Indemnity Act, which provided legal protection to officials for any
acts they might commit, and the Insurrection Act, which, among other provi-
sions, established the death penalty for administering illegal oaths. By the end of
that year, the government had suspended habeas corpus and was arresting key
leaders, including Samuel Nielson, Charles Teeling, and Thomas Russell, who
would remain incarcerated on a charge of high treason until 1802, longer than
any other leader of the United Irishmen.

Viewing these events from France—and through the prism of the French
Revolution—Wolfe Tone began to alter some of his earlier attitudes toward the
poor. He thoroughly revised his view of the Defenders, seeing them no longer
as "misguided and ignorant rabble" but as an admirably disciplined mass organization "whose object is the emancipation of their country, the subversion of
English usurpation and the bettering the condition of the wretched peasantry
of Ireland." He even opined in his diary that if "the men of property" in Ireland
refused to join the struggle for independence, "we can support ourselves by the
aid of that numerous and respectable class of the community, *the men of no property.*" In October 1796, Tone wrote a pamphlet aimed specifically at the Irish
peasantry—"the tillers and cultivators of the earth, by whose labour all the
other classes are supported and sustained"—that had even more radical implications. In it he applauded the French Revolution's alleged redistribution of three-
fourths of landed property and the fact that the peasantry of France had won for

"every man an estate more or less according to his means and his industry." He concluded by imploring Irish peasants to "shake of[f] the yoke and raise your-selves to the same station of ease and comfort as your brethren, the peasantry of France." Jettisoning his conservative views about property, he believed now that an Irish political revolution would of necessity involve some kind of social and economic transformation in the countryside.[46]

In June 1796, the Directory finally decided to move ahead on an Irish inva-sion, at least in part because of Tone's unflagging arguments. In July he met General Hoche and received a commission as *chef de brigade* in the French army. Tone, who since his youth had romanticized military pursuits, was immensely honored and genuinely looked forward to serving in action. His opportunity came in December, when a force of 43 ships and 14,450 troops sailed out of Brest harbor for Ireland. Unfortunately, the *Fraternité*, carrying Hoche himself, along with seven or eight other ships, was separated from the rest of the fleet, which reached the southwestern coast of Ireland at Bantry Bay on December 21, 1796. The landing, which was supposed to have taken place that day, was postponed to give Hoche a chance to catch up. "I am in undescribable anxi-ety," Tone wrote in his diary at the end of the day. "There cannot be imagined a situation more provokingly tantalizing than mine at this moment, within view, almost within reach of my native land, and uncertain whether I shall ever set my foot on it."[47]

Tone would not set his foot on his native land, at least not on this voyage. On December 22, the east wind picked up force and, as the ships attempted to make land, rain and snow created further disarray within the fleet. On December 24, the east wind became a storm and on December 27 the storm a hurricane. One by one, the remnants of the fleet headed back toward France, defeated by what came to be known in Irish lore as a "Protestant wind." As Tone bitterly observed, "England has not had such an escape since the Spanish Armada."[48]

The weeks and months after Bantry Bay were filled with more frustration for Tone, only partly offset by his reunion with his family, who joined him in Paris in May 1797. The Directory put a second Irish invasion attempt on indefinite hold, and when Hoche died of tuberculosis in September, things looked even more hopeless. Late in 1797, Tone held meetings with the leading figure in the French army, Napoleon Bonaparte, who, though polite, expressed more interest in invading Egypt than Ireland.

What Tone did not know, however, was that the Bantry expedition had altered the military situation in Ireland dramatically. By demonstrating that French support for the United Irishmen was neither a republican fantasy nor a loyalist nightmare, the failed invasion generated a wave of new support for the revolutionary cause. At the same time, by providing a frightening warning to the crown and the Ascendancy, it set in motion a drive toward vastly increased governmental repression. These two trends would come to a head in the rebellion of 1798.[49]

After Bantry Bay, the clandestine United Irish organization began growing rapidly, especially in Ulster, where membership doubled between January and April 1797. By June, it may have had as many as 120,000 members in the province. This rapid growth increased the determination of the government to destroy the movement, using all means at its disposal, before it could advance any further. Its efforts focused on Ulster, where, in the spring of 1797, General Gerard Lake, a veteran of the American War of Independence and the war with France, was directed to stamp out the revolutionary movement before French forces could return, which he did with zeal. As one of Lake's subordinates, Brigadier-General Thomas Knox, explained, "severe military execution alone" could bring victory, even though it would entail "spreading devastation through the most disaffected parts" of the province.[50]

Lake's operations in Ulster lasted for the rest of the year. His soldiers burned houses wherever arms were discovered or suspected, made mass arrests, and flogged suspects to extract information. Some men were tried, convicted, and executed for violation of the Insurrection Act, though many were also killed during the dragooning of Ulster itself. These tactics, which Camden described candidly as an effort to "strike terror" in the populace, achieved the desired results. The organizing efforts of the United Irishmen were badly disrupted, critical stocks of weapons seized, and many members and potential members frightened away from the movement. By early 1798, government officials believed that Ulster had been pacified.[51]

Officials also worked to aggravate an ongoing sectarian conflict in County Armagh that had already led to the emergence and growth of a new organization. The Orange Order, taking its name from William of Orange, who had defeated the Catholic-supported James II in the 1690s, had been founded in September 1795 by a group of lower- and lower-middle-class Anglicans worried about the growth of the Defenders and United Irishmen, but it soon began receiving support from the Anglican gentry in that county. Though they initially regarded it as a dangerous menace, government and military officials also came to see the Order as an essential, if unpredictable, ally. General Knox played a particularly important role in encouraging its growth. While recognizing that the Orangemen were "rather a difficult card to play," he nonetheless believed that despite "their licentiousness, on them must we rely for the preservation of our lives and fortunes should critical times occur." The very sectarianism that the United Irishmen and Defenders were striving so hard to overcome was, in Knox's view, essential to social stability.[52]

Both repression and sectarian violence intensified significantly in 1797 and early 1798. In May 1797, four United Irish members of the army at the Blaris camp near Belfast were court-martialed and executed. The next day, members of the Monaghan militia rampaged through Belfast, destroying the offices of the *Northern Star*, which was permanently silenced. Developments like this set off a debate among leaders of the United Irishmen. Some, notably Thomas Addis Emmet and William MacNeven, counseled patience, seeking to hold back a rebellion until French forces could return. Others, such as Samuel Neilson, Arthur O'Connor, and Lord Edward Fitzgerald, argued that a rising should be attempted before the movement was totally crushed. In June 1797, the national committee rejected the call for an immediate rising, but events thereafter began to shift the debate in the militants' direction. The suppression of the *Northern Star* led to its replacement in September by O'Connor's Dublin newspaper, the *Press*, a more revolutionary organ, which became wildly popular in the capital. Most important were the government raids of March 12, 1798, in which Emmet, MacNeven, and nearly all the members of the Leinster provincial committee were arrested. Government officials were satisfied with their preemptive strike, not only because it left the United Irishmen bereft of their most effective leaders but also because it vastly increased the likelihood of a premature rebellion, undertaken when "it would be more in our power to quell," as John Foster, Speaker of the Irish House of Commons, put it, "than if such an event happened when the enemy were off our coast." Foster's assessment was on the mark: with the arrest of Emmet and the others, the United Irishmen were almost completely in the hands of figures like Fitzgerald, Neilson, and John and Henry Sheares, who were determined to wait no longer for the French and began hastily to draw up plans for a rising for May. It would begin in Dublin, with the subsequent failure of mail coaches from the capital to arrive in other areas providing the signal for the launch of a general rebellion throughout the country.[53]

As it turned out, these plans went badly awry. On May 19, a party of the gentry-led Yeomanry corps broke into Fitzgerald's rooms and mortally wounded him in an exchange of gunfire. The following day, the government declared martial law in Dublin. The day after that, authorities arrested the Sheares brothers, leaving Neilson as the only important leader still at large, and they arrested him two days later. That evening, when the United Irishmen in Dublin began assembling to initiate the rising, they found that government forces had occupied their meeting points, barricaded bridges, and cut off communication with the surrounding area. Some 3,000 supporters who were marching toward the city dispersed. Efforts of the United Irishmen to assemble in the countryside around Dublin also collapsed without effective leadership and against the better-armed and trained forces commanded by General Lake. Rebel casualties were especially heavy at Tara, Carlow, and Curragh, where 300 unarmed men attempting to surrender were massacred on May 29.

Despite this, the rebellion began to spread. In County Wexford, insurgent forces, in the words of one participant, "swept o'er the land like a mighty wave." They defeated the militia at Oulart on May 27, going on to capture Wexford town, which they held for the next three weeks, establishing an improvised United Irish Directory as a working revolutionary government. The fighting in Wexford, where religious tensions had long been present, took on a sectarian character not seen in other areas of the country. Catholic insurgents carried out a mass execution of 93 Protestant prisoners in Wexford town and burned some 200 others to death in a barn at Scullabogue. But even in Wexford, the anti-sectarian and republican goals of the United Irishmen could be clearly seen. The Wexford Directory was explicitly nonsectarian, consisting of four Catholics and four Protestants, and the rebel military commander in the county, Edward Roche, repeatedly urged his followers to practice restraint. "Let not your victories be tarnished with any act of cruelty," he implored in a June 7 proclamation, "neither let a difference in religious sentiments cause a difference among the people."[54]

Meanwhile, in the now badly disorganized United Irish heartland of Ulster, it took the May 29 ousting of the entire provincial leadership and the appointment of new leaders, among them Henry Joy McCracken, to tip the scales in favor of a northern rising. Despite the fact that the rebellion here was, in the words of one participant, more "a forlorn hope, than a force having any well-founded expectation of a successful issue," an estimated 27,000 insurgents turned out in east Derry, Antrim, and Down. On June 7, having overrun government garrisons at Larne, Randalstown, and Ballymena, 4,000 United Irish combatants, under McCracken's command, launched an attack on Antrim town. Errors and miscues plagued the rebel forces, however, and what looked like a victory ended up as a rout. As McCracken's forces retreated, British troops looted and burned dwellings and tortured and executed prisoners, a process that culminated in the burning of Randalstown. Rebel attacks in County Derry on June 9 and County Down on June 12 proved similarly unsuccessful and were also followed by British mopping up actions that included hangings, torture, the mass rape of local women, and the burning of homes. Henry Munro, the rebel leader in Down, was hanged on June 16; McCracken was hanged on July 17.[55]

Defeat in a climactic June 21 battle on Wexford's Vinegar Hill, where as many as 200 women took part in the combat alongside their husbands, fathers, and brothers, paved the way for the end of the Wexford rebellion, which was, as in Ulster, followed by considerable brutality. Ironically, only after the insurrection had been decisively crushed in these areas did the long-awaited French forces arrive. The August 22 landing in north Mayo of 1,100 French troops under the command of General Jean Humbert triggered a fresh mobilization of United Irish supporters in that county, but by September this mobilization had been crushed in one of the most awful bloodbaths of the entire rebellion. While French soldiers were permitted to surrender and treated as prisoners of war, as many as 2,000 Irish rebels were slaughtered after the fighting had ended.[56]

Final Days

There was one last French effort. In October, the Directory dispatched a force of 3,000 soldiers to reinforce General Humbert, not aware that he had already surrendered. Wolfe Tone was with them, sailing on the flagship, the *Hoche*. After three weeks of fighting heavy winds, part of the fleet reached the northwest coast of Donegal, where they were met by an overwhelming British naval force. Several of the French ships were able to escape, but the crew of the *Hoche* fought a six-hour battle before finally surrendering. Recognized by an old Trinity class-mate serving in the British army, Tone was taken to Dublin in irons to face a military court martial.

On November 10, 1798, he entered the courtroom, proudly wearing his French uniform. Charged with treason, he readily acknowledged the prosecution's statement of facts, but requested the right to explain his actions. "The great object of my life has been the independence of my country. For that I have sacrificed every thing that is most dear to man," he told the court. "I have braved difficulty and danger; I have submitted to exile and to bondage; I have exposed myself to the rage of the ocean and the fire of the enemy." After all of these travails, he added, "it is little to say that I am ready to lay down my life." Tone's only request was that he be granted a military execution by firing squad, not hanged like a common criminal. His request was denied. After a trial lasting just over an hour, Tone was convicted and condemned to hang in two days' time. The following night, however, he cut his own throat. He died a week later.[57]

Thus ended the short but eventful career of Theobald Wolfe Tone. Many of his sympathizers mourned his passing and even some of his enemies regretted that such a talented young man had been brought to this kind of end. Few of his contemporaries, however, could have predicted at that moment that Tone would eventually be regarded as one of the most important figures in Irish history. This appreciation would only develop posthumously, on the basis of Tone's unpublished writings. Collected, edited, and brought into print by his widow, Matilda, in the United States in the 1820s, the *Life of Theobald Wolfe Tone* would provide later generations of Irish and Irish American nationalists with an inspirational narrative of courage, intelligence, and determination, as well as a body of nationalist writings on republicanism, democracy, and the evils of religious hatred. Just as important, the act of publicly "remembering" Tone would itself become a weapon of immense value for the project of Irish nationalism.[58]

Tone's life prefigured many of the themes and tensions that would resonate within Irish and Irish American nationalism over next two centuries. Although much would change over this long period, a number of issues that Tone grappled with would remain critical: Irish nationalists' uneasy relationship to movements for women's rights; their stance on class and racial inequality; the relationship of republican separatism to more moderate forms of nationalism; the role of exile in strengthening nationalist sentiments; and the relationship of Irish nationalists in America to American society and politics. These last two points, in particular, would take on even greater significance as the number of the Irish in the United States grew from some 500,000 in the 1790s to nearly 40 million by the 1990s. They could be seen as early as the opening years of the nineteenth century, when large numbers of United Irishmen began arriving in the United States.[59]

2

Irish Exiles in a New Republic,
1798–1829

In early November 1804, a ship from Bordeaux sailed into busy New York harbor. On board were a number of Irish passengers, a fact that would have by itself raised few eyebrows. Between the end of the American War of Independence in 1783 and the economic panic of 1819, nearly 200,000 emigrants from Ireland made their way to the United States, an impressive number given the huge obstacles—nearly continuous war between Britain and France, naval blockades, and British laws discouraging emigration—that stood in their way. The Irish were America's largest immigrant group in these years, constituting more than twice the number of immigrants from England, Scotland, and Wales combined.[1]

Aboard this particular ship was Thomas Addis Emmet, at forty-one the most famous surviving leader of the Society of United Irishmen. Emmet had not taken part in the 1798 rebellion for he had been arrested with a number of other United Irish leaders in March, two months before the fighting began. He spent the next four years in British prisons before being released. After a frustrating spell in Irish exile circles in Holland and France, he and his family sailed for the United States. Many other United Irish veterans, including Emmet's friends and fellow state prisoners, William Sampson and Dr. William James MacNeven, would soon join him in America. They added their numbers to a sizable group of Irish republicans, including Mathew Carey, William Duane, and John Binns.

Unlike Wolfe Tone, these individuals would live out the rest of their lives in the United States, and more than a few of them had illustrious American careers. MacNeven, born to a prosperous Catholic family in County Galway and educated in Prague and Vienna, would achieve renown as a physician and chemist in the United States. Emmet, from an elite Dublin Anglican background and regarded as one of Ireland's most brilliant lawyers even before joining the United Irishmen in 1792, would leave a permanent mark on American law, as

would Sampson, another accomplished attorney. All three became central figures within New York's growing Irish community. Carey, who had settled in
Philadelphia, would become a well-known publisher and one of the nation's first
political economists. By the early nineteenth century, his was the most important
publishing house in the country and when he retired in the 1820s, he did so with
what he termed "a moderate fortune." As editor of the influential Philadelphia
Aurora, Duane made countless political enemies but enjoyed the friendship of
presidents Thomas Jefferson and Andrew Jackson. Binns, another prominent
journalist and editor, would serve on Philadelphia's Board of Aldermen for more
than twenty years.[2]

These men were only the most famous of a large number of Irish exiles literally scattered across the globe. Beginning with the British government's crackdown on radicals in the mid-1790s and growing exponentially in the years
following the bloody end of the rebellion, thousands of United Irishmen and
their supporters left (or were forcibly transported from) Ireland for a host of
destinations that included France, Britain, and Australia, as well as the United
States. This scattering of United Irishmen had a profound effect on the political
and social landscape of Ireland, draining the country of its most democratic
and radical elements and paving the way for the resurgence of vicious religious
hatreds, especially in the northern province of Ulster. This exodus also had
profound and long-lasting effects on the various places that United Irishmen
settled.[3]

Nowhere was the impact greater than in America, where as many as 2,000
Irish radicals ended up making their homes. The exiles aligned themselves
closely with the Republican electoral upsurge that brought Thomas Jefferson to
power in 1800. They defended immigrants and freedom of expression against
the Alien and Sedition Acts, fought for religious tolerance and a separation of
church and state, and worked to get out the Irish immigrant vote on election
days. To American political life they brought a highly confrontational style
derived from what they saw as a life-and-death struggle between "democracy"
and "tyranny" back in Ireland. They were not always in accord on every issue.
They were divided over women's and workers' rights, just as they had been in
Ireland, and in the United States a major new political disagreement emerged
among them over the rapidly expanding institution of slavery. But on one point
they were in full agreement: their commitment to Ireland's cause. The exiles
built societies devoted to Irish independence, supported a reinvigorated Irish
movement for Catholic emancipation, and published a steady stream of books
and pamphlets designed to keep the flame of separatist republicanism burning
in America even as it grew dimmer in Ireland itself. In so doing they left a huge
imprint on the history of Irish nationalism in both countries.

Aftermath

The effects of the 1798 rebellion were profound. Most immediately, it confirmed many British officials' belief that they needed more direct forms of political control over their potentially unruly neighbor. The result was the Act of Union, passed by both the British and, after much debate, the Irish Parliament in 1800. This legislation, which took effect January 1, 1801, established a new political entity called the United Kingdom of Great Britain and Ireland. It abolished the historic Irish Parliament on College Green and gave Ireland direct representation at Westminster, with four bishops and twenty-eight peers in the House of Lords and one hundred MPs in the House of Commons. Though plans like this had been in circulation for decades, the fears that the rebellion sparked among both British officials and members of the Ascendancy finally made it politically feasible. William MacNeven was wrong when he later asserted that British political leaders had actually "stirred up" the rebellion in order "to supply the necessary pretext for effecting their nefarious design," but even Prime Minister Pitt admitted that the events of 1798 had handed him and his allies a powerful argument that only union could "provide for the internal peace of the country and secure the connection with Great Britain." As early as August 1798, he was emphasizing "the necessity of bringing forward the great work of union which can never be so well accomplished as now." According to a leading Ascendancy figure, George III had also signaled his approval for "using the present moment of terror for frightening the supporters of the Castle into a union." Though vigorously challenged by later generations of Irish nationalists, the Union would remain intact until 1921.[4]

The global result of the rebellion was a scattering of United Irishmen, Defenders, and other Irish radicals to numerous locales throughout the Atlantic world and beyond. These activists were typically young, literate, and highly opinionated: as a colonial official in Australia reported, radical Irish convicts there were eager "to recite the miseries and injustice of their punishment and the hardships they suffer." Though their exact numbers cannot be known, as a group they constituted an extremely significant example of the phenomenon of politically influenced emigration or, to use the term favored by the migrants themselves, exile.[5]

Some chose exile over prison or death even before the fighting had ended. By April 1798, for example, Walter Devereux, a Catholic supporter of the movement in County Wexford, had already seen more than enough curfews, arrests, and killings as the government worked to crush the United Irishmen in that county. "If the times are not Settled Before Next August I Certanley will then leave this Land of tiriney and Seek a land of Liberty," Devereux wrote to his brother John, a resident of Utica, New York. "I Certainley will go to you if life Permits Me to Do." As the rebellion swept over Wexford the following month, Devereux acted on this decision, traveling first to Liverpool and then, disguised as a sailor, to the Caribbean island of Martinique.[6]

Other United Irish supporters left Ireland only after months or even years in prison. France, still the revolutionary beacon, was a natural destination for many of them, and it was here that some of the most prominent leaders of the movement settled, at least for a time. Thomas Russell, for example, imprisoned without trial in 1796, was released from Scotland's Fort George in 1802 on the promise that he would immediately leave the country. He made his way to Paris, where he joined a thriving, though often divided, United Irish exile community that included Thomas Emmet's younger brother, Robert. Expelled from Trinity College for his radical political views in 1798, the younger Emmet had been an underground organizer for the United Irishmen in Dublin until forced to flee Ireland in May 1799. It was among the Paris exiles that Emmet, Russell, and others began to plan one last Irish rising, this one centering on Dublin.[7]

Though not able to obtain French military support, the conspirators secretly returned to Ireland in October 1802, linking up with a small force of United Irish guerrillas, led by Michael Dwyer, still operating in the mountains of County Wicklow, and with an underground rebel network that had managed to survive in Dublin, where they built up an arsenal of arms and explosives. An accidental explosion at one of their Dublin hideouts in July 1803 forced the conspirators into a premature rising, which was easily crushed. Dwyer was sentenced to transportation to the penal colony in Australia, while Emmet, Russell, and twenty others were sentenced to death by hanging. "Let no man write my epitaph," Robert Emmet was reported to have said in a dramatic speech from the dock on September 19, 1803, after the reading of his death sentence. "When my country takes her place among the nations of the earth, then, and not till then, let my epitaph be written." He was executed the following day. Thomas Russell, who had been one of the founders of the Belfast Society of United Irishmen in 1791 and was in many ways the most visionary of its leaders, went to the gallows on October 21.[8]

After this final effort, the United Irishmen in France dissolved into a series of acrimonious factional disputes. Some continued to lobby the French government for yet another invasion of Ireland, but without success. Napoleon did form an "Irish Legion" within the French army in 1803, but the factionalism of the exiles simply continued on within its ranks. Individual exiles, to be sure, distinguished themselves in the French army. Miles Byrne who had taken part in both the Wexford rebellion and the Wicklow guerrilla war, left Ireland for good after the failure of Emmet's conspiracy. He traveled to France, joined the Irish Legion, and went on to have an illustrious military career, both before and after

Napoleon's fall. But the Irish Legion itself gradually lost its Irish character (and in 1811 even its "Irish" title) and became simply a unit for foreigners serving in the French army, one, moreover, with a reputation for disorganization and insubordination. Meanwhile, the only formal political organization among the exiles, the Paris-based United Irish Society, ceased to exist in 1806.[9]

The situation for United Irishmen making their way to England and Scotland was very different, for they were migrating not to an allied partner in revolution but rather into what they saw as the very belly of the beast. Even before the 1798 rebellion, an Irish revolutionary underground had emerged in London, revolving around John Binns, a young orator who had migrated from Dublin in 1794 and quickly became a key figure in the London Corresponding Society and the larger world of English plebian radicalism. Along with his brother, Benjamin, Binns was soon joined by increasing numbers of Irish republicans driven out of their country from the mid-1790s onward by sectarian violence and government repression. A London branch of the United Irishmen was formed in 1797, one closely identified with the faction (led by Arthur O'Connor and Edward Fitzgerald) that was arguing for an immediate rising. The London-based radicals began planning for sympathetic action (such as kidnapping members of the Privy Council) to aid the approaching Irish rebellion and linked up with militants in the London Corresponding Society to form a new organization called the United Britons. The authorities, who kept themselves fully abreast of all of these developments through their network of informers, arrested Binns, Arthur O'Connor, and radical Armagh priest James Coigly for possession of seditious material in February 1798, and then began arresting many other members of the United Irishmen, London Corresponding Society, and United Britons in London and Manchester. Though Coigly was convicted of high treason and hanged, Binns and O'Connor were eventually acquitted. O'Connor departed for Paris, where he became a leading figure in the city's émigré community, while Binns set off for the United States in 1801.[10]

Underground Irish revolutionary activity in London culminated in 1802 with a conspiracy planned by an Irish-born naval hero named Colonel Edward Despard to spark a rising in the British capital itself; the conspiracy was discovered and Despard hanged. A revolutionary underground also existed in Scotland from as early as April 1793 when a Scottish radical named Thomas Muir became an honorary member of the United Irishmen while in Belfast, and, in December 1794, Glasgow republicans founded the Society of United Scotsmen, using the Irish organization as their model. United Irish émigrés, especially Presbyterian radicals from Ulster, helped to expand this organization dramatically in the years 1797–1803, and radical Irish influences were still apparent in the political agitation that spread through Scotland after the end of the Napoleonic wars. Gradually the United Irish influence waned in England and Scotland, where, unlike France or America, an emerging political vocabulary that stressed the fundamental opposition of social classes trumped the republican language of citizenship and rights that was so central to the vision of the United Irishmen. Still, continuing migration from Ireland to Britain in the nineteenth century meant that British and Irish radical movements would remain intertwined; thus, the demand for the repeal of the Act of Union held an important place in the British Chartist agenda in the 1840s, and Arthur O'Connor's nephew, Feargus, would become Britain's foremost Chartist leader.[11]

Australia, another important United Irish destination, was a special case, because the Irish radicals who ended up there did so as punishment for their activities and because they constituted such a large proportion of the early European settler population. The penal colony at New South Wales had been founded in 1788, just ten years before the rebellion, and at least 400—and possibly more than 600—United Irishmen and their supporters were transported there between 1799 and 1802, adding to the estimated 200 Defenders sent there in the decade after 1791. Since the entire European population of Australia at the opening of the nineteenth century was only about 4,500, Irish radicals represented 10 percent to 20 percent of that population. This group affected everything from educational systems and labor practices to the ethos of male mutual support that Australians call "mateship." Even the surveying of Tasmania and the locating of the colony's capital at Hobart Town was performed by a United Irish exile, James Meehan, transported to Australia for his role in the rebellion. The most significant thing the Irish veterans brought was a republican and radically egalitarian ethos into a country that remained formally a linchpin of the British Empire. In 1804, Irish convicts, many of them United Irishmen or Defenders, took part in a rebellion at Castle Hill, in what is today Sydney, the largest uprising in the history of transportation to Australia and the final United Irish rising worldwide. Locals rechristened the site of the rebellion "Vinegar Hill" in recognition of the sizable United Irish contingent taking part.[12]

Coming on top of the 30,000 or more lives lost in 1798, the exodus of thousands of Irish radicals, whether by choice or transportation, had a substantial impact on Ireland itself. It eliminated virtually an entire generation of dedicated and effective political activists whose lives had been devoted to making the isle a more egalitarian, less corrupt, and less sectarian place. Democratic politics atrophied and sectarian conflict returned with a vengeance, especially in the once radical province of Ulster, where violent clashes between the rapidly growing Orange Order and a new secret Catholic grouping calling themselves Ribbonmen broke out in the 1810s. "The North seems dead and rotting, like their flax when steeping in holes and ditches," William Drennan wrote to his sister, Martha McTier, describing Ulster in 1807. "A general stagnation diffused itself over national feelings," wrote the Catholic reformer, Richard Lalor Sheil, in 1823, describing Ireland in these years. "The public pulse had stopped, the circulation of all generous feeling had been arrested, and the country was palsied to the heart."[13]

United Irishmen in the United States

The nation most profoundly affected by the United Irish exodus, arguably even more than Ireland itself, was the new American republic, where more than 2,000 exiles eventually settled. The initial foothold of Irish radicals in American life began as early as the mid-1780s, when Mathew Carey took flight for Philadelphia. The young Catholic editor of Dublin's *Volunteers Journal*, who had already fled Ireland for France once before to avoid a likely sedition prosecution, did so again in September 1784 to escape trial for criminal libel against John Foster, Speaker of the Irish House of Commons. Obtaining a loan from the Marquis de Lafayette, whom he had met earlier in France, Carey began publishing the Philadelphia *Evening Herald* in 1785 and the *American Museum*, initially a pro-Federalist magazine, in 1787. His enthusiastic support for the French Revolution and his strenuous opposition to the Jay Treaty, however, brought him solidly into the Republican camp. Carey also founded the publishing firm that brought out the first American edition of the Catholic Douay-Rheims Bible in 1790 and, with great fanfare, the second American printing of Wollstonecraft's *Vindication of the Rights of Woman* in 1794.[14]

With the British crackdown on Irish radicals in the mid-1790s, the gravitational pull of the United States increased substantially. By 1795, not just Wolfe Tone but also Napper Tandy, Hamilton Rowan, and Dr. James Reynolds all found themselves in Philadelphia. Tandy, the celebrated Dublin radical whose activism went back to the Volunteers and support for the American revolutionaries in the 1770s, had fled Ireland in March 1793 rather than face trial for the felony of taking the oath of the Defenders and spent two years in England before turning up in Philadelphia. The fallout from the 1794 Jackson affair, in which William Jackson had solicited assistance from United Irishmen for a French invasion, brought Tone, Rowan, and Reynolds to America. Rowan, already imprisoned in Dublin for an allegedly seditious address to the Volunteers, escaped shortly after learning of Jackson's arrest in April 1794 and then embarked on a spectacular and dangerous voyage in a small fishing boat for the coast of Brittany. He spent the following year in France, leaving in disgust at the confusion and bloodshed of French politics under the Committee of Public Safety, and arrived in Philadelphia in July 1795. Reynolds was also in Philadelphia by August 1795 and the formation of a United Irish émigré group in America, focused on winning the French government's support of an Irish invasion, can be dated from this month. "A kind of seditious convention is now forming in America," reported the Dublin barrister and informer Leonard McNally in September, using personal letters obtained from Tandy's loyalist son to correctly identify Tone, Reynolds, Tandy, and Rowan as central to the communication "carried on between the leaders of the United here and persons in France, through the medium of fugitive friends."[15]

The exiles soon began to play an oppositional republican role in American politics as well. Tandy was an exception, believing that "having found asylum in America, from the persecution of tyranny in my own country, as an alien it would be ungrateful in me to take any active part in politics," and he left to join Tone in Paris in 1797. But Rowan and Reynolds agreed fully with Tone's acid criticisms of American politics and society under the Federalists. "I came here as I thought to a country of Liberty and equality," Rowan wrote bitterly to Thomas Jefferson in 1798, but "I do not find it such." They threw themselves into the political fray, playing a particularly important role in the fight against the Jay Treaty. Rowan organized meetings and petition drives against the treaty, drawing many of Philadelphia's newer Irish immigrants to the Republican cause. His views, according to Mathew Carey, were embraced by "thousands of kindly souls, who sympathize in his sufferings." Likewise, Reynolds, in Rowan's opinion, was participating fully in "the politics of America, and is as busy, as sincere, and as zealous" as he had ever been in Ireland.[16]

Joining the Philadelphia exiles in 1796 was William Duane, who had a more global career than any other Irish radical of his generation. Born to Irish parents in what would become Vermont in 1760, Duane grew up in Ireland after his family returned there shortly following his birth. In 1786, he set off for India, where he founded the *Bengal Journal* in Calcutta. He soon became a fierce opponent of British rule in India and, after 1789, an equally fervent supporter of the French Revolution, positions that naturally put him in hot water with British authorities, who imprisoned and then deported him in 1795 as a "dangerous incendiary." Arriving in London in the midst of the crackdown on radicals there, Duane immediately joined the London Corresponding Society and threw himself into the growing circle of United Irish supporters in that city, becoming a critic not only of British colonialism and repression but also of the harsh conditions experienced by British working people in industrializing cities like Manchester and Birmingham. Duane left for America in 1796, where he obtained work as assistant editor on Philadelphia's Republican newspaper, the *Aurora*.[17]

When the *Aurora*'s editor died in 1798, Duane took it over and within months turned it into one of the most influential newspapers in the United States. In the Federalist attacks on radicals over the next two years, epitomized by the Alien and Sedition Acts, Duane was indicted three times for seditious libel, threatened with deportation, beaten by a mob of military officers, and dragged through the streets by Federalist rioters. His courage in the face of these attacks made him a folk hero to political radicals, especially immigrants from Ireland, who sometimes referred to the heavily Irish neighborhoods of Philadelphia as simply "Duane's district." His continuing editorial efforts, moreover, contributed significantly to the Republican triumph in the presidential election of 1800. After his victory, Jefferson immediately halted the Sedition Law prosecution against Duane, later recalling the *Aurora* as "our comfort in the gloomiest days," while John Adams singled Duane out as one of a handful of individuals most responsible for his defeat. The once globetrotting Irish radical was by this time one of the most powerful figures within Philadelphia's dominant Democratic Republican Party.[18]

Not surprisingly, Jefferson's election drew many more Irish radicals to the United States. During Adams's administration, the American minister to Britain, Rufus King, had labored tirelessly to prevent the British government from releasing the one hundred or so Irish state prisoners (the most important leaders of the United Irishmen) to the United States, arguing that their "principles and habits" were "utterly inconsistent with any practicable or settled form of government." "I certainly do not think that they will be a desirable acquisition to any Nation," King wrote in a September 1798 letter to the British Home Secretary, "but in none would they be likely to be more mischievous than in mine, where from the sameness of language and similarity of Laws and Institutions they have greater opportunities of propagating their principles than in any other country." Meanwhile back in the United States, Adams's secretary of state, William Pickering, had ordered the drawing up of blacklists to prevent the immigration of those he termed "United Irish Desperadoes." Such men, at this point, were not interested in emigrating to the United States, discouraged by what they saw as the Federalist betrayal of the American Revolution and justifiably fearing that if they actually made it to America they would immediately be deported under the terms of the new Alien Friends Act. In the fall of 1798, MacNeven (unsuccessfully) petitioned the authorities for release "to go to the Continent," Emmet told them his preferred destination was "decidedly not America," and when Sampson was released for health reasons in 1799, he set off initially for Portugal. By the time that Emmet, MacNeven, and the others began to be released in 1802, however, the dramatic political changes that had taken place in America made it a much more attractive destination. The Sedition Law had expired on the day of Jefferson's inauguration in 1801 and in his successful plea to Congress for the repeal of the Federalists' 1798 naturalization laws, the newly elected president had asked, "Shall oppressed humanity find no asylum on this globe?"[19]

After 1800, many United Irish veterans began to give Jefferson a clear answer to his question: they saw America as precisely such an asylum. Released from a London prison in March 1801, John Binns was in Pennsylvania by July. Belfast's Samuel Neilson, the one-time proprietor of the *Northern Star*, sailed for

America in December 1802, though, weakened by a bout of yellow fever, he died in Poughkeepsie, New York, the following August. After his release from Fort George in 1802, Thomas Addis Emmet went first to Holland and then to France, but the factionalism of the Paris émigrés and the execution of his younger brother Robert turned his eyes toward America; Emmet arrived in New York in 1804. Upon his release from Fort George, William MacNeven went to Switzerland and then to France, where he served in the Irish Brigade of the French army until 1805. When it became clear to him that there would be no more French invasions of Ireland, he too left for America, arriving in New York on July 4, 1805. William Sampson moved from Portugal to France in 1799, where he lived for six years, then spent nearly another year in the large community of Irish exiles in the northern German port city of Hamburg. By 1806 he too was in New York.[20]

Most of these new émigrés, not surprisingly, aligned themselves closely with the Jeffersonian Republicans and, over the next quarter of a century, they bolstered the fortunes of that party considerably, helping to turn it into the dominant one in American political life. Though relatively few in numbers, the exiles exerted tremendous influence because of their concentration in the world of journalism, their extensive political experience, and their ability to speak for and organize the large and growing Irish community in America. Jefferson was grateful for the efforts of editors like Duane who helped him and his Republican successors, James Madison and James Monroe, occupy the presidency continuously until 1825. But the story was the same at the state and local level. Republican politicians like DeWitt Clinton in New York and Simon Snyder in Pennsylvania came to rely heavily on the efforts of the exiles every time elections approached. The émigrés brought to American politics a new and highly charged confrontational style derived from the bitter struggle back in Ireland. In April 1807, for example, Emmet published a series of letters in the *American Citizen*, praising New York gubernatorial candidate Clinton and denouncing his Federalist opponent, Rufus King (who had earlier blocked the Irish state prisoners' release to America), as a "royalist" who had schemed to "torture oppressed Ireland and keep her bleeding patriots in dungeons." By agitating consistently and effectively for an expansion of the franchise in the United States, just as they had in Ireland, and still seeking, as Emmet had put it earlier, "to make every man a consummate politician," the exiles contributed significantly to an even more important phenomenon in this era: the halting growth of American democracy. Though limited in crucial respects, the expansion of white manhood suffrage and the emergence of mass-based political parties were two of the most important political developments in the United States during the first few decades of the nineteenth century, and the United Irish exiles played an important role in both.[21]

To say merely that this process of democratization was limited, however, would be an understatement. The problem was not just that the benefits of the expansion of the franchise and growth of political parties were limited to white men, but that from the standpoint of many white women, democracy appeared to be reversing. During the years before and after the American Revolution, well-connected and elite women had been able to use the domestic spaces under their control, especially the parlor, to participate in political discussion and exert real political influence, while white women across the social spectrum staked out valued political roles as "republican mothers," preparing their sons for the duties and rights of citizenship. In the 1790s and early 1800s, some women took this a step further, enthusiastically embracing Wollstonecraft's call for women's rights and claiming a more direct role as what some of them called "female politicians," who strove to participate more fully in political debate. By the 1820s, the very expansion of white manhood suffrage and the rise of mass-based political parties, to which Duane, Emmet, and the others contributed, served increasingly to exclude women from the political sphere altogether. Their reputation among hostile Federalists as "the most God-provoking Democrats on this side of Hell" notwithstanding, few of the exiles raised their voices against this backlash. A partial exception was Wollstonecraft's Philadelphia publisher, Mathew Carey, but when Carey authored a pamphlet in 1831 on "the sufferings of seamstresses," which among other remedies proposed an expansion of education for women, his friend and fellow exile William Sampson wrote to him in protest. Educating women above their station, Sampson believed, would only "inspire them with pretensions very unfavorable to their peace and contentment."[22]

And yet there was an aspect of the democratization process that positively affected women as well as men and to which some of the exiles made an extremely important contribution: the growth of religious freedom. This was a victory won in the courtroom rather than at the polls, and the key actors were the United Irish lawyers rather than the journalists. Coming from Ireland, where an established Anglican Church and the denial of full rights to Catholics were still in place, the exiles agreed that such systematic religious discrimination would be absolutely unacceptable in the United States, and they waged an ultimately successful legal fight for free religious expression. Thus, in an 1813 case cited to this day in religious expression cases, William Sampson (a practicing Anglican) successfully defended a New York Catholic priest who refused to renounce his sacred obligation to maintain the secrecy of the confessional by testifying against one of his parishioners. Sampson's argument, delivered with deep emotion, derived directly from the history of Ireland, where "the rights, lives, liberties, and feelings of the catholics had been assailed through successive ages in every wanton form that avarice, vengeance and malignity could devise." In the new American republic, Sampson asserted, things had to be different: "every citizen here is his own country. To the protestant it is a protestant country; to the catholic, a catholic country; and the jew, if he pleases, may establish in it his New Jerusalem." The ultimate goal was "nothing but pure and perfect equality."[23]

In addition to achieving a historic legal victory for religious freedom and the separation of church and state, Sampson was expressing the belief, shared by virtually all of the United Irish exiles, that religious sectarianism had no place in the growing Irish community of the United States. This belief took him to court again in 1824, when he and Emmet (also an Anglican) jointly defended Irish Catholic weavers arrested for the violence that ensued in Greenwich Village when Irish Protestants carrying Orange Order flags marched through the neighborhood. Referring again to Ireland's bitter and violent history, Sampson told the jury that they must "avert the arm of the sanguinary bigot [the Orangeman] who would drench your country in blood." Deeply held anti-sectarian views like this also led the exiles to organize associations like the Hibernian Provident Society and the Shamrock Friendly Association, which were open to all Irish immigrants and Irish Americans regardless of their religious beliefs.[24]

The republican views of the exiles and their sometimes strident claims to speak for the Irish American community as a whole, of course, did not win support from all sectors of that community. Prior to the arrival of the United Irishmen and their supporters, Irish American leaders, Protestant and Catholic alike, tended toward political conservatism, especially in the larger cities where the exiles ended up. Wealthy Protestant merchants, for example, dominated the Friendly Sons of St. Patrick, America's first Irish voluntary organization, which maintained close ties with the Federalists. Well-heeled Irish Catholics were often no more sympathetic to the exiles' politics than their Protestant counterparts, a fact made clear on February 8, 1799, when William Duane, James Reynolds, and two other Irish republicans attempted to gather signatures for a petition opposing the Federalists' Alien Act at St. Mary's Catholic Church in Philadelphia. In what came to be known as the "Irish riot," St. Mary's prosperous (and staunchly Federalist) trustees led parishioners in physically attacking the radicals and driving them off the church's grounds. For their part, radicals fired back, denouncing Irish American Federalists as "pro-British" and "Orangemen," and over time their views carried the day. Even the social and political character of St. Mary's itself eventually changed, as newer working-class Irish immigrants began taking a more active role in its affairs—inspired partly by a United Irish priest named James Harold, who arrived in Philadelphia in 1811 after a decade spent in the penal colony of Australia.[25]

For all their unity on certain issues, the exiles were deeply divided on others. In the early years of the nineteenth century, Mathew Carey became one of the nation's most influential advocates for manufacturing, internal improvements such as roads and canals, protective tariffs, and a strong central bank, while other émigrés, such as Hamilton Rowan, clung to a more agrarian vision of America's economic future. In a partially related division, Philadelphia's Republican coalition saw considerable tension between one faction dominated by merchants and manufacturers (for whom Carey spoke) and another representing artisans and laborers, whose undisputed leader was William Duane.[26]

In a replay of disagreements that had first appeared among United Irishmen in Ireland in the early 1790s, the exiles also divided over the new journeymen's unions that were emerging in American cities in the early nineteenth century. This disagreement could be seen most clearly in the 1809–10 New York cordwainers' conspiracy trial, which grew out of efforts by journeymen cordwainers (shoemakers) in the city to prohibit the employment of nonunion journeymen and apprentices. When one employer refused to abide by these regulations, his workers went on strike; then, joined by twenty other master shoemakers, he swore out a complaint against the union's leaders, charging them under English common law with conspiracy to interfere with trade. The employers' goal, it seems clear, was not only to break this particular union but also to obtain a virtual legal ban on trade unionism in general. Arguing passionately for the workers was William Sampson, who drew on his understanding of Irish history to denounce "the spectre of the common law" itself as an oppressive British relic ("remnants of antiquated folly") that should have no legitimate role in a republic. Opposing counsel was Sampson's old friend and fellow state prisoner, Thomas Addis Emmet, who argued (successfully) that while trade unionism itself should not be banned, the common law doctrine of conspiracy did have a place in cases of disputes between employers and workers.[27]

Much more profound than this was a new disagreement that emerged among the exiles over the rapidly expanding American institution of slavery. Opposition to slavery and the slave trade had been a deeply held article of faith among virtually all United Irishmen in the 1790s. Transplanted to the United States, however, some of them ended up supporting the institution, or at least apologizing for its American incarnation. "Slavery is odious wherever it is practiced," wrote the United Irish veteran Denis Driscol in 1802, but in the United States, he continued, "slavery is freedom comparatively speaking." After he moved to Georgia and began editing the *Augusta Chronicle*, Driscol printed advertisements offering rewards for the capture of runaway slaves and defended the harshest forms of punishment for enslaved men and women, including the death penalty for burglary. Some United Irish veterans in America became slaveholders themselves. The family of James Bones, a one-time Antrim rebel turned successful Georgia linen merchant, owned at least fifteen slaves by the early 1820s. In 1819, Anthony Campbell, a United Irish exile in Natchez, Mississippi, placed a newspaper advertisement to obtain the return of a runaway slave, who had "been lately well whipped for theft," adding "the scars are not yet healed."[28]

At the other end of the spectrum were individuals like Thomas Addis Emmet, who remained passionately committed to the anti-slavery cause. Emmet chose settlement in New York over Virginia, primarily because the latter was a slave state, while New York had passed an act for the "gradual abolition of slavery" in 1799. In sharp contrast to Driscol or Campbell, he defended fugitive slaves in court and served as legal counsel to New York's Manumission Society, which sought to keep the issue of slavery before the public, assist individual African Americans in pressing for freedom, and provide formal education for New York's free black population. As with the pro-slavery exiles, there were a number of other United Irishmen in this camp, including Emmet's fellow New York residents William Sampson, William MacNeven, and David Bailie Warden, who believed throughout his life that slavery was the "grand evil in the United States." So it was with the earlier exile, Hamilton Rowan, who, back in 1796, began making plans to move from Philadelphia to the American interior. "I will go to the woods," he wrote to his wife, Sarah, that February, "but I will not kill Indians, nor keep slaves."[29]

Finally, there were those, such as Thomas O'Connor, who fell between these two poles. A Catholic from an old and respected Gaelic family, O'Connor had been given the United Irish oath by Wolfe Tone himself. In New York, he eventually became editor of the city's first Irish American paper, the *Shamrock*. In 1810, before his involvement with it, the *Shamrock* had carried advertisements for slave sales. This sparked angry responses from members of the exile community, including one émigré who wrote an indignant letter reminding readers of the radical Thomas McCabe's efforts to keep Belfast out of the slave trade. "Ireland justly boasts of never having participated in the slave trade and I hope none of her sons in this land of freedom will countenance the dishonourable traffic," he wrote. In response, the *Shamrock* stopped carrying the ads, and when O'Connor joined the paper as editor in 1814, he launched an editorial attack on slavery. Yet as the years went by, O'Connor began to express ambivalence over the institution. Slavery was morally wrong, he continued to believe, but more and more he came to feel that imagining its end was unrealistic. In Philadelphia, William Duane, John Binns, and Mathew Carey followed a similar trajectory, not actively defending slavery but gradually shedding the anti-slavery politics on which they had been reared. Duane's *Aurora* and Binns's *Democratic Press*, the city's leading Jeffersonian organs, were among the few Philadelphia newspapers that continued to print advertisements for the sale of slaves into the first decade of the nineteenth century. Yet Duane was also a leading proponent of allowing African Americans to enlist in the US army during the War of 1812, a move strongly opposed by southern Republicans, including President James Madison, who believed that arming free blacks was an open invitation to slave rebellion. Carey was also equivocal on the question. "Slavery in every form is an evil," he readily admitted in an 1829 essay, but those arguing for emancipation needed to be "aware of the immense difficulty of removing the evil."[30]

Remembering the Rebellion

One thing that the exiles did not shed in the United States was their commitment to achieving Irish independence. Even as the dream of an independent republic faded in Ireland after the defeat of 1798, their enthusiasm remained unabated. In their ongoing activism over the next three decades, they became the pioneers of Irish American nationalism and made a profound contribution to the transmission of the separatist republican vision to future generations in Ireland. In the early years of this period, the exiles' activism involved direct material aid to the revolutionary struggle at home. In 1796, for example, as plans for revolution in Ireland moved rapidly forward, a group of émigrés in America arranged to send gunpowder to Belfast carefully hidden in flaxseed cakes. In 1803, a faction of Philadelphia United Irishmen sent cartridges and pikes to Robert Emmet on the eve of the rising that he led that year.[31]

This early phase of activism also saw the birth of the American Society of United Irishmen, the first explicitly Irish nationalist body in the United States. Founded in Philadelphia in August 1797 by Duane, Reynolds, Rowan, Carey, and a number of other émigrés whose "love of freedom has not been lessened by what we have experienced of its effects, or of Ireland by our distance," the American Society of United Irishmen announced clearly that its goal was "to promote the emancipation of Ireland, and establishment of a republican form of government there." By May 1798 the organization had branches in Delaware, Maryland, South Carolina, New York, and Pennsylvania and counted some 1,500 members in the Philadelphia area alone.[32]

As the revolutionary tide receded, material and organizational efforts like those of the American United Irishmen became much less important than an ideological struggle over the memory and meaning of 1798. In Ireland itself, loyalist writers like Sir Richard Musgrave were already busy constructing an interpretation of 1798 that presented the rebellion in wholly sectarian terms, as the work of brutal and ignorant Catholics embarked on a long and violent crusade against Protestants. "It is not what is erroneously and ridiculously called emancipation that the mass of Irish Roman catholics want," Musgrave declared near the end of his mammoth and commercially successful *Memoirs of the Different Rebellions in Ireland*, which originally appeared in 1801. "It is the extirpation or expulsion of the protestants, the exclusive occupation of the island for themselves, and its separation from England, which they have aimed at from the beginning of Elizabeth's reign." In America, the United Irish émigrés put ink to

paper in a concerted effort to provide an alternative history, a heroic, nonsectarian, and republican version of the events of 1798. John Daly Burk, a middle-class
Protestant radical from Cork who had fled to America in 1796, was the first in
print, publishing in 1799 his *History of the Late War in Ireland*, which placed the
rebellion firmly in the context of the American and French revolutions. William
MacNeven published his *Pieces of Irish History*, which also included an essay by
Emmet, in 1807, arguing in Jeffersonian terms for an inherent right to revolution in the face of tyranny. William Sampson published the first edition of his
Memoirs in New York in the same year, adding new material for a second edition
ten years later. Taken together, these books, and those that came later, offered a
version of the rebellion that ran directly counter to the hostile loyalist version of
events being disseminated in Ireland.[33]

The 1798 rebellion, to be sure, was not the only historical topic that engaged
the American exiles' attention. Mathew Carey took on a more remote subject
in his 1819 book, *Vindiciae Hibernicae*, a systematic effort to refute a long-
held Protestant interpretation of the 1641 Irish uprising as an example of pure
Catholic savagery. Meanwhile, Robert Emmet's 1803 speech from the dock was
being performed on American stages as early as 1806, and the *Shamrock* told
the younger Emmet's story a number of times after it began publication in 1810.
Still, it was the ideological battle over the meaning of 1798—along with the
character and ideals of its leaders—that dominated the historical writings of the
exiles.[34]

In the end, the most important figure in this collective project of historical rec-
lamation was Matilda Tone. Her painstaking efforts to bring her late husband's
contributions to light culminated in the 1826 publication of the two-volume *Life
of Theobald Wolfe Tone*. This turned out to be a key event in the history of Irish
nationalism, for the work not only effectively presented the efforts of the United
Irishmen in a positive light but also constructed Wolfe Tone himself as the hero
he would become to later generations of Irish republicans on both sides of the
Atlantic.[35]

When Tone had gone into exile in the United States in 1795, Matilda and their
children had accompanied him. She disliked America as much as her husband,
describing in a September 1796 letter to Thomas Russell her poor health and
deep unhappiness in her new home. She must have been relieved to have joined
Tone in Paris the following year. But the years in France after Tone's suicide were
difficult ones for her. Rumors that she had married a brother of Napoleon circulated in Ireland in 1801, but these were just as unfounded as those in 1797
that reported her drowning at sea en route to France. Though alive and in good
health, Matilda remained unmarried and in financial straits for many years.
"Nothing can surpass the destitute condition in which the widow and children
of the late Wolfe Tone are left," Martha McTier wrote to William Drennan in

1802. Only in 1804 did Matilda begin receiving a long-promised pension from the French government.[36]

In 1816, Matilda Tone married Thomas Wilson, a Scottish radical she had known for many years, and the two made efforts to return to Ireland. The British government, however, still worried about her as a potential symbol and rallying figure for Irish republicans, rebuffed their efforts. They moved instead to the United States in 1817, settling just outside of Washington in 1819. In Matilda's baggage was Wolfe Tone's mass of unpublished papers—his autobiography, diaries, letters, and assorted political memoranda—as well as copies of his published articles and pamphlets.[37]

Matilda had been guarding this archive for a long time. Most of the material was already in her possession at the time of Tone's death. Some of it was in Philadelphia, where she had entrusted it to James Reynolds in 1796, before leaving America to join Tone in Paris. To her dismay, Reynolds lost or sold all of the material in his care, but Matilda and her son William were able to recover some of it on an 1807 trip to the United States. As early as December 1814, Matilda wrote to her sister, Catherine Heavyside, that she hoped to publish a collection of the papers at some point in the future. Thomas Wilson died in 1824, and the same year the *New Monthly Magazine* in London published a series of extracts from Tone's autobiography, followed in 1825 by an article on Matilda and her family in Paris. In an effort to respond to what she considered an inaccurate assessment of Tone's life and a disrespectful treatment of her own, Matilda, aided by William, turned finally to the work of arranging and editing Tone's papers. The final result was a two-volume work, more than 1,200 pages in length, published in Washington in 1826.[38]

What appeared in print had been shaped and molded in myriad ways: parts of Tone's autobiography had been excised, while materials from his other writings had been carefully selected, arranged, and added to the text. The first materials to be deleted in the process of editing—especially important in light of the book's American publication—were all of Tone's bitingly critical comments about the United States, its people, and its early Federalist leaders, who were by this time already national heroes. Also excised were details about Tone's difficult relationship with Matilda's parents and brother and his flirtations with other women. The goal of this editing job, of course, was to make Tone even more attractive to readers—and especially to potential future supporters of Irish republican nationalism—than he would have been otherwise. Tone's memoirs, William asserted in a preface to the *Life* that was approved, and very likely shaped, by his mother, would convince every fair reader of Tone's "purity and patriotism, whatever they may deem of his wisdom and foresight. No man who ever engaged so deeply and so earnestly in so great a cause, was so little influenced by any motives of personal ambition, or so disinterestedly devoted to what he thought the interest of his country." The task that Matilda and William had accomplished turned out to be an almost textbook example of this sort of imaginative ideological labor in the making of nationalist sentiment.[39]

Catholic Emancipation

The *Life* included Wolfe Tone's most important piece of political writing, *An Argument on Behalf of the Catholics of Ireland*. Focused as they were on Irish, just as much as American affairs, it is not surprising that in the 1820s, Matilda Tone and the other Irish exiles gave full support to the renewed campaign for Catholic emancipation, the repeal of the last remaining laws that excluded Catholics from sitting in Parliament, holding high offices of state, and serving as judges or county sheriffs. While such exclusions obviously affected upper- and middle-class Catholics most directly, they enshrined anti-Catholicism into the fabric of politics in a way that deeply offended much of the Catholic population of Britain and Ireland. William Pitt had hoped, and had convinced many Catholics in Ireland, that these laws could be abolished shortly after the Act of Union took effect in 1801, but large majorities in the House of Commons rejected petitions for Catholic emancipation in both 1805 and 1808. Things looked more hopeful in the second decade of the century. A bill authored by Henry Grattan, a life-long supporter of the cause, went down to defeat by just two votes in 1819 and, two years later, the Commons actually passed an emancipation act. Determined opposition from both the House of Lords and King George IV, however, killed the bill.

A new phase in the campaign began in 1823, when a Catholic lawyer and landowner from County Kerry named Daniel O'Connell, who had been working for emancipation since early in the century, established an organization called the Catholic Association. Though originally a Dublin-based caucus made up of the same mix of landowners, merchants, and professionals that had dominated the eighteenth-century Catholic Committee, the Catholic Association transformed itself within two years into a national mass-based membership organization without precedent in Irish history. Driven by O'Connell's powerful and highly charged rhetoric, the campaign established direct links with the Catholic episcopate and clergy, especially a new generation of politically minded priests then emerging in Ireland. Catholic clergymen became ex-officio members of all branches and played important roles as local organizers and as disseminators of information. Priests also played a critical role in what was perhaps O'Connell's greatest innovation, the "Catholic Rent" that permitted membership in the Catholic Association for just a penny a month, often collected at the church door. Mass enthusiasm was furthered when the organization broadened its goals to include not just fighting the legal restrictions facing well-to-do Catholics but also reducing tithes and ending Ireland's highly discriminatory administration of justice.

The campaign experienced a setback when the Catholic Association was banned in 1825, but continuing mass support became the basis for the breakthrough strategy of direct parliamentary combat to further the cause. O'Connell himself was originally skeptical, but when the Catholic landlord Thomas Wyse and a number of other activists demonstrated the power of the electorate in the general election of 1826 by achieving stunning victories for several pro-emancipation candidates, O'Connell became a convert to political action. His decision to stand in the County Clare by-election of 1828 and his overwhelming triumph there—even though as a Catholic, he could not legally sit in Parliament—finally convinced British policymakers that emancipation could be delayed no longer. Following an intense bout of negotiations, a Catholic Relief Act became law on April 13, 1829, winning for Irish and British Catholics the right to hold high public office and seats in Parliament and winning for O'Connell the popular title of "Liberator." Though the government simultaneously increased the property qualification for voting from forty shillings to ten pounds, thus dramatically reducing the total Irish electorate, few at the time denied the historic character of the victory.[40]

The campaign for Catholic emancipation became the last hurrah for many of the surviving United Irish veterans, both in Ireland and abroad, who saw in it at least partial fulfillment of what they had fought to achieve three decades earlier. In Belfast, William Drennan, the Presbyterian radical who had drifted away from the United Irishmen in the mid-1790s and thus took no part in the 1798 rebellion, was organizing pro-emancipation meetings as early as 1819. "Your object will be obtained and your name recorded in History," he predicted in a letter to O'Connell that year. Although Britain's chief secretary for Ireland knowingly exaggerated when he called for the suppression of the Catholic Association in 1825 because it was filled with those "familiar with the traitors of old times—Tone, Russell, and Emmett [*sic*]," his point had some validity in the American context. It was, in fact, three former United Irishmen—Sampson, Emmet, and MacNeven—who took the lead in founding the New York Friends of Ireland in July 1825 to raise money for Catholic emancipation, establishing the first of what eventually became twenty-four associations across the United States, along with four in Canada and one in Mexico. In contrast to the increasingly Catholic character of the movement in Ireland, these American associations drew considerable support from Irish Protestants, as well as from Americans without any Irish background, the most prominent of whom was George Washington Parke Custis, the first president's step-grandson. Sampson was especially adamant that the movement should retain its nonsectarian character, seeing the struggle as a matter of fundamental justice, not religion, and one that Americans, with their republican tradition, had a particular obligation to support. "I am a Catholic in this respect," said the Anglican Sampson, "that I would not honor any community that would change its religion, and prove renegado through fear or compulsion. It is that terror, tyranny, and persecution, that has made the Population of Ireland so truly Catholic; and it is the knowledge of that sacrilege, that places an honest man, particularly an American, on the side of Catholic Ireland." In Augusta, Georgia, a tight-knit community of United Irish veterans, most of them Ulster Presbyterians, also supported the movement for Catholic emancipation. In Philadelphia, Mathew Carey and John Binns—one a Catholic, one a Protestant, but both Irish republicans—jointly took the helm of the emancipation society that emerged there in 1828.[41]

Committed to a nonviolent strategy and strenuously disavowing any association with the traditions of 1798, leaders of the movement back in Ireland viewed support from men like this with deeply mixed feelings. O'Connell responded unenthusiastically to an 1825 address of support written by MacNeven, leading to a temporary disintegration of the New York organization. In 1829, a key Catholic Association leader, Richard Lalor Sheil, exulted over a contribution of $1,000 from the New Yorkers and referred glowingly to "our auxiliaries in America." In the same year, however, Thomas Wyse cautioned that the American associations had become the tool of MacNeven and other United Irish exiles who "had brought with them the burning sense of accumulated injury—the liveliest desire of retaliation,—a deep and solid detestation of the very name—of the very thought, of England." Wyse was relieved that emancipation had been won before such sentiments could begin to take hold back in Ireland itself. Had the campaign gone on much longer, he opined, "the violent party would have triumphed over the moderate: the American would have gained over the British." [42]

Emancipation was in fact achieved before the American associations could make much of an impact, but this did not prevent the old exiles from celebrating the event with gusto. At the 1829 St. Patrick's Day dinner of the New York Friends of Ireland, with emancipation clearly visible on the horizon, MacNeven compared the campaign to struggles on behalf of African slaves and the Greeks striving for independence against the Ottoman Empire. In Philadelphia, Binns emphasized the nonsectarian theme when he hailed the Catholic Relief Act's passage two months later. "The Catholics are no longer serfs," he proclaimed. "Our bells are ringing a merry peal for *Catholic* Emancipation from the Steeple of a *Protestant* Episcopal Church." In an address to the Philadelphia Friends of Ireland on Bastille Day that year, Binns placed the victory in the widest international republican context when he offered a toast to "the 4th of July, 1776; the 14th of July 1789; and the 13th of April, 1829—the anniversaries of the emancipation of the United States, France, and of Ireland." [43]

Not all the exiles lived to celebrate the victory, however. Late in 1829, the New York Friends of Ireland took the $1,000 that remained in their coffers to build a monument to the memory of Thomas Addis Emmet, who, as his friend Sampson put it, "did not live to behold the triumph of the Catholic cause, that happy accomplishment of one of the great measures to which he devoted fortune and life." Emmet had collapsed in a New York courtroom on November 14, 1827, and had died the following day. His funeral was one of the most impressive New York had yet seen, with James Monroe and DeWitt Clinton serving as pallbearers. "He came from a distant land, an exile, after long captivity, broken in his fortunes, crossed in his dearest hopes, pursued by malice, and branded as a malefactor, to whom the common rights of hospitality could not with safety be extended, and against whom the doors of society should be closed," Sampson had eulogized in a brief address to the New York Bar. "But when he came to know, and was judged by his own merits, and no longer by false report; prejudice died away; distrust was turned to confidence, and hate to love, and none were more ready to shed tears of affection on his bier than those who had been first taught to shun or revile him."[44]

The monument that Emmet's comrades built, however, did not quite fit Sampson's simple narrative of oppression and exile followed by acceptance and success. One of the most imposing in St. Paul's churchyard in lower Manhattan and still throwing (as MacNeven put it in 1833) "a melancholy grandeur on the cemetery," the monument has inscriptions not only in English and Latin but also in Irish Gaelic. In the sculpted image that adorns its front, an American eagle clutches in its talons an Irish harp. Rather than a symbol of what later generations would call assimilation or "Americanization," the Emmet monument illustrates both the synthesis of Irish and American republicanism that the United Irish exiles labored to effect and their abiding commitment to what they called "the cause of Ireland."[45]

3

Repeal, Rebellion, and American Slavery, 1829–1848

In 1829, it was finally won: the achievement of civil equality for Catholics, in Britain as well as Ireland, "emancipation" as it was called. This might have been the moment for Irish reformers to simply declare victory and rest on their laurels. But for many, at least those who thought of themselves as Irish nationalists as well as reformers, Catholic emancipation could only be seen as a partial victory. In New York City, the United Irish exile Thomas O'Connor welcomed reform but argued vigorously that this was no time to quit. "Our course is clear, we must continue to meet, we must agitate, we must enlist public opinion, we must enlist the world," he wrote on the eve of Catholic emancipation. "We will continue as a thorn in the side of England."[1]

Daniel O'Connell, the charismatic leader of the emancipation campaign, was not ready to quit, either. In the 1830s, he turned his attention to an even more daunting task: the repeal of the Act of Union between Great Britain and Ireland and the restoration of Ireland's ancient parliament that the act had abolished in 1800. Most of the surviving United Irish exiles in the United States and elsewhere supported the cause of repeal, just as they had that of Catholic emancipation. But O'Connell's outlook differed in profound ways from that of the United Irishmen. Rejecting both their secular republican political vision and their willingness to embrace physical force, he spoke for a new, more moderate, and more Catholic incarnation of Irish nationalism. In the United States, where an extensive network of repeal associations emerged in the 1840s, the tension between the exiles' republicanism and O'Connell's constitutional nationalism was present from the outset. But in America this tension was overshadowed by a far more significant conflict that exploded in the 1840s, one over slavery, abolition, and the civic and national identities of Irish immigrants in their adopted country. In Ireland, the decline of the repeal movement, combined with the inspiration provided by the European revolutions of 1848, put a small group of nationalists on the road to rebellion, a rebellion that generated significant, if somewhat inchoate, popular support in the United States.

O'Connell and the Movement for Repeal

O'Connell had long believed that Ireland would best be served by its own parliament, operating under a British monarchy. His very first political speech, in January 1800, had been delivered in opposition to the proposed Act of Union and he began publicly calling for repeal of the act as early as 1810. The struggle for Catholic emancipation and his own legal career occupied him over the next two decades, but following the 1832 British general election, O'Connell became the leader of the first Irish nationalist parliamentary party ever in the British House of Commons, composed of thirty-nine MPs pledged to working for repeal. During the 1830s, however, with the moderately reform-minded Whigs in power, O'Connell put repeal aside to focus on other measures. In his informal 1835 Lichfield House compact with the Whigs, he suspended the call for repeal in exchange for Irish municipal reform and reform of the tithe, the burdensome and, to Catholics and Presbyterians, deeply offensive tax on agricultural income that supported the established Church of Ireland.[2]

In April 1840, disappointed by the inadequacy of most of the enacted reforms, and with a Conservative election victory looming, O'Connell formed the National Association for Full and Prompt Justice or Repeal (renamed the Loyal National Repeal Association in 1841) to agitate directly for repeal of the Act of Union. This marked the stirrings of the first truly mass movement working to achieve a nationalist goal in Irish history. Building on the phenomenal success of his earlier "Catholic Rent," O'Connell set association membership dues at a penny a month, calling it the "Repeal Rent." Drawing on another lesson of the Catholic emancipation campaign—but in a sharp departure from the secular and nonsectarian politics of the United Irishmen—O'Connell cultivated a close relationship with the Catholic clergy and developed a rhetoric and policies that made Catholicism and Irish nationalism appear almost interchangeable. There was still a place for Protestants in the movement; in fact, thirteen of the thirty-nine repeal MPs elected in 1832 had been Protestants, and the Protestant landlord William Smith O'Brien would be a key leader in the Repeal Association from 1844 onward. But the general Catholic orientation of O'Connell's nationalism was clear to all. "The Catholic church is a national church," he declared at the opening of the repeal campaign in 1840, "and if the people rally with me they will have a nation for that church." This basic orientation shaped O'Connell's approach to the nuts and bolts of political organizing: "Be sure to have the approval of the Catholic clergy in every place you move to," he admonished his personal secretary in September 1842.[3]

O'Connell's break with the traditions of the United Irishmen went far beyond this: he was, in many ways, deeply and profoundly anti-republican. The nephew and eventual heir of a wealthy County Kerry landowner, he had attended Catholic schools in northern France in the tumultuous years from 1791 to 1793, fleeing the country on the very day of Louis XVI's execution. This background led O'Connell to identify strongly with at least some of the institutions of the ancien régime and to oppose the leveling, anti-monarchical, and anti-clerical aspects of the French Revolution. Though a subsequent spell studying law in London drew him to the edge of radical and free thought circles there, his deeper conservatism was apparent in his reaction to the failed French invasion at Bantry Bay in 1796: had the invasion succeeded, O'Connell wrote, it "should have shook the foundation of all property, would have destroyed our profession (Law) root and branch." His overarching goal—even more important to him than Catholic emancipation—was Irish autonomy, the restoration of a suitably reformed parliament in Dublin. The years from 1782 to 1800, the era of what was coming to be called "Grattan's Parliament," he saw as a kind of golden age. But, like Grattan himself, O'Connell believed strongly in the legitimacy of the British crown and in the importance of some kind of continuing constitutional connection between Ireland and Britain on matters of defense and empire. The emphasis on "loyalty" in the name of the Loyal National Repeal Association and O'Connell's devotion to the young Queen Victoria made this more than clear.[4]

He was also an adamant opponent of physical force, at least in Ireland. The government informer Francis Higgins claimed that O'Connell was a member of the United Irishmen in the late 1790s, and it is certain that he at least flirted with the organization while studying law in Dublin in 1797. By the time of Robert Emmet's Dublin insurrection, however, his opposition to revolutionary physical force had hardened into dogma. Emmet "merits and will suffer the severest punishment," he wrote in August 1803. "A man who could coolly prepare so much bloodshed, so many murders—and such horrors of every kind has ceased to be an object of compassion." O'Connell's views on revolutionary violence were not consistently pacifistic; he supported both the 1830 Belgian revolution that won independence from the Netherlands and the wars of liberation in South America, and he greatly admired Simón Bolívar, for whom the title "Liberator" had originally been coined. But in the Irish context, he was unalterably opposed to physical force as morally wrong and inevitably leading to disaster.[5]

Organizing for repeal got off to a slow start. Some of the Catholic middle classes and bishops who had been enthusiastic about Catholic emancipation were much less so about repeal, believing, as a Cork merchant put it, "that its attainment is impractible," and O'Connell himself was absorbed with his responsibilities as Dublin's lord mayor from November 1841 to October 1842. But in 1843, which O'Connell declared to be "the great Repeal year," the movement took off. Peaceful mass demonstrations, which had been important in the Catholic emancipation struggle, became even more so in the struggle for repeal. Between March and September 1843, a succession of unprecedented mass demonstrations was held. Several of these "monster meetings," as the press called them, attracted crowds of half a million or more, peaking on August 15 on the Hill of Tara, above its ancient Gaelic earthworks, where an estimated 750,000 people gathered to see O'Connell and demonstrate their support for repeal.[6]

At the same time, hovering over the movement was the stance of Sir Robert Peel's Tory government, which had taken office in 1841. In his five years in power, Peel tried hard to undercut Irish opposition by reaching out to moderate Catholics in Ireland, increasing government grants to the Catholic Maynooth College, for instance, and facilitating private bequests for Catholic religious and charitable purposes. O'Connell's movement stood as the largest single obstacle to this political strategy, however, and as the monster meetings continued over the summer, the government increased the strength of its Irish garrisons and watched carefully for examples of seditious language in the repeal press. Faced with yet another demonstration scheduled for October 8 at Clontarf and fastening onto the mention of a "repeal cavalry" and other military metaphors in announcements for the meeting, the government issued a proclamation forbidding it to take place. O'Connell obeyed the proclamation and called off the demonstration. Buoyed by this initial victory, the government arrested him and eight other prominent figures in the Repeal Association on the charge of sedition.[7]

Irish Immigration and the American Repeal Network

As these dramatic events unfolded in Ireland, the movement for repeal was rapidly developing an important wing in the United States as well. Surprisingly, it began not in the Irish centers of New York or Philadelphia but in the relatively new Irish Catholic community of Boston. As Thomas Mooney, who had worked with O'Connell in Ireland before setting off for America, characterized that community, it was "as yet but infantine" and employed mainly "in manual labour." Yet, he continued, despite their small numbers and paltry resources, the Boston Irish were "sensitively alive to the sufferings of their fellow countrymen."[8]

Boston emerged as an Irish nationalist center as Irish migrants to America were becoming more working class, more Catholic, somewhat more likely to come from provinces other than Ulster, and much more likely to end up in the industrializing northeast. Between the end of the Napoleonic Wars in 1815

and 1845—that is, the thirty years preceding the onset of the Great Famine—
somewhere between 800,000 and 1 million Irish men and women made their
way to North America, twice as many as in the entire previous two centuries. The
Irish accounted for a full third of all immigrants to the United States. Another
500,000 or so migrated to Britain, with approximately 30,000 obtaining government assistance to make the long voyage to Australia. Emigration became a mass
phenomenon for the first time in Ireland's history.[9]

The causes for this are not hard to locate. The end of Britain's long war with
France ended Ireland's war-induced prosperity, triggering an almost immediate
agricultural depression. Depression, growing competition from England, and
increasing mechanization also had disastrous effects on the ability of men and
women to earn wages by spinning textiles or weaving cloth at home, cottage
industries that had once given employment to as many as a million Irish small
farmers and peasants. The expansion of livestock grazing, the one bright spot
in the postwar Irish economy, also reduced rural employment substantially and
led to the transformation of potato plots and fields into grazing land for cattle
and sheep. Meanwhile Ireland's population was growing, doubling from 4 million in 1780 to 8 million in 1841. In the face of population growth, some farmers and better-off tenants tried to keep their holdings intact by passing them
on to just one heir rather than dividing land among many as they had in the
past. But this strategy dramatically increased the number of people in need of
employment.[10]

One result of these economic and demographic changes was the reemergence
of struggles over issues of rents, wages, and land use and occupancy. Although
rural protest was hardly new to Ireland, in the early 1820s it took a new and significantly more violent form with the Rockites (so-called because they claimed
to be followers of a mythical "Captain Rock"), an agrarian insurgency more
widespread than any Ireland had seen since the 1790s. Though economic misery
provides only a partial explanation for the Rockites' emergence, the movement
drew many adherents among hard-pressed peasants in southern Leinster and
eastern Munster, who used it to strike out against increasing rents, decreasing
wages, and the commercialization of agriculture, as well as against older injus-
tices like the tithe. A more important response over the long run, however, was
emigration. Transatlantic migration, in particular, was facilitated by the expansion of shipping that accompanied the end of the Napoleonic wars, the eventual
repeal of British passenger laws that had kept ship ticket prices high, and the
emergence of Liverpool as the focal point of trade between Britain and North
America. Concurrently, the construction of roads and canals within Ireland tied
more and more people to the market, gave them knowledge about the larger
world, and increasingly rendered emigration a reasonable response to economic
hardship.[11]

As transportation networks, market activity, and information spread throughout Ireland, the social and regional origins of emigrants gradually changed. Though they still tended to have more economic resources and skills than later Famine emigrants, poorer farmers and workers began to emigrate for the first time in these years. By 1836, for example, nearly two-thirds of all Irish immigrants arriving in New York were servants or laborers, up from under a third just a decade earlier. Ulster remained the main source of Irish emigrants through the 1830s, though more and more Ulster Catholics joined the Presbyterians who had traditionally dominated the flow out of the province. By the 1820s and 1830s, enthusiasm for migration had spread south into northern Leinster and Connacht, especially the counties of Longford, Meath, Sligo, and Roscommon, while particular regions within Munster, especially County Cork, began sending large numbers of emigrants as well. Since these areas were predominantly Catholic, Irish Catholic emigrants to America in the 1830s outnumbered Irish Protestants for the first time since 1700.

Immigrant settlement patterns in the United States began to shift as well. Previous Irish migrants had been drawn to New York and Philadelphia, where they accounted for a fifth of the approximately 100,000 residents in each city in 1820, as well as to the southern seaports of Baltimore and Charleston. Many of the earlier Ulster emigrants had also headed to the American backcountry: central and western Pennsylvania, western Maryland, the ridges and valleys of Virginia, and the piedmont of the Carolinas and Georgia. Now new economic opportunities, developing trade and transportation networks, and especially the demand for labor stimulated by industrialization and urbanization drew more and more Irish immigrants to the cities, canal towns, and industrial mill villages of the northeast and mid-Atlantic states, where the terms "Irish," "Catholic," and "worker" began to seem almost synonymous.[12]

Nonetheless, Irish America remained socioeconomically heterogeneous, and not only because of the continuing predominance of the early and relatively prosperous Protestant immigrants. The very presence of large numbers of new Catholic working-class immigrants opened up significant opportunities for at least some Irish Catholics as well. In Lowell, Massachusetts, for instance, a small Irish Catholic middle class began emerging as early as the 1820s, centered around the foreman of the first crew of Irish laborers in that mill village, a stone mason turned labor contractor, and a group of shopkeepers whose customers were mainly the transient Irish workers of the region. In Worcester, Massachusetts, substantial building contractors and master artisans were providing leadership to the Irish Catholic working-class community by the 1830s. In Kensington, one of the industrial suburbs growing up around Philadelphia, this process went further, for here a small group of Irish Catholic master weavers had become wealthy men by the early 1840s, when they faced off in a series of bitter strikes waged by their (also Irish Catholic) employees. By this time, New York and Philadelphia both possessed a sizable Irish American middle class, consisting of businessmen, lawyers, and other professionals—both Catholic and Protestant—who watched the arrival of the poorer immigrants with apprehension. Even in Boston, where most Irish were indeed working class, Thomas Mooney noted "the exception of those who keep little groceries, groggeries, and boarding-houses, and the like." The beginnings of the "lace curtain" Irish Catholic middle class were already visible.[13]

All of this had huge ramifications for the American Catholic Church, which grew rapidly and was increasingly dominated by men of Irish birth or ancestry. Although the federal government kept no statistics on church membership, historians estimate that in the two decades after 1830, America's Catholics increased from approximately 3 percent to 8 percent of the total population—making theirs the largest religious denomination in the country—and that the Irish made up a majority of the nation's approximately 1.6 million Catholics in 1850. The composition of the church hierarchy reflected this changing religious demography: as late as 1829, only one American bishop, in Philadelphia, was Irish, but by the eve of the Famine, Irish bishops led the dioceses of Boston, Chicago, Cincinnati, Pittsburgh, and, most notably, New York, where an outspoken Ulsterman named John Hughes was named bishop in 1842. In a related trend, earlier Irish American newspapers like the *Irish Shield* or Thomas O'Connor's *Shamrock*, which had generally been political and nonsectarian, were eclipsed by the rapid growth of explicitly Catholic newspapers and magazines, the number of which leaped from six to fifteen between 1836 and 1845 and included such widely read papers as the *New York Freeman's Journal*, the *Pittsburgh Catholic*, the *Philadelphia Catholic Herald*, the *Cincinnati Catholic Telegraph*, and the *Boston Pilot*.[14]

The leadership of United Irish exiles and other republicans in the Irish community was increasingly being challenged, not only by the growing social weight of Catholicism but also by emerging new leaders of the Democratic Party, especially in the large cities. Mike Walsh, the Protestant son of a United Irishman in Cork who became the leader of the "shirtless" or "subterranean" Democrats in New York, epitomized the new style of leadership, and conflict with the surviving exiles was inevitable. When the once-revered William Sampson ran for Congress as a Whig in 1834, working-class voters in the heavily Irish Sixth Ward, by now deeply loyal to the Democrats, handed him a humiliating defeat, with one newspaper's prediction that the old political exile "won't carry with him ten votes of Irishmen, or the sons of Irishmen in this city" coming in not too far off the mark. The very meaning of Irish identity was up for grabs, and secular and republican notions of what it meant to be Irish in America appeared to be losing out. Sampson seemed to some to be a relic of the past; the future belonged to figures like New York Bishop John Hughes and "shirtless" Mike Walsh.[15]

As the numbers and political influence of the Catholic Irish grew, so too did anti-Catholicism and anti-Irish nativism. Fomented by Protestant religious revivals, as well as by political turf battles and class-based prejudice, nativism grew steadily through the 1830s, strengthened by publications like Maria Monk's fabricated and salacious *Awful Disclosures* of life in a Montreal convent. Literature portraying Irish Catholics as superstitious, ignorant, and politically dominated by their priests—and thus intrinsically anti-republican in outlook—also fueled nativism, as did local conflicts between Catholics and Protestants over public school policies, such as the use of the Protestant King James Bible in classrooms. In the early 1840s, nativists began organizing politically, forming parties with names like "Native American" and "American Republican" to contest elections. The movement rose to a crescendo in 1844 when the American Republicans elected six congressmen and dozens of local officials in Boston, New York, and Philadelphia and when bloody and destructive anti-Catholic riots erupted over the school Bible issue in the Kensington and Southwark districts of the latter city.[16]

This was the social and political setting in which the American repeal movement arose and grew. On October 12, 1840, just six months after O'Connell founded the Repeal Association in Ireland, a meeting attended by as many as 2,000 people at Boston's Boylston Hall established the Friends of Ireland Society to provide financial and moral support for the repeal movement back in Ireland. As the Dublin-born British consul to Massachusetts, Thomas Colley Grattan, observed, it was not "the historical names" like Emmet or MacNeven but "the obscure Irish inhabitants of Boston" with "such patronymics as M'Hugh, M'Ginniskin, and Murphy" that took the lead. A fish packer, a coal and wood dealer, and a hack driver dominated this first meeting, with only Patrick Donahoe, editor of the *Boston Pilot*, and his assistant offering a touch of bourgeois respectability. The organization selected as its president John W. James, an eminent Yankee lawyer and son of a Revolutionary soldier, who had developed an enthusiasm for Irish causes and had led Boston's Catholic emancipation organization, the Hibernian Relief Society, back in the 1820s. But overall, as the condescending Grattan sneered, the founders of the American repeal movement were individuals "of no note or position."[17]

Nonetheless, the organization quickly established branches in South Boston, Charlestown, Roxbury, East Boston, and West Cambridge, drawing heavily on new Catholic immigrants to the city and its environs. By December 1840, repeal organizations had sprung up in mill and factory towns throughout Massachusetts and Rhode Island, as well as in Philadelphia and New York. As the movement grew, its social composition and political connections expanded as well. In Lowell, Massachusetts, for example, at least some middle-class Yankee Protestants joined middle- and working-class Irish Catholics in supporting the movement and in charging Britain with "intrigue, perjury, infidelity and tyrannical treatment of Ireland." In Philadelphia, the repeal organization was headed by an important local political figure, Judge Joseph Doran, who had been active in the city's Catholic emancipation organization. In New York, the Tammany organization threw open the doors of its hall for repeal meetings.[18]

New York was also the scene of the first stirrings of internal conflict within the movement. Robert Emmet, son of the United Irish exile Thomas Addis Emmet, had agreed to serve as president of the New York Friends of Ireland and presided over the initial meeting of the repeal organization in December 1840. But in the spring of 1841, O'Connell, at a meeting of the Repeal Association in Dublin, offered his thoughts on the 1798 rebellion, characterizing the United Irishmen as "weak and wicked men who considered force and sanguinary violence as part of their resources for ameliorating our institutions." When Emmet learned that O'Connell had called his late father, his martyred uncle (and namesake), and their republican comrades "miscreants," worthy only of the "contempt and indignation of mankind," he angrily resigned the presidency of the Friends of Ireland, which also passed resolutions disapproving O'Connell's remarks. The United Irish exile Thomas O'Connor, now seventy years old, decided to remain in the New York organization but, like many others, believed that O'Connell had been "wrong in making an unnecessary attack on the United Irishmen of 1798," so many of whom had perished in an effort "to confer full and not partial independence for Ireland" (a barbed reference to the more limited ambitions of O'Connell's movement). "Must we condemn them because they were more passionate?" O'Connor mused. "Forbid it." Tensions within the city's repeal movement peaked three months later when a group of younger and more militant activists left the parent organization to form the New York Young Men's Repeal Association.[19]

Despite these early tensions, the movement grew dramatically in 1841 and 1842, spreading south along the Atlantic coast and into the interior of the country. Thomas Mooney, working under the aegis of the New York Young Men's group, played a critical role in its growth, traveling to Ohio and from there into the South, as far as Louisiana, organizing repeal associations wherever he went. Meanwhile, the nation's leading Irish Catholic newspapers, especially the *Boston Pilot* and the *New York Freeman's Journal* (both of which had many readers across the country), publicized meetings and listed officers of and donors to the associations, aided by short-lived repeal newspapers that sprang up in several cities. The "repeal year" of 1843 saw still further growth. The Philadelphia branch collected $2,000 in a single week in June and, by the end of the year, repeal associations could be found from Maine to New Orleans to the western territory of Iowa.[20]

As the movement grew, efforts were made to establish some kind of permanent national organization. On Washington's Birthday in 1842, the first National Repeal Convention, the first nationwide gathering of Irish nationalists in American history, opened for a two-day session at Independence Hall in Philadelphia. Neither the meeting date nor the venue were accidental but rather reflected an effort to connect the movement to America's patriotic (and anti-British) heritage, a move also registered in the selection of the Boston Yankee John W. James as president of the convention. Delegations from twenty-six cities and towns were present, though the convention ended without creating a lasting organization. Still, the social background of the delegates indicated how the movement had changed in the sixteen months since it began. The convention was dominated by middle-class and successful Irish, many of them born in the United States, with a fair sprinkling of Americans from non-Irish backgrounds as well. Politicians and merchants, doctors and lawyers, journalists and building contractors had supplanted the fish packers and hack drivers who had founded the movement. The Philadelphia delegation alone included four physicians, an alderman, the city recorder, and the Pennsylvania state attorney general.[21]

This changing social class composition was not the only notable feature of the repeal movement. At least in the eyes of contemporaries, the American repeal associations seemed to break entirely new ground by providing avenues for the participation of women. In August 1841, Thomas Mooney organized a committee within the Young Men's Repeal Association to approach New York's "ladies, and solicit their countenance and support in favor of the good cause." The following month, Philadelphia's repeal association admitted as full members sixteen "lovely young ladies" who had donated money and whose "patriotism and virtues cannot be too much extolled." Boston and Charleston, Massachusetts, and several southern associations as well soon began reporting on women's financial contributions and their attendance at meetings. While there were no women among the 202 delegates at the first National Repeal Convention, women's enthusiasm for the cause was already being acknowledged in its deliberations. When John T. Doyle of New York proposed that a committee be established to address the people of England on the subject of repeal, other delegates strenuously opposed this as a humiliating and obsequious petitioning of Britain. The debate on the question was vigorous but ended abruptly when John C. Tucker of Boston commented that if "he should vote for it the men of Boston would scout at it, and he would not dare to look at the women." At this point Doyle withdrew the resolution, with Tucker remarking, "the charm was in his allusion to the women." Though his comments were meant to be humorous, the power of the joke lay in the reality of women's support for repeal.[22]

In 1843, women dramatically expanded their involvement in the movement. That October, a group of Philadelphia women joined a newly formed repeal association, quickly raising £50, which they sent to O'Connell's eldest daughter, Mrs. Christopher Fitzsimmons, in Dublin. Explaining to her "how large a space the cause of Ireland fills in the affections of the women of America," they compared their own activism to that of women in "our revolutionary struggle," who, they maintained, "took a prominent though not obtrusive part." The *Public Ledger*, Philadelphia's leading newspaper, estimated that of the 3,000 city residents attending a repeal meeting in November, 300 to 400 were women. Meanwhile women in both Providence and Boston were taking an increasingly large role in fundraising, leading the *Boston Pilot* to praise this "novel and striking feature in the American agitation."[23]

In fact, the phenomenon of women's social activism in American cities of this era was far from novel. As early as the 1790s, from New York City and Boston to Utica, New York, and Petersburg, Virginia, middle-class and working-class women, black and white, Protestant, Catholic, and Jewish, had thrown themselves into creating a wide variety of charitable, religious, and reform organizations. The women who joined the repeal campaign in the 1840s were thus building on a substantial tradition of American women's social activism. But the phenomenon was indeed "novel and striking" in comparison with Ireland, where women's involvement in the Repeal Association was confined to observing meetings from the gallery at the Dublin Corn Exchange. O'Connell had actually read Mary Wollstonecraft in the 1790s, agreeing with her that "the mind has no sex, and that women are unjustly enslaved," and during the campaign for Catholic emancipation in the 1820s, he had specifically appealed to women contributors. But he never believed that they should exercise political power. Now he welcomed financial support from American women, expressing "gratitude to the ladies involved," but did not use it as an opportunity to encourage the participation of Irish women in the movement.[24]

Protestants were also welcomed in the American repeal associations. In Savannah, Georgia, a port city with a growing Irish population, a Protestant, George B. Cumming, and a Catholic, Michael Dillon, jointly led the repeal organization, whose mainly working-class members also included a significant minority of non-Irish Americans. In February 1841, the Boston Repeal Association announced that its membership was open to all, "without distinction of sect or party." And in September, Brooklyn repealers wrote to O'Connell, noting that "our countrymen here, of all creeds, and Americans of all ranks, join us." A Philadelphia repealer emphasized the point the same month, writing to a Dublin associate of O'Connell that "one of the most insidious and not least dangerous of the calumnies" put forth by "enemies of Ireland" was "that the Repeal Movement both in Ireland and in this country is *exclusively Catholic in origin and object*—that the *Pope* is the author and abettor of it." The city's Repeal Association reinforced his point in January 1842 when they selected a native-born Protestant, Democratic politician William Stokes, to succeed a second-generation Irish American Catholic, Judge Joseph Doran, as their president. The following month, the first National Repeal Convention endorsed "An Address to the People of Ireland" that envisioned an Ireland that had "education without sectarian jealousies, religion without tithes, peace without Ribbonmen and without Orangemen." Not surprisingly, since one of its authors was the old United Irishman Thomas O'Connor, the address looked to a future in which "Protestant and Catholic would be brethren and *Irishmen*; all would be happy." "In America there were many friends of Ireland both amongst the residents and the natives," a visiting American told a Repeal meeting in Dublin in 1842, "and men of every clime, creed and denomination."[25]

Yet, despite the attraction of Protestants (both Irish and non-Irish) to the movement, it remained predominantly Irish and, even more important, predominantly Irish Catholic. The deeply anti-sectarian vision of the United Irish exiles was in decline and Irish nationalism in America, as in Ireland, was beginning to take shape as a movement closely linked to the Catholic Church. This was clearly revealed during the movement's first scandal, which centered on Thomas Mooney, traveling organizer of the New York Young Men's Repeal Association. On May 21, 1842, the *Catholic Telegraph*, official weekly of the Cincinnati diocese, broke the story that Mooney had attempted to seduce a married woman in Natchez, Tennessee, adding the "melancholy" observation that "so many should prove reckless of the high trust reposed in them, and instead of aiding to shield their helpless Ireland from the darts of her enemies, should add by their misconduct to her many afflictions." When Mooney denied the accusation, the Young Men's group appointed a Catholic priest, the Reverend John Power, to investigate. Power ruled that the evidence was inconclusive and Mooney's supporters managed, over protest from the association's officers, to pass resolutions exonerating him. The officers then resigned en masse, which led to conciliatory efforts that resulted in the creation of a new unified New York Association headed by Thomas O'Connor—and Mooney's hasty departure for Boston. Significantly, neither side in this debate challenged the authority of representatives of the Catholic Church to make charges against leaders of the Irish nationalist movement or to investigate and pass judgment on them.[26]

The Mooney scandal may have slowed the movement's growth in America, but not by much. By the time the second National Repeal Convention, attended by 405 delegates from thirteen states, opened its proceedings at New York's Broadway Tabernacle in September 1843, the movement had captured public attention far beyond the Irish immigrant community. Holding the gavel was no less a public figure than Robert Tyler, eldest son of the president of the United States, John Tyler. Other well-known figures, including the Whig journalist Horace Greeley, New York's former Whig governor William H. Seward, former Democratic president Martin Van Buren, and Democratic politicians James Polk and James Buchanan, also spoke out in support of the cause, as did President Tyler himself. "I am a decided friend of the Repeal of the Legislative Union between Great Britain and Ireland," he had said in July 1843. "I ardently and anxiously hope that it may take place, and I have the utmost confidence that Ireland will have her own Parliament in her own capital in a very short time."[27]

Why were such prominent non-Irish Americans attracted to the cause of repealing the Act of Union? Certainly a political calculus was at work for some of them, even if anti-repeal newspapers like the *New York Herald* exaggerated the importance of "broken down politicians and office-hunting speculators of both parties" in the associations. The Tammany machine in New York had been working hard to attract Irish immigrants to the Democratic Party for years. Opposing the newly powerful forces of nativism and of temperance offered one way to do this, but so did the relatively cost-free strategy of support for repeal. Tammany and the Democrats had no monopoly on political opportunism. John Tyler, for example, who had suddenly become president after William Henry Harrison's death in 1841, was a politician in desperate need of a constituency. A one-time Democrat who had already been expelled by the Whigs, Tyler had much to gain and nothing to lose by supporting the movement, as did other long shots for the 1844 presidency, such as Lewis Cass of Michigan and Colonel Richard M. Johnson of Kentucky.[28]

The support that presidential hopeful Lewis Cass gave to repeal was also influenced by an ideological force that remained powerful in America in the 1840s: Anglophobia. A Democrat from Michigan who had served as minister to France under both Van Buren and Tyler, Cass was a well-known and scathing critic of the British navy's intrusive search practices at sea and had published a widely read pamphlet denouncing these as an affront to America's national honor. Anglophobia increased in the early 1840s as British imperial wars in China and Afghanistan and, in particular, Britain's November 1840 naval victory over Egyptian forces at St. Jean d-Acre in Syria prompted concern among many American political leaders. A widely publicized February 1841 House Foreign Affairs Committee report, authored by the South Carolinian Francis W. Pickens, characterized Britain as a sinister international menace, moving "steadily upon her object with an ambition that knows no bounds." All of this inclined some Americans to see the Act of Union as just another example of British imperial aggression. Irish independence "will most surely be accomplished," wrote Josiah Abbott, a Massachusetts corporation lawyer in 1843. "Seven millions of true-minded Irishmen cannot always be held in bondage." Irish American repealers benefited from this Anglophobia by presenting themselves as loyal Americans who shared with numerous other Americans an antipathy to the British.[29]

Finally, O'Connell's international stature as a liberal political leader and his success in achieving Catholic emancipation through peaceful means drew some non-Irish Americans to the cause of repeal. In the United States, O'Connell was one of the most admired European politicians of his day. In the American Whig Party, aspiring politicians sometimes even modeled their oratory on his, along with that of the Anglo-Irish leaders Henry Grattan and Edmund Burke. O'Connell's moderate political liberalism also drew support from Whigs. A figure like Seward, for example, could deeply deplore the radicalism of the French Revolution (and by association that of the United Irishmen), while admiring O'Connell, who, he wrote, carefully steered Ireland "between the dangers of Anarchy and the pressure of Despotism."[30]

The repealers who met in New York certainly had grounds to feel satisfied with the support their movement and leader had achieved. But clouding the proceedings was the awareness that Robert Peel's government was on the verge of suppressing the Repeal Association in Ireland. Recognizing this, the delegates displayed a willingness to embrace physical force that greatly dismayed O'Connell himself. They greeted the entrance of a group of aging United Irish exiles, including John Caldwell and Thomas O'Connor, with rapturous applause. When a national executive committee of five members was established to coordinate action in the event of a crisis in Ireland, O'Connor's son, Charles, received praise when he compared the new body to the Directory of the old United Irishmen. One wealthy Irish American offered to contribute $1,000 toward financing an invasion of Canada if Peel used force against O'Connell, and even the normally pacifistic John W. James called for the shipment of American arms to Ireland to aid "the finest peasantry in the world" in resisting Peel, triggering wild cheers among the delegates.[31]

This kind of talk, however, set off alarm bells for some of the delegates present. When the term "physical force" was used in one resolution, Dr. Edmund Bailey O'Callaghan, a member of the Albany delegation, rose in dissent—and in so doing brought to the surface some of the more complex transnational connections involved in the repeal movement. Born to a Catholic family in County Cork in 1797, O'Callaghan had migrated to Quebec in the 1820s. In the 1830s he joined Louis-Joseph Papineau's Patriote Party, a movement of French Canadians locked in a bitter political fight with the British colonial government, and began editing the party's Anglophone newspaper, the Montreal *Vindicator*. Working tirelessly to attract Irish Catholic immigrants to the Patriotes, O'Callaghan drew parallels between Britain's oppressive treatment of French Canada and of Ireland, compared Canadian Tories to "Orangemen," and saluted Papineau himself as the "O'Connell of Lower Canada." As tensions reached a boiling point, O'Callaghan called openly for revolution, but British troops easily crushed two poorly organized rebellions in 1837 and 1838. Hundreds of rebels were killed, imprisoned, or transported to Australia, while others, including O'Callaghan and Papineau, fled to the United States. By 1843, then, O'Callaghan was both a political exile and living testimony to what he saw now as the folly of taking up arms against the British Empire. A fervent convert to O'Connell's vision of moral force, he spoke eloquently on the subject at the New York convention. In the end, such views carried the day: the new executive committee finessed the whole issue by interpreting "physical force" to mean "monetary contribution."[32]

With over 400 convention delegates, a good deal of money to spend, and considerable American sympathy, the repeal movement had hit its high point. To be sure, both the numbers involved and amounts of money collected pale in comparison with later Irish American nationalist movements, and the repealers' heavy reliance on non-Irish political leaders indicated that the interweaving of Irish American ethnic identity and Irish nationalism, which would characterize some of these later movements, had not taken form. Still the American movement had made its mark. "The spirit which has been shown in this matter, the money which has been sent and interest manifested in the success of their efforts," observed a writer in Philadelphia's *Public Ledger* in June 1843, "prove that the Repealers of this country are hand and heart with their friends abroad."[33]

The Irish Diaspora and Repeal

O'Connell's fight for repeal was the first Irish nationalist movement to attract significant support throughout the Irish diaspora. A number of branches appeared in Canada, for example. Halifax, Nova Scotia, boasted an active association in the mid-1840s, and Irish repeal supporters there eventually joined forces with the liberal Reform Party to defeat a long-established Tory regime in the province in the 1847 elections. In Toronto, more conservative Catholic clergymen played a prominent role in the movement, apparently supporting Irish nationalism at least partly as a way of cementing the allegiance of new Irish Catholic immigrants to the church.[34]

Even Australia, a destination for some 50,000 Irish emigrants between 1836 and 1850, was affected by the agitation. In late 1842, a branch of the Repeal Association was organized in Sydney. Though never particularly strong, the organization's emergence reflected the complex debates within the overlapping but distinct Irish and Catholic communities in this distant outpost of the British Empire. The Scottish Catholic editor of the *Australasian Chronicle,* W. A. Duncan, vigorously opposed repeal of the Act of Union, arguing that removing Irish members from the imperial parliament would give free rein to Anglican and Tory interests and thus potentially harm Australian and other colonial

Catholics; but this provoked a sharp rebuke from leaders of the Irish Catholic community, who, though relatively prosperous and somewhat suspicious of the new forces of democracy being unleashed by O'Connell, supported repeal out of a growing sense of their own Irish identity. This fusion of Catholic and Irish identities would characterize Irish nationalism in Australia well into the twentieth century.[35]

In Britain, repeal organizations sprang up not only in the two great centers of London and Birmingham but also in the northern cities of Manchester, Leeds, Liverpool, and Preston, and in the Scottish cities of Glasgow and Edinburgh. Although repeal leaders in Liverpool and Manchester were a socially conservative group who effectively discouraged Irish immigrants there from supporting trade unions or Chartism (the British working-class movement then in the midst of its fight for universal manhood suffrage), in other places these movements significantly overlapped. Robert Crowe, an Irish-born tailor working in London, later recalled that in the heady year of 1843, all "my spare time was divided between . . . the repeal movement under Daniel O'Connell, and the Chartist or English movement under Feargus O'Connor."[36]

Although workers like Crowe may have supported both Chartism and repeal, however, the leaders of these two movements were at each other's throats. Feargus O'Connor, the son of a United Irishman and nephew of the famous United Irish leader Arthur O'Connor, had begun his political career as a supporter of O'Connell and was elected to Parliament as a repeal MP from County Cork in 1832. In 1833, however, he openly challenged O'Connell's strategy of working with the Whigs, his decision to postpone parliamentary debate on repeal, and, at least by implication, his leadership of the entire movement. O'Connell carried the day on this occasion, but just barely, and when, in 1835, O'Connor was barred from Parliament because he failed to satisfy the property requirements, O'Connell declined to come to his defense. The following year, O'Connor published a book denouncing the man he called not a "Liberator," but a "Dictator." In 1837, he started what soon became a hugely influential radical British newspaper—named the *Northern Star* in homage to United Irishmen—and was the dominant figure in British Chartism from that time until the movement's collapse in 1848.[37]

From the mid-1830s onward, O'Connell bitterly opposed O'Connor on many issues but especially on the latter's willingness to talk of physical force to win the People's Charter. While professing to support the basic thrust of the Charter and generally sympathetic to British working people, O'Connell denounced Chartism on several occasions, citing what he saw as its intolerance, propensity toward violence, and social radicalism. The extent to which O'Connell's hostile stance prevented the Chartist movement from effectively recruiting among Irish immigrants in Britain is not entirely clear. But the conclusion that Irish nationalism in Britain was thoroughly intertwined with British political and social conflicts in this era is inescapable.[38]

If this was true in Britain, it was even more so in America, where the repeal movement was thoroughly absorbed in the 1840s by one of the country's debates over the question of slavery. This was inevitable, for Daniel O'Connell was not only the leader of a great national movement to repeal the Act of Union but also a leading figure in the international movement to abolish slavery. As the decade progressed, he increasingly knitted these two concerns together in an effort to persuade American repealers (and Irish Americans generally) to support abolition. The results were explosive.[39]

Irish Nationalism and American Slavery

If O'Connell had in most respects broken with the legacy of the original United Irishmen, the great exception was his opposition to slavery. He was every bit as steadfast in his anti-slavery convictions as Tone, Russell, or Emmet, and for him it was not just a matter of personal belief but of political action. O'Connell's anti-slavery activities went back to the 1820s, when he had backed the Liverpool merchant and Quaker abolitionist James Cropper on a plan to develop a textile industry in southern Ireland that could trade manufactured cotton goods for sugar from India, simultaneously reducing Irish poverty and British dependency on slave-produced West Indian sugar. In the 1830s, he gave frequent speeches at anti-slavery gatherings in England and Ireland and played an important role in the parliamentary debates that won the 1833 Slave Emancipation Act, which provided gradual abolition of slavery in the British colonies, and he had an even more central role in the debates that led in 1838 to the full abolition of the subsequent system of "apprenticeship" in the West Indies. Turning his attention thereafter to the problem of slavery in the United States, O'Connell worked with the new British and Foreign Anti-Slavery Society, which focused its efforts on the fight against American slavery, engaged in a highly publicized London *Times* debate with the slaveholding American ambassador to Britain Andrew Stevenson, and labored unsuccessfully in Parliament to prevent British recognition of the new slaveholding republic of Texas. Running through all of O'Connell's rhetoric in these years was a powerful critique of the hypocrisy of an American republic that asserted "all men are created equal" while also accepting the legitimacy of human bondage.[40]

American abolitionists, especially the young men and women calling for the immediate and unconditional end to slavery who rose to prominence in the early 1830s, were well aware of O'Connell's stance and lionized him for it. Beginning in 1832, with the first issue of his newspaper, the *Liberator*, William Lloyd Garrison, the most famous of the new abolitionists, quoted extensively from O'Connell's anti-slavery speeches; Garrison's later campaign for the "Dissolution of the American Union" and the *Liberator*'s 1842 motto, "No Union with Slaveholders," were both strongly influenced by the language of the Irish repeal movement. In 1833, African American abolitionists meeting in New York's Abyssinian Baptist church honored O'Connell as the "uncompromising advocate of universal emancipation, the friend of oppressed Africans and their descendants, and of the unadulterated rights of man." Many Irish American nationalists were also aware of O'Connell's anti-slavery commitments but found them a cause for concern, not celebration. In February 1838, a group of Philadelphia Irish Americans that included the United Irish veteran John Binns wrote to O'Connell to register their distress at an anti-slavery speech in which he had attacked white Americans who resided in slave-owning states. "Instead of their being the highest in the scale of humanity, they are the basest of the base, the vilest of the vile," O'Connell was reported to have said, and the Philadelphia group asked him to explain why he had "libeled" (their term) "their Native American fellow Citizens."[41]

Such disagreements, however, remained of limited significance until a group of American and Irish abolitionists began making systematic efforts to link directly the cause of repeal with the cause against slavery. It began at the World Anti-Slavery Convention, held in London in June 1840, which significantly increased contacts between British, Irish, and American anti-slavery advocates and led to the emergence of an important, if loosely structured and often contentious, transatlantic network dedicated to ending slavery in the United States. The convention itself was a tumultuous affair, dominated by a fight over the London hosts' refusal to recognize and seat American women delegates. Garrison and several other men in his organization, the American Anti-Slavery Society (AASS), protested the convention's action by joining the excluded women in the visitors' gallery. Though he also supported (somewhat reluctantly, by his own later admission) the women's efforts, O'Connell participated fully in the proceedings, giving what Garrison called a "scorching, blistering, burning" speech against American slavery on the last day of the convention. O'Connell also spoke about the critical need for Irish Americans to support abolition, leading the Irish-born New York Quaker abolitionist James Canning Fuller to approach him about the possibility of issuing a direct appeal to their fellow countrymen in the United States. "I believe he could do more to put down slavery in America than the convention can effect," Fuller wrote soon afterward. "Some of our Irish brethren there are the principal supporters of slavery, and if we would issue an address to them we should soon have powerful coadjutors." O'Connell agreed to write such an address and, though he did not immediately follow through, he emerged from the convention with a clear sense of the distinctive role he might be able to play in the transatlantic abolitionist movement.[42]

The convention also gave a badly needed shot in the arm to anti-slavery activities in Ireland itself, and in its wake, a number of American abolitionists, including Garrison, Lucretia Mott, and Nicholas P. Rogers from the AASS and James Birney and Henry B. and Elizabeth Cady Stanton, representing a breakaway rival soon calling itself the American and Foreign Anti-Slavery Society, toured the country. Irish abolitionists, many of them Quakers and Unitarians, who had organized the Hibernian Anti-Slavery Society in 1837, generally leaned toward the Garrison group, and when his associate, John A. Collins, arrived in Dublin in May 1841, Collins not only strengthened that support, but also stressed the urgency of reaching out to the Irish in America. "I regret to tell you that many of your countrymen, coming out of ignorance, readily join the pro-slavery ranks," he told a meeting of abolitionists in Dublin. "You must not allow this to be! Ireland must not swell the ranks of slavery!" But it was the subsequent visit of the African American abolitionist Charles Lenox Remond that did the most to focus Irish attention on this point. In a triumphant Irish speaking tour that stirred echoes of Olaudah Equiano's a half century earlier and became a model for those of Frederick Douglass and other black abolitionists, Remond studiously avoided discussion of factional disputes and focused clearly and directly on the evils of slavery and racial prejudice. He powerfully affected his audiences, first in Dublin, where he spoke at six meetings filled, as he put it, "to suffocation," and then in Waterford, Wexford, Cork, Limerick, County Clare, and Belfast.[43]

At his final Dublin lecture, the Irish abolitionist Richard Davis Webb read a document that he and Remond had prepared. Entitled *Address from the People of Ireland to Their Countrymen and Countrywomen in America,* the document began by proclaiming "admiration" for the United States and expressing the hope that the emigrants had found "happiness and prosperity in the land of your adoption." Turning to slavery, the document denounced its existence not only as sinful but also as deeply hypocritical in a nation that proclaimed a belief in the "inalienable rights of man." Finally the address turned prescriptive, calling on Irish Americans to "*unite with the abolitionists,* and never cease your efforts until perfect liberty be granted to every one of her inhabitants, the black man as well as the white man." The final ringing sentences made an effort to directly link Irish and Irish American identity with the struggle against slavery and racial prejudice. "Irishmen and Irishwomen! Treat the colored people as your equals, as brethren. By all your memories of Ireland, continue to love liberty—hate slavery—*cling by the abolitionists*—and in America you will do honor to the name of Ireland." As he proceeded on his Irish tour, Remond carried this document with him, presenting it to his audiences for them to sign, which they did in large numbers. In July, the Irish abolitionist Richard Allen reported that 15,000 Irish men and women, including 43 Catholic clergymen, had signed the address. By the end of 1841, it boasted nearly 60,000 signatures. Although Daniel O'Connell was one of the last to sign the document and the Repeal Association that he led played no role in its circulation, abolitionists sought to highlight his support of the Irish Address, making it almost seem as though he was its author, and downplaying the roles of Remond, Webb, and others.[44]

In December 1841, Remond returned to the United States with the Irish Address, which was soon reprinted in abolitionist newspapers, and on January 28, 1842, Garrison read the document to a crowd that reportedly included a large number of "Irish inhabitants of Boston and vicinity" at the city's Faneuil Hall. Though the speakers included abolitionist luminaries Garrison, Remond, Frederick Douglass, and Wendell Phillips, the highlight of the meeting was the powerful speech delivered by James Canning Fuller. "Irishmen!" he thundered. "I know what feelings and sufferings bring an Irishman to America. What did you come from the other side for? *Oppression* drove you here, and you came for universal liberty." Irish immigrants were "republicans by choice," rather than by the accident of American birth, he told the crowd, and thus had "more responsibility" to labor for the anti-slavery cause. His speech ended in much cheering. The Irish Address, Fuller and his comrades hoped, would provide the key to achieving a breakthrough to Irish Americans in general and supporters of the rapidly growing American repeal network in particular.[45]

It was not to be. The Catholic press, increasingly the voice of the American repeal network, quickly put as much distance as possible between itself and the movement to abolish slavery, questioning the authenticity of the Irish Address and combating any efforts, as the *Boston Pilot* put it, "to bring the Irish into the vortex of Abolitionism." Far from recognizing commonalities between the oppression of Ireland and that of African American slaves, the *Pilot* asserted the existence of "a worse slavery in Ireland." New York's Bishop John Hughes, who, though not a repeal association member, had considerable influence among American repealers, also publicized his opposition to the Irish Address. Hughes accepted nineteenth-century Catholic teachings on slavery, which held it to be a legitimate social relation that could be justly maintained, but he instead advanced the argument that the Irish Address represented a form of foreign interference in American affairs. "I am no friend to slavery, but I am still less a friend to any attempt of *foreign origin* to abolish it," he wrote, going on to express anger that abolitionists had singled out Irish Americans as a "distinct class" within American society for their efforts. "The duties of naturalized Irishmen or others, I consider to be in no wise distinct or different from those of native born Americans," Hughes asserted, essentially charging abolitionists with asking Irish immigrants to overthrow a deeply rooted social institution of the very nation that had welcomed them to its shores.[46]

This was the position taken by the movement itself at the February 1842 convention of repeal associations in Philadelphia. Meeting at Independence Hall on

Washington's Birthday, the repealers were intent on demonstrating their loyalty to America and their identity as American citizens. On the first afternoon of the convention, Boston delegate Isaac H. Wright put forward a resolution that "the friends of Ireland in America, will not be diverted from giving at their Repeal Meetings, their whole hearts and minds to the proper objects of such meetings, by the introduction of any topics of discord, connected with the domestic institutions of this country." Southern delegates actually argued strenuously against this resolution because they feared it would hinder their ability to make explicit their *defense* of slavery at repeal meetings, but in the end a version of Wright's motion passed, essentially pledging the movement to ignore the Irish Address or whatever future anti-slavery pleas O'Connell himself might make.[47]

Most local repeal associations took this position over the next two and a half years but with some important regional variations. While New England, New York, and Philadelphia associations initially remained silent, in the slave South and in border free states, the first reaction was to attack. The Cincinnati repeal association condemned abolitionists as "traitorous to the Constitution" and in the mining town of Pottsville, Pennsylvania, a meeting of repeal supporters who described themselves as representative of the "local working population" responded to the Irish Address by raising fears of racial "amalgamation," expressing outrage that it called "upon us and our wives and daughters to look upon the negroes as '*brethren*' and to join with and espouse the cause of abolition." In Wheeling, Virginia, repealers strongly denounced "attempts that were made by abolitionists to link themselves with the friends of Ireland in America" and, in New Orleans, repealers went so far as to denounce O'Connell as "a political renegade," deserving nothing less than the "execrations of all sober, upright and enlightened American citizens." Attempting to explain such sentiments, Thomas Mooney, then organizing for repeal in New Orleans, wrote directly to O'Connell. Opining that American slaves were better off than the Irish poor and that slavery would probably "wear away" on its own, he advised his leader to put aside abolition and focus on the "single object" of repeal, prompting O'Connell back in Dublin to express sadness that his old friend "should seem to have become infected with the atmosphere by which he was surrounded" and "had become a kind of mongrel between freedom and slavery." The Reverend James McGarahan, an Irish American priest from Mobile, Alabama, also offered explanations, delivering a contribution of £50 from the Mobile repealers to O'Connell in person, while simultaneously trying to convince him that African American slaves were not ready for freedom since they were "idle, ingovernable and incapable of managing their own affairs."[48]

Such efforts backfired, only increasing O'Connell's commitment to speaking out against American slavery. Blending equal measures of principle and pragmatism, he was initially reluctant to push the issue too hard. He publicized his religious disagreements with Garrison and other evangelical abolitionists and continued to accept American repealers' contributions, even when accompanied by pro-slavery or anti-abolitionist resolutions (though he also consistently registered his disagreement with such missives). In March 1843, he went so far as to propose a vote of thanks to the pro-slavery American repealer Robert Tyler over the objections of James Haughton, an abolitionist active in the Irish Repeal Association, who castigated the American president's son as "one of the greatest enemies of Irishmen and Irish liberty on the face of the earth." But when confronted, in May 1843, with a powerfully argued defense of abolition sent to him by the Pennsylvania Anti-Slavery Society, O'Connell gave a speech that he hoped would finally prod the American repealers into joining the battle against slavery. "I pronounce every man a faithless miscreant, who does not take a part for the abolition of slavery," he charged, focusing attention directly on his fellow countrymen in America. "Over the broad Atlantic I pour forth my voice saying 'Come out of a such a land, you Irishmen; or if you remain, and dare countenance the system of slavery that is supported there, we will recognize you as Irishmen no longer.'" Changing course from his previous willingness to accept American financial contributions when accompanied by pro-slavery statements, O'Connell added that he wanted no more "bloodstained money."[49]

Faced with such passionate words, the main body of the American repeal movement did as much as it could to ignore them, blame them on the abolitionists, or disavow them, usually citing their own deep loyalty to America and its institutions. Neither the *Boston Pilot* nor the *New York Freeman's Journal* even printed O'Connell's speech. Other papers did, and again regionally distinct reactions emerged, with slave-state repeal organizations responding most vehemently to O'Connell's strictures and, in a few cases, even disbanding as a result of them. In Charleston, for instance, epicenter of the 1832 nullification crisis, the repeal association simply voted itself out of existence, asserting its loyalty not to the United States, but to the section of the country in which the institution of slavery was fundamental. "As we must choose between Ireland and South Carolina," one member proclaimed in support of dissolving, "we say *South Carolina forever!*" Associations in Natchez, Mississippi, and Milledgeville, Georgia, also disbanded, and the southern associations that soldiered on took an extremely hostile stance toward O'Connell.[50]

Two repeal associations in the section of the country most sympathetic to abolition passed resolutions endorsing O'Connell's opposition to slavery. "While we sincerely sympathize with the oppressed and downtrodden inhabitants of Ireland, and every nation where British tyranny bears sway," the repeal association of Little Falls, New York, proclaimed in July 1843, "as citizens of a free State, we would not forget the bondsman of our own land, the slave, who is bound to his American master by a tie that nothing but death can sever."

According to the local press, however, this resolution "was carried by a very small majority of voices, and they not Irish." Only in one locale, strongly anti-slavery Burlington, Vermont, did Irish American members decisively support a repeal association resolution expressing full support for O'Connell's "noble sentiment on the atrocious system of slavery." Father Jeremiah O'Callaghan, an Irish American priest who authored the resolution, explained that once the question of slavery had been raised, "he would not let it pass without expressing his entire concurrence with Mr. O'Connell in his compassion for the slave, and his detestation of slavery."[51]

The repeal movement in the critically important center of Philadelphia split down the middle. At a July meeting of the Philadelphia Repeal Association presided over by the Democratic politician William Stokes, Robert Tyler condemned O'Connell's speech as the work of British abolitionists who had no sympathy "for any body but the cannibal negro on the shores of Africa," a statement that prompted the audience to offer three cheers for him and three cheers for his father, the president. But, as a local abolitionist observed, "a respectable and perhaps large minority" of the organization's members objected to these views. A month later, these dissenters organized a rival association, the Association of the Friends of Ireland and Repeal, under the leadership of Judge Doran, the first leader of the original Philadelphia association. The new organization authorized Doran to send O'Connell £50 along with resolutions of full support; and Doran closed with an implicit endorsement of O'Connell's anti-slavery stance by honoring him as "the deliverer from bondage of my father's land and the fearless and consistent champion of the rights of man throughout the world." At a Dublin Repeal Association meeting shortly thereafter, O'Connell thanked Doran for "this highly prized token of sympathy and affectionate regard" while dismissing Stokes as a "man more in love with slavery than with Ireland." In October, the new repeal organization created a stir by accepting a contribution from Robert Purvis, Philadelphia's leading African American abolitionist.[52]

But the breakaway Philadelphia group and the even more explicitly anti-slavery associations in Little Falls and Burlington were out of step with the American repeal movement as a whole. The New York convention in September 1843 was divided over the question of physical force and the creation of an executive committee but not over slavery, which was excluded entirely from discussion. In presiding over the convention, Robert Tyler became the public face of repeal while Stokes and a host of other pro-slavery figures played important roles. In the South, some of the repeal associations that had disbanded started up again. Slavery and abolition were off the table.

This overwhelming, if not quite unanimous, refusal of the American repeal movement to follow O'Connell's strenuous urgings to embrace the anti-slavery cause can be explained in part by racism and the refusal of southern repealers to speak against the dominant institution of their region. Some (especially workers) may have been worried that freed slaves would provide competition to Irish workers. Catholics in the movement were undoubtedly influenced by Catholic teachings legitimating slavery and, more specifically, the role of Bishop Hughes and the Catholic press. Some Catholics may also have been offended by the anti-Catholicism of various leaders of the abolitionist movement. Many Americans, of course, feared and hated abolitionists and the repeal movement echoed this. Some saw abolition as a British-inspired conspiracy to hurt the American union. The Democratic Party loyalties (and thus strongly anti-abolitionist politics) of some repeal supporters were important, and this was reinforced by the direct involvement of explicitly pro-slavery politicians. Finally, at least for the Irish-born and Catholic supporters of the movement, a strong desire to win full social acceptance in their new land undoubtedly played a role. This sentiment, reflected in the frequently made objection to being addressed by the abolitionists as a "distinct class" in American society, strengthened alongside the growth of political nativism. Opposing abolition appeared to be a way for Irish Americans to demonstrate, in the face of such nativism, that they were worthy American citizens.[53]

The Collapse of the American Repeal Movement

The central importance of this last point can be seen in the event that ended up destroying the American repeal movement, a speech that O'Connell gave in Dublin on March 30, 1845. O'Connell began his speech with the kind of rhetorical attack on slavery to which the American repealers had grown accustomed. But he quickly turned his attention to foreign policy and, in a new departure, took a forcefully pro-British stance in a major international dispute brewing between Britain and the United States. If Britain would simply repeal the Act of Union and grant Ireland its legislative independence, O'Connell promised, it could count on complete Irish support in what appeared to be an impending war with the United States over the Oregon territory.[54]

O'Connell, who had served three months in prison after a May 1844 conviction for seditious conspiracy (the House of Lords overturned the conviction in September) seemed to many a changed man when he left Richmond Penitentiary. He had always been willing to engage in the politics of compromise, but now, nearly seventy years old and in apparent physical decline, he exhibited a cautiousness that dismayed many in the repeal movement. That movement's momentum had been disrupted by the trial and brief imprisonment of several of its key leaders, which may also have prompted O'Connell's exploration of new initiatives. Among these new initiatives was a willingness to provide full support to British foreign policy objectives—even Robert Peel's foreign policy objectives—in exchange for repeal of the Act of Union.

While this was occurring in Ireland, the United States was in the midst of a presidential election in which American territorial expansion was the major issue. Taking office in early 1845 was the Democrat James K. Polk, who had finished a highly jingoist campaign highlighted by the slogan "All Oregon!" Polk supported the annexation of both the entire Oregon country up to the border of Alaska, which Britain and the United Stated had occupied jointly since 1827, and the independent republic of Texas, which Britain saw as a buffer against American expansionism. Polk's positions, laid out belligerently in a saber-rattling inaugural address, set off alarm bells in Britain, and Peel responded with an angry speech of his own to Parliament, upholding Britain's rights in Oregon and pledging to defend those rights with force. The two nations eventually settled the Oregon dispute with an 1846 treaty establishing the forty-ninth parallel as America's northern border in the west and, in the end, Britain stood by and watched as the United States annexed Texas and fought a war with Mexico to acquire that nation's entire northern half. But for a number of months in 1845, war between Britain and the United States seemed like a real possibility. This was the tense diplomatic atmosphere existing on March 30, when O'Connell gave his speech that killed the American repeal movement. "The throne of Victoria can be made perfectly secure—the honour of the British empire maintained—and the American eagle in its highest point of flight, be brought down," he proclaimed. "Let them but give us the parliament in College Green, and Oregon shall be theirs."[55]

The response in the United States to what came to be called the "American Eagle" speech was immediate and disastrous. American politicians and newspapers (and not just nativist ones) denounced it. In the South, repeal associations that had weathered the disputes on abolition and slavery quickly disbanded. Thomas Barrett, the leader of the New Orleans Repeal Association, dissolved his organization in May, according to a local newspaper editor, "in consequence of the course pursued by O'Connell." Associations in Baltimore and Norfolk, Virginia, also disbanded, citing the need, as the Baltimore repealers put it, to place their "patriotic devotion beyond the reach of suspicion." In the North, repeal associations did not disband but almost unanimously lashed out against O'Connell and asserted their patriotic loyalty to the United States. Even the stalwart John W. James admitted that "O'Connell's rhetoric is out of joint," though he urged his fellow Bostonians to separate O'Connell from the larger cause of repeal and carry on. The Boston association agreed to do so (though they also passed a resolution denouncing O'Connell and pledging "their allegiance to this land of freedom"), as did associations in New York and Philadelphia. But even in the North, O'Connell's "American Eagle" speech eventually took its toll, for it placed too much strain on Irish Americans seeking full acceptance within their adopted country. O'Connell's "denunciations against slavery might be tolerated," wrote a northeastern repealer in the *Boston Pilot* in May 1845, "but never let him touch a feather in our eagle of liberty under whose fostering wing so many of his fellow-countrymen have found shelter and protection." By the end of 1846, the American repeal movement was dead.[56]

Young Ireland and 1848

Meanwhile, in Ireland O'Connell was coming under heavy criticism from a different quarter, a small but influential group of middle-class intellectuals that came to be known as Young Ireland. The nucleus of the group had taken form in October 1842, when three aspiring young lawyers, Thomas Davis, Charles Gavan Duffy, and John Blake Dillon, established a weekly newspaper called the *Nation* to give support and publicity to the repeal movement. Diverse in their religious and regional backgrounds (Davis was a Munster Protestant, Duffy an Ulster Catholic, and Dillon a Catholic from Connacht), what united them was a commitment to a vigorous Irish cultural nationalism that included, but went far beyond, O'Connell's campaign to repeal the Act of Union. Though never a clearly articulated movement, Young Ireland quickly drew in several other highly talented individuals, including a middle-aged Catholic lawyer from an impoverished rural Tipperary background named Michael Doheny; the Ulster-born son of a Presbyterian minister named John Mitchel; James Fintan Lalor, the son of a prosperous Catholic farmer in Queen's County; and Thomas Francis Meagher, who came from a Catholic mercantile family in Waterford. Significantly older than this youthful group, the Protestant landlord William Smith O'Brien came to play an important part in their circle as well.[57]

Though operating within the framework of the repeal movement until 1846, this group had a number of commitments not shared by O'Connell. Heavily influenced by Thomas Carlyle and by continental European romanticism, Young Irelanders argued for an essentially ethnic (even primordial) view of the Irish nation. In a series of articles in the *Nation* in 1842 and 1843, for example, Davis put forward the idea that Irish nationality was nothing less than "a spiritual essence." Young Irelanders spoke, in particular, of the need to promote a national literature and to revive the Irish language, then experiencing rapid decline. Though Irish had actually been O'Connell's first language and he could speak it fluently when necessary, he did not support its revival, stating in the 1830s that "the superior utility of the English tongue, as the medium of all modern communication, is so great, that I can witness without a sigh the gradual disuse of Irish." In practice, Young Ireland was never able to implement its goal of an Irish language revival, but the issue remained central to their embrace of a "Celtic" Irish identity.[58]

The identity they embraced was Celtic, but not Catholic. In fact, it was their militantly nonsectarian stance and their criticism of O'Connell's Catholic orientation that created the most friction among them. The Anglican Thomas Davis, in particular, stressed the need for Protestant participation in the Irish nation to fully realize its potential, a stance that struck some Catholic Irish nationalists as an arrogant assertion of Protestant superiority. Whether or not this was a fair assessment, this nonsectarian commitment led the Young Irelanders to endorse the principle of government aid to mixed Protestant and Catholic schools in 1845, which O'Connell, like the Catholic episcopate, opposed. This issue, as much as their criticisms of O'Connell's pragmatism and willingness to compromise, and the suspicions that he harbored about their designs on his leadership, led to a showdown between the Young Ireland group and the majority of the Repeal Association in July 1846.[59]

Young Irelanders also diverged from O'Connell in embracing the principle of physical force, not just as a right of defense but in theory as "an assertive force." In June 1843, with the government's repression of the repeal movement looming on the horizon, Davis responded to the absolute nonviolence propounded by a Quaker repealer, Ebenezer Shackleton, with an editorial entitled "The Morality of War." In the same tense month, the *Nation* published a poetic glorification of the United Irishmen entitled "Who Fears to Speak of '98?" The Young Irelanders were no more actually contemplating revolution at this point than O'Connell himself; but in July 1846, responding to their criticisms of his efforts to build a new alliance with the Whigs, O'Connell seized on their theoretical defense of revolutionary violence and proposed a requirement that all Repeal Association members renounce the use of force. The Young Irelanders refused to do so, and in a highly charged two-day meeting, the Repeal Association came face to face with the issue.[60]

Significantly, in Young Ireland's assertion of the right of revolution, the example of America loomed very large. In the most famous speech of his career, at the meeting of the Repeal Association that sealed the split in the movement, Thomas Francis Meagher offered a defense of "the sword" by appealing to heroic rebels like Andreas Hofer, William Tell, and—last but not least—George Washington. "Abhor the sword? Stigmatize the sword?" he asked rhetorically. "No, for at its blow, and in the quivering of its crimson light a giant nation sprang up from the waters of the Atlantic, and by its redeeming magic the fettered colony became a daring, free Republic." O'Connell's son, John, had responded to this line of argument the previous day by noting that the American Revolution had been defensive rather than "assertive," and, moreover, had resulted tragically in the expansion of American slavery.[61]

American slavery itself (or, more precisely, the links between repeal and abolition) was yet another issue that divided O'Connell from Young Ireland. The Young Irelanders had for some time opposed O'Connell's strong stand against slavery (his "transatlantic philanthropy," as they dismissively put it), arguing that the people of Ireland suffered just as much as African American slaves and that the immediate task at hand was to liberate Ireland, not abolish slavery. Few joined the Young Irelander John Mitchel in actually defending the institution of slavery, but they did oppose O'Connell's repeated anti-slavery appeals for undermining the movement's support in America. "Repeal must not be put into conflict with any party in the States," asserted a *Nation* editorial in early 1844. "The men of the southern states must not have their institutions interfered with, whether right or wrong." At a Repeal Association meeting the following year, Thomas Davis expressed his dismay at O'Connell's "American Eagle" speech. "Notwithstanding the slavery of the negro," commented the *Nation* at the time, America "is liberty's bulwark and Ireland's dearest ally." These disagreements came to a head four months later when the *Nation* endorsed the position of Richard Scott, a Dublin solicitor, who argued strenuously that the Repeal Association should leave it to the Hibernian Anti-Slavery Society to criticize American slavery. As the Young Irelander Michael Doheny later recalled, O'Connell's stand on "the 'infamous institution' of slavery"—his sarcasm was unmistakable—was one of the few points in the first half of the 1840s on which the Liberator's "wisdom was questioned and condemned." While not as important as other issues underlying the split, the ongoing debate over abolition widened the divide between O'Connell and the Young Irelanders, providing grist for their view that his leadership was hurting the cause of repeal.[62]

As they turned away from the Liberator, Young Irelanders came to embrace and promote the legacy of an individual that they considered to be his antithesis, Theobald Wolfe Tone. It was Tone's opposition to sectarianism and his embrace of revolution—and his heroic willingness to die for the cause of Ireland—that most attracted Young Irelanders to him. What they knew of him came directly from the *Life of Theobald Wolfe Tone* that Matilda Tone had published two decades before. Though the book had received good reviews on publication, it was only with the emergence of Young Ireland that a kind of cult of Tone began to take shape. Thomas Davis initiated a project to lay a memorial stone on Tone's grave at Bodenstown, setting his burial place on its way to becoming a major nationalist pilgrimage site by the 1860s. On the eve of his sudden death from scarlet fever in 1845, Davis was corresponding with Matilda Tone about his plans to write his own short biography of Tone.[63]

Tone's *Life* was not the only book that influenced and inspired the Young Irelanders. Charles Gavan Duffy, for instance, had been introduced both to journalism and to the physical force tradition by the memoir of United Irish veteran

Charles Teeling, a book that had been published in 1828. United Irishmen such as Thomas Cloney, Joseph Holt, and Hamilton Rowan had all published memoirs by 1840, joining earlier volumes by William MacNeven and William Sampson. Tone's moving and witty *Life* may have held pride of place on their shelves, but the Young Irelanders' rediscovery of the United Irishmen was also aided by the publication of Richard Robert Madden's monumental seven-volume work, *The United Irishmen: Their Lives and Times*, the first volume of which appeared in 1842, just months before the establishment of the *Nation*. Extremely hagiographical, Madden's work had a profound influence on the Young Irelanders.[64]

Young Ireland ignored Madden's most important political commitment, which was the abolition of slavery, not Irish nationalism. Born in Dublin in 1798, the son of a successful Catholic silk merchant, Madden joined the British Anti-Slavery Society in 1829. When Parliament abolished slavery in the empire four years later, he secured posts in the Caribbean, first as a special magistrate in Jamaica, where he won the enduring hostility of the planters because of his efforts to rein in their continuing brutal treatment of freed slaves, and later in Cuba, where he served as the first Commissioner for Liberated Africans. Along the way, Madden turned out a stream of writings against Cuban slavery, the international slave trade, and the slavery-like apprenticeship system in Jamaica. He was particularly concerned with reshaping Irish American attitudes on slavery, and his signature appeared at the very top of the Irish Address on slavery that William Lloyd Garrison presented in Boston in 1842. Madden traveled to the United States a number of times during these years, meeting abolitionists and prominent Irish émigrés, and it was on one of these trips, in the winter of 1835–36, that he met the elderly William MacNeven. It was MacNeven, by now one of the few surviving United Irishmen—and one who fully shared Madden's anti-slavery convictions—who encouraged Madden to become the historian of the organization.[65]

Madden's *The United Irishmen*, based to a great extent on the memories and documents preserved by widows and children of United Irishmen permanently settled in the United States, created a full pantheon of heroes for Young Irelanders to revere. On the other hand, their embrace of Tone and the other United Irishmen as nationalist heroes did not necessarily mark their acceptance of the radical democratic politics that the society had actually propounded. Their historical memory was highly selective on this point, and their break with the outlook of their forebears went beyond the question of slavery. "I am one of the people, but I am no democrat." Meagher maintained. "I am for an equality of civil rights—but I am no republican." Even Davis, for all his admiration of Tone, felt that his 1791 argument "on behalf of Catholics" was premature; only by 1829, in Davis's view, had the Irish Catholic masses proved through their activism that they were worthy of emancipation.[66]

The middle-class intellectuals of Young Ireland also repudiated the traditional ways and means of Irish popular mobilization—from the mass-based, but secretive, organizing of the United Irishmen and Defenders to the Catholic orientation and open membership of the Repeal Association—and instead tried to mark out a totally new path to political change. After breaking with O'Connell and withdrawing from the Repeal Association in July 1846, they formed the Irish Confederation, a network of exclusive clubs intended to enroll "not an undistinguished mass of supporters, but only such Irishmen as thoroughly understand the principles it professes." Although the Chartist leader Feargus O'Connor wrote in support of Young Ireland's struggle against his old adversary, O'Connell, the Confederation firmly rejected any alliance with British Chartists: "We are neither so insane nor so vile, as to join them in their designs against life and property," Mitchel declared.[67]

Events of 1847 and 1848 began to change this orientation. In the winter of 1846–47, the Irish potato crop failed entirely, following a partial failure in 1845. The number of deaths due to starvation and disease climbed dramatically in the countryside, combining with massive emigration to reduce the size of the Irish peasantry considerably. The wrenching effects of this catastrophe on Irish nationalism would be profound over the long run, but almost overnight, the repeal question that had dominated Irish politics for most of the decade seemed irrelevant. The situation was magnified by O'Connell's death in 1847 and the disorganization in the Repeal Association that followed. Could the new Irish Confederation fill this political vacuum?[68]

Only if it began to think and move in radically new ways, its leaders decided. Central in staking out a new direction was John Mitchel. Responding to the growing catastrophe in the countryside and drawing on the land reform proposals of his colleague James Fintan Lalor, Mitchel began to systematically link the causes of agrarian and political revolution. In October 1847, he appealed to tenant farmers to withhold all produce for their own consumption, and in December he called on peasants to arm themselves and prepare for insurrection. When Duffy closed the pages of the *Nation* to Mitchel's writings favoring rebellion, he quit the Confederation's policy committee and began to call for immediate armed action by the peasantry; after all, Mitchel opined, Ireland was already "actually in a state of war—a war of 'property' against poverty—a war of 'law' against life." In the first issue of the new newspaper that he founded in February 1848, the *United Irishman*, Mitchel headed the leader column with Wolfe Tone's 1796 paean to "the men of no property."[69]

And then, into this mix came news of a revolution in Paris that had toppled the regime of Louis Philippe and established a French republic, triggering revolutions across Europe. Highly attuned to the historical resonances involved, leaders of the new Irish Confederation (and even some repealers) greeted the

1848 French revolution with the same kind of rapturous enthusiasm that the radicals in Belfast and Dublin had greeted that of 1789. For the first time, Young Irelanders like Mitchel, Meagher, Lalor, and even the landlord O'Brien raised the demand that had been so central to their United Irish heroes: the demand for a fully independent Irish republic. Mitchel no longer sought "a golden link, or a patchwork parliament or a College Green chapel of ease to St. Stephen's—but an Irish republic, one and indivisible." Lalor echoed these sentiments, writing that his goal was "not the constitution that Wolfe Tone died to abolish, but the constitution that he died to obtain—independence; full and absolute independence for this island, and for every man within this island." Even Duffy, while continuing to stand by the original demand for an independent Irish Parliament under the British crown, said that he would support the founding of an Irish republic by force if Britain continued to resist this demand. Equally striking was the rapidly growing social egalitarianism that accompanied this revival of the republican ideal: "The life of a labouring man is exactly equal to the life of one nobleman," Mitchel wrote in the *United Irishman*, "neither more nor less."[70]

The British government, traumatized by the revolutionary currents coursing through Europe as well as by the turmoil surrounding the Chartist struggle in Britain, would not let such talk go on much longer. Repression came quickly, with the speedy arrest, trial, and conviction of John Mitchel in May 1848, under a new Treason Felony Act. To the shock of many throughout Ireland, Britain, and the United States, the court sentenced Mitchel to fourteen years' transportation to Australia. For the first time, activists in the Irish Confederation began to think seriously about actual rebellion. They began to organize clubs that they hoped could form the nucleus of a revolutionary army. A war council from these clubs, consisting of Dillon, Meagher, Richard O'Gorman, Thomas D'Arcy McGee, and Thomas Devin Reilly, was elected, and plans were drawn up for a rising that would occur after the harvest. As part of these plans, the council dispatched Mitchel's young brother, William, and a solicitor named Martin O'Flaherty to organize potential supporters in the United States. As Duffy recalled years later, the emissaries to America carried their credentials ("a commission signed by four persons, whose names would be recognized by the Irish in the United States") smeared with gunpowder and stuffed into a loaded pistol, so "that it might be fired off in case of arrest."[71]

But Irish nationalists in America were already organizing. Mesmerized by newspaper accounts of revolutions in Europe, they began working to provide support to what they saw as an inevitable rising in Ireland. Many Americans greeted the February 1848 revolution in Paris with enthusiasm (the United States, in fact, was the first nation to recognize the new French provisional government) and Irish nationalists sought to use this enthusiasm to their advantage. In the United States, 1848 was an election year and, in an already familiar pattern, numerous politicians were anxious to offer rhetorical support for the Irish cause. Some congressmen took "the opportunity of Publick Meetings, convened for the expression of sympathy for the new French Republick, to make the most violent and unjust attacks upon Her Majesty's Government, more especially as regards their Policy towards Ireland," reported the alarmed British chargé d'affaires in Washington, "and to express the ardent hope that the 'glorious scenes' enacted at Paris may, ere long, be repeated in that Country."[72]

Seemingly out of nowhere, a new organization, the Irish Republican Union (IRU), was established in New York "to promote revolutions for the establishment of Republican Governments throughout Europe, especially in Ireland." The IRU hastily developed a plan for the formation of what it called an Irish Brigade. "The real wants of Ireland, are a want of Republican spirit, and a want of military science," according to one member of the organization; the IRU would provide these "in the person of a few thousand Americanized Irishmen, who are now ready and willing to embark in her battle." The IRU's leaders also hoped that the new government in France would give military assistance to an Irish rebellion, as an earlier French government had in the revolutionary decade of the 1790s. Both the vigorous militancy and the historical resonances of the moment were encapsulated in the pen name chosen by the IRU member who reported on its activities for the *Boston Pilot*: "Tone."[73]

The IRU's plans, however, hit roadblocks almost immediately. France, under considerable diplomatic pressure from Britain, refused to assist Irish revolutionaries in any way. Equally important, influential American supporters of the Irish cause, such as Robert Tyler, opposed the formation of the Irish Brigade as a clear violation of the American constitution. Speaking at a Philadelphia meeting, Tyler forcefully argued that Ireland could be supported only in ways "consistent with our duties as American citizens." Responding to these roadblocks, the IRU quickly shifted gears, pledging to provide aid to Ireland "in every way in our power, not in violation of the laws, or prejudicial to the national position of the glorious land of our adoption." After all, the whole point of intervention in Ireland, as stated in a resolution adopted at a Tammany Hall assemblage of some 2,000 men and women, was the extension to that "oppressed land of that republican freedom, which all happily enjoy in these United States." The powerful Irish drive for acceptance in America, which more than any other factor had led to the collapse of the repeal network, also provided a strong check on the aspirations of would-be revolutionaries in 1848.[74]

Redefined in this way as a kind of American assimilation project, the movement attracted numerous politicians, who, as noted in the ever-cynical *New York Herald*, "look more to the ballot boxes of the United States than the cartridge boxes in Ireland." The first meeting of what they called the American Provisional Committee for Ireland became, according to the *Herald*, "a regular auction for

Presidential votes; and whigs, locofocos, barnburners, were all there, bidding over each other for the Irish vote." New York's mayor presided over the meeting, with assistance from the mayors of Brooklyn and Jersey City, the local district attorney, and the entire New York Board of Aldermen. Horace Greeley was chosen as a vice president of the organization, which displayed its revolutionary credentials by electing Robert Emmet, who had angrily quit New York's repeal society back in 1841, as its president and treasurer.[75]

News of John Michel's conviction, which reached America in June, however, prompted a sharp change in the mood, as well as in the social composition, of the emerging movement. In Philadelphia, the aging United Irishman, John Binns, chaired a meeting attended by a group of workingmen who carried the Irish tricolor—mounted on a pike. In New York, a meeting of the IRU resurrected its plans for an Irish Brigade, reconfigured as a stealth force of waves of pretended returning emigrants (but actually veterans of the war against Mexico) who would train and drill their countrymen for a rising after the harvest. Even this plan for a secret invading army could be given a pro-American, assimilationist cast; Thomas Mooney, the one-time repeal organizer who was now a convert to physical force, called it the surest way to "plant the Republican Tree of America on the Hill of Tara." But this New York meeting attracted a very different crowd from earlier ones. "Here were neither office-seekers nor popularity-hunters," observed a sympathetic *Boston Pilot* journalist, "but the most honest mechanics and labourers, and men fully determined to go to Ireland, to 'conquer or die.'" A parallel development occurred in Britain, where Chartists took the lead in calling for demonstrations in industrial towns in northern England and Scotland, as well as in London, to protest Mitchel's conviction.[76]

The arrival of William Mitchel and Martin O'Flaherty generated further excitement and helped broaden the movement far beyond the ranks of the IRU and the American Provisional Committee. At a mammoth August 14 meeting at Vauxhall Gardens in New York, Emmet and Greeley, heading up a new nine-member Directory, pledged to raise $1,000,000 for an Irish "military chest." General James Shields, a County Tyrone native who had commanded troops in the US war against Mexico, committed his life to the cause, while Bishop Hughes contributed $500. In Boston, Irish nationalists formed their own Directory, chaired by another convert to physical force, John W. James. And in Canada, British colonial authorities maintained full military readiness, on guard against an incursion by Irish American nationalists, perhaps acting in alliance with the exiled remnants of Papineau's Patriote movement. But most eyes were on Ireland itself. "As we write," declared the breathless editor of the *Boston Pilot*, "polished pikes may glitter in the sun, and browned rifles be leveled with quick eye and steady hand by the Patriot Irish troops against the English foe."[77]

In fact, by the time he wrote these words, it was already over. The British government, drawing on highly accurate intelligence from its dense network of informers, moved against the rebels before they had time to act, suspending habeas corpus and flooding Dublin with troops on July 21. Thomas Francis Meagher and John Blake Dillon persuaded the reluctant William Smith O'Brien to lead a rising, but failing to recruit supporters in the southern countryside and hampered by strong opposition from the Catholic clergy, a ragtag group of only about one hundred insurgents made its final stand against a contingent of police at a farmhouse near Ballingarry, County Tipperary. Two rebels were killed, the rest dispersing when military reinforcements arrived, and the rebellion collapsed. Some leaders escaped to France or America, but O'Brien and several others were tried, convicted of treason, and (after Parliament commuted their initial death sentences) sentenced to transportation in 1849. By this point, the Irish revolutionary movement in America had long since collapsed. News of the rebellion's end "seems to have put a stop to the movements of 'sympathizers' altogether," reported the relieved British chargé d'affaires from Washington in October 1848. "Sympathy is indeed still expressed for the cause by a great number of the American newspapers and pity for the fate of the rebel leaders, though this has been latterly somewhat seasoned with contempt."[78]

An Exile's End

On March 5, 1849, Charles Hart, a minor Young Irelander and Dillon's brother-in-law, paid a visit to eighty-year-old Matilda Tone at her home just outside of Washington. Unlike many of the more successful United Irishmen—and unlike the middle-class and assimilating Irish Americans who had dominated the movement for repeal—Matilda Tone had never ceased regarding herself as an exile. She peppered Hart with questions about "poor old Dublin" and expressed sorrow that she had never been able to even visit Ireland again after leaving in 1795. "Oh, don't expatriate yourself, don't expatriate yourself," she exclaimed when Hart said he was thinking about remaining in America. "Here I am for thirty years in this country and I have never had an easy hour, longing after my native land." Matilda Tone died less than two weeks after this meeting. Hart took her advice and returned to Ireland in December.[79]

Matilda Tone's deep sense of exile and displacement would emerge as a dominant theme for the Fenians, the Irish physical force republicans who would build a powerful transnational movement for Irish independence during the 1860s and 1870s. The Fenians drew support and sustenance from a new tidal wave of emigrants, many of whom also viewed themselves as exiles fleeing the Great Irish Famine.

4

The Fenian Movement, 1848–1878

Over the course of 1848, as many as 91,000 Irish men, women, and children disembarked in New York City, North America's main point of entry for emigrants from Europe. Most of them were fleeing the hunger and disease of the Great Irish Famine, which had begun in 1845. Some of the arrivals quickly set off for other parts of the country, but many others stayed in the city. By the mid-1850s, the rapidly growing metropolis contained some 175,000 people who had been born in Ireland, more than a quarter of the city's total population. New York and its immediate environs by this time held nearly as many Irish-born people as the city of Dublin. Thousands of the new arrivals congregated in the congested slums of the Five Points neighborhood in lower Manhattan, an area that, in the words of Bishop John Hughes, housed "the poorest and most wretched population that can be found in the world—the scattered debris of the Irish nation."[1]

As the Famine took its deadly toll, the annual number of Irish emigrants to the United States increased dramatically, peaking in 1851, when more than 221,000 arrived in the country. But immigration continued at extremely high levels even after the worst years of the "great hunger" had passed. All in all, over 3 million Irish emigrants made their way to the United States between the beginning of the Famine and 1890, shaping Irish and American life in myriad ways and marking a new phase in both Irish and American history.

The Famine proved critical to the evolution of Irish nationalism. First, the most important Irish nationalist organization of the mid-nineteenth century, a separatist republican organization called the Fenian Brotherhood, recruited very heavily among the Famine migrants, especially in America, but also in Britain and Canada. Second, several important Irish nationalist intellectuals of these years, particularly the Young Ireland veteran and exile John Mitchel, put forward a powerful interpretation of the Famine that charged the British government with the deliberate starvation of the Irish people. Though modern historical research does not support this interpretation, the effectiveness with which Mitchel and others propounded it became one of the most important ideological foundations for the rebuilding of revolutionary separatism in the 1860s and beyond.[2]

The Fenians, who expressed this sentiment most forcefully, dominated Irish popular politics during the 1860s. Though a secret, oath-bound society committed to revolution, condemned by the Catholic Church as well as by much of the growing Catholic middle class, the Irish Republican Brotherhood (IRB), as the Fenian organization was known in Ireland, drew thousands of young men to its ranks, recruiting especially heavily among urban tradesmen, laborers, and white-collar workers. Its program included not just independence but also the establishment of a thoroughly democratic Irish republic that many of its supporters hoped would set the stage for an even more sweeping program of social and economic reform. In 1867, with the prompting and significant support of Irish Americans, the Fenians made an effort to launch a full-scale revolutionary war in Ireland. Though this effort was unsuccessful and led to the organization's decline, the movement left a powerful legacy for the next several decades, compelling the British government to respond with important social and political reforms and inspiring Fenian veterans to build a variety of other movements, including urban trade unions, a constitutional (but highly aggressive) movement for Irish home rule, and a powerful agrarian reform organization called the Irish Land League.[3]

The American history of Fenianism was significant as well. However much they differed from one another in their ideological perspectives, all previous Irish nationalist organizations in the United States had been essentially offshoots of already existing organizations or movements in Ireland. In contrast, the preliminary organizing for what became the Fenian Brotherhood actually occurred in the United States in the 1850s, mainly within Irish exile circles in New York. The American and Irish Fenian organizations were founded nearly simultaneously in 1858–59 and from then on were in constant communication, if not always in strategic or tactical agreement. American Fenians, in addition to playing a key role in the 1867 Irish rising, took military actions of their own, most notably dramatic armed attacks on British-controlled Canada in 1866, 1870, and 1871. In America, the organization was legal, public, and open, and even its apparent violations of the nation's neutrality law brought little in the way of response from the federal government. Though the American Fenians were (like their counterparts in Ireland) condemned by the American Catholic Church and by some within the growing Irish American middle class, their organization had as many as 50,000, mainly working-class members by its peak in 1865, which, with an estimated number of supporters at over 200,000, made it the first mass-based Irish nationalist movement in American history. In America, too, the organization left an important legacy, with Fenian veterans going on to build trade unions, labor reform movements, American Land League branches, and Irish revolutionary organizations like the Clan na Gael later in the nineteenth century. But the Fenians' most important and original legacy was in helping to hone a separate and distinct ethnic identity among the Irish, intensifying their sense of social and cultural difference from the mainstream of American life. The radical character of the Fenian break with the past can best be understood as part of its emergence from Great Irish Famine.[4]

John Mitchel and the Famine

The Famine was the result of several interrelated factors, both natural and social in character. The natural element was provided by a fungus, *Phytopthora infestans,* which first appeared in Ireland, along with much of western Europe, in 1845, destroying some 30 percent to 40 percent of the Irish staple crop, the potato, and triggering a tremendous amount of suffering among the rural poor. In 1846, the crop was nearly totally destroyed, and full-fledged famine became widespread. The effects of the blight lessened somewhat in 1847, holding out the hope that the worst was over; however, since many families had already consumed their seed potatoes, the harvest produced only about 10 percent that of pre-Famine years. Then the blight returned with a vengeance in 1848, wiping out nearly the entire crop. It continued, though at a somewhat lesser level, through the early 1850s.[5]

Over a million people died, some from outright starvation, many more from exposure and diseases like typhus, diarrhea, and dysentery that mercilessly struck a weak and malnourished people. There were significant geographic and social variations in the way the Famine dealt out death. The rural poor—including small farmers; cottiers, who sold their labor for a bit of land to work on their own; and wage-earning agricultural laborers—died in disproportionately large numbers. Predictably, poor children died in the greatest numbers; less predictably, men died in greater numbers than women. Though the effects of the Famine could be seen throughout rural Ireland, it was the western parts of the country, especially the province of Connacht and the western counties of Munster, that were most affected.[6]

The Famine's horrific scale stemmed partly from the simple fact that so many people were living barely on the edge of survival in the best of times. From 1750 to 1845, the population in Ireland had grown at a rate of about 1.3 percent a year, significantly faster than in other countries in Western Europe. By the beginning of the 1840s, the country had some 8 million people, a large and increasing proportion of them living in poverty. Population growth itself was not the cause of the catastrophe, but the great dependence of large numbers of the poor on a single staple crop exposed them to potential disaster if that crop were to fail—which is precisely what happened in the mid-1840s.

The response of the British government to this catastrophe was inadequate and misguided, shaped by widely held stereotypes about the "character" of the Irish Catholic poor and a deep commitment to the tenets of a laissez-faire political economy. Things were not so bad in 1845, when the potato crop failure was less than total and when Sir Robert Peel's Conservative government provided a level of relief sufficient at least to prevent mass starvation. When the blight first appeared in fall 1845, Peel had been prime minister for four years. Though it had been his government that had cracked down on Daniel O'Connell's repeal movement, and though he now ignored O'Connell's appeal for a temporary suspension of grain exports from Ireland, Peel did understand the potential human and political consequences of continuing distress. He used government coffers to purchase food abroad and set up a Special Relief Commission to distribute it and subsidize the voluntary work of local relief committees. He also passed legislation to finance public relief works, mainly on roads and irrigation projects. These were all long-established policies in dealing with Irish food crises, though they were now undertaken on a much larger scale than ever before.[7]

Peel's policies, however, were flawed. In 1846, his government permanently halted the purchase of food from abroad, interpreting an increase in private corn imports that summer as a vindication of its withdrawal from any further interference with the international grain market. Moreover, the government's reliance on local landowners to provide relief—aided by generous loans and subsidies from the government—led to a situation in which many of these landowners appeared to be entirely evading their own financial responsibilities. Some landowners also used public works projects to improve their estates at the taxpayers' expense and favored their own dependents over other local people more in need of assistance (actions widely reported in the British press), and this led a large section of the British public to the conclusion that Peel's policy had been too generous to both Irish landowners and the Irish poor.

The worsening conditions of the following year, intensified by unusually cold weather in the winter of 1846–47, became the responsibility of Lord John Russell, who came to power in June 1846 as leader of a Whig Party that was even more committed to the orthodoxy of laissez-faire than the Conservatives. Responding to the severity of the situation, Russell did continue funding for the public works programs, which leaped from 250,000 to some 750,000 workers between fall 1846 and spring of 1847, and he even introduced state-supported soup kitchens, utilized by 3 million people by July 1847; but both were seen as temporary emergency measures and had been ended by September of that year. In their place, reflecting the widespread British view that "Irish property must pay for Irish poverty," Parliament introduced the principle of "local chargeability" into the Poor Law Extension Act of 1847. The new economic pressures on landowners—squeezed between higher taxes and tenants who could no longer pay their rents—led many of them to resort to eviction. An estimated 500,000 people were evicted between 1849 and 1854. For many of these people, the poorest and most vulnerable within the Irish rural population, eviction was the last straw. Meanwhile the so-called Gregory clause of the new Poor Law, which denied workhouse relief to anyone holding more than a quarter-acre of land, encouraged thousands of others to simply abandon their land. The experience of eviction, coming on top of everything else, left many of those who survived with a deep and consuming bitterness that made them natural recruits for physical force Irish nationalism in the ensuing decades. "I do not care to speculate as to the number of the class of evicted tenants scattered through the United States," wrote John Francis Maguire, the Cork journalist and nationalist politician, after touring North America in 1868, "but wherever they exist, they are to be found willing contributors to Fenian funds, and enthusiastic supporters of anti-British organisations."[8]

Perhaps such individual and shared memories of suffering and loss would have drawn Irish emigrants to the Fenian movement even without the writings of nationalist intellectuals who interpreted the Famine as an act of pure British aggression against the Irish people. But the wide dissemination of such writings made the emergence of revolutionary nationalism all but inevitable. The central point of the nationalist argument was that the Famine was the direct result of a conscious and deliberate effort to starve the people systematically in order to ensure the maintenance of British rule. Most historians today, while often highly critical of British policy, dispute this view, emphasizing instead the vociferous commitment of several key British officials to laissez-faire economic thought and the view of others that the Famine was the work of what British treasury head Charles Trevelyan called "an all-wise and all-merciful Providence" that would lead to a moral regeneration of the Irish people—exacerbated by a banking crash in the fall of 1847 that blocked the possibilities of more effective government action. Still a number of nationalist writers advanced the incendiary charge of what today would be called "genocide," none more effectively than the New York–based journalist and Young Ireland exile John Mitchel. Though Mitchel himself was to have a peripheral and often contentious relationship with the Fenians, the success with which he put forward his interpretation of the Famine in the 1850s accounted for a great deal of the Brotherhood's appeal in the following decade. In this sense, his later claim to be the "father of Fenianism,"—or, more precisely, "the principle of Fenianism"—was accurate. Mitchel's intellectual labors in the 1850s, like those of Matilda Tone in the 1820s, illustrate the point that Irish American nationalism was never just a matter of money or guns, meetings or petitions; it was also an ongoing work of political imagination.[9]

Mitchel's conviction and transportation for the newly created crime of treason-felony in May 1848 had set off the sequence of events leading to the disastrous rebellion that July. By the time of the rebellion itself, Mitchel was a prisoner in Bermuda, where he remained for ten months before being transported to the prison island of Van Dieman's Land (now Tasmania), off the southeastern coast of Australia. In June 1853, he managed to escape, sailing first to Sydney and then on to San Francisco. He arrived in New York to a hero's welcome in November and quickly resumed his interrupted career in revolutionary journalism, founding a weekly newspaper, the *Citizen*, in January 1854. It was in the pages of the *Citizen* that Mitchel's most famous work, *Jail Journal*, first appeared in serial form.[10]

"May 27, 1848," his first installment tersely opened: "On this day, about four o'clock in the afternoon, I, John Mitchel, was kidnapped, and carried off from Dublin, in chains, as a convicted 'Felon.' " *Jail Journal* was, by any standards, a remarkable work of autobiographical and political literature. In its pages, Mitchel not only told a compelling personal story, but also conveyed an entire social and political worldview that was paradoxically both resolutely republican and deeply conservative. Like a number of his fellow Young Irelanders, Mitchel was a devotee of the Scottish essayist, Thomas Carlyle, who provided him with the intellectual ammunition for a full-scale attack not only on Britain's domination of Ireland but on modern civilization as a whole, in which basic human relationships had been reduced to the "cash nexus." Mitchel's sweeping conservative critique of modernity led him to embrace republican revolution in 1848 and also to defend American slavery as an idealized alternative to the inhumanity of laissez-faire capitalism.[11]

In *Jail Journal*, however, Mitchel was adamant that Britain's treatment of Ireland during the Famine had not been the result of laissez-faire capitalism—nor of mere anti-Irish bigotry—but rather of a deliberate campaign to subjugate Ireland once and for all through mass starvation and forced emigration. This proved to be the most enduring element of Mitchel's entire body of writing. More effectively than any other author, he propounded the idea that the British government, through its inadequate relief policies and by allowing food to be exported from Ireland, had been guilty of genocide against the Irish people. "A million and a half of men, women, and children were carefully, prudently, and peacefully slain by the English government," he wrote in *The Last Conquest of Ireland (Perhaps)*, a fuller elaboration of his argument that he published in 1860. "They died of hunger in the midst of abundance which their own hands created." "The Almighty, indeed, sent the potato blight," Mitchel conceded, "but the English created the Famine."[12]

Such views had been widely held among the veterans of the 1848 rebellion. Thomas D'Arcy McGee, for example, had labeled the Whigs' relief policies

"2,000,000 ministerial murders" and asserted that the Irish were being "exterminated as a people." But the vehemence with which Mitchel advanced his case resonated deeply among many in Ireland and even more among the Famine migrants of the diaspora, especially in the United States, where Mitchel resided through much of the 1850s and 1860s. As the Irish Fenian enthusiast John O'Leary lamented four decades later, "nearly all Mitchel's writings after this time [1848] (which are far his greatest in style, and indeed in almost every way) were published in America, and little read at the time—as indeed they are far too little read yet—in the country which he had had been forced to leave." But simple locale of publication was not the only issue here. Deeply wounded by loss of family, friends, and homeland, and finding a life of little more than hardship, poverty, and discrimination in America, many Famine immigrants were predisposed to embrace the fervently anti-British views of a figure they regarded as a fellow exile. "Our nation is scattered abroad like the Jews, and trampled at home as no people, or tongue, or nation, Jew or Gentile, ever was before," Mitchel wrote in the *Citizen* in 1854. The impact that such language had on this "scattered" people was incalculable.[13]

The New York Exiles

After his arrival, Mitchel also began to play an active role in Irish republican circles in New York. Back in Ireland, nationalist activity during the 1850s centered on agrarian reform as, after a brief flurry of conspiratorial activity that culminated in a small and unsuccessful rising in County Waterford in September 1849, republicanism went into a kind of hibernation. As he set off from Ireland to make a new life in Australia in 1855, Charles Gavan Duffy, the Young Ireland veteran, declared that he saw "no more hope for the Irish cause than for the corpse on the dissecting-table." "And so the years passed on, leaving Ireland where she was, disgusted, disheartened, and, to all outward appearances, entirely apathetic," recalled John O'Leary years later, labeling the mid-1850s "the 'deadest' time in Irish politics within my memory, and perhaps within the memory of any man now living." New York City in the 1850s, on the other hand, was alive with Irish revolutionary activity. Mitchel was joined there by numerous other '48ers, most prominently John O'Mahony and Michael Doheny, as well as by those arriving in America after the failed 1849 conspiracy. "The result of the abortive insurrection of 1848," an astute British observer of the Irish American scene observed some years later, "was to change the base of Irish revolution from Ireland to America."[14]

Exiled after the defeat of the 1848 revolutions throughout Europe and drawn by the generally enthusiastic American support for those revolutions, well-known European nationalists or republicans like Giuseppe Garibaldi and Lajos Kossuth also made highly publicized American tours in the early 1850s. Kossuth's barnstorming tour of December 1851 to July 1852, an effort to win US diplomatic and military assistance for a new Hungarian revolt against the Hapsburg empire, was spectacular: huge crowds welcomed him almost everywhere he went and he even addressed the House of Representatives, the first foreigner to be invited to do so since the Marquis de Lafayette a quarter of a century before. Several thousand exiled '48ers from the German states also arrived in the United States over the course the 1850s, sparking a revival of American trade unionism, while filling the ranks of the free soil movement and various free thought societies and Turnvereins, gymnastics associations, in many of the cities where they settled.[15]

Rubbing elbows with these political émigrés in increasingly cosmopolitan cities like New York, Chicago, and St. Louis, Irish republicans also gave them their support. John Mitchel, for example, trumpeted the cause of republican revolution not only in Ireland, but throughout continental Europe as well, lamenting in 1849 that "Hungary is *down*—Venice, Rome and Baden, all down, and the Kings and Grand Dukes are everywhere rampant," but optimistically predicting that "the blood of men fighting for freedom is *never* shed in vain" and that "the avenger knoweth his day and his hour." A group of Irish American republicans styling themselves "the Irish volunteers" joined German Turners, American trade unionists, and others in the huge procession welcoming Kossuth to New York in December 1851. These transplanted European radicals shared many of the same opponents, especially John Hughes, recently elevated to the position of archbishop, who denounced the European '48ers as "red republicans." Indeed, throughout his entire time in New York Mitchel waged an almost continuous war of words with Hughes. Meanwhile, some of the Americans who rallied to Kossuth made similar gestures to the Irish '48ers. In October 1851, Charles Sumner, the newly elected Free Soil senator from Massachusetts, appealed to President Millard Fillmore to offer political asylum to William Smith O'Brien "and the other Irish exiles," citing American efforts on behalf of Kossuth as a precedent.[16]

Though openly organized Irish republican nationalism had collapsed in the United States after the 1848 debacle, secret Irish republican clubs in New York continued to have a vigorous, if often faction-ridden, existence. Military companies that the Irish Republican Union had organized in 1848, for instance, folded themselves into the New York state militia at the end of 1849 and were formally recognized as part of that body's 9th Regiment the following year. Meanwhile, the previously open and public IRU transformed itself into an organization called the Silent Friends, operating as a secret body within the 9th Regiment. The Silent Friends spurred the formation of new Irish military companies, such as the 69th and the 72nd, with the long-term goal of using Irish American military training on behalf of Irish independence. By 1853, however, bitter factionalism had led to the total collapse of this organization.[17]

In April of the following year, John Mitchel helped organize a new revolutionary body in New York, the Irishmen's Civil and Military Republican Union, which also reached out to Irish American members of the New York state militia. In addition, Mitchel approached the Russian ambassador to ask for arms to support an Irish rising. The previous month, Czarist Russia had gone to war against Britain, France, and Turkey in the Crimea. Despite considerable popular Irish enthusiasm for the British war effort, Mitchel and other Irish republicans in America believed that the departure of British troops from Ireland to the Crimea might make this a propitious moment to launch an insurrection. This reprise of Wolfe Tone's diplomatic entreaties to the French minister in America led nowhere, and the new organization collapsed entirely when Mitchel left New York for Tennessee at the end of the year. There he founded the *Southern Citizen* to agitate for the reopening of the African slave trade.[18]

Filling the vacuum left by Mitchel's departure were two other key Irish '48ers. One of these was the self-educated Tipperary lawyer, Michael Doheny, who had managed to evade arrest after the rising, making his way first to Paris and then to New York, where he published one of the first accounts of these events, *The Felon's Track*, before returning to the practice of law. The other was John O'Mahony, the son of a County Cork gentleman farmer, who had also escaped to Paris, moving to New York in January 1854, after hearing that Mitchel had relocated there. In March 1855, these two exiles founded the Emmet Monument Association. The effort to wrap their new organization in the legacy of a famous United Irish martyr was readily apparent; less obvious to some was the revolutionary intent built into the bland-sounding name, a coded reference to Robert Emmet's 1803 statement from the dock that only when Ireland took her place among the nations of the earth should his epitaph be written. The only "monument" that the Emmet Monument Association intended to erect was an independent Irish republic.[19]

Though it had branches in a number of cities, the new organization had its national directory based in New York, where it soon counted as many as 2,000 members among the Irish regiments and companies of the state militia. According to one of these members, they were mainly young single men "free from family obligations, such as having a wife, mother, or others, depending upon them for support." By June 1855, they were drilling once a week, "ready to serve at a moment's notice" in an invasion to secure "the freedom of Ireland." Despite their efforts at secrecy, however, the British ambassador soon learned of the New York activity and fired off an angry letter to US Secretary of State William Marcy, complaining of "the existence of Clubs composed of the Irish population in that City for the purpose of enlisting and drilling volunteers to effect an insurrection in Ireland." The ambassador believed that New York's Irish American militia regiments, as well as many members of its police force, "had been corrupted and that their aid was counted upon by the conspirators of New York in their projected rebellion." Like Mitchel before them, Doheny and O'Mahony tried to seize the opportunity presented by the Crimean War, approaching the Russian consul in New York with the goal of obtaining transportation and arms for Irish Americans to fight in Ireland. The Russian consul went so far as to forward the request to St. Petersburg, but the war ended before anything could come of it.[20]

In Boston, activists organized a body called the Massachusetts Irish Emigrant Aid Society, which—despite the charitable connotations of its name—convened in August 1855 to discuss methods to advance "the cause of liberty in our native land." The Boston group had far-flung affiliates, including a Cincinnati organization called the Robert Emmet Club; twenty members of that club were arrested in early 1856 for encouraging the migration of Americans to foment revolution in Ireland, in violation of the 1818 Neutrality Act. But New York remained the main center of activity, and when the Boston group decided to hold a second and larger convention in December 1855, they met in New York, selecting none other than the ex-president's son and repeal veteran, Robert Tyler, as their chair. The convention itself was the scene of considerable conflict between Doheny and the Boston group, with charges and countercharges of being British agents hurled by both sides.[21]

Members of the Emmet Monument Association, at this point, had no contacts on what they called "the other side," but this was about to change. In the summer of 1855, Joseph Denieffe, a young tailor who had arrived in America four years earlier, returned to his native Kilkenny, partly to see his ailing father but also with "carte blanche" from Doheny "to do what you can for the organization." He soon began recruiting "intelligent young men," mainly tradesmen, white-collar workers, and small proprietors, first in Kilkenny and its environs, then in Dublin. Some of these men had taken part in the 1849 conspiracy and, according to Denieffe, gave "their hearts and all their energies" to preparing for another rising. Though modest in scale, Denieffe's efforts marked the first time the impetus for Irish revolutionary organizing emanated from America rather than from Ireland.[22]

Other offshoots of American exile groups began to appear in various parts of Ireland. A New York organization called the Shamrock Benevolent Society, for example, dispatched an Irish-born American citizen by the name of Fallon to Ireland, carrying cash and secret passwords—though he was arrested in Westmeath and sentenced to seven years in prison for his activities. Much more significant were the so-called Phoenix Societies. In 1856, a young man named Patrick J. Downing returned from New York to the west County Cork market town of Skibbereen, an area hit particularly hard by starvation and emigration. Here, with help from a young hardware store clerk (and son of an evicted tenant farmer) named Jeremiah O'Donovan Rossa, he established a body called the Phoenix National and Literary Society of Skibbereen, modeled after an organization of the same name that had been founded by Irish republicans in New York four years earlier. Other Phoenix Societies appeared across Ireland in the mid-1850s, unconnected to one another but drawing on the New York society for their highly evocative name if nothing else. Though focused more on self-improvement and sociability than on revolution at the outset, these societies encouraged intense nationalist political discussion among the young tradesmen and clerks who were drawn to them. Many of these young men would end up as Fenians, and the phoenix itself—the mythical bird that rose from its own ashes—would eventually become the unofficial symbol of the Brotherhood.[23]

A rising that the Emmet Association had planned for September 1855 never materialized, but two years later a massive rebellion in the northern and central parts of the Indian subcontinent that contemporaries called "the Indian mutiny" created a stir among New York's Irish republicans. They welcomed the Great Rebellion of 1857 with enthusiasm, and at least some of them registered a growing sense of common grievances under British rule that was becoming more salient even than perceived racial difference. Inspired by the Indian rebellion as well as by an increase in Anglo-French tensions that followed the Crimean War, Doheny and O'Mahony undertook a new initiative. They sent a letter to James Stephens, another veteran of 1848, asking him to take charge of building an organization in Ireland—funded by Irish American contributions—that would begin preparing for revolution. It was this initiative that led to the formation of the Fenians.[24]

But if the original plan, the funding, and the very name of the Fenian organization all came from America, the structure that it adopted as an oath-bound secret society came from the world of revolutionary exiles that Stephens had absorbed in the seven years that he resided in Paris. A supporter of both the February and June 1848 revolutions in France and a strenuous opponent of the efforts to bring Louis Napoleon to the head of the French government, he had lived and worked among the secret societies of socialists, communists, and republicans in the city. Stephens made a full study of the theory and practice of these organizations, which were at the center of democratic revolutionary activism in the decade after 1848, combining what he learned with what he regarded as the specifically Irish republican tradition of the United Irishmen and 1798. Though never a socialist, in Paris he also began to propound a deeply egalitarian social vision that focused on the betterment of the common people.[25]

Stephens was back in Ireland when the New York exiles contacted him, and he gave them a generally positive response to the "proposed co-operation of our transatlantic brothers." Before accepting "this great personal responsibility," however, Stephens insisted on a guaranteed stream of financial support from America (£100 a month for at least three months). Irish American financial support was absolutely essential to the project because, as he wrote to Doheny, in Ireland "the men of property are not with us." Drawing on his observations of Parisian republican politics, Stephens also demanded "unshackled" control of the Irish body, asking to be accorded the position of what he called its "provisional dictator."[26]

The Fenian Brotherhood

When the New York exiles agreed to these terms, a new revolutionary nationalist movement was born. On St. Patrick's Day, 1858, Stephens, Thomas Clarke Luby (another veteran of the 1848 rising), Garret O'Shaughnessy, Joseph Denieffe, and Peter Langan convened the first meeting of the Irish Republican Brotherhood in Langan's Dublin lumberyard, swearing an oath of allegiance to "the Irish Republic, now virtually established." Within a few months, most of Denieffe's earlier Kilkenny recruits had joined the new organization, as had a number of the members of the Phoenix National and Literary Society in west Cork. "The same spirit of enthusiasm spread to other counties," Denieffe later recalled, "and very soon the men of Munster were out nights on the hillside and on lonely roads drilling." In Dublin, the organization also grew rapidly, drawing especially on skilled workers and laborers in the city's building trades. Across the Atlantic, the exiles began sponsoring fundraising events in New York in January 1859 and, by April, had organized themselves under a strange and distinctive name: the Fenian Brotherhood.[27]

The name was proposed by a key figure among the New York exiles, John O'Mahony—a product of his research. A Trinity College graduate, O'Mahony was a serious scholar of Gaelic literature and language, and three years after his arrival in New York, he had published a copiously annotated translation of Geoffrey Keating's seventeenth-century *History of Ireland*, in order, as he put it, to "fix the minds of the disinherited sons of the Clanna Gaedhail, wherever scattered, upon that green land which is their ancestral birth-right." "Fenian" was an Anglicization of the Irish word *Fianna*, the warriors of the ancient Celtic warrior chief, Fionn Mac Cumhail, or Finn MacCool, that O'Mahony had celebrated in his annotations to Keating's *History*. The founders of this new organization were intensely conscious of the need to emphasize its roots in a deep (if largely invented) history of nationalist struggle. With the appellation "Fenian," they invoked a far deeper history than that of the Emmet Monument Society, and the term quickly caught on on both sides of the Atlantic. Since members of the Irish

Republican Brotherhood in Ireland avoided using its formal name, usually referring to it simply as "the organization" or "the brotherhood," both the Irish and
the American organizations came to be popularly known as "Fenians."[28]

Throughout their history, the two organizations were linked in a way that
would have been inconceivable even a decade or two earlier. Part of the reason
for this was technological. The quarter-century between the late 1840s and the
early 1870s was an era of astonishingly rapid improvements in transportation
and communication. The railroad, the steamship, and the telegraph, all widely
adopted in the 1850s, brought more and more of the world into the domain
of an international capitalist system, stimulating both mass production and the
emergence of the modern corporation. These same developments also helped
make Irish republicanism a more fully integrated transatlantic movement than
it had ever been before. The complex transatlantic organizing that went into the
planning of the 1867 rising, for example, would have been much more difficult
without the working telegraph cables that had recently been laid beneath the
North Atlantic or the oceangoing steamships that allowed Fenian envoys to
travel quickly between New York, Dublin, and London.[29]

The Fenians' effort to link their struggle with an ancient warrior tradition—
or even with Tone, Emmet, and the United Irishmen sixty years earlier—was a
work of intellectual invention, but their connection with Young Ireland was real
and direct. This fact laid the groundwork for one of the Fenians' most dramatic
and effective early gestures: the transatlantic funeral of the Young Ireland veteran, Terence Bellew McManus. McManus, like John Mitchel, had been a prisoner in Van Dieman's Land, but together with Thomas Francis Meagher, he had
also managed to escape, making his way to San Francisco, where he remained for
the rest of his life. When he died there in 1861, California Fenians devised a plan
to send his body back to Ireland for burial. Excitement grew steadily throughout Irish America as McManus's body, which had been placed in a metal-
lic coffin, made its way via Panama to New York. On September 15, a police
escort, a marching band, and ten men from each company of the state militia's
69th Regiment accompanied the coffin to the Old St. Patrick's Cathedral on
Mulberry Street, where, despite some misgivings, Archbishop Hughes conducted a funeral mass.[30]

Back in Dublin, James Stephens was initially unhappy with the plan to bring
McManus's body to Ireland, fearing it could trigger a premature rising. But he
could do little to stop the Irish Americans. As Denieffe later put it, "after all the
large cities in America had taken it up and finally decided in carrying it out,
he had no other course open but to acquiesce." By the time the coffin reached
Dublin in November 1861, thousands of the city's residents were lining the procession's route to Glasnevin Cemetery. At McManus's graveside, an American
Fenian read a eulogy written by Stephens that began by describing "the anguish

of the exile doomed to die and leave his bones for ever in a foreign land," but ended on a hopeful note: "As the stricken mother takes her latest martyr to her breast," she gave those living the "faith and stern resolve to do the work for which M'Manus died." Thus evoking a physical force republican tradition that stretched from the United Irishmen to Young Ireland, Stephens's words announced the Fenians as the legitimate heir to this tradition: "the Irishmen of to-day are true as any of their predecessors." The McManus funeral was one of the signal events of nineteenth-century Irish republicanism—as well as being part of the longest wake in Irish history—and helped make the political funeral an important part of the republican movement's tool box. More immediately, as the constitutional nationalist A. M. Sullivan lamented, it "gave the Fenian chiefs a command of Ireland which they had not been able to command before." From this point until 1865, the growth of the organization was extremely rapid.[31]

The American Civil War, which began the year of McManus's death, provided a major stimulus to the Fenian movement in America. For one thing, it ended in a single stroke the bitter disagreements over slavery and states' rights that had roiled the ranks of Irish nationalists in the northern states since the early nineteenth century. John Mitchel had already left New York for the South (though he happened to be in France when the war broke out) and his example was followed by Robert Tyler, who had remained active in America's Irish nationalist circles through the mid-1850s, while continuing to defend slavery. With Confederate guns firing on Fort Sumter, Tyler faced arrest for treason and, as his enraged Philadelphia neighbors built a bonfire in front of his home and hanged him in effigy, he and his family beat a hasty path toward the safety of his father's Virginia plantation. Meanwhile Fenians in Chicago and other cities gave enthusiastic support to the Union cause. Some of them, unlike most Irish Americans (or northern white Americans generally), began to voice support for African American emancipation as well.[32]

Many Irish and Irish American men also began to enlist in the Union army. By the end of the war, nearly 150,000 of them had served under the flag of the United States. Some joined up to prove their loyalty in the face of persistent anti-Irish nativism; others were enticed by the enlistment bounty and a steady wage in a time of high unemployment. Fenians, who enlisted in significant numbers, wanted to acquire training in arms and military tactics that they hoped to use soon in Ireland; they also sought to recruit other soldiers to the Irish revolutionary movement. This motivation, of course, could lead men to enlist in the armies of either North or South, and some Fenian circles did appear among the 20,000 or so Irish who served in the Confederate military. But the Union cause naturally drew those with the deepest ideological commitment to republicanism and the large number of Union veterans in the Brotherhood actually hindered its ability to organize in the South after the war ended. Thomas Francis Meagher, who had praised both "the sword" and the "daring, free Republic" whose birth it had facilitated, began encouraging Irishmen to enter the Union army shortly after Fort Sumter and soon joined up himself, putting together a company of infantrymen attached to New York's 69th Regiment. Following the First Battle of Bull Run, he organized the Union army's Irish Brigade. Meagher himself had resisted earlier entreaties from Doheny and O'Mahony to join the Fenians, but his Irish Brigade was filled with them. The Lincoln administration even encouraged Fenian efforts to organize in the army, hoping to counteract Democratic Party influence among Irish American Union soldiers.[33]

The war itself led to an increase in Fenian strength, and by 1863, the Brotherhood was ready to hold its first national gathering. Attending the Fenian convention, held in Chicago in November, were 300 delegates representing 63 "circles" scattered across the continent; at this meeting, the participants created a new organizational structure, including a Head Center (O'Mahony) and a five-man Central Council, and issued what it called a "Declaration of Independence" for the Irish Republic. The convention raised the profile of the organization dramatically, transforming it from "neither more nor less than a myth," in the view of one participant, to a body of "power and influence." Within months, Chicago's Irish nationalists hosted an even more impressive public event, the so-called Fenian Fair, which raised over $50,000 for the Brotherhood.[34]

Chicago's Fenian Fair illustrates a critical dimension of the organization in the United States: its largely working-class membership and its deep connections with the Civil War–era labor movement. The emergence of a national labor movement in the towns and cities of the northern states was one of most important developments of these years and labor's growth was especially impressive in Chicago, where native and foreign-born workers (mainly Irish and German) organized a dozen new trade unions, established a city-wide central labor assembly and weekly labor newspaper, engaged in numerous strikes, and began waging a political campaign for the eight-hour day. Chicago's trade unionists participated enthusiastically in the Fenian Fair, with the Chicago Typographical Union, the Horseshoers' Association, and the Tailors' Fraternal Union all marching in the opening parade and the city's Iron Molders Union presenting the Fenians with a McCormick reaper to be carried in the procession. Such deep connections between Fenians and trade unionists were common throughout the industrializing East and Midwest in the Civil War and immediate postwar period.[35]

Irish American women were prominent at the Fenian Fair, selling tickets, serving meals, playing music, and directing the crowds. Their efforts were echoed at the national level in February 1865, when Ellen O'Mahony, sister of the Brotherhood's leader, founded an organization called the Fenian

Sisterhood, which sponsored balls and other social events to raise money for the movement. The Fenian Sisterhood marked another step in the growing political engagement and inclusion of Irish nationalist women in America that had begun with their participation in O'Connell's repeal network. This trend was apparent in Ireland as well, with the Fenian-inspired poetry and journalism that Ellen O'Leary and several other women writers began publishing in the 1860s. At a deeper level, however, the emergence of the Fenians should probably be seen as a step backward, toward the exclusion of women from the inner world of Irish and Irish American republicanism. The Fenians' imaginative construction of a highly masculine, military identity for themselves would seem to deny all outlets for women's political activism beyond those efforts, as contemporaries put it, to "excite men to action." The Fenians, after all, identified themselves not just as a "brotherhood," but as a brotherhood of warriors. They even masculinized their mythical forerunners, viewing themselves as the soldiers of Finn, a male warrior chief, rather than (as many previous nationalists had) the sons of the (female) Erin.[36]

Back in Ireland, developments were unfolding quickly. In the wake of the McManus funeral, Stephens and another '48er, Thomas Clarke Luby, began building up the Fenian organization. They attracted attention from the police, as well as opposition from the Catholic hierarchy and from middle-class nationalists like A. M. Sullivan, a former Young Irelander who now edited the *Nation* as a strictly constitutional organ. In November 1863, Stephens started his own newspaper, the *Irish People*, triggering criticism from O'Mahony and others in the American organization, who argued for a strict policy of secrecy in Ireland. But the newspaper helped bring tens of thousands of young men in Ireland into the fold, along with large numbers in Britain's Irish immigrant community and even in the British army. By 1865 Ireland appeared to be ripe for a renewal of revolutionary struggle, while the American Fenians claimed over 50,000 members, many of them battle-hardened veterans who were ready to give assistance to a new Irish rising.[37]

But it was not to be. A group of Irish American veterans had already landed in Ireland, and a number of experienced ex-Union army officers, led by Colonel Thomas Kelly, had set up a military council in Dublin when, in September 1865, the British government began a preemptive crackdown on the IRB that led to the capture of key figures like John O'Leary, Jeremiah O'Donovan Rossa, and, within a short time, Stephens. Those Fenian leaders who were still at large had little choice but to call off the rising. As Irish Fenians regrouped, some of their American counterparts looked for another way to strike at Britain's domination of Ireland, turning to the British colony of Canada. In so doing, they triggered the first major political split within the ranks of the American group.

Attacks on Canada and the 1867 Rising

The main advocates of a military attack on Canada were Colonel William R. Roberts and Thomas W. Sweeny who, at a special Philadelphia meeting of the Fenian Brotherhood in October 1865, overthrew O'Mahony and set up what they called a Senate of the body to move ahead on this initiative. It is hard to imagine a figure more unlike the scholarly O'Mahony than William Roberts. Emigrating from County Cork to New York in 1849, Roberts was an economically motivated immigrant, not a revolutionary exile, and he achieved a great deal of success in the United States in the dry goods business. His motives in joining the Brotherhood are not entirely clear, but he quickly developed a strong personal following in the organization.[38]

Not to be outflanked, O'Mahony's faction of the organization struck Canada first, with a poorly executed assault by several hundred men on Campobello Island, in New Brunswick's Bay of Fundy, in April 1866. Their goal was to seize and hold the island as a way of harassing Britain, but American military forces intercepted and dispersed the raiding party before it could reach its destination. The main effect of the attempted raid was entirely unintended, prompting New Brunswick's legislature to finally vote to join the Confederation of British North America, thus strengthening British interests in North America.[39]

The following month, the Roberts wing of the Fenian Brotherhood launched its assault on Canada from Buffalo and St. Albans, Vermont. Their force of about 800 Fenians, many of them Union army veterans, was commanded by Colonel John O'Neill, a County Monaghan native with substantial Union army experience, first as a cavalryman, later as an officer with the 17th Regiment of the US Colored Infantry. The Fenians crossed the Niagara River and fought a short and victorious battle on June 2 with the Canadian militia at Ridgeway, in what is now the province of Ontario. "We come among you as the foes of British rule in Ireland," the invaders announced, in a proclamation signed by Thomas Sweeny. "We have taken up the sword to strike down the oppressors' rod, to deliver Ireland from the tyrant, the despoiler, the robber." The Canadian authorities naturally saw things differently and US president Andrew Johnson agreed, condemning the invasion and dispatching federal troops to block a second and significantly larger invading force under Sweeny's command. The Roberts wing of the Brotherhood had suffered a major blow to its prestige and power.[40]

The 1866 split in the American organization, coming in the wake of the British crackdown on the IRB, also weakened the movement in Ireland. The Fenian military council in America leaned heavily on Stephens to call the Irish rising that he had been promising for months and, when he again prevaricated, they deposed him and took matters in their own hands. Fighting broke out in March 1867, but—long anticipated by the British government, which had riddled the movement with spies—the rising never really got off the ground. O'Mahony's supporters tried to send rifles, ammunition, and even cannons to Ireland, but by the time the ship with this weaponry arrived, the brief skirmishes in County Kerry, Cork City, Limerick, and Dublin that constituted the rebellion had ended.[41]

Even though the rising was a military failure, it was far from the embarrassing disaster that the 1848 rebellion had been and it actually ended up helping to renew the physical force revolutionary tradition. This outcome stemmed partly from the response of the British government, which handed out long prison sentences to the rising's leaders and the death penalty to a group of Fenians attempting to free two key IRB figures from a prison van in the British city of Manchester in September 1867. Following the botched effort, which led to the death of a police officer, the government tried, convicted, and publicly executed three men (soon to be known as the "Manchester Martyrs"). Executions for Irish republican activity had not been carried out since the hangings of Robert Emmet, Thomas Russell, and their co-conspirators in 1803, and they immediately created widespread outrage in Ireland. Catholic priests who had once condemned the Fenians now said masses for them. The failure of the 1867 rising also hurtled a new phalanx of Irish exiles to American shores. "From the date of the [1798] Irish rebellion to the present hour every successive agitation or disturbance has driven its promoters, its sympathisers, or its victims, across the ocean," observed John Francis Maguire after his North American visit of 1868, "and thus, from year to year, from generation to generation, has an anti-English feeling been constantly quickened into active life, and been widely diffused throughout America."[42]

In the short run, transnational factionalism was the order of the day. In 1868, the IRB's Supreme Council in Ireland broke off connections with the American Fenians, on whom it blamed the defeat of the previous year. In 1870, Colonel John O'Neill rallied some of these American Fenians for another attack on Canada, this one launched from the Lake Champlain area of Vermont. This raid was another failure: the organization was riddled with informers and President Ulysses Grant exploded at a May 1870 cabinet meeting that he planned "to issue a proclamation against such proceedings as those of the 'Irish Republic' the 'organization of a Government within the U.S.' the 'holding of a Congress,' and the 'assumption of the power to raise armies and fit out expeditions.' " Grant went on to say that "this thing of being a Citizen of the U.S. for the purpose of voting, and being protected by this Gov. and then claiming to be Citizens of another Gov. must be stopped." O'Neill's small band had barely gotten across the border when they were driven back by federal forces and O'Neill was arrested.[43]

A more complicated situation arose when British rather than US authorities arrested American citizens of Irish birth. Throughout the 1860s, Britain held to the doctrine that citizenship was inalienable and regarded Irish immigrants who had become US citizens under American naturalization law as continuing to have an obligation of "perpetual allegiance" to Britain. While in ordinary times this could seem like a somewhat arcane issue, in the context of Fenian raids and rebellion it meant that Irish-born American citizens arrested in Ireland, Britain, or Canada could be charged with the crime of treason. In the wake of the 1867 rising, a number of American citizens, most famously John Warren and Augustine Costello, were tried and sentenced to long terms in British prisons. The American Fenian Brotherhood and its supporters took up their case, with the goal not only of securing their release but also of heightening the international tensions between the United States and Britain that had been simmering since the Civil War. But though Warren, Costello, and some of the others were eventually set free, the Fenians' larger goal was undercut in 1870, when Parliament passed a law permitting a British-born subject to "divest himself of his birth-allegiance, and adopt another citizenship." With this legislation, informally known as the Warren and Costello Act, and with an international agreement finalized the same year, American and British governments settled their long-running dispute on a friendly basis. Though international law on the right of expatriation had been significantly advanced, so too had harmonious Anglo-American relations, much to the disappointment of the Fenians. [44]

O'Neill and the Fenians launched one final raid on Canada in 1871, linking up with a rebellious group of Métis (a people of mixed Indigenous and European descent) in Manitoba, but the raid proved to be another disaster and O'Neill was arrested by US authorities yet again. After this, the American Fenian Brotherhood experienced a steady decline, though the group managed to stagger on until the mid-1880s.[45]

The Clan na Gael

New forces were already at work that would soon lead to a revival of physical force nationalism in America. Among the post-1867 wave of exiles to the United States was John Devoy, who would become one of the country's most influential Irish nationalists. Born in County Kildare in 1842, Devoy served in the French Foreign Legion in Algeria in 1861, returning to Ireland the following year to take charge of the IRB's efforts to infiltrate the British army. Arrested in 1866, he was released from prison in 1871, after agreeing to go into exile. Upon arrival in the United States, he immediately threw himself into Fenian circles in New York, where he would remain a towering figure among Irish American nationalists for the next fifty years. The growing assemblage of post-1867 Fenian exiles also included Thomas Clarke Luby and Jeremiah O'Donovan Rossa, who settled in New York after time in British prisons.

The goal of these new exiles was to bring some kind of organizational order to the chaos that was American Fenianism. Both Devoy and O'Donovan Rossa were unhappy with the ties that New York Fenians had established with Tammany Hall, controlled by political boss William M. Tweed, and O'Donovan Rossa even once ran unsuccessfully against Tweed for a seat in the New York State Senate. Meanwhile, though advised by his old friend, the ex-Fenian and *Boston Pilot* editor, John Boyle O'Reilly, to forget about Irish nationalism, Devoy found his way into an organization called the Clan na Gael.[46]

Established in June 1867 by the *New York Herald* journalist Jerome J. Collins and a group of Fenians disillusioned by the factionalism of the Brotherhood, the Clan's original goal was simply to reconcile the quarreling Fenian factions and revive the organization. Eventually despairing of this, however, they turned to building up their new organization. Devoy, who began working for the *Herald* shortly after arriving in the city, emerged as a key figure within the Clan. The Clan, sometimes calling itself the United Brotherhood, shrouded itself in secrecy, rituals, and coded communications, attempting to rectify what its leaders saw as the mistakes of the Fenian Brotherhood, which, they felt, had become too public and open an organization. The Clan was organized into local "camps" and regional districts and was headed by a national executive. Like previous nationalist organizations, it was strongest in the large cities of the Northeast and Midwest, but camps could be found in smaller towns and in western states as well.[47]

In the 1870s, the Clan embarked on a number of schemes to advance the cause of the Irish revolution. They contracted with an engineer named John Holland, originally from County Clare, to build a submarine for use against the British navy. The Clan subsidized Holland for five years, spending $60,000 on the project, though only one of the three boats he designed for the organization ever became operational. When tensions between Russia and Britain threatened to boil over during the 1877–78 Russo-Turkish War, Devoy approached the czar's ambassador in Washington with a request for military aid, which was declined. The Clan had more success in hiring a New England whaling ship, the *Catalpa*, for a daring rescue of a group of Fenian prisoners held in Australia in 1876, an accomplishment that would achieve an almost mythic reputation. By 1877, when it established formal links with the IRB in Ireland, the Clan had nearly 10,000 members and a treasury of $50,000. Though small compared with its Fenian predecessor, it was nonetheless by far the largest nationalist organization in either Ireland or the Irish diaspora at that point in time.[48]

Fenianism in the Wider World

Both the Fenians and the Clan na Gael established footholds, some more secure than others, throughout that diaspora. Australia had Fenian prisoners, and a kind of anti-Fenian (and more generally anti-Irish Catholic) hysteria took shape after a mentally ill Irish Australian named Henry O'Farrell attempted to assassinate Prince Alfred, Queen Victoria's son, during the first ever royal visit to Australia in 1868. Although O'Farrell was said to have shouted, "I'm a Fenian—God Save Ireland," as he shot the prince in the back, the truth is that he had no political associations of any sort. A similar situation existed in New Zealand, where what became known as the "Fenian riots" actually reflected intense—but highly localized—ethnic and class tensions, not Irish revolutionary activity. Fenian organizations did appear in both Australia and New Zealand in the 1870s, and a representative from Australasia even participated in the Revolutionary Directory that linked the Clan na Gael and the IRB after 1877; but the number of active Fenians in the antipodes remained insignificant.[49]

The situation was very different in Britain, which, after Ireland and the United States, had the largest Fenian contingents. The National Brotherhood of St. Patrick, founded in 1861 in Dublin "to secure the national independence of Ireland, whether by parliamentary agitation or other means," had outposts in London, Liverpool, and numerous Lancashire factory towns, and it served as a kind of front group for the IRB in Britain. Thomas Clarke Luby, organizing for the Brotherhood in England and Scotland in 1865, believed he "must have addressed, in those countries, a short time, mark, before we were arrested, at least twelve or fifteen hundred men." Luby later recalled speaking to them "fiery stuff about the coming time and the *diversion* and destruction they could make in England." In 1866 and 1867, Fenians in Britain linked up with British radicals in the Reform League, then agitating for an expansion of the franchise to British working-class men.[50]

Perhaps the most surprising case was Canada, where Fenian ranks grew steadily over the course of the 1860s in places like Toronto and Montreal, despite the American Fenian border raids of 1866. The movement even weathered the backlash that followed the 1868 assassination of the popular Irish Canadian politician, Thomas D'Arcy McGee, the one-time Young Irelander who had become a vocal champion of the British Empire and a bitter enemy of Fenianism. In fact, it was the fear of further Brotherhood raids from the United States that persuaded Canadian authorities to refrain from a full crackdown on the Canadian Fenians, allowing them to develop, as in the United States, a formidable public presence. Ironically, it was the overwhelming defeat of the 1870 attack that brought the Canadian Brotherhood's growth to an end; the humiliation of that debacle was more than the organization could withstand.[51]

Everywhere Fenians could be found, it appears, they attracted urban and working-class men (with a strong component of white-collar workers) to their ranks. While American Fenian and Clan na Gael leaders were typically doctors, lawyers, or journalists, rank-and-file activists were mainly working class. The largest single camp of the Clan na Gael in the 1870s was located in what contemporaries called the "worker city" of Troy, New York. Troy had earlier boasted an active circle of the Fenian Brotherhood in the 1860s and, at least according to Devoy, the city's mayor, chief of police, and comptroller were all members of the Clan na Gael in the 1870s. Sometimes labor leaders themselves emerged as important figures in the Clan, the most famous of whom was Terence V. Powderly. Son of an Irish immigrant, mayor of Scranton, Pennsylvania, and future national leader of the Knights of Labor, Powderly was in the 1870s the "senior guardian" of Camp 470 of the Clan na Gael. His energetic work on behalf of the Clan drew many working-class adherents throughout northeast Pennsylvania in the late 1870s and early 1880s.[52]

Some Fenian leaders, while embracing such supporters, firmly rejected the notion that workers should challenge their employers—or the propertied classes more generally—in either Ireland or the United States. "Our movement was mainly one of the masses, not against the classes, but unfortunately without them," John O'Leary later reflected, and it is true that many prominent Fenian leaders focused their sights on a purely political revolution for independence from Britain, without thinking much about social or economic issues or grievances. But other Fenian leaders, in both Ireland and America, tried not only to recruit "the men of no property" but also to put forward social and economic policies that spoke to their needs. James Stephens believed throughout his life that "unless the Irish land were given to the Irish people, Irish national independence was not worth the trouble and sacrifice of obtaining it." Though never articulating a coherent program of land reform, the Fenians' Dublin newspaper, the *Irish People*, denounced both landlords and graziers and called in general terms for land redistribution that would facilitate the spread of peasant proprietorship. Making an economic, along with a political, case for their rebellion, the IRB's Proclamation of 1867 declared that "the soil of Ireland, at present in the possession of an oligarchy, belongs to us, the Irish people, and to us it must be restored."[53]

Meanwhile, in the United States, there were clear links between Fenians and various labor and third-party efforts. For instance, Colonel Patrick Guiney, a Fenian supporter, abolitionist, and Civil War hero, ran for Congress in 1866 on an independent workingmen's ticket, pledged to winning the eight-hour day. Though initially ambivalent about the Fenians, Karl Marx came to regard them with tremendous respect, going so far as to appoint a young Fenian named

Joseph P. McDonnell as Ireland's official representative on the general council of the International Workingman's Association. Two American Fenians,
John Masterson and Robert Blissert, were also important figures in the First
International, where they worked closely with socialists, anarchists, and assorted
labor reformers. For men like these, the achievement of an Irish republic was just
a step toward much more sweeping social and economic change.[54]

Broadly popular, at least for a time, the Fenian Brotherhood and Clan na
Gael brought thousands of ordinary Irish and Irish Americans to the cause of
physical force republicanism, in spite of opposition from the Catholic hierarchy
and important elements in the Irish and Irish American middle classes. In so
doing, they prepared the way for the even more powerful transatlantic nationalist movement that would appear on the scene in the early 1880s, the Irish and
American Land Leagues.

The New Departure in America, 1878–1890

By 1878, a new direction was badly needed for republican nationalists in both Ireland and the United States. Neither the Irish Republican Brotherhood nor the Clan na Gael was growing, but their problems ran much deeper than this. Though Fenianism in both countries had drawn heavily on the support of urban and rural working people and had expressed in a general way their aspirations for a better life, the absence of a coherent or clearly articulated social program rendered the movement on either side of the Atlantic incapable of responding effectively to what appeared to be the dominant questions of the day. In the United States, this was what an Ohio politician called the "overwhelming labor question," which, as evidenced by the smoldering ruins of trains and rail yards left by the Great Railroad Strike of 1877, "has dwarfed all other questions into nothing." In Ireland, it was the land question, a problem intensified by a series of poor harvests beginning in 1877 that, combined with a general agricultural depression spreading throughout Western Europe in the later 1870s, presented the threat of a tragic replay of the Great Famine. Many Irish and Irish Americans wondered what Irish republicans, or nationalists more generally, had to say about such questions.[1]

The new direction that emerged was mapped out in the United States. In July 1878, Michael Davitt, a member of the Irish Republican Brotherhood's Supreme Council, arrived in America; he had recently been released from Britain's Dartmoor prison, where he had served seven years for gunrunning. The child of County Mayo tenant farmers evicted during the Famine, Davitt had grown up in the Lancashire industrial town of Haslingden, where, at age eleven, he had lost an arm working in the cotton mills. These early experiences gave him an acute sensitivity to the problem of economic inequality and a deep commitment to social justice that were rare among the mainly middle-class leaders of the IRB. In New York, Davitt met with John Devoy, the most important leader of the Clan na Gael in the United States, with whom he hammered out a new plan for the

Irish republican movement, one that put aside the physical force strategy that appeared to have reached a dead end. Instead, they would give conditional support to a group of Irish members of the British House of Commons who were working to achieve a greater degree of political autonomy for Ireland, a goal that was now being called Home Rule. This approach would be combined, Davitt and Devoy decided, with an effort to radically restructure the Irish land system, ending the dominance of large landlords and providing avenues for tenant proprietorship of the land. This radical rethinking of republican orthodoxy would come to be known as the New Departure.[2]

The land question grew more urgent as agricultural conditions deteriorated in Ireland over the course of 1879, triggering a three-year explosion of agrarian protest known as the Land War. Beginning in the far western county of Mayo, where local activists like James Daly had been working for several years to organize tenant farmers, the movement spread rapidly throughout Ireland's southern provinces and into Ulster. As it did, tenant demands for a short-term reduction of rents and greater security of tenure were transformed into a condemnation of Irish landlordism in general. Though the leaders of the campaign attempted, with partial success, to prevent a return to the violent tactics of previous agrarian movements, the Land War was nothing if not confrontational. Highlighted by mass meetings and marches, fiery rhetoric, and the concerted refusal of tenants to pay rent except when forced to do so "at the point of a bayonet," the Land War also embraced as one of its main tactics the refusal to work for oppressive landowners and the complete social ostracization of the movement's opponents. Though this tactic was not original, it was given a new name taken from a County Mayo land agent who became its first victim, Captain Charles Boycott.[3]

Returning to Ireland, Davitt helped found a new organization, the Irish National Land League, in October 1879, to provide coordination and direction to the still unfocused movement. Assuming formal command of the Land League in 1880 was the new leader of the parliamentary Home Rule forces, a charismatic Protestant landlord from County Wicklow named Charles Stewart Parnell. The intertwined issues of land and labor, the question of Home Rule, and the figure of Parnell himself would dominate Irish nationalist politics in both Ireland and the United States for the rest of this tumultuous decade.

The American Land League

In early 1880, Parnell journeyed to the United States, the birthplace of his mother, to raise funds for famine relief, land agitation, and Home Rule. His three-month tour through the East, Midwest, and Upper South was an unqualified success, raising over £70,000 and generating tremendous American enthusiasm for the cause. From this point on, funds from the United States became the lifeblood of the Home Rule Party (renamed the Irish Parliamentary Party in 1882), allowing it, for example, to provide allowances to many of its otherwise unremunerated MPs. While the American Irish were Parnell's main supporters, in an echo of O'Connell's repeal network four decades earlier, Americans from non-Irish backgrounds also rallied to his leadership and party. Local politicians, Protestant clergymen, and business people turned out for him in many of the sixty-two towns and cities that he visited, and his address to the US House of Representatives (the first by a foreigner since Hungarian nationalist Lajos Kossuth had spoken to this body in 1851) gave the movement a major boost. The success of his American tour prompted Timothy Healy, an up-and-coming Irish politician and journalist, to hail Parnell as "the uncrowned king of Ireland." It also prompted Michael Davitt to return to America for a tour of his own, traveling the country and organizing support for the Irish Land League in towns and cities from Boston to San Francisco.[4]

Though American enthusiasm for Parnell's mission may have echoed that for O'Connell's repeal campaign, the goals of the Home Rule movement were actually much less ambitious. It is true that Parnell could sometimes sound like a radical separatist, as in Cincinnati, where he allegedly said—perhaps attempting to appeal to Fenians in the crowd—that the Irish people would not "be satisfied until we have destroyed the last link which keeps Ireland bound to England." In fact, however, Home Rulers did not seek a repeal of the Act of Union or the reestablishment of an independent Irish Parliament under the crown—let alone a fully independent republic, as the Fenians wanted. What they sought was rather a devolved government within the Union, in which the British Parliament would transfer certain limited responsibilities to an Irish executive formed from an elected Irish legislative body. Both the Union and British sovereignty over Ireland would remain intact.[5]

Equally important, Irish America had changed in important ways in the forty years since O'Connell's repeal campaign. By 1880, the Irish-born population had risen to 1.8 million and even larger was the American-born second generation, which reached a staggering 3.2 million in this year, the first year that the US Census counted the children of immigrants. Both the Irish- and American-born overwhelmingly labored in working-class occupations. But while unskilled day labor for men and domestic work for women were still common, by 1880 more and more men, especially among the second generation, occupied skilled positions, working as iron molders, machinists, bricklayers, and carpenters. Working-class life, even for those in the skilled trades, remained precarious, as demonstrated by the mass unemployment and wage cuts that accompanied the depression of the 1870s. Nonetheless as the US economy grew in the late 1870s and early 1880s, many Irish immigrant and Irish American workers began to improve their positions, through both individual bargaining in a tighter labor market and membership in trade unions, which expanded rapidly after the losses of the depression years.[6]

By the 1880s, the social and occupational diversity that had already character-ized Irish America forty years earlier was even more clearly discernible. An Irish Catholic middle class, composed mainly of merchants and professionals, could be found in many cities, especially in the Midwest and West, where the Irish gen-erally found greater economic opportunity and avenues for advancement than in the more settled cities of the East. But even in New York, there was a substantial Irish Catholic middle class, its higher reaches mixing with the city's increasingly cohesive urban elite. With the 1880 election of Irish-born millionaire William R. Grace as the first Catholic mayor of New York, the arrival of the "lace curtain" Irish had become a fact of political—as well as economic and social—life. It was a heterogeneous Irish America that gave its welcome to Parnell.[7]

Enthusiasm and local activism soon gave birth to a new national organization. In March 1880, a group of Irish Americans, meeting in New York on the eve of Parnell's return to Ireland, organized a body they called the American Land League, more formally the Irish National Land and Industrial League of the United States. They elected as their president James J. McCafferty, a young law-yer from Lowell, Massachusetts, whose only qualification (at least according to Davitt) was that "he was supposed to be the handsomest man in New England." Despite such questionable leadership choices, the convention marked a kind of turning point. Irish nationalism, over the next few years, became a genuine mass movement in the United States, surpassing in numbers and influence even that of the Fenians at their Civil War peak. Branches of the American Land League sprang up in towns and cities across the country to provide support for the agrar-ian reform and Home Rule movements in Ireland, seen by many in the United States as thoroughly intertwined. By early 1882, the Land League had organized more than a thousand branches across the nation and had raised over $500,000 for the cause, drawing especially heavy support from Irish American working people.[8]

The significance of all this did not lie in numbers and money alone. The Irish nationalist movement's real achievement in the early 1880s was to bring together three currents of protest that up until this point had generally been separate: the revolutionary republicanism that began with the United Irishmen and was now expressed by the IRB in Ireland and the Clan na Gael in the United States; the efforts of parliamentary leaders from O'Connell to Parnell to achieve repeal, or now Home Rule; and the social and economic struggles of the rural and urban poor, stretching from the eighteenth-century Defenders to the Land War. Close to the center of this transnational conjuncture of forces was a radical New York journalist named Patrick Ford, whose widely circulated weekly newspaper, the

Irish World and American Industrial Liberator, served as the voice of the most politically active part of the Irish American working class.[9]

The *Irish World* had supported trade unions, strikes, and labor reform movements like the Greenback-Labor Party as early as the 1870s. In the early 1880s, the paper began drawing parallels between the land struggle in Ireland and the labor struggle in the United States, arguing that monopoly was the central social problem in both countries. "The cause of the poor in Donegal is the cause of the factory slave in Fall River," Ford wrote, in a characteristically transnational key. In some areas of the country, particularly the industrial districts of New England, the anthracite mining regions of Pennsylvania, and the hard rock mining and railroad communities of the Far West, mainly working-class branches of the American Land League quickly arose that adhered closely to Ford's views, in some cases virtually merging with local assemblies of a rapidly growing national labor reform organization called the Knights of Labor. In these areas, the Land League and the Knights together articulated a radically class-conscious perspective that posited a deep and fundamental conflict between those they called the "producing classes" (workers, small business owners, and small manufacturers) and "monopolists" (large industrialists, railroad owners, and especially bankers). Ford and his supporters saw the latter as posing a fundamental threat to the social order, for they seemed to be coming to control not only the land of Ireland but American industry and finance as well.[10]

The idea that Irish nationalists could have something pertinent to say about American economic inequality was not entirely new. As early as February 1848, a group of Irish nationalists in New York had met to organize a Tenant League to combat rapidly rising rents in the city. Rather than the more familiar drawing of contrasts between a "republican" America and a "despotic" Ireland, speakers here sketched explicit parallels between American and Irish conditions. One expressed horror "at the rapid strides of the same system of landlordism, which, in his native country, Ireland, has led to the destitution of the masses, and has driven them to seek refuge in this country." Another condemned a shared "system of landlordism" as "one of the most blighting curses that ever was inflicted on the human race," not just in "poor starving Ireland." Though New York's Tenant League had collapsed by the end of the 1840s, some of its proposals were reintroduced by other American land reform organizations in the 1850s. Still, the cross-Atlantic parallels that Ford sketched in the pages of the *Irish World* were fresh and gripping.[11]

A key ally of Ford was the American economic reformer, Henry George, whose 1879 book, *Progress and Poverty,* would become the most widely read volume of political economy of the nineteenth century. Focusing attention on what he called the "great enigma of our times," the growth of poverty in an age of industrial progress, George identified land monopoly as the root of the problem and proposed a "single tax" on land values as the solution. While denying any "necessary conflict between capital and labor," he believed that objections to "the combination of workmen for the advance of wages" were "baseless" and strongly supported the emerging labor movement, making numerous converts to his ideas within its ranks. Equally important, he became a leading supporter of the Ford wing of the Land League, writing pamphlets on the Irish land question and serving as the *Irish World*'s correspondent in Ireland in 1881. In turn, both Ford and Davitt worked hard to publicize *Progress and Poverty*, and Irish American working-class supporters of the Land League became one of George's first constituencies.[12]

To be sure, not everywhere did labor radicals control the Land League. In the rapidly growing western commercial city of Denver, Colorado, for instance, the local branch of the organization was led by members of the emerging Irish American middle class. Some within this group actually opposed the local trade unions and the Knights of Labor, prompting one Denver labor leader to charge them with being "specialistic liberators." In New York City, middle-class conservatives also dominated the Land League's leadership, and the city's leading Irish newspaper, the *Irish American*, reflected their outlook, taking a generally conservative stance in both American politics and the politics of Irish nationalism. A similar situation could be found in other large cities, such as St. Louis, Philadelphia, and Pittsburgh.[13]

Even in these cities, however, a strong connection existed between the emerging labor movement and the struggle against the Irish land system. In Denver, for example, many Irish American workers gravitated not to the Land League branch but to the leadership of a local Irish radical named Joe Murray, who had lived a life far removed from the lawyers, politicians, and businessmen who dominated the city's Land League. Born in poverty near Dublin in 1843, Murray migrated with his family to Manchester, where he labored in the mills, acquired the rudiments of an education in a night school, and became active in Irish republican circles. But, sharing the international republican outlook of James Stephens and other founders of the Fenian movement, he also became a corresponding member of Guiseppe Garibaldi's Carbonari, and in 1859, he left Manchester to fight with the Redshirts for Italian independence. Two years later, he accepted a commission as an officer in the 69th New York Regiment, the most famous unit of Meagher's Irish Brigade. Like many of his fellow Irish nationalists in the Union army, Murray was fighting to defend republican principles in America while simultaneously preparing his countrymen in arms for the coming battle to establish an Irish republic.[14]

After the war, Murray moved to New York, where he worked as a bookkeeper and joined the city's Fenian movement. But his social views took a new turn in the later 1860s. He became a follower of Horace Greeley, attracted by that reformer's belief in organized economic cooperation as "the application of Republican principles to Labor, and the appointed means of reducing laboring classes from dependence, prodigality and need." In 1870, Murray took up farming in Colorado as a founding member of the cooperative Union Colony at Greeley, an intellectual hothouse peopled by ex-Chartists and abolitionists, free thinkers, and financial radicals whose influence served to strengthen Murray's growing radicalism. In 1878, he left the Republican Party to join the Greenback Party and by 1881 was an organizer for the Colorado Knights of Labor. "A soldier of liberty on the battlefields of two continents," as one admirer described him, Murray was no narrow Irish nationalist but rather a fighter for national determination as an international principle and a believer in radical social and labor reform as integral to Irish republicanism. Confronting Thomas Brennan, a one-time officer of the Irish National Land League, at a Denver meeting in the winter of 1883, Murray disagreed with Brennan "that the struggle in Ireland is one of race," arguing instead that "it is a class war." As Murray saw it, "it was not only the poor of Ireland who were suffering from the tyranny of despotic and capitalist rule but that the poor of all countries were enslaved thereby; and that the cry would soon be—is now in fact—for the equality of all mankind."[15]

Other locales experienced similar class and ideological tensions. In Worcester, Massachusetts, middle-class conservatives dominated the local Land League branch, but working-class nationalists were also a presence, challenging their leaders on any number of occasions. In Pittsburgh, middle-class figures, mainly from the Irish province of Leinster, dominated one branch of the League while working-class radicals, mainly from Munster, dominated another. And in New York, labor and reform leaders put forward their own version of Irish nationalism as an explicit alternative to that of the local Land League leadership, with no small measure of success. In January 1882, for example, some 12,000 trade unionists met at Cooper Union to back the so-called No-Rent Manifesto then being promulgated by the Land League in Ireland. Under a banner declaring that "the No Rent battle of Ireland is the battle of workingmen the world over," nationally prominent labor reformers like Robert Blissert, George McNeill, and Peter J. Maguire drew attention to what Maguire, leader of New York's carpenters, called "the similitude of the slave system at home and abroad." In the wake of this meeting, New York labor activists formed the city's Central Labor Union. The first plank of its declaration of principles stated that land should be "the common property of the people."[16]

It was in New York that some of the most radical dimensions of Irish American nationalism came to the surface. In 1882, Dr. Edward McGlynn, pastor of the sprawling working-class parish of St. Stephen's in lower Manhattan, began to champion both Michael Davitt's newly announced land nationalization plan for Ireland and Henry George's single tax reform for America. In the Anti-Poverty

Society that he founded and in his powerful sermons and speeches, he developed a distinctively Irish and Catholic version of the social gospel. "Christ himself was but an evicted peasant," McGlynn told a rally for Davitt organized by the Central Labor Union in June 1882. "He came to preach a gospel of liberty to the slave, of justice to the poor, of paying the full hire to the workman."[17]

Labor and economic issues were not the only new elements in this mix. Irish radicals in America also endorsed a new departure in the relationship of women to nationalist and social reform movements in these years. In the 1880s, both Irish and Irish American nationalism were influenced by a dramatic expansion of women's activism. In New York City, Ford's *Irish World* backed women's rights along with labor and land reform. In addition, Fanny Parnell (Charles's sister) and Jane Byrne organized the Ladies' Land League in the city in October 1880, taking what an early twentieth-century Irish feminist would call "the most important step since the start of the movement." Over the next two years, active Ladies' Land League branches, usually independent of male control, appeared in a number of American cities. Organizing a branch of the Ladies' Land League in November 1880, Irish American women in Worcester raised $5,000 for the cause over the next two years, a significantly larger amount than that provided by the city's more numerous male branches. Moreover, the women here defied the more conservative and clerically oriented local male leadership by sending these funds directly to the radical editor Patrick Ford rather than to the central Land League treasury, managed by the Reverend Lawrence Walsh of Connecticut. "The land of every country belongs to the people of that country," the Worcester women proclaimed. "Thousands for independence, not one penny for rent." In Denver, Irish American women organized a Ladies' Land League branch in late 1881; here men in the movement voiced enthusiasm for "working with the Ladies."[18]

Michael Davitt, who had been impressed by the American women's activism and by Fanny Parnell in particular ("thorough politician, able speaker, earnest manner," he noted), proposed the establishment of a parallel organization in Ireland, arguing that it could continue the Land War if the League's male leaders were imprisoned. Though opposed by Charles Stewart Parnell as "a dangerous experiment," the Irish Ladies Land League was set up in January 1881, led by Anna Parnell, another of his sisters. Over the next year and a half, the Ladies Land League held public meetings, provided accommodations for evicted tenants, and distributed Land League literature, despite substantial clerical opposition. This was the first time that Irish women had formally entered a nationalist movement, and Anna Parnell became the first woman to occupy a prominent position in Irish public life.[19]

"In the Irish Land League cause, the best men were the women," Henry George opined in 1883 and George's supporter, Father McGlynn, became a vigorous champion of women's rights as well. In 1882, McGlynn defied the conservative bishop of Cleveland, Richard Gilmour, by speaking to a Land League branch in that city whose women members had been excommunicated by Gilmour for their activism. In turn, many Irish American women activists rallied behind McGlynn: his Anti-Poverty Society attracted a disproportionately large number of women supporters in the 1880s and 1890s, and women were prominent in the rallies organized to defend the radical priest after he was excommunicated in 1887. The Denver branch of the Land League also denounced Bishop Gilmour after his excommunication of the women activists. As one Catholic member of the branch put it, he could not condemn Gilmour "as a man or as a Catholic, but he would denounce the action of any man, whether priest, bishop, or pope, who opposed the Irish people in their struggle for liberty." As another Denver activist proclaimed, "it was not for kings or priests to dictate to the Land League."[20]

This public defiance of the Catholic hierarchy illustrates yet another dimension of radical Irish nationalism in this period: it encouraged a growing independence from clerical influence that shaded off into secularism and anti-clericalism among at least some Irish Americans. Without ever repudiating the church, the *Irish World*'s Patrick Ford was highly critical of the Catholic hierarchy through the early to mid-1880s. If the pope opposed the struggle for the Irish nation, Ford argued in 1884, then the Irish should simply ignore the pope. Philip Bagenal, an astute English observer of American society in these years, believed that the *Irish World*'s popularity indicated that the church was losing its influence among the American Irish. McGlynn's excommunication, although later reversed, probably accentuated the trend toward secularism among his Irish American supporters.[21]

The Politics of Race

Perhaps most significantly, the rise of the Land League marked a significant change in the racial thinking of Irish nationalists in America and particularly in their relationship to the tradition of American reform associated with abolitionism and the struggle for African American equality. While Irish American nationalists had been overwhelmingly hostile to abolitionism (even if most were not actively pro-slavery), the Land League struggle, and particularly the efforts of the *Irish World*'s editor Patrick Ford, did much to transmit the moral and political values of this movement to Irish America as a whole.

Born in Galway in 1837, Ford was a Famine emigrant, coming to Boston with his parents in 1845. He attended St. Mary's Catholic School in that city but was too poor to complete his education. At the age of fifteen, Ford took a job as a printer's devil for William Lloyd Garrison's *Liberator*. Garrison had a profound influence on Ford, who quickly developed an enthusiasm for both abolition and journalism. In 1861 he began editing a short-lived abolitionist paper of his own, the *Boston Tribune*. Following service in the Union army, Ford took over the editorship of the *South Carolina Leader*, a Republican newspaper that fought for African American rights in the Reconstruction South. Failing with this and a second paper, the *Charleston Gazette*, he moved to New York in 1870, where he established the *Irish World*, which he edited until his death in 1913.[22]

In embracing the causes of American labor reform, Irish land reform, and Home Rule, Ford drew explicitly on his abolitionist and Radical Republican heritage. The fight against slavery, he told his readers time and again, was the seedbed from which all the post–Civil War reform struggles had emerged, and he used the pages of the *Irish World* to lionize his former employer, Garrison, and his friend, the abolitionist and labor reformer Wendell Phillips. Veteran abolitionists and African American civil rights leaders responded in kind. The aging James Redpath, a Scottish-born Presbyterian who had long believed that Irish poverty was the result of Catholic profligacy, radically revised his views after traveling in Ireland as a correspondent for the *New York Tribune* at the height of the Land War in 1880. After returning to America, Redpath threw himself into the work of the American Land League, touring the Northeast and Midwest on its behalf and drawing thousands of Irish Americans to the cause with his fiery speeches. T. Thomas Fortune, the crusading young African American journalist, was another convert to the Land League, encouraging black Americans to support the Irish cause and, in 1887, proposing the creation of an Afro-American League "to be organized on the same plan" as that of the Land League. While noting the troubling existence of extreme "prejudice against color [among] our Catholic Irish fellow-citizens," Frederick Douglass also voiced support for Irish Home Rule, asserting in 1883 that "England to-day is reaping the bitter consequences of her own injustice and oppression."[23]

Ford used the *Irish World* to fight against the powerful currents of racism within the labor movement, the Land League, and Irish America as a whole. Expressing sadness that many Irish Americans had taken "an attitude of seeming hostility to the friends of human freedom" during the struggle against slavery, he sought to radically reorient Irish American attitudes. "Welcome the colored brother in the Land League," he editorialized. "He is a marked example of a defrauded workingman." Ford's choice of words here bears close examination. Despite his commitment to women's rights, Ford, like most labor reformers of this era, envisioned the "working class" in thoroughly masculine terms. Irish American and African American men were "brothers," for each was a "defrauded workingman." This was the kind of assertion of identity across the color line that few Irish Americans had ever even contemplated.[24]

In a similar fashion, Ford asserted a fundamental Irish and Irish American identity with colonized peoples around the globe. Devoy had struck this note at the time of the New Departure, calling on Parnell to take up the "advocacy of all struggling nationalities in the British Empire and elsewhere" as one of the conditions for cooperation, but Ford made it a central preoccupation of his weekly paper. The *Irish World* referred to Indians under British rule as "fellow subjects" and "brown Irishmen" and, in a striking reversal of the terms employed by much of the American press, labeled the British, not Africans, as "barbarians" for their invasion of the kingdom of Ashanti. Within the boundaries of the United States, Ford took a similar stance on Indigenous resistance to an expansionist American empire. His response to the Lakota, Arapahoe, and Northern Cheyenne victory at the Battle of the Little Big Horn in 1876 had been to publish two letters from Wendell Phillips condemning General Custer and to run an editorial denouncing as "unmanly cant" the characterization of the battle as a "massacre." "If *Sitting Bull* is a savage, *John Bull* is a hundred times a greater savage," Ford wrote, defending the Lakota leader against the venomous attacks on him in the American press. "The simple fact is that he stood between his people and extermination." The "colonization column," a weekly feature of the *Irish World* in these years, offered a running commentary on the identity Ford sought to establish between Irish and Irish Americans and other peoples struggling against "Anglo-Saxon colonialism" around the globe.[25]

In such statements and journalistic practices, Ford was not simply expressing sympathy for downtrodden peoples that he saw as fundamentally different from himself. Rather, the language that he deployed expressed a common identity with these peoples based on what he understood to be a shared experience of colonialism and oppression. Indians were "brown Irishmen"; Native Americans, Africans, and the Irish were all victims of colonial "savagery" and "barbarism"; African Americans and Irish Americans were "brothers." How many Irish immigrants and Irish Americans followed Ford down this road is impossible to determine, though his influence during this period was great. Drawing readers from across the country as well as in Ireland, England, and Scotland, the *Irish World* claimed a circulation of 35,000 by 1876 and of 60,000 by 1882. While it would be naive to assume that all (or even most) of Ford's readers agreed with his radically new conception of Irish American identity, at least some proportion of them must have grappled with his challenging ideas.[26]

One should not overstate the changes in Irish American racial attitudes that occurred in this period, including those of Irish American nationalists. When Michael Davitt visited San Francisco in 1880, for instance, he was greeted by a delegation of laboring men led by Denis Kearney, the Irish immigrant leader of California's Workingmen's Party, which stood at the center of the state's anti-Chinese campaign. Kearney ended every speech in this period with the party's slogan, "The Chinese Must Go!" Though critical of what he called Kearney's "dictatorial tactics," the Belfast-born Fenian veteran Frank Roney was another

San Francisco labor leader who combined a commitment to Irish nationalism with an embrace of the anti-Chinese movement. It was Roney who developed a plan in the early 1880s to adopt the tactic used in the Land War in the city's anti-Chinese movement, the boycott of businesses employing Chinese labor. "I thought that if our working people were only one-quarter as sincere in their desire to be rid of Chinese cheap labor as the Irish had proved to be in getting rid of Captain Boycott the victory would be as substantial in one case as it was in the other," he later recalled.[27]

The early 1880s, the very years of the Land League's meteoric ascent, also saw a dramatic upsurge of violent white working-class agitation against the Chinese throughout the western states, a campaign that contributed to the passage of the first major piece of federal legislation restricting immigration in American history, the 1882 Chinese Exclusion Act. The themes of Irish nationalism, land monopoly, worker exploitation, and anti-Chinese racism came together in the writings of Henry George, who had penned one of his earliest newspaper articles against the Chinese and whose racial hostility toward them never abated. Undoubtedly, many Irish American workers followed George's example in supporting both the Land League and the movement against the Chinese. "We do not oppose the Chinaman on account of any race prejudice," Patrick Ford defensively claimed in hailing the passage of the Exclusion Act, though his denial surely would have sounded hollow to the Chinese laborers for whom America's gates were about to close.[28]

But Ford's tireless efforts to connect Irish nationalism with the African American struggle for equality was profound, and it may have been one of the most important factors shaping the stance toward black workers taken by the Knights of Labor. The most important national labor organization of the nineteenth century, with a membership of over 750,000 in 1886, the Knights of Labor enrolled large numbers of Irish Americans and was led by Terence Powderly, an Irish Catholic machinist and one-time mayor of Scranton, Pennsylvania. Powderly, who had been a leader of the Clan na Gael in the 1870s, was a devoted enthusiast of the New Departure and was elected a vice president of the American Land League in 1881. The racial outlook of the labor organization that he headed does not lend itself to easy summary. Viciously anti-Chinese in the western states (the Knights stood at the center of what was called an "abatement campaign" to forcibly drive Chinese workers out of the region's lumber and mining camps), in the South the organization pursued much more racially egalitarian policies that eventually drew some 60,000 African American men and women to its ranks. At the opening session of the Knights' 1886 convention, held in Richmond, Virginia, Powderly began the proceedings with a fiery denunciation of racial discrimination against African Americans in the South and throughout the United States.[29]

The International Reach of the Land League

As with earlier moments in the history of Irish nationalism, enthusiasm for the Land League was not only to be found in Ireland and America. On the west coast of New Zealand, for example, branches of both the Land League and the Ladies' Land League appeared in 1881 and (as in the United States) these expressed more than a small dose of anti-clericalism. Middle-class leaders of New Zealand's Liberal Party, who had initially endorsed Irish Home Rule, drew back as the more radical implications of the Land War received increasing attention in the local press, but working-class Irish immigrants soldiered on in support of the movement, organizing meetings and sending a steady stream of funds to Davitt back in Ireland. The Irish in Australia also contributed heavily to the Land League in the early 1880s.[30]

Canada presented an even stronger parallel with the situation in the United States. Middle-class Irish Catholics in cities like Toronto rallied to the Land League as part of their larger quest for acceptance and upward mobility, while trade unionists and leaders of the Canadian assemblies of the Knights of Labor (which was extremely strong in Ontario, with pockets of strength in other provinces as well) embraced Patrick Ford's wing of the movement and sent funds directly to the *Irish World*. In industrializing Canada, like the United States, the Irish land struggle brought many Irish workers into support for a broader vision of labor radicalism.[31]

Outside Ireland and the United States, the Land League sank its deepest roots in Britain. This is not surprising given Davitt's boyhood in Lancashire and his concerns with the needs and goals of British workers generally. Agrarian issues, moreover, had occupied an important place in British working-class radicalism since the days of Tom Paine, and by February 1881, Davitt was urging Parnell to "take steps in England to instruct the working class with regard to ... the Irish land question." For tactical reasons, Parnell accepted the idea of an alliance between Irish nationalists and British workers, and in March, the National Land League of Great Britain came into being, under the presidency of Justin McCarthy, the vice chairman of the Home Rule Party. The new organization spread rapidly among Irish immigrants in England and Scotland and, as in America and Canada, links with working-class radicals were apparent early on. One of the British Land League's most tireless activists, for example, was H. M. Hyndman, who went on to found the Democratic Federation in June 1881, a central position of which was support for the Irish land struggle. That organization changed its name to the Social Democratic Federation in 1883, developing into a key organization in what became known as the "socialist revival" among British workers in the last decade of the nineteenth century.[32]

In light of all of this, it is not surprising that Michael Davitt chose Britain as the place to unveil a radical new economic plan. In Liverpool on June 6, 1882, he called for a policy of sweeping land nationalization as the only effective way to implement the Land League's slogan, "the land for the people." Addressing a large and enthusiastic crowd several days later in Cork, Davitt linked this economic policy with a political objective significantly more radical than the limited goal of Home Rule: "what Ireland wants is the nationalization of the land administered in Dublin by an Irish Parliament." He then set off for America again in an effort to internationalize the Irish land question, placing it in the context of a larger crusade for social justice.[33]

The Land League's Decline

It was at this point that the entire transnational movement began to unravel. A committed Irish republican like John Devoy could advance the demand for peasant proprietorship as a tool for recruiting Irish tenants to the nationalist cause, and he also believed that the British government's inevitable refusal to meet this demand would lead to polarization, revolution, and eventually political independence; but he saw Davitt's embrace of sweeping public land ownership as closer to socialism (which he opposed) than to nationalism. From another corner of this complex movement, Parnell was simultaneously backing away from any form of agrarian agitation. In the so-called Kilmainham Treaty that he hammered out with the Liberal government of William Gladstone in May 1882 (after the government had outlawed the Land League and imprisoned Parnell, Davitt, and its other leaders), he shifted his attention from the land question altogether to the parliamentary struggle for Irish Home Rule. Although he continued to pay lip service to the goal of peasant proprietorship, Parnell directed his energies toward a more narrowly political fight. The founding of the Irish National League to replace the now-suppressed Land League in October 1882 solidified this direction. Tightly controlled by Parnell, even the name of the "National League" reflected his desire to abandon the agrarian struggle. Over the rest of the decade, the League would serve purely as a kind of electoral machine for the Irish Parliamentary Party.[34]

A parallel development soon took shape in the United States. On April 25, 1883, the American Land League was officially dissolved at a meeting in Philadelphia. Over the next two days, a new organization, the Irish National League of America, was established. Rejecting not only Davitt's land nationalization plan but any kind of social or economic program—for either Ireland or the United States—this new organization was dominated completely by members of the Clan na Gael, and it remained so through the rest of the decade.

Deeply unhappy with the control of this ostensibly constitutional grouping by committed revolutionaries, more moderate (and generally more affluent) Irish Americans formed yet another organization, the Irish Parliamentary Fund Association, led by a wealthy Irish-born banker named Eugene Kelly. Despite their differences, both groups sent funds to Parnell's party through the 1880s, doing much to finance the parliamentary fight for Home Rule. Meanwhile, Irish American workers, many of whom had been deeply inspired by the Land League, generally kept clear of both organizations. Working people also generally avoided the Clan na Gael, an important faction of which now rejected the whole thrust of the New Departure in favor of a bombing campaign in Britain. In Patrick Ford's opinion, the broad international social movement heralded by the New Departure was now dead.[35]

The more narrowly defined Irish Home Rule movement, on the other hand, continued to make significant strides. In a single fundraising tour in 1883–84 that took them to Australia, New Zealand, and across the United States, the Home Rule leaders John and William Redmond did much to make their party the apparent voice of a tightly linked Irish diaspora. The party's international network of financial and moral support, combined with Parnell's political skills and the discipline that he imposed on his parliamentary colleagues, helped shaped William Gladstone's decision to pledge his Liberal Party to the Home Rule cause in December 1885. Shortly after his party's electoral victory the following February, Gladstone introduced a Home Rule bill in Parliament that Parnell hailed as "the final settlement." The bill went down to defeat in the House of Commons, splitting the Liberal Party and bringing the Conservatives (who now identified themselves as the party of so-called Unionist opposition to Home Rule) back to power. Nonetheless, it was an encouraging sign to Home Rulers, who looked forward to another effort the next time Liberals returned to government.[36]

Despite the dominance of the Home Rule agenda, reverberations from the Land League crusade continued to be felt in Britain and America through the rest of the decade and beyond. In Britain, land nationalization became a key demand of H. M. Hyndman's Social Democratic Federation. Land reform meetings, modeled after those in Ireland, continued to take place across the Scottish highlands in the 1880s, putting a Scottish labor leader, Kier Hardie, on a road that led first to Henry George's single tax program and eventually to socialism and the founding of the British Labour Party.[37]

In America, in addition to the rise of the Knights of Labor, whose membership peaked in 1886, a key event was Henry George's campaign that year for mayor of New York, heading the ticket of a new political organization called the United Labor Party. Large numbers of New York City's Irish American workers rallied behind George's challenge to Tammany Hall. Although he lost the election,

George polled a remarkable 68,000 votes, significantly more than the third-place candidate, a young Theodore Roosevelt. Both Patrick Ford and Father McGlynn worked in the George campaign, which was also backed by the Central Labor Union and the New York local assemblies of the Knights of Labor. McGlynn's participation in this campaign and his subsequent refusal to explain his position led to his excommunication by the Vatican in 1887, but a massive outpouring of support from his Irish American parishioners revealed the lingering appeal of the priest's distinctive brand of radicalism. Meanwhile, Davitt himself continued to be a frequent visitor to the United States, given enthusiastic receptions at conventions of the Knights of Labor and later the American Federation of Labor (AFL). Though rejecting socialist-backed proposals for the nationalization of the means of production, the national convention of the AFL passed a resolution in 1894 calling for the "abolition of the monopoly system of land holding" in the United States that could have been written by Davitt himself.[38]

In Ireland, the Land League's legacy was more muted. The Land War initiated a process of agrarian reform by the British government that led, by 1903, to its decision to buy out the Irish landlords and provide a dramatic expansion of land ownership for one-time tenants. This reform process dramatically undercut Irish agrarian radicalism. Michael Davitt continued to maintain a broad range of social and political commitments that involved, among other causes, labor and women's rights, Indian nationalism, and Zionism. But his reluctance to challenge Parnell's leadership gave Parnell a free hand over Irish nationalism—until his precipitous fall from power at the beginning of the 1890s.

6

Home Rulers and Republicans, 1890–1916

On November 17, 1890, two days of uncontested testimony detailing the long romantic relationship of Charles Stewart Parnell, charismatic leader of the Irish Parliamentary Party (IPP), and Katherine O'Shea came to a close with a divorce decree granted to O'Shea's husband (and Parnell's political associate), Captain William H. O'Shea. Unionist and Conservative opponents of Home Rule savored the moment, heaping ridicule and indignant condemnation on the man once called the "uncrowned king of Ireland." "A bad case in a bad class of cases," opined one Conservative member of the House of Lords, "inasmuch as it showed an abuse of friendship, a habitual depravity, and an elaborated system of deceit, which are happily of rare occurrence even in such cases." In the view of the vociferously anti–Home Rule *Times*, the evidence of "domestic treachery" and "long continued deception" that was revealed in court could only be compared to "the dreary monotony of French middle-class vice, over which M. Zola's scalpel so lovingly lingers."[1]

The first reaction in the Irish Home Rule Party, in sharp contrast, was to rally around their leader. At a great meeting in Dublin's Leinster Hall on November 20, attended by a number of the Irish Party members, Parnell's lieutenant, the MP Tim Healy, offered a ringing defense of his leadership that focused not on the O'Shea scandal itself but on the political imperatives facing the party. "Is it now in this moment within sight of the promised land that we are to be asked to throw our entire organisation back once more into the melting pot?" he asked. "I say that the Irish party are sovereign in their own domain, and if the English people are willing to cede us our rights and liberties upon domestic questions, I say of all questions that this is a domestic question." For Ireland, Healy concluded, "Mr. Parnell is less a man than an institution." He should not be ousted because of "a temporary outcry over a case that in London would be forgotten tomorrow."[2]

However, when Gladstone, responding to strong nonconformist Protestant pressure in the ranks of the British Liberal Party, announced that the Liberal-Nationalist alliance was now in grave danger, the Irish Party made an abrupt reversal, formally asking Parnell to resign as leader in December 1890. Despite the gathering storm of opposition from Gladstone, Ireland's Catholic hierarchy, and the majority of his own party, Parnell refused to step down. When the party removed him by vote and replaced him with Justin McCarthy, he formed his own party with a small group of supporters. Attempts to reunite the two factions of the movement failed, and in March 1891, the anti-Parnellites, as they came to be known, established a new fundraising organization, the Irish National Federation, in opposition to the Irish National League, which was still dominated by Parnell. Controlled tightly by the Irish Parliamentary Party, the National Federation sought to form local branches in every constituency in Ireland, combating Parnell wherever it could. In his speech to the new organization's first meeting, Healy, who had become the leader of the anti-Parnellite forces, ridiculed Parnell's claim to "leadership of the Irish race" as an absurd pretension. "I would never consent for one hour to remain in the party of which Mr. Parnell was the leader. I will never tolerate him. I will never consent to him in any shape or form."[3]

Reflecting the role of one of the most powerful of the forces arrayed against Parnell, the new organization gave pride of place to Ireland's Catholic Church. "Every priest who has been prominent in the national movement was present at the meeting," claimed the *National Press*, the newly launched anti-Parnellite newspaper that sought to be the voice of conservative Catholic nationalism. "The four Archbishops [of Ireland] blessed the infant in its cradle. Almost every bishop in Ireland concurred in its benediction." The *Times* noted that this first meeting marked "the formal and definite entry of the priesthood upon a struggle for the national movement" and went so far as to characterize the Irish National Federation as "essentially the organization of the Church for political purposes." Meanwhile, Parnell barnstormed through Ireland, fighting desperately to regain the party's leadership, a battle he continued until his sudden death on October 6, 1891.[4]

Even Parnell's death, however, did not end the split. His supporters regarded him as yet another martyr to the Irish national cause and they organized a funeral at Glasnevin Cemetery in Dublin, attended by over 100,000 people, which became one of the greatest political demonstrations of the nineteenth century, overshadowing even the MacManus funeral of 1861. The key issue, they proclaimed here and in a manifesto issued shortly afterward, had nothing to do with Parnell himself, but rather with the right of the Irish Party to elect its own leaders without the interference of British "friends" like Gladstone. A young and ambitious MP, John Redmond, emerged as the leader of the Parnellites. The Home Rule movement would remain bitterly divided along these lines for the rest of the 1890s.[5]

Home Rulers Regroup

In the United States, Irish American nationalists watched the unfolding of the Parnell split with consternation. "The fall of Parnell seemed at the time a death-blow to Ireland's future," remembered New York's Dr. Thomas Addis Emmet some years later. "I was almost on the verge of despair for Ireland's future." Not surprisingly, Irish American financial support for the Home Rule Party dried up almost overnight. Over most of the previous year, the party had been receiving approximately $1,000 a week from American supporters; within days of the split, the weekly take fell to $10. "The action of the guillotine was not more prompt or killing than that of this outbreak of dissension in Ireland upon our mission," recalled T. P. O'Connor, part of an Irish Party delegation then in the midst of a fundraising tour of the United States. Though the delegation had raised almost £8,000 at a single New York meeting on the eve of the divorce trial, by the end of the tour, all the meetings were "failures." When O'Connor spoke privately with Irish Americans, moreover, he became aware of "a violent division of opinion— some of the Irishmen were anti-Parnellite, some as fiercely Parnellite." "I could see all around me the fatal extension of the conflict at home to our race in America," O'Connor sadly concluded. And it was not just the middle-class Irish American leaders of the Home Rule organizations who were affected. "Even the porters in the hotels, who had been profuse in their kindly attention to us before the debacle, now turned on us surly looks." Contributions from Irish nationalists in Australia declined dramatically as well, forcing the Home Rule Party to rely almost entirely on fundraising in Ireland and among the Irish in Britain.[6]

Before long, Irish American Home Rulers began to regroup. First to organize were the anti-Parnellites, who came together on May 7, 1891, at New York's Hoffman House. They formed the Irish National Federation of America (INFA) "for the purpose of aiding in the advance of Home Rule for Ireland and for representing in this country the Irish people under the leadership of the majority of the Irish members of Parliament." The INFA modeled itself on, and was directly linked to, the Irish National Federation in Ireland. Recognizing the important role that historical references could play in their movement, especially at moments of crisis like this, the INFA decided to elect Emmet as their president. A prominent New York physician, Emmet was the grandson and namesake of the famous exiled United Irishman, Thomas Addis Emmet, and the grandnephew of the Irish revolutionary martyr Robert Emmet. He had taken no part in Irish nationalist politics up until this point, and he later ruefully admitted that it was the historical resonance of his name rather than any "peculiar fitness for the position" that had led to his election. As Dr. William B. Wallace put it in his nominating speech, Dr. Emmet was "the only man of Irish blood in the country who could hold the position as president for twelve hours without some one going for his head."[7]

Emmet turned out to be a competent and vigorous leader, and the INFA grew quickly. By February 1892, branches had been established not only in the East Coast centers of New York, Philadelphia, Baltimore, and Boston, but also in midwestern cities like Cleveland, Detroit, Indianapolis, and Cincinnati. Like its counterpart in Ireland, the INFA benefited tremendously from the support of the Catholic Church. New York's conservative Archbishop Michael Corrigan became a prominent supporter of the organization, and in other towns and cities, the clerical influence was even more pronounced. In Worcester, Massachusetts, the meeting that established the local branch of the INFA was held at the Catholic Institute in St. John's parish, and a popular local priest, Father Thomas J. Conaty, was elected as treasurer. "We are organizing Branches of the National Federation here in every parish," reported an enthusiastic Cincinnati official in June 1892. "The parish priests are assisting us very much."[8]

Even more striking than the clerical influence was the decisive role that men of wealth and standing took in the leadership of the organization. In addition to electing the well-to-do Emmet as its president, the organization picked the millionaire John Byrne as president of the board of trustees and Eugene Kelly, another millionaire who headed the Emigrant Savings Bank, as its treasurer. When Kelly died in late 1894, the INFA's Board of Trustees elected John D. Crimmins, one of America's wealthiest builders and contractors, to succeed him. Though Crimmins had started his working life as a gardener, by the late 1870s he owned the firm that had constructed much of New York's elevated transit system, sometimes employing as many as 12,000 workers. Rounding out the leadership group, as vice presidents, were two of Irish America's leading professional men: Philadelphia attorney Michael J. Ryan and St. Louis physician Dr. Thomas O'Reilly. To be sure, many working-class Irish Americans also gave their support to the INFA. Worcester's Irish American workers backed the local branch of the INFA, and in 1892 Emmet spoke to an enthusiastic meeting of 800 Irish American miners in Scranton, Pennsylvania, organized by the national leader of the Knights of Labor, Terence Powderly. But in ways markedly different from the moment of the New Departure and the Land League, neither working people nor their advocates played any role in the INFA's leadership.[9]

By the end of 1893, the INFA had established 150 branches across the nation. A number of public rallies were held, including a hugely successful mass meeting at the Academy of Music in New York City in March 1893, where New York's well-known Irish American member of Congress, W. Bourke Cockran, served as the featured speaker and where some $3,000 was raised. Nevertheless, defeat of Gladstone's second Home Rule Bill in the House of Lords (after passing the House of Commons) in September 1893, continuing conflict within the ranks of the Irish Parliamentary Party, and the onset of a major economic depression all severely hampered the INFA. Its annual operating funds fell from more than $33,000 in 1893 to just $5,500 the following year. "There is nothing to be got from the States just now," complained Irish Party leader Justin McCarthy in December 1894. The INFA continued to maintain a formal existence through the rest of decade, but for all practical purposes it was dead.[10]

Though a discouraging blow to the Irish Party, the defeat of the 1893 Home Rule Bill in Parliament helped bring to the surface new trends within

Irish nationalism on both sides of the Atlantic. In the wake of the defeat, Eoin MacNeill, Douglas Hyde, and a small group of other Irish-language enthusiasts founded an organization called the Gaelic League. Drawing on men and women from a mainly urban lower-middle-class background in Ireland, the League ran language classes and sponsored social gatherings, including a large national festival called An tOireachtas, which began in 1897. The organization also put out a newspaper, *An Claidheamh Soluis*, and sponsored the publication of Irish-language poetry and prose. By 1908, there were 671 branches of the League in Ireland, up from just 80 ten years earlier. Though formally nonpolitical and open to Unionists as well as nationalists, the Gaelic League had distinct political undertones. Like the Gaelic Athletic Association, which had emerged in the previous decade with the goal of reviving traditional Irish sports and games, the League's assertion of the enduring value of Irish culture and civilization eventually set many of its members on a path toward more explicit nationalist politics. As one Dublin member who would follow this path recalled, the Gaelic League "really aroused the spirit of Nationality that up to then was latent within me."[11]

The League soon reached out to the Irish in America, viewing them as a particularly valuable source of funds. As early as 1895, the organization was requesting financial assistance from the "various and disconnected Irish language societies outside of Ireland," and with the founding of the Oireachtas in 1897, Hyde and MacNeill issued a direct "appeal to our fellow countrymen [in America] to provide us with the necessary financial assistance to carry the project to a successful issue." These appeals culminated in Hyde's highly publicized speaking and fundraising tour of the United States in 1905–6. By this time though—and in spite of its formal avoidance of nationalist politics—one of the League's most important sources of American support came from the physical force revolutionaries of the Clan na Gael. Daniel Cohalan, for example, a leading figure in the Clan, gave speeches at New York Gaelic Society meetings, hosted Douglas Hyde at his New York home, and served as chairman of the finance committee of the Gaelic League in America "The work of the Gaelic League is in line with the objects of the Clan na Gael," stated a circular the organization put out during Hyde's speaking tour. "It is preparing the mind of the country for the supreme effort which will lead to the final triumph of the Gael."[12]

By 1905, the Clan na Gael's prospects were beginning to improve, but during the 1890s, physical force republicans in America had been as deeply divided as their constitutional opponents. The Clan, which had assumed dominance among Irish American republicans in the 1870s, was split between the so-called Triangle group, centered in Chicago and led by Alexander Sullivan, and John Devoy and his followers in New York. From 1889 on there were actually two distinct organizations calling themselves Clan na Gael and the sensational Chicago murder that year of a Devoy associate, Dr. Patrick Cronin, revealed how intense the rivalry had become. Those supporting Sullivan, who also called themselves the United Irishmen, constituted the larger of the two groups, led after 1894 by a Brooklyn building contractor named William Lyman. Putting out a newspaper called the *Irish Republic,* this group also helped establish a public front group, the Irish National Alliance, created in Chicago in September 1895, which leveled a barrage of criticism against anything smacking of constitutionalism. The Lyman group even worked to establish a rival to the IRB in Ireland itself. Calling itself the Irish National Brotherhood, the group made some recruits in Ireland and among Irish nationalists in London, most notably a young poet named William Butler Yeats. But it never managed to replace the IRB and both the Irish National Brotherhood and the Irish National Alliance were virtually dead by the end of the 1890s, leaving the field open to Devoy.[13]

As for the constitutional nationalists, only after 1900, when the main factions of the Irish Parliamentary Party reunited under the leadership of the Parnellite leader John Redmond, did its prospects in America begin to improve. In fact, the anti-Parnellite John Dillon's decision to step down in favor of Redmond, which prepared the way for reunification, was prompted at least partly by the hope for a renewal of American financial support. Rank-and-file support for Home Rule now took off in Ireland, where William O'Brien's newly formed United Irish League had 1,000 branches and more than 100,000 members by August 1901. Meanwhile, the United Irish League of America (UILA), its namesake, was founded in 1901 to replace the moribund INFA. The use of the term "United Irish" was a conscious effort to establish a direct genealogical link with the Society of the United Irishmen—despite the fact that both Irish and American groups rejected the goal of an independent republic and the strategy of physical force for which the original organization had been famous. And—though irritating republican separatists to no end—this kind of discursive work seemed to pay off. Heartily endorsed by Patrick Ford's *Irish World*, the UILA quickly formed branches in the New York area and, soon thereafter, throughout the country. Redmond toured the United States in late 1901, focusing much attention on the new organization and on the renewed dynamism in the Irish Home Rule movement. By the end of 1902, the UILA claimed over 200 branches throughout the United States and had raised at least £10,000 for the Irish Parliamentary Party.[14]

Over the next decade, the UILA played a critical role in financing the IPP. The American organization provided approximately £50,000 to the party during these years, leading Redmond's British opponents to caricature him as the "Dollar Dictator." In the 1910–12 period, the IPP's strategy, backed up by Irish American financial support, began to show real results. The British election of 1910 made it clear that the Liberal Party desperately depended on Redmond and the IPP to remain in power. Responding to this new political situation, as well as to the House of Lords' rejection of their budget the previous year, Liberals reformed the upper house in 1911 so that it could only delay, no longer veto, legislative bills. In April 1912, a new Irish Home Rule bill was introduced in Parliament. Irish Americans across the nation, finally seeing the attainment of Home Rule on the horizon, now rallied behind the UILA. Membership soared and leading American politicians from William Howard Taft to Theodore Roosevelt to Woodrow Wilson went on record with pro–Home Rule statements. The parliamentary wing of the nationalist movement was at high tide in the United States as well as in Ireland.

Varieties of Home Rule Social Thought

But what did Irish America's constitutional nationalists stand for beyond a greater degree of legislative autonomy for Ireland? What was their vision of a post–Home Rule Ireland? Their ideas about religion and the role of the Catholic Church, a central institution within both Irish and Irish American life, provide a good place to start. Surprisingly perhaps, John Redmond and the other IPP leaders had devoted very little thought to the role of the Catholic Church within a post–Home Rule social order, leaving no official party position on this crucial matter. In consequence, there was a wide range of opinion within the American Home Rule movement on the question. At one extreme was Patrick Ford. Though the editor had once been a vocal critic of the church hierarchy, he changed course dramatically after 1886. As he repudiated his earlier radicalism and moved toward the political center, Ford also drew closer to the church. As early as 1887, Ford was attacking his erstwhile allies, Henry George and Edward McGlynn, partly for their economic radicalism but also for their criticisms of the Catholic hierarchy. From this time until his death in 1913, Ford consistently lined up behind the church, viewing that institution as a guardian of public morality and as a bulwark against social radicalism.[15]

At the other end of the spectrum was John Quinn. A successful New York lawyer and active Irish constitutional nationalist in the early twentieth century, Quinn was perhaps best known as a patron of the arts. His vigorous support for artistic freedom led him toward an extremely critical view of the Catholic Church's interference with the arts and what he perceived as its domination of Irish and Irish American intellectual life. "You will never be able really to make a successful art movement in Ireland until you have accomplished two things—broken the power of the church and secured an educated audience," he wrote to W. B. Yeats, in 1906. "Perhaps I should have said only one thing, namely broken the power of the church, because when the power of the church is broken education will come."[16]

The center of gravity in the UILA lay somewhere between these two poles. It is significant that just one of the eight New York City members of the UILA's National Executive Committee in 1904 was a priest, suggesting that Catholic clergymen did not exercise much formal power within in it. The UILA was very much a secular organization. In fact, its main American supporters resembled Ireland's middle-class Home Rulers who, while overwhelmingly Catholic in religion, had long been immersed in British political and cultural life, admired what they saw as that nation's liberal political ideals, and were secularist in their basic outlook. They were disturbed, to be sure, by the anti-Catholic bias that they perceived in English culture, but they believed that this bias would be eliminated by the establishment of a partially autonomous Irish legislature. They had little sense of Ireland as a distinct civilization and hoped that its post–Home Rule institutions would be modeled along English liberal lines, so that Ireland could be given its deserved standing as a full partner in the British imperial enterprise. Such views were widely held among Irish American Home Rulers as well, and not only by Quinn who was well known for his strong identification with English civilization.[17]

If this cultural stance could lead to a devaluation of Irish culture, it could also help shape a powerful vision of Catholic-Protestant unity. This vision accounted for the unwillingness of most of America's Home Rulers to consider even the temporary partition of Ireland proposed by the Liberal Party in 1914, in response to an increasingly militant Unionist movement, with a reinvigorated Orange Order at its heart. "While the Orangeman differs widely from the Irish Catholic, each of them resembles the other more than anybody else in the world," the Irish American politician Bourke Cockran wrote in 1914. He went on to argue that the Catholic hierarchy in Ireland needed to take the lead in reassuring northern Protestants that it did not seek to create a Catholic state.[18]

The Home Rulers' views on social class and on socialism were as significant as their ideas about religion. On the whole, the UILA leaders were, like the INFA leaders before them, individuals of wealth and standing, and many of them had been previously active in the INFA. Thus, at the turn of the century, the building magnate and INFA veteran John D. Crimmins played a key role in organizing a so-called millionaire committee, a group made up of what John Redmond revealingly called "the better class of Irish men of New York," to coordinate financial contributions to the IPP. The group disbanded after the UILA got on its feet, but the UILA continued to attract support from upper- and middle-class Irish Americans. Among key New York figures, John Quinn was a wealthy corporate lawyer, and both Cockran and Judge Martin J. Keogh were men of considerable means.[19]

The situation in New York was paralleled in numerous other cities, where many of the "lace curtain" Irish found a prominent place in the UILA. In Philadelphia, the prominent and well-to-do lawyer Michael Ryan continued to play a central part in the UILA, as he had in the INFA. Even in towns dominated by Irish American blue-collar workers, the UILA attracted atypical men of wealth. In the solidly Irish American mining town of Butte, Montana, John D. Ryan, the head of the Anaconda Copper Mining Company, was an important financial supporter of the movement, as was F. Augustus Heinze, the famous German American "copper king." The Home Rule movement there, according to one of its leaders, Patrick Brophy, was supported by "the best Irishmen in Butte"—"the best material of our people," rather than the "masses of Irish."[20]

The social composition of the UILA's leadership helps to explain its response to the dramatic growth of class conflict and labor radicalism in this period. The American Socialist party grew steadily after its 1901 founding, particularly after 1908, when it began establishing deep roots in immigrant working-class neighborhoods in large cities around the country. In New York, a lively left-wing bohemian culture also began to take shape, with its center in Greenwich Village. Perhaps most important, the industrial landscape was torn apart by large strikes, especially those by western hard rock miners at the opening of the century, textile workers in Lawrence and other mill towns, and Jewish and Italian garment workers in New York in the years between 1909 and 1913.[21]

Irish America was in no way isolated from these developments. In the 1890s, Irish American shoe workers in Massachusetts had been crucial in providing the American socialist movement with some of its first electoral victories. The Western Federation of Miners, dominated by Irish immigrants and Irish Americans, adopted socialism as its official policy in 1903. Though generally supporting the Democrats, Butte's Irish American workers voted in large numbers for the socialists in 1903 and, in 1911, even helped elect a socialist as the city's mayor. Meanwhile, in New York City, the left-wing sojourner James Connolly established the Irish Socialist Federation specifically to appeal to Irish American workers in the city.[22]

Connolly was a child of the Irish diaspora, born to impoverished immigrant Irish parents in the Edinburgh slum of Cowgate in 1868. The nephew of a Fenian, he became a socialist after reading Marx in the 1890s. In 1896, Connolly moved to Ireland, establishing an organization called the Irish Socialist Republican Party and editing its weekly newspaper, the *Workers' Republic*. In 1903, disappointed with the party's lack of progress in Ireland, he moved to America to organize the Irish Socialist Federation (ISF). He remained in the United States until 1910, when he returned to Ireland to lead the new Socialist Party of Ireland.[23]

It is easy to dismiss the influence of Connolly and the ISF, given its small membership and the extremely low socialist vote in the Irish neighborhoods of New York. Yet the possibility of socialist influence among the city's Irish working people was always present. On Connolly's first speaking visit to New York in 1902, for example, every seat in the large Cooper Union Hall was filled. Bitterly fought strikes involving New York's Irish American teamsters and public transport workers in the early twentieth century also brought some of them into contact with friendly socialists. And few could deny the heroic mystique that attached to Connolly, Elizabeth Gurley Flynn, James Larkin, and other Irish or

Irish American labor radicals, especially those associated with the militant and colorful Industrial Workers of the World (IWW). In the early 1910s, William O'Dwyer, an immigrant from County Mayo and member of the city's hod carriers union, was captivated by the activities of "the IWWs, the Socialists, here and in the West." As O'Dwyer recalled many years later, "their programs, the articles that were written on them, the daily news that was carried on them and the magazine articles—those things happened to bring us to a realization of the things that were wrong in our civilization."[24]

The prospect of socialism's spreading influence among Irish American workers seemed to haunt the middle- and upper-class leaders of the UILA. Though they may have been divided on the role of the church, Patrick Ford and John Quinn were of one mind in their condemnation of militant labor activity and socialism. By the early twentieth century, Ford had left his radicalism far behind and opposed trade unionism, strikes, and all other forms of assertive labor activism. His *Irish World* held up "self-made" men of wealth like John Crimmins as individuals for workers to emulate and denounced socialism as immoral and atheistic. In a similar vein were Quinn's comments on the radical culture of Greenwich Village, expressed in a 1917 letter to the poet, Ezra Pound:

> I don't know whether you know the pseudo-Bohemianism of Washington Square. It is nauseating to a decent man who doesn't need artificial sexual stimulation. It is a vulgar, disgusting conglomerate of second and third-rate artists and would-be artists, of I.W.W. agitators, of sluts kept or casual, clean and unclean, of Socialists and near Socialists, of poetasters and pimps, of fornicators and dancers and those who dance to enable them to fornicate—But hell, words fail me to express my contempt for the whole damned bunch.

In light of such attitudes it is hardly surprising to find the New York Municipal Council of the UILA denouncing the visiting Irish labor radicals, James Larkin and Cornelius Lehane, for their socialist speeches in 1914.[25]

Hostility to labor radicalism did not necessarily mean opposition to moderate forms of trade unionism or to progressive labor reform measures. New York Acting Mayor John Purroy Mitchel, for example, played a conciliatory role in the 1910 New York garment strike, criticizing the anti-union bias of the courts and condemning the "violent and disorderly" activities of "both sides" in the dispute. Tammany Hall leader Charles F. Murphy was in many ways a genuine progressive, a supporter of women's suffrage and progressive labor legislation. Both of these politicians were closely identified with New York's Irish Home Rule movement. But both also regarded anything more radical than progressive labor legislation and what was called "pure-and-simple" trade unionism as beyond the pale.[26]

Murphy's support for women's suffrage raises the question of the relationship of women to constitutional Irish nationalism in the United States. Although Irish American women had not been active in the INFA in the 1890s, they took on important roles in the UILA from its very beginnings. Of the 149 New York City delegates to the second national convention of the UILA in 1904, for example, 11 were women, including Mary O'Flaherty, who was elected to the National Executive Committee of the organization. At the same convention, Chicago's John F. Finerty, accepting reelection as president of the UILA, devoted much of his speech to calling on Irish American women to join the movement, drawing thunderous applause. That he did so while invoking the memory of one of the key battles of 1798, the battle at Vinegar Hill, only increased his speech's powerful effect:

> We must never forget that the women of the Irish race have been the priestesses of the Irish race, we must not forget the breach of Limerick, where they hurled back the grenadiers (applause), we must not forget the slopes of Vinegar Hill, where, green flag flying, and with the shells of General Lake bursting, they bled and died side by side with the men of their race (applause) . . . . I say to the women of our race who are assembled here and who may assemble elsewhere, that they can do much for our cause.[27]

The situation in America represented a sharp contrast with Ireland where only a single branch of the United Irish League (UIL), the so-called Young Ireland Branch, admitted women. The gender exclusivity of the UIL in Ireland not only marked a retreat from women's nationalist activities in the Land League era but also indicated how out of touch the leadership of the organization was with a critical new development in Irish life, growing support for the women's suffrage movement. The movement had originated among middle-class Protestant women back in the 1860s and had grown only slowly in the late nineteenth century. In the first decade of the twentieth, the pace of activism quickened, as growing numbers of educated Catholic women for the first time began to give support to the movement. Far from embracing this trend, both IPP leader John Redmond and his deputy, John Dillon, remained strong opponents of women's suffrage and the party played a crucial role in preventing parliamentary action on votes for women in Britain.[28]

Yet on this point the Irish leaders faced considerable opposition, both from suffragists in Ireland and from Irish American women in the Home Rule movement. When Redmond traveled to the United States in September 1910, for example, UILA women told him that they would not provide him with funds unless he changed his position on the vote. Though they did not prevail on this occasion (Redmond left America with over $100,000 in election funds), women had made their presence felt within the movement. The women of the UILA were undoubtedly among those participating in the huge May 1912 suffrage demonstration in New York, for one of that demonstration's central demands was the extension of the vote to Irish women in the Home Rule bill introduced that year. Irish American women nationalists came to the fore in the tumultuous events of 1914. In March of that year, a large meeting was held at Carnegie Hall to protest "the dismemberment of the Island," a reference to Liberal Prime Minister Asquith's plan for a partition of Ireland. The meeting had been called, according to Bourke Cockran, "exclusively by women"—UILA activists.[29]

In their unified and vigorous condemnation of labor radicalism and militant working-class activity, then, Irish American Home Rulers broke sharply with some of the most important ideas of the New Departure. But in their generally secular orientation, their encouragement of women's participation, and their support for women's suffrage, they illustrated the continuing vitality of at least part of the radical legacy of the Land League of the early 1880s.

The Republican Outlook

If parliamentary nationalism occupied center stage in the opening years of the twentieth century, it did not do so unopposed. Moderate Home Rulers were dogged by constant criticism from revolutionary separatists in the Clan na Gael. The Clan had been discredited after its British dynamite campaign in the mid-1880s and had experienced bitter and debilitating factionalism during the 1890s, but in July 1900, at what its members called their "great Convention" in Atlantic City, the organization came together under the leadership of John Devoy, New York's Daniel Cohalan, and Philadelphia's Joseph McGarrity. The Clan asserted its commitment to the goal of an independent republican Ireland and proclaimed that "the only policy which it believes will attain that object is physical force." Constructing political legitimacy through historical remembrance, the organization traced the lineage of both its republican aims and its physical force strategies directly to the United Irishmen of the 1790s. "The object of the Clan is the complete independence of the Irish people and the establishment of an Irish Republic, and to unite all men of our race in all lands who believe in the principles of Wolfe Tone and Emmet." Like these two revered martyrs, the Clan pledged itself "to the principle that physical force is the only engine a revolutionary organization can consistently and successfully use to realize the hopes of lovers of freedom in lands subject to the bonds of oppression."[30]

Devoy and Cohalan had taken very different paths into the organization. The County Kildare–born Devoy was an almost archetypal Irish exile; though nominally a Republican, he cared little for American life or politics. "I respectfully decline the honour of being classed as 'an American,' " he had written in 1878—though he ended up residing in America for more than fifty years. Cohalan was different in every way. Twenty-five years younger than Devoy, he was a second-generation Irish American, born in Middletown, New York, in 1865. The son of a building tradesman-turned-factory owner with strong Irish republican views, Cohalan had the advantage of his prosperous family as he made his way in life. By the time of the Clan's Atlantic City convention, he was a successful New York City lawyer and was beginning to involve himself in the world of Democratic Party politics. Cohalan would go on to become a principal officer ("Grand Sachem") of the powerful Tammany Society and a political advisor to Tammany leader Charles F. Murphy; he would be appointed to the New York State Supreme Court in 1911.[31]

Using Devoy's weekly newspaper, the *Gaelic American*, to attack the IPP, the UILA, and the very objective of Home Rule, the Clan called for physical force to establish a fully independent Irish republic. Though overshadowed by the larger and more respectable UILA, the Clan had built a national membership of about 40,000 by 1910 and had a huge influence beyond its numbers. The Clan also provided crucial financial support for nationalist cultural and political movements in Ireland, such as the Gaelic League, the Gaelic Athletic Association, and the Irish Republican Brotherhood. [32]

Yet when it came to their thinking about the critical social issues of the day, the Irish revolutionary nationalists in America were less radical than might be imagined. Their ideas about "proper" women's roles are a good example. The Clan na Gael permitted women supporters to join its women's auxiliaries but, in marked contrast to the broad participation of women in the UILA, these organizations were clearly marked as subsidiary ones, dominated entirely by men. Mary J. O'Donovan Rossa, widow of the Fenian Jeremiah O'Donovan Rossa and a member of the Clan's women's auxiliary, expressed the dominant view within the Clan when she wrote to Devoy in fall 1915 that women's auxiliaries "must be absolutely under obedience to the authorised men and take willing guidance from them." O'Donovan Rossa supported women's suffrage, conceding that "every woman does these days." But she nonetheless proclaimed herself "old-fashioned enough still to cling to the notion that men are the lords of creation and women at their best when kindly cooperating in all that reason and conscience approve, and under guidance, with modesty, not self-asserting." When it came to women in the movement, she "would give the men a *despotism* over them and ban whoever murmured."[33]

Women's roles in the movement were limited by the continuing military orientation of the Clan and its essentially fraternal character, features that it inherited from the Fenians. According to the ritual of the Clan, the "incoming brother" was to be handed a sword and greeted with these words: "The sword is to impress on you that Irish freedom can be secured only by force—that our duty is to nerve and strengthen ourselves to wrest by the sword our political rights from England." A similar situation existed in the republican movement in Ireland. Though the women's republican organization, Cumann na mBan ("the league of women"), played an important role in the emerging revolutionary challenge to British rule, this role was carefully defined and limited by men.[34]

It is difficult to know how many women actually joined the Clan's auxiliaries. Certainly some were so committed to the Irish struggle that they were willing to put up with this kind of systematic subordination and others may have simply accepted the subordination as "natural." But many women who sympathized with the ultimate goals of the movement may have had qualms not only about the constrained roles of women within it but also about the violent methods advocated by the revolutionary republicans, methods that conflicted sharply with the idealized conception of womanhood that many Irish American women must have held. As one UILA supporter later explained, "we women have hesitated to give our adherence to the physical force party, not that we did not sympathise to the utmost with its aims, but that in our capacity as conservators of the race we hoped to call a halt to the immolation of Irish youth."[35]

A similar conservatism marked the Clan na Gael's views on the labor question. Although the organization attracted numerous Irish American working-class men, as had the Fenians in the 1860s, it was almost totally indifferent to the question of class inequality. Devoy got along well with James Connolly during Connolly's time in America, mainly because both men shared a hostility to what they regarded as the timidity of the Home Rule movement. Like Connolly, Devoy often asserted that well-to-do Irish Americans were unlikely to be staunch nationalists, simply because they were too self-interested and contented. But Devoy was no more sympathetic to Connolly's socialist views than he had been to Michael Davitt's agrarian radicalism back in the 1880s. Indeed, with the exception of his support for the New Departure, the Fenian leader demonstrated a striking consistency over his long career: he steadfastly resisted all efforts to dilute pure nationalism with any kind of social program. This marked a similarity with the position of republican separatists in Ireland. Because they drew support from an unstable coalition of agrarian radicals, urban workers, and the Catholic lower-middle class, they strenuously avoided articulating any social program that would set these groups off against each other.[36]

Others in the Devoy wing of the movement took an even more conservative position. In the garment strike that engulfed the city of New York in 1910, New York Supreme Court Justice John W. Goff, a prominent Irish separatist, handed down a sweeping injunction against the workers that, for the first time in the state's history, permanently restrained strikers from peaceful picketing and prohibited them from interfering in any way with those seeking to work. Samuel Gompers, the president of the American Federation of Labor, called Goff's ruling an example of the "tyranny of autocratic methods of concentrated capital and greed."[37]

This socially conservative stance could also be seen in the Clan's views on Catholicism. The church's growing importance in both Irish and Irish American life caused later generations of separatist revolutionaries to back away from the secular, sometimes anti-clerical, stance of the first generation of Fenians. Nowhere in the ranks of the Clan na Gael could be found the kind of anti-clericalism exhibited by John Quinn or, before him, the supporters of Henry George and the Land League. Even the socialist James Connolly exhibited an apparently sincere respect for the role of the church in Irish history and culture, striving in his writings and speeches to prove that Catholicism and socialism were compatible. The more radical ideas and programs of the Land League era, then, played almost no role at all in the social thought of America's revolutionary separatists between 1890 and 1916. Class inequality and socialism were simply not matters of concern for most of them while in their ideas on gender and religion they appeared to be more conservative than their counterparts in America's Home Rule movement.[38]

Yet, in at least one area the Clan did break new ground and seemed considerably less parochial than at first it would appear. This was its support for the anti-colonial movements then emerging in many parts of the world. This was not a totally new development, of course. Irish republicans in both Ireland and the United States had welcomed the 1857 Great Rebellion against British rule in India, and support for Indian independence had been an important part of the New Departure and of the journalism of Patrick Ford. But this trend developed considerable force in the first decade of the twentieth century, as emigration from India to the United States began. Clan members actively supported the agitation of Indian nationalists, such as the merchants Amar Singh and Gopal Singh, who toured the United States in 1906. This was a matter of considerable concern to the British Foreign office, which had actively discouraged Indian migration to America precisely because it feared that Indian nationalists would find sympathy for their cause among Irish Americans.[39]

Clan members demonstrated their anti-colonial orientation by embracing an Irish nationalist leader for whom an expansive anti-colonialism was absolutely fundamental. Sir Roger Casement, a Protestant Anglo-Irishmen, who had been born in County Dublin in 1864, joined the British colonial service in 1892. On duty in Africa, he became a key figure in uncovering and publicizing European atrocities in the Congo Free State. Casement grew increasingly skeptical about imperialism generally, particularly its claim to be a progressive force, "civilizing the natives." Sent by the British government to the Amazon in 1910 to investigate the labor practices of a British rubber company, Casement found a situation that "far exceeds in its depravity the demoralization of the Congo regime at its worst."

Though knighted in 1910, he retired from the colonial service three years later, embittered by the abuses that he had uncovered and dismissive of the civilizing claims of imperialism generally. From this point on, he focused his attentions on Ireland, his native land. However, he saw its predicament as a particular example of a global system of exploitation and domination that affected the peoples of the Congo and the Amazon just as much as they affected the Irish.[40]

In July 1914, Casement came to America, where his speeches generated a great deal of interest not only within the ranks of the Clan na Gael, but across the spectrum of Irish American nationalism. While in New York, he stayed with Home Ruler John Quinn and he accompanied Bourke Cockran to the national convention of the Ancient Order of Hibernians in Norfolk, where he gave a speech in support of the new Irish Volunteer movement. But the Clan na Gael was Casement's home base in the United States, and the organization arranged a very successful speaking tour that took him to Philadelphia, Baltimore, Buffalo, and Chicago, along with New York. By this point, the influence of the Clan within both Irish and Irish American nationalism had already begun to grow significantly.[41]

Toward the Easter Rising

The years from 1912 to 1916 witnessed an almost complete reversal in the fortunes of constitutional and republican nationalism in the United States, triggered initially by the rise of militant Unionist resistance in Ireland to the possibility of Home Rule. Previous Home Rule bills in 1886 and 1893 had also generated opposition, but the much better prospects for this third bill shaped a new, and considerably more violent, tone to the resistance. Based mainly in Ulster, but with a charismatic Dublin lawyer, Sir Edward Carson, as their leader and strong British Conservative Party support, Unionists began their protests even before the bill was introduced. In September 1911, a demonstration of 50,000 Orangemen and Unionists warned Liberals against using the recent reform of the House of Lords to implement Home Rule and, four months later, the Orange Order requested licenses from magistrates to begin conducting armed drills. In April 1914, two days before the bill was introduced, Conservative Party leader Bonar Law declared that he could "imagine no length of resistance to which Ulster can go in which I should not be prepared to support them." On September 18, 1912, nearly 500,000 men and women, representing virtually the entire adult Protestant population of Ulster, signed parallel documents, the Ulster Covenant and the Declaration, pledging armed resistance to the implementation of Home Rule. In January 1913, a paramilitary body called the Ulster Volunteer Force (UVF) was created to carry out the pledge; led by retired British army officers, the UVF soon counted nearly 90,000 members.[42]

Rather than confront this increasingly militarized Unionism head on, Herbert Asquith's Liberal government hesitated. Asquith did not discipline officers at the main British army camp in Ireland when they declared in March 1914 that they would resign rather than fight the UVF; nor did he take action against the UVF the following month, when, in a spectacular case of gunrunning, the organization brought 25,000 rifles and 5 million rounds of ammunition that they had purchased in Germany into several Irish ports. Instead of directly confronting resistance to their legislative agenda, government officials began to discuss some sort of temporary partition of the island (excluding all or some of Ulster's nine counties from the Home Rule framework) as a way of compromising with Unionists.

In response, Irish nationalists underwent a process of militarization of their own, founding the Irish Volunteers in Dublin in November 1913 as a kind of mirror image of the UVF. Though formally commanded by the Gaelic League moderate, Eoin MacNeill, members of the Irish Republican Brotherhood constituted an influential minority on the Volunteers' organizing committee from the outset. Irish republican leaders in America were initially skeptical of this new initiative, but the Clan na Gael officially endorsed the Volunteer movement in June 1914. It was this that brought Casement to America in July: his objective was to raise money and solidify support among Irish Americans for the Volunteers.

If the Home Rule crisis and the growing militarization of the conflict in Ireland were beginning to alter the balance of forces between parliamentary and republican nationalists in America, the outbreak of World War I in August was an even more important catalyst. John Redmond's decision to support the British war effort and accept a postponement of Home Rule transformed the Irish nationalist movement in America, undermining support for the UILA and leading to a sharp rise in the fortunes of the revolutionary wing of the movement. By the end of August 1914, the *Irish World*, previously steadfast in its support for constitutional nationalism, was voicing strong criticism of what appeared to be Redmond's inclination to encourage the enlistment of Irish men in the British army: "No 'King's Shilling' for Irishmen" read one headline in the paper. Such sentiment increased dramatically the following month, when Redmond, having received the government's assurances that it would enact Home Rule at the conclusion of the war, asserted in the House of Commons that it was the "duty" of Irishmen "to take their place in the firing line in this contest."[43]

Irish Americans who had supported Redmond in the past now turned angrily against him. In the fall of 1914, UILA supporter Dr. Gertrude B. Kelly, a well-known New York physician and women's suffrage advocate, emerged as an important figure in this shift, couching her anti-war and anti-imperialist arguments against Redmond in highly charged—and decidedly gendered—language:

May I, as a woman, an Irishwoman and a physician, spokeswoman of hundreds, thousands of my sisters at home and abroad, ask our leaders what it is they propose to Ireland to do—commit suicide? Admitting for the moment that this is a "most righteous war"—not "a war of iron and coal"—a war between titans for commercial supremacy—why should little Ireland have to do what the United States, Switzerland, etc. do not? Is Home Rule to be secured for the cattle and the sheep when the young men of Ireland are slaughtered, the old men and the old women left sonless, the young women obliged to emigrate to bring up sons for men of other climes.

On its face, Kelly's conceptualization of gender appeared to be traditionalist and conservative, assuming the permanence of women's roles as wives and mothers and of their domestic duty to "bring up sons for men." But in Kelly's case, domestic discourse was deployed in a way that implicitly explained and justified, as an absolute necessity, women's political activism.[44]

Not everyone in the UILA agreed with such views. John Quinn was unwavering in his support of Redmond and the British war effort, as was Bourke Cockran, who believed that "the English people are fighting the battle of civilization." But as the months passed, theirs was increasingly a minority viewpoint among the ranks of Redmond's erstwhile supporters. "The general impression here is that Redmond is either a bungler or a traitor," wrote an unhappy New York Home Ruler in early 1915. "The UIL in New York city has been reduced to a skeleton." The UILA was in such bad shape by this time that, in a total reversal of the long-established direction of cash flows, it required financial assistance from the Irish Parliamentary Party to support its activities.[45]

Irish and German American organizations began holding joint anti-war rallies in the summer and fall of 1914, hardly surprising given the long history of interaction between these two large immigrant groups in the United States, and for some Irish Americans, denunciation of Britain's war shaded over into support for its enemy, Kaiser Wilhelm II's Germany. In 1915 and 1916, James K. McGuire, the one-time mayor of Syracuse, New York, and an important figure in the state's Democratic Party, penned a number of newspaper articles and a pair of popular books, *The King, the Kaiser and Irish Freedom* and *What Could Germany Do for Ireland*, detailing the benefits that would accrue to Ireland from a German victory in the war.[46]

In May 1915, a secret military council within the Irish Republican Brotherhood in Dublin began to take this kind of thinking one step further as they started to plan an Irish rebellion that they hoped could draw on both Irish American moral support and German material assistance. Tom Clarke, a fifty-seven-year-old Fenian veteran, who had spent most of his adult life in prison or in America, was central to this group. Raised in County Tyrone, Clarke had migrated to the United States when he was twenty-one and soon became involved with the Clan na Gael. He was arrested in England during the Clan's 1883 bombing campaign and served fifteen years of a life sentence in British prisons. He returned to the United States after his release in 1898, but in 1907 he moved to Dublin where he quickly became an influential figure, much admired by a younger group of republican militants who were striving to rejuvenate the IRB. In 1915, this group made contact with a young poet and schoolmaster named Patrick Pearse and several other key leaders in the Irish Volunteers, though they concealed their plans from the Volunteers' commander-in-chief, Eoin MacNeill. Pearse had spent much of the first half of 1914 on a fundraising tour of America, where he had established contacts of his own with Joseph McGarrity and other Clan leaders and returned exhilarated by their enthusiasm for an Irish rebellion. In January 1916, the socialist labor leader James Connolly, who had returned to Ireland from his own long American sojourn five years earlier, joined the conspiracy as well.[47]

Given this web of American connections, along with the fact that in 1915–16 the United States was still a neutral power, it was logical that the Clan na Gael would became a conduit for communication between the IRB conspirators and the German government. A committee of the Clan met with Count Johann von Bernstoff, the German ambassador to the United States, to request arms and officers in support of the planned rebellion. The Clan also brought Roger Casement, who was still in America, into these discussions and Casement played a critical role, developing strategic ideas, writing a long letter to the Kaiser, and lending his international prestige to the conspiracy. Von Bernstoff endorsed the proposal, Germany agreed to supply the arms, and Casement set off for Germany in an effort to recruit an "Irish Brigade" among British army prisoners of war. These echoes of Wolfe Tone's 1796 journey from America to France were not lost on Casement himself. As he prepared to leave New York, according to his host John Quinn (who knew nothing of the conspiracy), Casement "constantly referred to the Tone thing and several times he said 'I am Wolfe Tone. I am the reincarnation of Wolfe Tone.'" The parallels would not end there.[48]

Figure 1 Detail of the Thomas Addis Emmet monument, St. Paul's churchyard, New York. Photograph, 2010. Courtesy of Susan Stuart.

Figure 2 William Duane, Irish radical and Jeffersonian Republican. Engraving, 1802. Courtesy of the Library of Congress.

Figure 3 Daniel O'Connell, Irish leader of the campaign to repeal the Act of Union.
Lithograph, 1847. Courtesy of the Library of Congress.

Figure 4 Facsimile of the banner of an American Repeal association.
Lithograph, 1842. Courtesy of the Library of Congress.

Figure 5 John Mitchel, Young Ireland exile and political journalist. Lithograph, 1848. Courtesy of the Library of Congress.

Figure 6 1866 Fenian raid near Ridgeway Station, Ontario. Lithograph, 1869.
Courtesy of the Library of Congress.

Figure 7 Fenian exiles, including John Devoy and Jeremiah O'Donovan Rossa, in 1871. Lithograph, 1871. Courtesy of the Library of Congress.

Figure 8 New York procession for the Fenian exiles, February 1871. Lithograph, 1871. Courtesy of the Library of Congress.

Figure 9 Michael Davitt, transatlantic Irish Land League organizer. Photographic print, 1881. Courtesy of the Library of Congress.

Figure 10 Henry George, political economist and supporter of the Land League.
Photographic print, 1898. Courtesy of the Library of Congress.

Figure 11 John D. Crimmins (center), a key figure in the Irish National Federation of America and the United Irish League of America. Photographic negative, c. 1900. Courtesy of the Library of Congress.

Figure 12 Friends of Irish Freedom leaders, Judge John Goff, John Devoy, and Judge Daniel Cohalan, with Éamon de Valera, president of the Provisional Irish Republic. Photographic negative, 1919 or 1920. Courtesy of the Library of Congress.

Figure 13 Marcus Garvey, president of the Universal Negro Improvement Association and supporter of Irish republicanism. Photographic print, 1924. Courtesy of the Library of Congress.

Figure 14 American women protest in support of the Irish Republic.
Photographic negative, 1920. Courtesy of the Library of Congress.

Figure 15 Matilda Tone's headstone, Green-Wood Cemetery, Brooklyn. Photograph, 2010. Courtesy of Susan Stuart.

The Irish Revolution, 1916–1921

James Connolly was the last to be executed. Returning to Ireland from America in 1910, he had thrown himself into a whirlwind of labor and socialist activism. Serving first as the Ulster organizer for the Irish Transport and General Workers Union (ITGWU), Connolly, after the imprisonment of fellow labor activist James Larkin, became the leader of the Dublin workers during their bitter 1913 lockout. In 1914, he became acting general secretary of the ITGWU and commandant of its Irish Citizen Army, which had been set up to defend workers from violent attacks by the Dublin Metropolitan Police during the lockout. Connolly strongly condemned the fighting that began in Europe in 1914 as an imperialist war, though he subsequently came to see the war as providing the opportunity for an insurrection against British rule in Ireland. In early 1916, he committed the Citizen Army to participation in the Easter Rising and went on to command Dublin's rebel forces during Easter Week itself. Badly wounded in the fighting, he had to be carried into the yard at Kilmainham jail, where he was executed by firing squad on May 12, 1916.[1]

Unlike the rebellions of 1798, 1848, or 1867, the Rising of 1916 opened the door to a full-fledged and partially successful war for Irish independence. The Rising itself was small in scale, involving only about 1,600 rebels, mainly Irish Volunteers with smaller numbers from Connolly's Citizen Army and from the women's republican organization, Cumann na mBan, whose members served mainly as doctors, nurses, and messengers during the fighting. The rebels quickly captured a number of key government sites in Dublin, and in front of the General Post Office, Patrick Pearse read a proclamation establishing what they called the Provisional Government of the Irish Republic. "Supported by her exiled children in America and by gallant allies in Europe," the document stated, Ireland "now strikes in full confidence of victory." British troops moved into Dublin and, after a week of fighting, the insurrection ended, leaving about 450 people (mainly civilians) dead before the leaders of the Rising surrendered. By most accounts, the views of ordinary Irish people toward the rebellion ranged from indifference to outright hostility.[2]

What changed public attitudes were less the actions of the rebels than those taken by the British government. Most people in Ireland probably assumed that the leaders of the Rising would be given prison sentences, perhaps long ones, like those handed down to Young Irelanders in 1848 and Fenians in 1867. Instead, fifteen men were charged with treason during wartime, given speedy and secret trials in military courts, and then, to the shock of many, executed by firing squad. Although support for separatism in Ireland had been growing since the beginning of the Home Rule crisis in 1912, the executions of the Rising's leaders accelerated the shift in public opinion. And though British authorities and Irish Unionists regarded the executions as both legal and appropriate in a time of war, the widespread perception of these men as nationalist martyrs in the tradition of Wolfe Tone and Robert Emmet shattered the Home Rule Party and gave physical force republicanism a moral authority that it had not possessed for decades. This newfound sense that the separatists' claims were based on fundamental principles would be the foundation for the Irish War of Independence. It also paved the way for the greatest outpouring of support for Irish republicanism that the United States had ever seen.

The War of Independence

The British government followed up on the executions of the Rising's leaders with other actions that proved equally damaging to its cause. Roger Casement, who had been arrested two days before the Rising as he disembarked from a German submarine off the coast of County Kerry, was executed in August, despite international pleas for clemency. Martial law was declared throughout Ireland, causing much hardship and leading to the widespread opinion that a whole nation was being punished for the action of a handful of militants. The government also arrested numerous republican suspects, some 3,500 at the outset—though it quickly released 1,500 of them, indicating how little evidence it actually had against them. Another 1,800 were interned without trial, an action that did more to undermine the political legitimacy of the government than to stamp out the rapidly growing republican movement. Meanwhile the government refused to back off from its earlier decision to temporarily exclude parts of Ulster from Home Rule, and the Irish Party, though deeply opposed to this action as inevitably leading to the permanent partition the island, was unable in 1917 and 1918 to come up with an effective strategy to combat it.[3]

The main beneficiary of this sea change in Irish public opinion and the Irish Party's ineffectiveness was a political organization founded by Arthur Griffith in 1905 called Sinn Féin ("Ourselves"). Relatively insignificant until this time, Sinn Féin had not been involved with the Rising but it seemed to offer a viable political outlet for those supporting a united and independent Ireland. Operating as a constitutional and nonviolent political organization, Sinn Féin also strongly opposed Redmond's party and it opposed the enlistment of Irishmen into the British army, positions that led it to victories in four by-elections against the Irish Party in early 1917. Later that year, Éamon de Valera, the most senior surviving leader of the Easter Rising, who had just been released from prison, was elected president of Sinn Féin. Born in New York in 1882, de Valera was yet another product of the Irish diaspora.

A 1918 parliamentary bill to extend military conscription to Ireland triggered a massive outpouring of protest throughout the country. The conscription crisis provided the final blow to the Irish Party. John Dillon, who had assumed leadership of the party following Redmond's death, protested the bill by walking out of Parliament, but this response was widely seen as meek and ineffectual in comparison with Sinn Féin, which emerged at the helm of a powerful extra-parliamentary movement in the streets to fight the drafting of Irish men. The November 1918 armistice prevented the implementation of Irish conscription, but as the war came to an end, Sinn Féin was positioned to reap the political benefits of its militant stance.

Still, the sheer scale of the party's postwar ascendancy startled many. In the general election held in December 1918, Sinn Féin captured 73 out of 105 Irish seats in the British Parliament, utterly decimating the Home Rule Party (which won only six), although its leaders stated that they would not actually take up seats in a "foreign" parliament they refused to recognize. The first general election since 1910, the most widely franchised election yet in Irish history (since women over the age of thirty could vote for the first time), and the last election in which citizens of the whole island of Ireland voted together, the 1918 vote was hailed as a crucial democratic mandate by those seeking a fully independent Irish republic.

True to its pledge to abstain from the British Parliament, Sinn Féin established a new Irish Parliament (Dáil Éireann in Irish Gaelic) in Dublin in January 1919, which immediately declared Irish independence. Not surprisingly, Unionists (who had won twenty-six seats in the December election, all in Ulster) refused to attend the Dáil's opening session, as did those representing the remnants of the Irish Party. Meanwhile, the Irish Volunteers gradually transformed themselves into the Irish Republican Army (IRA), the military arm (as they saw it) of the Provisional Irish Republic that had been proclaimed in front of the General Post Office in 1916. Determined to end British rule in Ireland and rejecting the idea of partition, the IRA was commanded by Michael Collins, who led it in a highly effective guerrilla war against the British army from 1919 to 1921, as well as against Britain's hastily recruited special auxiliary forces, often referred to as the Black and Tans.

Collins was also an important political leader during this period, since de Valera, the president of the Dáil (and thus of the proclaimed Irish Republic), embarked on a mission to generate American support in April 1919, remaining in the United States for the next eighteen months. During this period, the Dáil, despite being outlawed in August 1919, established a highly effective administrative and judicial apparatus at both local and national levels that did much to gradually undermine the authority of British rule throughout the southern parts of Ireland.

The Anglo-Irish War of 1919–21 was marked by considerable ruthlessness on both sides. So-called active service units of the IRA carried out numerous ambushes of British soldiers, while the squad that Collins personally commanded carried out systematic assassinations of British security agents and civil servants. Meanwhile, retaliating for one such wave of assassinations in November 1920, British soldiers opened fire on a group of Gaelic football spectators at Dublin's Croke Park, killing twelve of them and wounding many others. The most infamous atrocities were the work of the belligerent, poorly trained, and undisciplined Black and Tans, who committed arson, looting, torture, and cold-blooded murder in their efforts to subdue the country. Reports of these atrocities led to a substantial weakening of support for the war in Britain and a Labour Party commission condemned the British military role in the conflict.[4]

A series of other wrenching events punctuated the conflict, none more important than the hunger strike of Terence MacSwiney, a well-known republican activist and intellectual and the Lord Mayor of Cork. On August 12, 1920, at the height of fighting, British forces arrested MacSwiney at a Cork IRA meeting. Denying Britain's legal authority in Ireland and demanding release, the Lord Mayor began a hunger strike. The British government, however, refused to release him and MacSwiney continued his hunger strike for seventy-three days, before dying in London's Brixton prison on October 24. Newspapers throughout Europe and the United States carried news of his ordeal on an almost daily basis. By dramatically personalizing the struggle in Ireland, MacSwiney's hunger strike played a critical role in swinging world and British opinion in favor of some kind of agreement that would end the war. A truce was announced the following July.[5]

Irish American Republicans in Peace and War

Although not accompanied by violence, the rapid growth of Irish nationalism in the United States between 1916 and 1921 possessed a drama that in some ways rivaled events in Ireland. In these five short years, revolutionary Irish republicanism became a movement of immense proportions. A new mass organization

called the Friends of Irish Freedom (FOIF), founded by Clan na Gael leaders
John Devoy, Joseph McGarrity, and Daniel Cohalan in 1916, claimed nearly
300,000 members by 1919, and its later rival, the American Association for
the Recognition of the Irish Republic (AARIR), would grow even larger. By
1921, the AARIR, founded by de Valera during his eighteen-month organizing campaign in the United States, had 700,000 members and had raised over
$10,000,000 for the republican movement in Ireland. As a veteran activist of
these years recalled, "sentiment in favor of the Irish Republic swept over this
country so strongly that it was felt in every city and town in the nation. It permeated all walks of life."[6]

The FOIF had been organized six weeks before the Easter Rising, at the so-
called Irish Race Convention in New York in March 1916. Reflecting the growth
in support for Irish republicanism since the Home Rule crisis and Redmond's
endorsement of the war, the convention counted more than 2,000 American
men and women in attendance. Though ostensibly an open event, Clan leaders
had made sure that those in attendance at the convention were critics of limited
Home Rule and fully committed to "bringing about the National Independence
of Ireland." The convention chose the composer Victor Herbert as its president
and set about building a public organization, with local chapters across the
United States. Leaders of the FOIF encouraged women's participation in the
new body, and already existing Irish American organizations were permitted to
take out associate memberships. Regular meetings of the local chapters helped
to educate and mobilize Irish Americans across the nation to take part in whatever activities were deemed necessary to advance the cause. Despite its public
presence, the new organization was dominated by the Clan na Gael: every one of
its officers and fifteen of its seventeen executive committee members belonged
to the Clan.[7]

Naturally the FOIF's first tasks were to rally support for the Easter Rising and
then to protest the British execution of its leaders and the declaration of martial law in Ireland. By late April 1916, huge meetings were being held all along
the East Coast, with especially large ones in Boston and New York. In May, as
news of the executions arrived in America, thousands of Irish Americans who
had previously supported the moderate Home Rule movement—or not been
involved in nationalist activities at all—began to rally to the leadership of the
FOIF. At coordinated nationwide meetings on May 8, the new organization
effectively channeled the widespread anger at the executions and almost overnight became the most important Irish nationalist organization in the United
States. The extent of the shift in attitudes could be seen in a packed Carnegie
Hall meeting on May 14, where John Devoy shared the platform with Bourke
Cockran, who repudiated his earlier support for Redmond and Home Rule. The
FOIF issued statements thanking Germany for its support of the Rising and did

much to develop working relationships with the German American Alliance and other anti-war German American organizations. It also worked strenuously to prevent the entry of the United States into World War I on Britain's side, calling for strict neutrality, and, in so doing it helped shape the thinking of many Irish Americans on the most pressing political question facing the American people as a whole in 1916 and early 1917.[8]

Among Irish Americans in the labor movement, the position of the FOIF had a particularly significant impact, especially as President Woodrow Wilson's administration began to make concrete preparations for entry into the war. Some labor leaders, most notably Samuel Gompers, president of the American Federation of Labor (AFL), firmly backed the government's preparedness efforts, reasoning that political support would give labor new influence in Washington. Other voices in the AFL, including socialists and German Americans, strongly disagreed, calling for US neutrality and endorsing efforts at mediation of the conflict. But more important than either of these two groups within the AFL were trade unionists of Irish birth or ancestry. Many had been close allies of Gompers before the war, but now they broke ranks. The 1916 Irish Race Convention and the campaigning of the FOIF had an especially large impact on their thinking.[9]

As a result, 1916 saw a major debate within the labor movement on the critical questions of war and peace. Across the nation, a kind of counter-preparedness movement took shape, frequently spearheaded by Irish American leaders of local labor councils. In San Francisco, the powerful (and overwhelmingly Irish American) Building Trades Council (BTC) prohibited its members from taking part in a local preparedness parade organized by the city's chamber of commerce. In July 1916, the BTC's leader, Limerick-born P. H. McCarthy, appeared at a large rally, caustically denouncing both the parade and its business organizers. The Easter Rising and the execution of its leaders added intensity to such feelings, leading many labor activists to view with deep revulsion American efforts to prop up what they saw as an immoral British imperialism. The heavily Irish American Chicago Federation of Labor bitterly condemned what it called "the domination of the Celtic people of Ireland by alien people and powers" and issued a protest against the "the summary execution of Celtic persons taken as prisoners of war." Other trade councils across America followed suit; the executions only intensified their opposition to the preparedness campaign.[10]

The political activism of the Friends of Irish Freedom and Irish American labor leaders, along with that of older ethnic associations like the Ancient Order of Hibernians, triggered a double-edged response from the Wilson administration. Running for reelection in November 1916, Wilson publicly denounced Jeremiah O'Leary, one of the most vociferous and pro-German among his Irish American critics. At the same time, the Democratic president sought ways to placate Irish Americans who were so important to the political party that he led.

In March 1917, Colonel Edward M. House, Wilson's main foreign policy advisor, drafted a memorandum for an Imperial Conference meeting in London, noting that "there are many reasonable and intelligent Americans of Irish extraction who feel very strongly on this subject, and who might be persuaded to lend their assistance with all honesty to a settlement of this question at the end of the war." A month later, following the US declaration of war on Germany, Wilson's secretary of state instructed the ambassador to Britain to bring up the Irish question directly with Prime Minister David Lloyd George, noting that "the failure so far to find a satisfactory method of self-government for Ireland" was "the only circumstance which seems now to stand in the way of an absolutely cordial cooperation with Great Britain by practically all Americans."[11]

The US declaration of war on Germany on April 6, 1917, introduced a new set of difficulties for Irish American republicans. In San Francisco, P. H. McCarthy and most of the city's other Irish American labor leaders gradually fell into line in support of the war effort. The Chicago Federation of Labor also changed course after the declaration of war, voting 140 to 59 to support Gompers's prowar stance, while previously anti-war labor councils in New York and St. Louis took a similar course. A parallel shift occurred in the Clan na Gael and Friends of Irish Freedom, which also began backing away from direct criticism of the Wilson administration. The political chill that came over America in the war years was palpable, and Irish republicans, like anti-war socialists and German Americans, were at risk from a government that saw Irish revolutionary agitation as directly counter to its war aims. Federal authorities suppressed Jeremiah O'Leary's newspaper, *Bull*, in October 1917, and in early 1918 barred the *Irish World* and Devoy's *Gaelic American* from the mails. They also arrested O'Leary and several other republican leaders and subjected Irish nationalist organizations to increased surveillance and harassment. As a result, the Clan na Gael and the Friends of Irish Freedom began to downplay their call for immediate Irish independence and to avoid criticism of US war policy. Only one organization marked out a different path in these years: a small but important group called the Irish Progressive League (IPL).[12]

The IPL was founded in New York in the fall of 1917, in an effort to fill the political vacuum left by the retreat of the established organizations like the Clan and the FOIF. Between this date and November 1920, the IPL, which boasted a core membership of about 150 people mainly in the New York area, took on a variety of tasks. It established an Irish National Bureau in Washington, DC, drew up a blacklist of members of Congress who were unsympathetic to Irish independence, and raised money to establish what the IPL called an Irish "embassy" in the capital. In the spring of 1918, with the threat of conscription into the British army looming over Irish men, the IPL focused its efforts on the crisis, sending a delegation to the White House and holding meetings denouncing the new British conscription act. In the wake of the November 1918 armistice, the December 1918 Sinn Féin electoral victory, and the January 1919 convening of the Dáil, the IPL held meetings and published literature demanding American recognition of the proclaimed "Irish Republic" and protesting the British imprisonment of Sinn Féin leaders. The organization had a particularly high profile in New York, where it built significant popular support in the city's Irish American working-class neighborhoods through a program of almost nightly street corner meetings in Brooklyn, Manhattan, and the Bronx. This was the IPL's primary significance: it kept the Irish republican cause alive in a period marked by governmental intimidation and nationalist retreat.[13]

Almost as important, from the outset the Irish Progressive League saw itself as acting within a tradition of American working-class reform and radical activity dating back to the Land League in the early 1880s. This can be seen not only in its name, with its implication that "progressive" domestic social reform needed to go hand in hand with Irish independence, but in its first decision: to endorse the Socialist Party leader, Morris Hillquit, in his campaign for mayor of New York in the fall 1917 election. Throughout its short history, the IPL was notable in attracting enthusiastic support from a wide variety of socialists, left-wing progressives, and radical labor activists. Supporters of the IPL and featured speakers at its meetings included not only Hillquit but also socialist and anti-war crusader Norman Thomas; labor activist and suffragist Leonora O'Reilly; Nora Connolly, eldest daughter of James Connolly; James Maurer, president of the Pennsylvania State Federation of Labor and a socialist member of Congress; and Joseph D. Cannon, an organizer for the Western Federation of Miners who had been one of the leading trade union opponents of American intervention in the war. None of these figures was solely interested in the Irish question and a number of them were not even Irish Americans; all saw their support for the declared Irish republic as part of a larger struggle for peace, social reform, or workers' betterment.[14]

The IPL was also distinctive for its broadly anti-imperialist perspective on the Irish question. The Irish cause, IPL activists believed, was thoroughly intertwined with those of Indian and Egyptian nationalists in particular, and a number of them were members of organizations like the Friends of Freedom for India. Support for anti-imperialist movements also extended, for at least some IPL members, to support for Marcus Garvey's Universal Negro Improvement Association (UNIA), the pan-African movement that achieved prominence in the United States in the years after World War I. Garvey had founded the UNIA in his native Jamaica in 1914, moving it to the Harlem neighborhood of New York two years later, and over the next few years the UNIA grew dramatically. "The UNIA," proclaimed the IPL's Helen Golden, after meetings with that organization's leaders in 1920, "has inaugurated a history making movement" whose goal of "eliminating all race prejudice" deserved the support of all Irish republicans. Other IPL activists linked their cause with that of the Bolshevik revolution. "Self-determination and freedom are doctrines that cannot be bounded, walled or hedged. They are universal and limitless," wrote one IPL activist in a sweeping critique of those "armchair Irish nationalists" who opposed the new Soviet government in Russia.[15]

Perhaps of even greater significance was the fact that the IPL was the first Irish nationalist organization in America to be led mainly by women. Five individuals dominated the organization from its birth until its merger with the AARIR in 1920. One was the poet and journalist Peter Golden, an immigrant from County Cork. But the other four were women: Golden's spouse, Helen Golden; the Irish feminist émigré Hanna Sheehy-Skeffington (widow of Francis Sheehy-Skeffington, a well-known Irish pacifist, republican, and feminist, who had been arrested and summarily shot by British troops while trying to prevent looting during the Easter Rising); Margaret Hickey; and Dr. Gertrude Kelly. "Most of my support has been from [women's suffragists], radicals and progressives— and very little from the Irish," Sheehy-Skeffington wrote to Peter Golden after a speaking tour in 1918.[16]

Gertrude Kelly's career illustrates many of the strands that came together in the IPL. Kelly had been born near Waterford, Ireland, in 1862, arriving in America in 1873. In the 1880s, she began medical training, eventually becoming a distinguished surgeon, and supported Henry George's single tax movement. In the early twentieth century, she was active in the women's suffrage movement and was arrested during World War I for participation in an anti-war demonstration. Kelly was a member of the Friends of Freedom for India and the Friends of New Russia, which, in 1917–18, agitated for the immediate American recognition of the new Soviet government. But the central focus of Kelly's political life through the early 1920s was Irish nationalism. She was a leading figure in the UILA in New York in the early twentieth century, though she bitterly denounced Redmond's decision to lead Ireland into support for Britain's war effort. From 1916 on, Kelly moved toward the revolutionary wing of the nationalist movement and, in the fall of 1917, she helped found the IPL.[17]

From Versailles to the Truce

Though the Friends of Irish Freedom had kept a low profile after the American entry into the war, with the November 1918 armistice the organization took up its agitation again, proclaiming the week of December 8–15 to be "Irish Self-Determination Week" and holding a number of large meetings around the country. A second FOIF-sponsored Irish Race Convention met in Philadelphia in

February 1919, where speakers also demanded "self-determination" for Ireland, adroitly framing their cause in terms that Woodrow Wilson had made famous the previous year, and the convention appointed a delegation to meet with the president the following month to encourage him to raise the Irish question at the upcoming Paris peace conference. The meeting did not go well—Wilson later confided to his legal advisor that he had felt like telling the Irish Americans to go to hell—but in its wake the delegation selected three of its most distinguished members (Kansas City labor lawyer Frank P. Walsh, former mayor of Chicago and governor of Illinois Edward F. Dunne, and attorney and one-time Philadelphia UILA leader Michael J. Ryan) to present the Irish case directly at the peace conference. This group, styling itself the American Commission on Irish Independence, arrived in Paris on April 11.[18]

Although the delegates' initial efforts in Paris appeared promising, their decision to make a side trip to Ireland, where they were hosted by Sinn Féin and leaders of the Dáil and delivered widely reported speeches favoring an independent republic, gave the mission a partisan flavor that probably hurt its chances for success. In any event, Wilson, who was seeking British support for his vision of a postwar order revolving around a League of Nations, was disinclined to press Lloyd George on other questions. Nor did Wilson believe that "self-determination," as vague and elastic as the concept might be, should be applied to the Irish case, which he saw as purely a British domestic problem. The Versailles Treaty that emerged from the conference in June 1919 contained no mention of Ireland, and the fighting there continued.[19]

The failure at the Paris peace conference had important ramifications for both American politics and postwar international relations, bringing many Irish Americans into strong opposition to the Versailles Treaty and its proposal for a League of Nations. When the Senate Foreign Relations Committee took up hearings on the treaty in August, all three members of the American Commission on Irish Independence appeared as hostile witnesses, joined by 112 other Irish American leaders. On its final vote in March 1920, the Senate rejected the Versailles Treaty, with the FOIF helping to shape the isolationism that would characterize important aspects of American foreign policy in the 1920s and 1930s.[20]

By this point, the guerrilla war in Ireland was well under way, and Americans sympathetic to the republican cause began to look for other ways to support it. In April 1920, Patrick McCartan, the Provisional Irish Government's envoy to the United States, hearing rumors of an impending military action by British troops in Dublin, called for protests by America's Irish nationalists. Gertrude Corless, a New York City journalist, responded by organizing a group of Irish American women volunteers to travel to Washington and set up pickets at the British embassy. In a meeting at the Hotel Lafayette (which had been headquarters of the women's suffrage lobby), the protesters formed the American Women Pickets for the Enforcement of America's War Aims, referencing (as the second Irish Race Convention had done) Wilson's proclaimed support during the war for self-determination for small nations. They continued their demonstrations at various sites in Washington throughout the spring, following the suffragist strategy of refusing bail when arrested.[21]

New York also saw significant actions by the group. On July 31, 1920, fifty Women Pickets helped organize a demonstration at Chelsea's Pier 60, on the west side of Manhattan, to help send off Australia's Archbishop Daniel Mannix, an immensely popular figure in the Irish nationalist movement, who was sailing for Ireland on a British ship, the *Baltic*. Mannix's popularity reflected the growing web of international connections shaping Irish nationalism in this period as well as revealing significant differences between nationalist movements in various locales. From the 1880s on, Irish nationalism in Australia had, unlike the movement in the United States, come increasingly under the control of Catholic clerics, who often led and spoke for nationalist organizations. While the Irish-born Mannix was typical of the Australian movement in this regard, he diverged from it in his espousal of the most militant forms of Irish republican nationalism. Mannix had been a central figure in the successful 1916–17 campaign to prevent Britain from extending conscription to Australia, and by 1920, he was a leading backer of Sinn Féin and the Irish revolution. Though the Irish in Australia, many of whom leaned toward support for Britain, did not necessarily embrace Mannix's political views, these views endeared him to an increasingly interlocked transnational network of Irish republican activists, a network that included the American Women Pickets.[22]

When Terence MacSwiney began his hunger strike in August 1920, the New York Women Pickets were among the first groups in the United States to respond, beginning a daily vigil at the British consulate on August 24. On Friday, August 27, they moved their protest to Pier 60, where they knew the *Baltic* would be docking after its return voyage. In a well-publicized maneuver, the British navy had arrested Archbishop Mannix at sea to prevent him from reaching Ireland, and the Women Pickets hoped to persuade Chelsea's predominantly Irish longshoremen to boycott the ship (or, more precisely, to refuse to unload its cargo) as a symbol of British imperialism.[23]

Their efforts were astoundingly successful. Holding a banner reading "The *Baltic* Is Dirty and Stands for Tyranny—Let Tyranny Rot Till It's Rotten," five members of the Women Pickets sparked a walkout of the Irish American longshoremen that closed not only Pier 60 but also the docks of all the other British lines on Manhattan's West Side. Declaring a boycott on the cargo of all British ships in port, the longshoremen demanded nothing less than the immediate release of Terence MacSwiney from prison and they remained on strike for the next three and a half weeks. Involving about 3,000 men in all, the strike spread to Brooklyn and Boston, with longshoremen as far away as Philadelphia, Newport News, New Orleans, and Galveston threatening to join the walkout. The Women Pickets organization, meanwhile, went on to provide primary leadership for the action, raising a strike fund for the longshoremen and coordinating women volunteers for daily picket duty.[24]

The long tradition of American labor support for Irish nationalism may have influenced those who walked off their jobs in August 1920. But the longshoremen's background in Ireland may have also influenced them, for it seems likely that many were relatively recent arrivals to America. In the first fifteen years of the twentieth century, more than 20,000 Irish emigrants entered the United States annually, up to one-quarter of them settling in the New York City area. Because they came from rural areas, they possessed little in the way of industrial skills and ended up working in economic sectors such as construction, teamstering, and longshoring. By 1920, the majority of Chelsea's Irish dockers were young "new immigrants," rather than more settled second- or third-generation Irish Americans.[25]

Unskilled recent Irish immigrants, many of them peasants or recently proletarianized agricultural laborers from the west of the country, seem to have provided the social base for the most extreme forms of nationalism in the United States in this period. The experience of economic inequality and material deprivation in both Ireland and America, combined with a widely held perception of emigration as exile, may well have led Chelsea's dockers not only to support the goal of revolutionary nationalism (represented by MacSwiney and the IRA) but also to support or engage in some of the most militant tactics available to nationalists, the hunger strike and the industrial strike for political ends. In engaging in such tactics, the dockers pitted themselves against the British shipowners and the more moderate nationalists and even their own union leadership.[26]

Perhaps the most surprising aspect of the strike was the support that Chelsea's African American longshoremen gave to it. On the first day of the boycott, a large crowd moved from pier to pier, calling on dockers working on British ships to walk off the job. But when the crowd came to Pier 56 it looked like the action might come to an abrupt end, for there was little reason to think that the black dockers who worked on this pier would join. But they did join and supported the boycott for its entire duration.

This undoubtedly surprised many Irish nationalists. It was not only that anti-black racism had been a central feature of Irish American life for decades; it was also, more specifically, that ethnic and racial conflict had long dominated the New York docks. Although the International Longshoremen's Association did not exclude African American dockers from union membership, intense (and often violent) pressure from white longshoremen, especially the Irish, kept them from working on many piers, particularly those that paid the highest wages. Thus, although the 1920 census counted over 5,000 black longshoremen in New York City, in Irish-dominated Chelsea, African Americans were able to find work on only a single pier, the Atlantic Transport Line's Pier 56. The rapid growth of New York's black population during the war years heightened racial tensions, and there were numerous cases of white attacks on black dockworkers. What would cause the latter to support this action?[27]

To begin with, leaders of the boycott made direct appeals to the African American longshoremen. Though the first day's action appears to have been spontaneous, after that, leaders systematically reached out to black dockers. Signs prepared by the American Women Pickets for use by African American pickets bore slogans such as "Ireland's Fight Is Our Fight! Up Liberty, Down Slavery" and "The Emancipation of the Irish Is the Emancipation of All Mankind," which attempted to universalize the Irish struggle, making it emblematic of the struggle against colonialism generally. Other signs were more specific: "Roger Casement Exposed the Congo Crime and Brought the First Relief to Africa. Ireland for the Irish. Africa for the Africans." The American Women Pickets prepared similar signs, with slogans in Italian, for use by Italian longshoremen on the docks.[28]

The ultimate key to African American support was the direct intervention of Marcus Garvey, then nearing the height of his popularity and influence. By the early 1920s, the Universal Negro Improvement Association that Garvey led had chapters in thirty American cities, 65,000–75,000 dues-paying members, and African American supporters that may have numbered in the millions. According to a federal agent who had infiltrated the UNIA, shortly after the boycott began, Garvey sent an aide, the Reverend J. W. Selkridge, "down to the docks to urge all the Negro longshoremen not to load British ships." Selkridge played a critical organizing role throughout the strike, working closely with Helen Golden, the Irish Progressive League leader who was also active in the American Women Pickets.[29]

Garvey's intervention reflected the tremendous influence that the Irish revolutionary struggle had had on his political thinking. The Irish revolution provided the major ideological example for Garvey's dramatic shift from apostle of self-help to African American nationalist and anti-colonialist. In his formal dedication of Liberty Hall, the UNIA's meeting place on 138th Street in July 1919, Garvey proclaimed that "the time [had] come for the Negro race to offer up its martyrs upon the altar of liberty even as the Irish [had] given a long list from Robert Emmet to Roger Casement." Indeed, the very name "Liberty Hall" reflected Garvey's appreciation for the Irish struggle, for he had named it after Liberty Hall, Dublin, the headquarters of Connolly's Irish Transport and General Workers Union and one of the sites from which the Easter Rising had been launched. The influence of the Irish revolution, combined with Garvey's particular admiration for MacSwiney, accounted for his decision to back the Irish dockers' boycott.[30]

But there were limits to Garvey's influence among New York's African American longshoremen. On September 10, the British steamship lines turned to a proven labor strategy used by American employers: they hired 250 African American strikebreakers to work on Pier 60. The Irish American strikers quickly gathered at the International Longshoremen's Association (ILA) local union headquarters at 23rd Street and 11th Avenue but were told there that all of the African American dockers who had been hired were union members and that their hiring was proper, since the ILA had not authorized the strike.[31]

Clearly something had to be done. Two days later, on September 12, a Garvey aide named Adrian Johnson and Women Pickets' leader Helen Golden met with representatives of the Irish strikers and the foreman of the black dockers who were breaking the strike on Pier 60. The foreman put the position of his men clearly: while they were willing to participate with "the Irishman in the strike for liberty by virtue of it being a Common Cause akin to that of the Aethiopian people," they were nonetheless concerned about the "apathetical treatment extended to them in normal times on various piers on which . . . wages were highest." The men demanded that "some proper arrangements be made to ameliorate their period of unemployment and to guarantee them a confraternal consideration with the Irish Workers in the Cause of Liberty which they conjointly are striving to attain."[32]

That evening, a delegation of fourteen Irish dockers and their supporters, led by the Irish American lawyer and Farmer-Labor Party leader, Dudley Field Malone, appeared at a UNIA meeting at Liberty Hall in Harlem. According to a federal agent who was present, Malone and others "spoke in high terms of Garvey and his movement and pledged their support." But the defining moment of the evening came with a statement by the Irish longshoreman and strike leader Patrick McGovern, who, according to Adrian Johnson, "pledged his acceptance of the proposition set forth in the complaint of the Colored Longshoremen."[33]

What occurred on the New York docks provides a window on the largest and most far-reaching implications of the Irish revolution. Just as Irish republicanism was becoming a movement with a strong transnational dimension, so it could also become a force for—at least temporarily—overcoming some of the deepest racial divisions in American life. As Garvey himself put it in his statement to the Irish dockers' representatives on September 12, although one could always find "narrow-minded individuals" and "color prejudice" on both sides of the color line, "liberty was common to all mankind, irrespective of creed or color."[34]

The radical class, gender, and racial politics of the Irish Progressive League and the American Women Pickets and events like the 1920 dockers' boycott were not typical of the Irish nationalist upheaval in the United States in these years, but neither were they unique. In Boston, a similar mix of anti-imperialism, left-wing progressivism, and support for women's suffrage shaped the city's Irish republican movement in ways that differentiated it from the more socially conservative Friends of Irish Freedom. In fact, there were even more radical figures at work in the larger movement, individuals who saw the IPL as too moderate a political force. The Irish labor activist James Larkin, for example, a resident of the United States from 1914 to 1923, believed that the IPL was far too limited in its objectives. He dismissed its American socialist supporters (like Morris Hillquit) as representatives of the right wing of the Socialist Party and felt that its leading Irish members, Hanna Sheehy-Skeffington and Nora Connolly, had abandoned their earlier socialist convictions entirely. Larkin believed that the IPL was more interested in recruiting American socialists to the struggle for an independent Ireland than in converting the American Irish to socialism and, in March 1918, he organized the James Connolly Socialist Club in New York as a left-wing alternative to it. Similarly named groups emerged across the country in these years: in Butte, Montana, for example, the Pearse-Connolly Irish Independence Club, founded in late 1916 after a visit by Larkin, played a critical role in building the militant Metal Mine Workers Union, which waged a bitter strike against the biggest copper mine owners the following year.[35]

Meanwhile, Irish American women activists, like Golden, Kelly, and Leonora O'Reilly, continued to forge links between Irish nationalism and American feminism, the early twentieth-century wave of which was cresting with the achievement of the vote for women in August 1920. That fall, O'Reilly formed the Irish Women's Consumers League, which helped direct a boycott of British goods by, among other tactics, staging a dramatic reenactment of the Boston Tea Party. Other Irish republican feminists formed links with the National Woman's Party, then just beginning a fight for an Equal Rights Amendment to the US Constitution. When Muriel MacSwiney, widow of hunger striker Terence MacSwiney, arrived in New York in December 1920, she was greeted not only by a committee from the mayor and a delegation from the International Longshoremen's Association but also by Jeannette Rankin, the Montana feminist and anti-war activist who in 1916 had been the first woman elected to the United States Congress.[36]

None of this should be seen as surprising. The Irish republican movement in America, after all, was peaking at a moment of worldwide crisis and upheaval. It was almost bound to forge alliances and develop ideologically in ways that its leaders could neither predict nor control. In a global context of a Bolshevik revolution in Russia, socialist revolutions in Hungary and Germany, an unprecedented strike wave in the United States, the victorious culmination of the women's suffrage campaign in Britain and America, the dramatic rise of Marcus Garvey's pan-African movement, and the growth of anti-colonial agitation in

India and Egypt, the Irish revolutionary movement in America was bound to be drawn in new directions. Many of these directions, however, were profoundly disturbing to the mainly Irish and Irish American leaders of the movement, and probably to a majority of the rank and file as well. FOIF leaders like Cohalan and Devoy were especially troubled by links that some Irish American republicans were forging with labor radicals and feminists. In late July 1920, a month before the MacSwiney strike began, the leaders of the Friends of Irish Freedom had expelled the Irish Progressive League from associate membership in the organization for the offense of "holding Irish meetings without the approval of the Friends." That action drew a sharp rebuke from Helen Golden, directed at Cohalan and others she labeled "sorry politicians."[37]

The main challenge to the FOIF's control of the Irish nationalist movement in America, however, came not from the radicals of the IPL but from the republican political leadership of Ireland, specifically Éamon de Valera, who resided in the United States for much of 1919 and 1920. Part of the conflict was personal in nature; de Valera later remarked that "big as the Country is, it was not big enough to hold the Judge [Cohalan] and myself." But the larger issue was whether the nationalist movement in America should be led and directed by Americans, like Cohalan, with an American perspective on policies and events, or alternatively by elected representatives of the Irish republic, like de Valera himself. This conflict led to a disastrous inability to influence either Republican or Democratic election platforms at their national conventions in the summer of 1920. At the Republican convention, rival Irish nationalist groupings were in such disagreement that the party ended up dropping all references to Ireland in its platform. With no need to compete with the Republicans, Democrats followed suit.[38]

By fall, a major split in the movement was looming. Following an unsuccessful effort to wrest leadership of the FOIF from Devoy and Cohalan, de Valera began laying plans for a national organization that he hoped would bring new activists into the movement. The American Association for the Recognition of the Irish Republic was founded at a meeting in Washington in November 1920 and it quickly overtook the FOIF in both membership and fundraising capacity. At its peak in late 1921, the AARIR claimed over 700,000 members, making it the largest Irish nationalist organization in American history.[39]

The IPL immediately folded itself into the AARIR, with Peter Golden becoming one of its main traveling organizers. Other liberals and progressives, such as the labor lawyer Frank Walsh and San Francisco's Father Peter Yorke, also took on leading roles in the new group. But the AARIR was far from a bastion of radicalism. The stridently anti-labor New York Judge John Goff, for instance, moved from the FOIF to the AARIR and the equally anti-labor Los Angeles corporate attorney, Joseph Scott, played a central role in the organization in the West.

Presiding over the AARIR as a whole was another southern Californian with a revered Irish republican name, Edward L. Doheny. The nephew of the Young Ireland leader, Michael Doheny, Edward Doheny was most widely known as an oil tycoon in California and Mexico. No friend of labor or progressive causes in either country, Doheny was worth an estimated $100,000,000 at the time of his AARIR presidency, making him one of richest men in America.[40]

By the time de Valera left the United States for Ireland in December 1920, other groups were working on other aspects of the Irish question. Oswald Garrison Villard, editor of the liberal *Nation* magazine, organized an eight-person body called the American Commission on Conditions in Ireland. The commission, which included such well-known progressive figures as Chicago settlement house pioneer Jane Addams and Nebraska Senator George W. Norris, held public hearings that were widely covered in the press and published in their entirety in the *Nation*. Its final report, issued in March 1921, painted a bleak picture of conditions in the country and provided gripping documentation of British atrocities committed during the war. Another new organization, the American Committee for Relief in Ireland, presented an equally dramatic account of distress, raised over $5,000,000 for Irish relief, and in 1921 received a written endorsement from the new president, Warren G. Harding, who wished it "the fullest measure of success" and observed that "knowledge of distress in Ireland makes quick and deep appeal to the more fortunate of our land where so many of our citizens trace kinship to the Emerald Isle."[41]

But it was de Valera's AARIR that dominated the field. The new organization established a national headquarters in Washington, DC, and a propaganda office in Chicago, which began publishing a series of pamphlets designed to build support for the Irish republican cause. State and local organizations grew rapidly, drawing many deserters from the FOIF, and, as de Valera had intended, many newcomers to Irish nationalism as well. The AARIR coordinated the sale of Irish republican bond certificates, raising more than $5,000,000 this way, though only about half of that amount made it to Ireland. To be sure, the organization never achieved its principal goal, US recognition of the Irish provisional government, but for a time it became an extremely powerful force in Irish American life. Measured by either membership figures or the intensity of mass enthusiasm, nothing on this scale had happened before—nor, for that matter, would it ever happen again. Irish American nationalism had hit high tide.

8

The Long Wait, 1921–1966

In 1922, in the midst of the fighting that would be called the Irish Civil War, Peter Golden, the New York poet and stalwart of the Irish Progressive League and American Association for the Recognition of the Irish Republic, penned one of his final poems. Entitled "A Prayer for Ireland," it ruminated on "the brooding horror" of a war in which two factions of a movement that had just brought the greatest imperial power in the world to the negotiating table now fought each other with devastating brutality. Golden's short poem concluded with a prayer, as well as a melancholy look back at the power of an Irish republican movement (both in Ireland and the United States) that seemed to collapse almost overnight, amid calls on both sides in the Civil War to "fight to the end":

> The end of what? And who shall gain?
> Those who are slain—Can Ireland lose?
> Almighty Father, give them light
> That they might right and just may choose.
>
> And lift this Nation in Thy Name,
> Up from the shame of civil woe.
> Bring back again in peace and love,
> The glory of a year ago.[1]

Many Irish republicans in the United States shared Golden's dismay and disappointment, and such feelings only grew in the years following the Free State's 1923 victory in the Civil War. From their point of view, there was much to be disappointed about. To start with, there was the new oath of faithfulness to the British crown that all Free State officials had agreed to swear. Though many Irish Americans had trouble understanding the importance of what appeared to be a mere formality, those who upheld the vigorous strain of republicanism going back to the American and French Revolutions and the United Irishmen approached such symbolism with deadly seriousness. The idea of swearing fidelity to any monarch—let alone a monarch who represented the face of British colonialism in Ireland—was simply abhorrent. There was also the question of Irish national unity (or lack thereof), for though twenty-six counties of Ireland had achieved something resembling de facto sovereignty, six counties in the northeast of the island were now bound closer to the United Kingdom than ever before.

Then too there was what contemporaries called "the social question." Though republicans like Peter and Helen Golden had worked closely with the Irish and American socialist left, most were not socialists themselves, and the new Irish communist movement, led by James Connolly's son, Roddy, was at this point an insignificant force among nationalists. Still, republicans from Wolfe Tone onward had argued that part of what they were fighting for was a better life for Ireland's rural and urban poor, a life sufficient in material terms to end what nationalists—and many others—regarded as the curse of emigration. The new Free State government, partly because of economic forces outside its control and partly because of its own free trade and business-oriented outlook, did little to alleviate the high levels of poverty and emigration that continued to mark Irish life in the 1920s and early 1930s.

Because the 1916 Proclamation of the Republic had called for an Irish government "elected by the suffrages of all her men and women" and for "equal rights and equal opportunities, for all its citizens," and because leading feminists like America's Alice Paul, Ireland's Hanna Sheehy-Skeffington, and Britain's Sylvia Pankhurst had all been active supporters of the independence struggle, most republicans assumed that an independent Ireland would be one in which the cause of women's equality would make further advances. Here too they were to be disappointed. Despite a 1922 constitution that established formal gender equality, the close relationship of Free State political leaders with the Catholic hierarchy produced nearly the opposite effect. The 1924 Juries Bill allowed women, but not men, to apply for exemption from jury service because of their all-important "domestic duties," and it was followed in short order by the prohibition of divorce in 1925 and the 1929 Censorship of Publications Act, which gave the state the power to ban all published material, including information on birth control.[2]

Peter Golden died in Denver, on a cross-country lecture tour, in March 1926, but the deep disappointment that many other Irish nationalists in the United States shared with him led them to pose the question of whether the impressive republican presence of 1919–21 (when as many as a million people joined American-based organizations supporting Irish independence) could be rebuilt and a republican vision brought back to life. For the next four decades, the answer seemed to be a simple and resounding no.[3]

The Civil War

The guerrilla conflict known as the Irish War of Independence came to an end on July 11, 1921, when a truce between the Dáil and the British government went into effect. Following direct meetings between Dáil President Éamon de Valera and Prime Minister Lloyd George that failed to produce a settlement, more formal talks between representatives of the two bodies began in October. After an intense bout of negotiations, a document known as the Articles of Agreement for a Treaty between Great Britain and Ireland was signed in London on December 6. The Government of Ireland Act, a last-ditch effort to implement the old goal of Home Rule, which the British Parliament had passed the previous year, had already led to a partition of Ireland and, in fact, a newly established Unionist-dominated parliament, representing six of the nine historic counties of Ulster, constituted as "Northern Ireland," was already meeting in Belfast. Because of this reality on the ground, and the fact that the terms on which the London negotiations took place clearly specified that they would determine only "how the association of Ireland with the community of Nations known as the British Empire may be best reconciled with Irish national aspirations," there was absolutely no hope that a united or fully independent Irish republic could come out of the talks. But the Dáil's negotiators, led by Michael Collins and Arthur Griffith, worked to get the maximum degree of Irish independence possible from Lloyd George's government.[4]

What they got in the Anglo-Irish Treaty was partial recognition of southern Ireland's sovereignty, reflected in the term "Irish Free State," with far more actual autonomy and self-government, despite some significant military and economic limitations, than the old Home Rule Party had ever even tried to achieve. What they did not get was a republic, either in name or in fact. The Lloyd George government, concerned as much about the potential effect such a concession might have on the British possessions of India, Egypt, and South Africa as about Ireland itself, had insisted on the Free State remaining a "dominion" within the British Empire and on an oath of faithfulness to crown and commonwealth that all Irish officials would be required to take. Although the Treaty included a provision for the establishment of a Boundary Commission to examine and possibly adjust the border between Northern Ireland and the Free State, the Irish negotiators had accepted partition at least for the time being as a fait accompli.[5]

The negotiating team returned to Dublin, arguing strenuously that this was the best possible deal that could be achieved at this time. The Treaty "gives us freedom," Collins asserted, "not the ultimate freedom that all nations desire and develop to, but the freedom to achieve it." Many in the Dáil disagreed. Partition was not the main issue of debate here, since both pro- and anti-Treaty deputies believed that the new state of Northern Ireland would be too small and economically insecure to last long on its own. But the limits on Irish autonomy and the symbolic oath of fidelity to what republicans regarded as a corrupt and foreign institution deeply repelled them. Was this "Free State" to be all there was to show for a deeply remembered history of struggle and sacrifice that stretched from Wolfe Tone to the hunger striker Terence MacSwiney? The latter's sister, Mary MacSwiney, who had spent much of 1920 and 1921 touring the United States for the republican cause, became perhaps the single most effective opponent of the Treaty, denouncing those who supported it as abandoning the principles of 1798, 1848, and 1916. "I ask you to vote in the name of the dead to unite against this Treaty," she pleaded with her fellow deputies during the Dáil debate. "The issue is not between peace and war; it is between right and wrong." In the end, all six of the women in the Dáil—five of them close relatives of martyred patriots—voted to reject the agreement.[6]

On January 7, 1922, the Dáil voted. In an extremely close contest, sixty-four members voted in favor of the Treaty, while fifty-seven voted against. Rather than accepting ratification, however, the Dáil's president, Éamon de Valera, led his followers in a walkout from the body, after which Collins was elected chairman of what came to be called the Provisional Government. The Irish Republican Army was as deeply divided as the Dáil: after its own split in March, pro-Treaty members of the IRA quickly became the core of Collins's Free State army, while anti-Treaty "Irregulars" demonstrated the depth of their convictions in April by arming themselves and occupying the Four Courts and several other important buildings in Dublin. A general election in June solidified the position of the pro-Treaty party, which took fifty-eight seats to the thirty-six of anti-Treatyites, with another thirty-four seats going to smaller parties, all of them supporting the Treaty, but the Irregulars refused to end their occupation of the Four Courts. Buoyed by a perceived popular mandate—but also heavily influenced by a British threat to attack the building if the Free State did not— on June 28 Collins's troops launched an artillery attack on the Irregulars, many of whom were their former friends and comrades, triggering a civil war that spread through the country and lasted until the following May. Though the Irregulars, taking the name Irish Republican Army for themselves, fought with determination and had strong support in particular regions of the country, especially the west, they were overwhelmed by the greater firepower of the Free State army (which used weaponry loaned by the British government) as well as by the hostility of the Catholic Church, which threatened them with excommunication.[7]

Pointing to the vote in the Dáil and in the general election, Free State leaders interpreted the Civil War as a contest between pragmatic pro-Treaty "democrats" on the one hand and essentially anti-democratic republican purists on the other.

Their claims for "democracy," however, downplayed the very large dose of coercion involved in the sequence of events that led to the outbreak of fighting. To be specific: the negotiators who signed the Treaty in December, the majority of the Dáil members who ratified it in January, and the Irish voters who supported pro-Treaty candidates in June all did so with the very real threat of renewed and all-out war with Britain hanging over them if they did not. Lloyd George was absolutely clear that in a renewed conflict Britain would press on to a complete military victory. Under these circumstances, it is difficult to interpret these decisions as the expression of an unalloyed democracy. In fact, it may be better to see the Free State less as the voice of a democratically expressed Irish popular will than as the partially coerced representative of the British Empire. If this was true, then the Civil War could itself be seen as a continuation of the previous guerrilla war between Britain and the IRA and the Free State victory as a proxy British victory in a war of colonial retention. Many contemporaries (and not just hardcore republicans) saw it this way, which helps explain both the ongoing existence of the IRA and the rise of de Valera's vigorously anti-Treaty (but constitutional) Fianna Fáil party just a few years later, a development shaped by the impact of the Depression on the Irish electorate as well.[8]

Though estimates of the Irish Civil War's death toll vary widely, it is certain that more people died in this conflict than in the War of Independence that had preceded it. Although it claimed to act on the basis of a democratic mandate, the Provisional Government's own legitimacy was called into question by its tactics, which included the internment of over 10,000 people without trial, Collins's establishment of a short-lived military dictatorship in the summer of 1922, and the summary reprisal executions of seventy-seven anti-Treaty prisoners the following December. Collins himself was killed in an IRA ambush in August 1922, but his successor, William T. Cosgrave, intensified the government's military offensive, affirming at one point his willingness to kill as many as 10,000 people to establish stability in Ireland. Though the fighting ended on May 24, 1923, when IRA Chief of Staff Frank Aiken ordered his organization to dump its arms, real stability was only achieved in the later 1920s.[9]

In the United States, as in other countries where significant numbers of Irish could be found, the Irish nationalist movement quickly divided between pro- and anti-Treaty factions. The announcement of the initial truce with Britain in July 1921, not surprisingly, took the wind out of the sails of Irish American nationalism almost immediately. Irish American activists followed press reports of the London negotiations closely, but the time for meetings, rallies, and demonstrations had clearly passed. Moreover, the fact that it was Britain that had called for the truce seemed to mark a significant political victory—which some Irish American nationalists, willfully or not, misinterpreted as a military victory—for their cause. In Philadelphia, Joseph McGarrity's *Irish Press* heralded the "many

Irish victories" and "heavy casualties among English forces" in the weeks immediately preceding the truce, implying that a handful of IRA guerrillas had actually defeated the British Empire on the battlefield. In any event, it was understood by all that London and Dublin, not New York, Chicago, or Boston, were to be the centers of action for the moment.[10]

Many nationalists in the United States, of course, still deeply distrusted the British. Despite his personal antipathy to de Valera, the now elderly Irish American nationalist John Devoy welcomed de Valera's rejection of Britain's initial offers in July and August, drawing forceful attention to the role played by British coercion throughout the negotiating process. "Permit the oldest active Fenian living to congratulate you and Dail Eireann on prompt and effective answer to Lloyd George's challenge and his threat to resume massacres," Devoy stated in a telegram to de Valera. "Your action is a trumpet call to race in America which will bury differences and bring united action to enable Republic to defend Irish people in bitter struggle before them." In the end, however, Devoy's personal distrust of de Valera led him to endorse the Anglo-Irish Treaty signed in December. While "we believe and know that a Republic can be the only final solution for Ireland," he wrote in his newspaper, the *Gaelic American*, on December 17, "we are not going to accept as the leader of that movement a man who tried to destroy it." Not surprisingly, Devoy's wing of the secret Clan na Gael took a similar stance, as did the Friends of Irish Freedom, the once sizable mass organization that Devoy led with New York Judge Daniel Cohalan.[11]

The Friends of Irish Freedom went through a tortuous few days, initially protesting the Treaty as "an insult to the dead who died fighting for an independent Irish Republic"; soon, however, they issued a statement that endorsed its terms as the best that could be obtained while pointedly noting that since it had been signed under the coercive threat of renewed war, "the compromise made can never be held morally binding, upon this or future generations of the race." Like Devoy and his wing of the Clan, the Friends continued to offer support (though sometimes adding criticisms) to the Collins and Cosgrave governments through the bloody months of Civil War that followed. In the invective it hurled at its Civil War–era opponents, Devoy's *Gaelic American* displayed Irish American nationalism's most narrow-minded and bigoted side, denouncing anti-Treatyites Mary MacSwiney and Hanna Sheehy-Skeffington as "viragos" and "unbalanced women," de Valera as a "dead Jew," and the compromise plan that he offered at one point in the negotiations (the so-called Document No. 2) as a "Jew's Crown Republic." Comments like these led Peter Golden to describe Devoy as the "most foul and sinister" figure produced by Irish nationalism in more than a century.[12]

Other Irish Americans were far less reticent than Devoy or Cohalan in their initial enthusiasm for the Treaty. Even within the ranks of the American Association for the Recognition of the Irish Republic, which officially opposed the Treaty, there was a great deal of sentiment in its favor, a point that numerous branches communicated directly to Michael Collins himself. "History will record you as the George Washington of Ireland," wrote one AARIR officer in the Bronx, noting that 85 percent of the members of his branch supported the Treaty. Many Irish American nationalists accepted Collins's argument that the Free State was but a way station on the road to a republic; others simply felt that it was not their place to express an opinion one way or the other on the matter. If the Treaty satisfied Collins, wrote one New Yorker, then "it ought to satisfy those in America, who were 3,000 miles away when the real fighting was being done." A virtual onslaught of editorial comment in American newspapers in favor of the Treaty undoubtedly played a role in shaping Irish American opinion, as did the personal persuasiveness of Free State leaders who hosted Irish American visitors. Mary MacSwiney observed sadly that many such visitors "went to Ireland republicans and came back Free Staters."[13]

Much the same was true in other important areas of Irish global settlement, areas where republicanism had been a major force just six months before. Australia's leading Irish nationalist newspaper, the *Freeman's Journal*, wholeheartedly endorsed Collins's logic that the Treaty was "a stepping stone to better things"; following the Dáil's ratification, the *Journal* predicted that "Mr. de Valera must eventually bow to the inevitable, no matter how badly his dreams have been shaken." The two leading Irish Catholic newspapers in Ontario, Canada, concurred, with the *Catholic Register* hailing the Treaty as the end of "seven long centuries" of British rule in Ireland and the *Catholic Record* dismissing de Valera as "impervious to reason and lost to the sense of realities." Alluding to Robert Emmet's powerful 1803 speech from the dock, asking that no one write his epitaph until Ireland "takes her place among the nations of the earth," another Canadian paper offered this front-page headline: "Robert Emmet's Epitaph Can Now Be Written."[14]

The outbreak of fighting in Dublin in June prompted mainly incomprehension and revulsion on the part of Irish nationalists in Australia and Canada as well as in the United States, where in the words of Sinn Féin's New York representative, the republican cause went "from an all high rating to a near zero" almost overnight. Anti-Treatyites managed to take full control of the AARIR in May 1922, but only by driving out two successive national presidents. The effects of these purges, and the bloody Civil War itself, on the organization were disastrous, as thousands of its members simply headed for the doors. As early as March 1922, labor lawyer (and de Valera's American legal advisor) Frank Walsh believed that the AARIR was "absolutely shot to pieces." Three years later, its membership, which had approached 700,000 in 1921, had fallen to just 13,870. Devoy's barbed comment that the organization had more letters in its name than supporters was not too far off the mark.[15]

Surprisingly perhaps, some new recruits entered republican ranks for the first time, including several prominent Americans from non-Irish backgrounds. The motivations of such recruits, however, varied tremendously. At one extreme was the journalist Charles Edward Russell. One of the most famous and widely read of the Progressive-era "muckrakers" who exposed the excesses of early twentieth-century American capitalism, Russell had been a founder of the National Association for the Advancement of Colored People and a leading member of the Socialist Party. He joined the ranks of the Irish republican movement at the very late date of 1923. In the tradition of earlier American reformers like Horace Greeley and abolitionist James Redpath, and contemporaries like Jane Addams and *Nation* publisher Oswald Garrison Villard, Russell's commitment to Irish republicanism was, as he put it, "not hereditary," and he was an active supporter of a wide range of international causes in the 1920s, including Zionism, Filipino independence, and Italian anti-fascism. "Of course, I am a friend of the Republican movement in Ireland," he wrote to Britain's Home Secretary in 1926, protesting the latter's refusal (at the Free State's request) to allow him to enter the country. "I am a friend of every Republican movement everywhere in this world. To my mind any other form of government in the twentieth century is a grotesque absurdity."[16]

Like Marcus Garvey, Russell also deeply admired what he saw as Ireland's long memory of its own resistance and its distinctive tradition of self-sacrifice—and he himself contributed to the memorialization of martyrdom and resistance with his poems in honor of Wolfe Tone, Patrick Pearse, and his friend Mary MacSwiney. "Ireland stands before the world today as a nation whose people have lived and died that liberty should not become extinct from the world," he told an AARIR meeting in Cincinnati in 1926. But his support for Irish republicanism was also driven by his angry opposition to British imperialism throughout the world, not just in "what is called, by a figure of speech, the Free State of Ireland."

> I hate Great Britain. I hate it and everything connected with it and the life of it. My feeling is not hereditary; it is caused by seeing how things worked around the fringes of that rotten empire. I have seen what Great Britain and its practices have meant to India, where it has been a curse; what it has meant to China as the evil genius of the entire East, where not one filthy trick and not one evil thing has set foot that Great Britain hasn't instigated. It is the champion of oppression, and, what is worse, it does its evil under the smug pretense of doing good.[17]

A very different kind of Irish republican recruit was twenty-one-year-old Chester Alan Arthur III, who, as the grandson of President Chester Arthur, was part of another long tradition, one that went back to George Washington Parke Custis, the first president's step-grandson who had been an influential supporter of Irish Catholic emancipation in the 1820s, and Robert Tyler, the son of a president who became a leader of Daniel O'Connell's American repeal network in the 1840s. Arthur discovered the republican cause while traveling with his wife as a tourist in Civil War Ireland. Caught up in the romance of the anti-Treaty cause, he was incensed at what he saw as the brutality and, he claimed, drunkenness, of Free State soldiers. "Imagine arming drunkards with English rifles and setting them to fight their own brothers who are keeping to their oath of fealty to the Republic!" he wrote to a family friend from war-torn County Kerry in July 1922. Arthur went on to serve as secretary to the Irish republican delegation in Lausanne, Switzerland, and, after returning to New York, became a popular speaker at republican events until he lost interest in the cause.[18]

It is tempting to dismiss a figure like Chester Arthur III, as one of his closest friends did in a mocking letter conceding that Arthur was caught up in "all the fascination of Irish revolutions and other honeymoon pastimes," but begging Arthur, "if you can't *stay* out of jail, at least . . . *get* out enough to take care of your correspondence." But the services that he performed for the republican movement in Ireland, Switzerland, and America were highly valued by its leaders. In a series of what he called "pro-Irish Republic" articles and letters in the *New York Times* and the *New York Herald* in 1922 and 1923, Arthur truly became—"mostly through my name," he was quick to admit—"the first writer to break the boycott of the conservative papers." With missives to the International Red Cross condemning the Free State executions that began, "I am an American, my grandfather having been President of the United States," he was assured of getting at least a polite response.[19]

More typical than either Russell or Arthur were the men and women of the Massachusetts MacSwiney Clubs. Founded in 1921 to support the independence struggle and named in honor of the martyred republican mayor of Cork, the clubs never hesitated for a moment on the Treaty, taking an uncompromising stand against, in the words of Pittsfield's Mary O'Kane, "the hypocrites who betrayed Ireland's sacred cause." Even as the republican cause declined precipitously nationwide, the Massachusetts clubs thrived, carried along by intensive organizing work, personal connections with Mary MacSwiney and Terence's widow Muriel, and creative coalition building. The MacSwiney Clubs were alone among Irish American nationalist organizations in linking up with French Canadian separatists in Quebec—going so far as to tell leaders of Quebec's Patriotic League that "should it come to an armed struggle between you and the British imperialists be assured that our sympathy will not be merely platonic." In phrases surely designed to bring back memories of the Fenian attacks on Canada in 1866 and 1870, Pittsfield's John F. Kelly assured Montreal's Anatole

Vanier that if his organization ever decided to raise "the standard of an independent Canada or Quebec, all hell cannot prevent our volunteers from swarming over the border. Long live free Quebec!" But there was a quid pro quo involved here: while "we are in full sympathy with a movement for liberty anywhere and by any race," Kelly told Vanier, "obviously the sympathy reaches a maximum where the movement is so directed that it cooperates with our efforts for the country of our ancestors."[20]

Building their organization throughout Massachusetts (Pittsfield, Plainfield, Fall River, and Northampton all had clubs); developing contacts with similar groups in Connecticut towns like Bridgeport, Waterbury, and Danbury; and using advertisements placed in New York's anti-Treaty *Irish World* to encourage kindred organizing in places as far away as Illinois, Indiana, and Minnesota, the clubs waged an ongoing propaganda war, did a great deal of fundraising, and coordinated a boycott of British and Free State goods. In marked contrast with John Devoy's anti-Semitic outbursts, leaders of the MacSwiney Clubs enthusiastically hosted a talk by a visiting IRA volunteer named Robert Briscoe, who, as "a young man, Irish born, a Jew, and a Mason," would be sure to open the eyes of "those that believe the Republican cause is exclusively a Catholic one." Irish American women were active as both officers and rank-and-file members of the clubs, playing a particularly important role in the boycotts as well as in raising up a "fund for widows and orphans" of IRA volunteers. That activity, along with fundraising for the dependents of republican prisoners in Free State jails, became more and more central to the clubs as the Civil War wound down in defeat for the anti-Treaty cause.[21]

The Irish Free State and Its Opponents

W. T. Cosgrave, who had succeeded Michael Collins as leader of the Free State government in 1922, remained head of state for the next ten years, winning the first election following the Civil War in August 1923 at the helm of a political party called Cumann na nGaedheal ("party of the Irish"). De Valera and his fellow anti-Treatyites, many of them still in prison, held on to the name Sinn Féin (and de Valera to the hopeful title, "president of the Irish Republic") and received the second largest number of votes, though since they refused to accept the legitimacy of the new government or to swear the required oath of fidelity to the British crown, those who were elected to the Dáil declined to take up their seats. As a result, Cumann na nGaedheal formed a government without effective opposition, though the Irish Labour Party, with just fourteen seats to the governing party's sixty-three, did its best to oppose what it regarded as Cosgrave's anti-worker policies. Cumann na nGaedheal began the work of building a new nation in the midst of this ongoing and bitter, if no longer lethal, conflict. The basic rift between the pro- and anti-Treaty positions remained the most salient one in Irish politics for years to come.

Was the Cosgrave government, despite its compromises with the British imperial state, the expression of an Irish nationalism? Without a doubt, and, despite its origins in a period of revolutionary struggle, it can be seen as the most recent iteration of Ireland's constitutional nationalist tradition. That tradition stretched back to the Irish Parliamentary Party, Home Rule, and (before that) O'Connell's repeal movement, while the anti-Treatyites could trace their own lineage back to the physical force republicanism of the United Irishmen. But in the 1920s, another gulf formed within Irish nationalism: between a distinctively southern (twenty-six county) nationalism and an island-wide nationalism that embraced (and would increasingly be shaped by) nationalists in the new political unit of Northern Ireland. Those on both sides of the Treaty and Civil War, for all the deadly disagreements between them, shared a basically southern viewpoint, one that emphasized political and economic development and cultural revival in the twenty-six counties, while leaving northern nationalists more or less on their own.[22]

Over the course of the 1920s, the constitutional and southern nationalists of Cumann na nGaedheal began the work of state building, work that included everything from large-scale electrification projects like the gigantic Shannon Scheme, completed in 1929, to repainting all the country's letter boxes green. The creation of stable and democratic institutions (albeit ones based on British models, despite their Irish names) is generally seen as the greatest achievement of Cumann na nGaedheal nationalism, along with the building of a respected, unarmed police force called the Garda Síochána, no small accomplishment given the large number of firearms circulating in post–Civil War Ireland. The government's inability to revive the slowly dying Irish language is usually regarded as its greatest failure.[23]

The leaders of Cumann na nGaedheal surely must be ranked among the most conservative revolutionaries in modern history. The Unionist and pro-business *Irish Times* approvingly described Cosgrave as "neither a wild-eyed revolutionary nor a long-haired poet," but as a figure who "dresses generally in somber hues, wears a bowler hat and looks rather like the general manager of a railway company," and the resemblance of the new taoiseach (or prime minister) to a business executive went well beyond his fashion choices. Strictly adhering to the economic orthodoxy of the day, Cosgrave and his ministers seemed driven by an obsession to balance the national budget, spending little on badly needed social welfare or housing and actually cutting the old age pension rate by a shilling a week in 1924. Although a long debate took place during the 1920s about the relative merits of free trade and protectionism, the government remained unalterably committed to a policy of free trade. Not surprisingly, the Free State economy continued to be based on agriculture, but in pursuing an "agriculture for export" policy, the government helped create a new, wealthy, and power-ful class of large landowners in the cattle industry. This group benefited most from the government's economic policies during the 1920s, while the posi-tion of small farmers and urban workers changed little or actually deteriorated. Economic stagnation was the hallmark of the decade and, as a result, emigration, which had come to a virtual halt in the years of war and revolution, resumed at very high levels. The prosperity that many Irish nationalists had assumed would result from political independence never materialized.[24]

Hopes of cultural nationalists for a revival of the Irish language were also dashed. Although officially bilingual, the state basically left the issue of lan-guage instruction to the schools. While some of these did some teaching in Irish, the government's failure to require the use of Irish in the conduct of poli-tics and business meant that English continued to predominate. In the area of family life, the government allowed the norms of Catholic teachings to take primacy. This was not simply a result of the overwhelming Catholic character of the population (accentuated now by the departure of the Protestant-majority six counties of Northern Ireland), but by the church hierarchy's successfully demanding a kind of "payback" for the essential support it had provided dur-ing the independence struggle. Irish feminists and their allies occasionally won victories in these years, as in their successful resistance to a government effort to exclude women entirely from juries in 1927. But in its gender politics, just as much as in its economic policies, the conservatism of the Cosgrave government was clear.[25]

From the standpoint of the long-term future of Irish American national-ism, however, even more significant than the Free State's conservative class and gender policies was its unwillingness to effectively challenge the partition of the island or alter the political status of Northern Ireland. When the Boundary Commission established by the Anglo-Irish Treaty began its proceedings in 1924, Northern Ireland's Prime Minister James Craig demonstrated his dis-dain by simply refusing to send a representative. The commission managed to stagger on but concluded its proceedings a year later by recommending only very minor changes to the border. At that point, the Free State's representative, Gaelic scholar Eoin MacNeill, resigned in protest, charging that the commission had deliberately misinterpreted the relevant Treaty articles. His protest proved utterly ineffectual and, as a result, the border remained as it was in 1920: a ger-rymandered political artifice designed to ensure a permanent Protestant and Unionist majority in the northeastern section of the island. Reflecting its essen-tially southern nationalist outlook, the Cosgrave government simply turned its attention to other matters.[26]

Despite all of this, those Irish American nationalists who had supported the Free State government during the Treaty debate and Civil War continued to do so now. In 1923, the leaders of the Friends of Irish Freedom, Daniel Cohalan and Diarmuid Lynch, traveled to Ireland, where they were enthusiastically welcomed by the Free State's leaders. In an essay published the same year, Cohalan proposed a campaign to develop links between Ireland and the United States, "not alone on sympathetic and racial lines, but also cultural, historic, commercial and economic—and above all, governmental—lines," and the Friends' leaders were elated when the Coolidge administration granted diplomatic recognition to the Free State government in October 1924. Though the failure of the Boundary Commission to modify partition was a great disappointment to Cohalan, following another trip to Ireland, he published an article in the *Gaelic American* marveling at the progress that Cosgrave's government had made in economic development and in creating stable parliamentary institutions.[27]

The Friends, to be sure, did not uncritically support every Free State policy initiative. The organization sharply criticized the Cosgrave government's application for membership in the League of Nations as a "blunder," arguing that the move could well "deprive it of the sympathy and support of millions of Americans of Irish blood." In 1924 the Friends even expressed dismay at what they called the "imperialist tendencies" of the Free State, illustrated by its ongoing cooperative relationship with Britain. Still these criticisms, harsh as they may seem, never tempted the Friends to break with the Cosgrave government or to switch their support to de Valera's republican opposition. Whatever the vicissitudes of its relationship with the Cosgrave government, the organization witnessed a sharp decline over the course of the 1920s. Its new initiatives, such as public organizing against the National Quotas Immigration Act, which Congress passed in 1924, failed to generate the kind of enthusiasm that support for Irish independence had and the onset of the Depression hurt the organization as well. By 1931, the Friends of Irish Freedom, which had embraced nearly 100,000 members a decade earlier, had been reduced to a mere 539. The organization formally disbanded in 1935.[28]

The Irish Free State found a more imposing supporter in the figure of the old Fenian exile John Devoy. Devoy visited Ireland in the summer of 1924, where he received an official welcome by a Distinguished Visitors Committee headed by William Butler Yeats, as well as by Cosgrave himself. It must have been an emotional moment for the eighty-one-year-old political agitator, who had made only one secret visit to Ireland since his exile began in 1871. "My heart has been in Ireland all the time that I have been in America," he told a New York banquet held in his honor two days before setting sail. When he died in Atlantic City four years later, the London *Times* called Devoy "the most bitter and persistent, as well as the most dangerous, enemy of this country which Ireland has produced since Wolfe Tone." Though he had lived in the United States for nearly sixty years, Devoy's body was shipped to Ireland where, after a full state funeral, it was interred in Dublin's Glasnevin Cemetery, near the graves of O'Connell, Parnell, and Collins, as well as that of San Francisco's Young Ireland exile, Terence Bellew McManus.[29]

The pro-Treaty wing of the Clan na Gael that Devoy had led followed the Friends of Irish Freedom in its rapid decline during the 1920s. Though claiming majority support in every locale except Rhode Island, Philadelphia, and San Francisco, and especially strong in New York City, the Devoy (or "Old") Clan had been badly hurt by the decision of Irish Republican Brotherhood in 1922 to recognize Joseph McGarrity's "reorganized" anti-Treaty Clan as its American affiliate. The Devoy group continued to hold meetings, publish the *Gaelic American,* and engage in fundraising for the Free State through the Friends of Irish Freedom. It also held commemorations of the Easter Rising and the birthdays of Wolfe Tone and Robert Emmet, participated in annual St. Patrick's Day events in New York and other cities, and turned out to welcome distinguished Irish visitors like the one-time Provisional Government army chief, General Richard Mulcahy, in 1925. Although the Old Clan continued to sputter along into the 1940s, for all practical purposes it was dead long before then. Serving as the American cheering squad for the government of an established nation-state—especially one as conservative as that headed by W. T. Cosgrave—may have been simply too much of a stretch for an organization that, since its founding in 1867, had considered itself the main standard-bearer of Irish revolutionary republicanism.[30]

Faced with the decline of these traditional nationalist organizations, the Free State government made strenuous efforts to reach out more directly to the Irish diaspora, particularly in America, harnessing the latest available communication technologies to do so. Cosgrave used the new medium of radio to broadcast the first of what would become annual St. Patrick's Day messages to America in March 1926. His first "live" radio address to the United States, in 1931, attracted a particularly large audience across the nation, as much for the marvel of the technology as for the content of his speech. Even in Chicago, where anti-Treaty sentiment remained strong, according to a somewhat breathless newspaper account, those "of Irish extraction gathered, singly or in groups, about the radio loud speakers that caught up the phrases of President William Cosgrave in Dublin, and, eliminating time and space, brought them echoing firmly and steadily into hundreds of homes." In light of such an "epochal occasion," the "first trans-oceanic address from the Emerald Isle," it was logical that the address was heard "with intense interest" by both supporters and opponents of the taoiseach.[31]

Anti-Treaty forces also made efforts to reach out to Irish America in these years, especially after Fianna Fáil, the new political party led by Éamon de Valera, prepared to reenter the Irish electoral mainstream. As early as 1923, de Valera had begun to reevaluate Sinn Féin's policy of abstentionism (refusing to take seats that it won in the Dáil), pondering how republicans might somehow participate in the parliamentary institutions of the Free State without abandoning the principles that they had fought for in the Civil War. If only the oath of fidelity to the crown could be removed, then "the question of going in or remaining out would be a matter purely of tactics and expediency," he had written to Mary MacSwiney that year. "I have always been afraid of our people seeing principles where they really do not exist." In late January 1926, having failed to persuade Sinn Féin to modify its abstentionist policies over the previous two months, he announced that he was personally prepared to enter the Dáil if no oath was required, fully realizing that this position would lead to a break with the majority of his party. "Those of us who hold that the new policy advocated by Éamon de Valera is wrong in principle and disastrous in policy, can no longer support him as head of the government we believe in," MacSwiney wrote in a letter reporting on these events to her American friend, Charles Edward Russell. "For the President of the Republic to enter the Free State Parliament even if the oath were removed and by so doing tend to stabilize and sanction British rule in Ireland, would constitute a gigantic farce, and would give the lie to everything we have said since 1922."[32]

A vote of no confidence and de Valera's resignation from Sinn Féin in March was followed two months later by his announcement of the formation of a new political party, Fianna Fáil ("Warriors of Destiny"), which in the June 1927 Dáil elections thoroughly eclipsed the older republican party, winning forty-four seats to Sinn Féin's five. Faced with a new law that required all members of the Dáil to either sign the oath or give up competing in elections altogether, de Valera and the other newly elected Fianna Fáil deputies simply signed their names without reading the words, and in a "snap" election held that September, they strengthened their position further, winning fifty-seven seats with an astonishing 35 percent of the total votes cast. Cosgrave's party managed to hold on to power for another five years, but the Free State was now a functioning multiparty democracy. The achievement should not be minimized: men and women who had fought on opposing sides of the Civil War just five years earlier now fought out their differences in a parliamentary chamber rather than in country road ambushes or deadly artillery attacks. De Valera's new initiative had brought impressive results.

In the United States, support for the new initiative among most of those who considered themselves Irish republicans was also impressive. Mary MacSwiney had hoped against hope that the anti-Treaty AARIR would "stand firm" against de Valera's new policy and that an Irish Republic could yet be achieved, "with the help of God, and our own perseverance, in our own day and generation." But the majority of those in the American organization saw things differently; according to a report received by Fianna Fáil leaders, support for the new party in the AARIR was "overwhelming."[33]

Irish American nationalists both inside and outside the AARIR also provided financial support for de Valera's *Irish Press*, responding generously to his pleas in 1928 and 1929 for help in starting "a daily newspaper representing our views." The name of the paper that began rolling off the presses in September 1931 was taken from Joseph McGarrity's republican weekly published in Philadelphia in the tumultuous years from 1918 to 1922 and reflected the respect with which de Valera and his lieutenants treated Irish Americans, who were critically important to the paper's early success. In turn, the *Irish Press*, which was addressed mainly to Ireland's working people and made particularly effective appeals to women voters, played an important role in Fianna Fáil's electoral victory in 1932. Not surprisingly, de Valera, who would remain in power as taoiseach until 1948, continued Cosgrave's practice of giving annual radio addresses to the American Irish on St. Patrick's Day. Fianna Fáil, like Cumann na nGaedheal before it, relied on Irish America for both financial and moral support.[34]

So too did the IRA. The organization had "dumped," rather than surrendered, its arms at the end of the Civil War, and its Chief of Staff Frank Aiken announced that it would now "stand by as the situation develops." Another opportunity to overthrow the Cosgrave government never presented itself in the 1920s, but the IRA continued to exist as a body of mainly young, working-class men who were embittered by the results of the Civil War and felt bypassed by the economic policies of the Free State government. Overwhelmingly Catholic in composition (volunteers would sometimes salute when passing churches), the IRA's leadership was nonetheless sincerely committed to the nonsectarian credo lying deep within Irish republicanism, continuing the Fenian tradition of annual pilgrimages to the Bodenstown gravesite of the Protestant and militantly anti-sectarian republican Wolfe Tone, for example.[35]

More flexible ideologically than the republicans of Sinn Féin, many in the IRA greeted de Valera's new political initiative with enthusiasm. Aiken himself left the IRA to help found Fianna Fáil, becoming a trusted de Valera advisor, while many rank-and-file volunteers helped canvass voters in the elections of 1927, 1932, and 1933. Firmly committed to the constitutional path and believing the only legitimate force in any society could be that of the state, de Valera eventually turned against the IRA, arresting, interning, and even executing volunteers for various crimes and banning the organization outright in 1936. Faced with this kind of repression, along with a host of Fianna Fáil policies that undercut its appeal—once in power de Valera abolished the oath of faithfulness to the crown, waged a successful "economic war" against Britain, eliminated British naval bases from Irish ports, and in 1937, passed a new constitution that made Éire (as the twenty-six county Free State was rechristened) a republic in everything but name—and torn apart by its own ideological divisions, the IRA lost momentum in the later 1930s.

The IRA's main American support group, McGarrity's "reorganized" wing of the Clan na Gael, was not much better off. McGarrity, a successful Philadelphia businessman, never tired in his republican activism, continuing to bankroll a whole series of IRA initiatives—including a notorious bombing campaign in Northern Ireland and Britain in 1939—until his death in 1940. This undoubtedly had much to do with his origins: unlike Devoy, Cohalan, Golden, or any other major figure in the ranks of Irish American nationalism, McGarrity had emigrated from one of the six counties that was now part of Northern Ireland. His persistent and dedicated activism went far beyond revulsion at the symbolic oath of fidelity to the crown; for McGarrity the deeper problem was that *his* Ireland was just as much a part of what was now called the "United Kingdom of Great Britain and Northern Ireland" as it had been before the independence struggle. Moreover, Catholics, who constituted about a third of the population in the region, suffered under a highly discriminatory Unionist government, often called the Stormont regime after the imposing Parliament building that opened at Stormont, just outside Belfast, in 1932. This was, as Northern Ireland's Prime Minister James Craig put it baldly two years later, "a Protestant Parliament and a Protestant State." McGarrity probably felt he had no choice but to soldier on.[36]

The anti-Treaty Clan as a whole was in bad shape, experiencing considerable demoralization and a sharp decline in membership and financial contributions after the end of the Civil War. The "non spectacular nature" of the struggle in the 1920s and 1930s, in the view of one observer, led to feelings of "apathy and disgust" among some Clan members, a problem that the increasingly frustrated IRA leadership tried to combat by regularly sending envoys to the United States to reorganize and reinvigorate the body. The situation improved a bit in the later 1920s and early 1930s, as what one supporter called "new blood" in the form of young IRA veterans of the Civil War began emigrating to the United States, helping to revive the fortunes of the Clan in a number of locales, especially New York City. Mixing political discouragement at the outcome of the Civil War with economic hopes for a better life, these new immigrants were not classic political exiles—and some surely wanted to put Irish republicanism as far behind them as they could. But within their ranks were those who almost immediately gravitated to the Clan and helped revitalize it. For newcomers like Mike Quill, Gerald O'Reilly, and Michael Flannery, the Clan was probably as much a social and cultural resource as a political organization, a way for individuals typically from a rural background in the far west of Ireland to get their bearings in a sometimes overwhelming city of 5 million people.[37]

Even this new blood could not stop the hemorrhaging of the Clan na Gael. A massive public opinion backlash over the 1939 bombing campaign, persistent rumors about the IRA's discussions with representatives of Hitler's Germany as late as 1940, and McGarrity's death in June of that year all wreaked havoc on the organization. Across the political spectrum and across the pro- and anti-Treaty divide, Irish American nationalism lay in shambles as the Second World War approached.

Residual Influences

Nevertheless, Irish nationalism possessed a kind of residual influence in the United States during the Depression decade, if for no other reason than that so many Irish Americans in so many walks of life had been profoundly shaped by its core values during the years of (or preceding) the Irish revolution. The American labor movement provides perhaps the best example of this phenomenon. Irish American workers, who had long occupied leadership positions in the craft unions of the American Federation of Labor, also played an important part in the industrial union upsurge of the 1930s, which brought millions of new mass production workers into the labor movement and culminated in the founding of the Congress of Industrial Organizations (CIO) in 1938. The experience of CIO organizing marked a political "coming of age" for immigrant workers from a variety of backgrounds and places: Jews and Italians in the East, Poles and Slavs in the Midwest, Mexicans in southern California. But it was often the Irish, industrial pioneers with the deepest experience in the labor movement in America or abroad, who emerged as leaders of the new unions.[38]

One of these was John Brophy; he had been a leading progressive figure in the United Mine Workers (UMW) in Pennsylvania during the 1920s, advocating the formation of an independent labor party and the nationalization of the coal industry before losing the 1926 election for the UMW presidency to John L. Lewis. A decade later, Lewis hired Brophy as national director of the newly created Committee for Industrial Organization, and he went on to play a critical role in the strikes and organizing drives of some of the most important of the new industrial unions, including the United Auto Workers, the United Rubber Workers, and the United Steel Workers. Other important Irish American labor leaders of the 1930s included James Carey and Albert Fitzgerald of the United Electrical Workers; Harry Bridges, a rank-and-file leader of the dramatic and bloody 1934 West Coast waterfront strike that gave birth to the International Longshoremen's and Warehousemen's Union; National Maritime Union leader

Joseph Curran; New York City's Transport Workers Union leader Mike Quill; and Philip Murray, Vincent Sweeney, and Joseph P. Molony of the United Steel Workers. Murray, who had been born in Lanarkshire, Scotland, to Irish immigrant parents, would succeed Lewis as president of the CIO in 1940. Experienced in the traditions, tactics, and ideals of organized labor, Irish American labor activists like these often became, as Carey and autoworkers' leader Walter Reuther later put it, "missionaries of industrial unionism."[39]

A variety of intellectual and political influences were at work on such individuals, inspiring them in some cases to devote their entire lives to work in the labor movement. For some, including Carey and Murray, Catholic social thinking played an important role, especially Pope Pius XI's 1931 encyclical calling on Catholics to build corporate associations in industries and professions for the common good, a stance that many working-class American Catholics interpreted as a mandate for industrial unionism. But an early exposure to Irish nationalism (in Ireland or the diaspora) played an important role in the political formation of a number of others. Brophy, for example, who had been born in 1883 in the industrial city of St. Helens, Lancashire, was strongly affected by the political outlook of his Irish immigrant father, a coal miner who was an enthusiastic supporter of Home Rule and the Irish Land League, and some of some of Brophy's earliest memories included visits to St. Helens by Michael Davitt and T. P. O'Connor, Liverpool's Irish Nationalist MP. After the family emigrated to Pennsylvania, Brophy would read Patrick Ford's *Irish World* aloud to his father, acquiring knowledge of the wider world from its coverage of contemporary labor and political issues but also entranced by the stories of Irish rebellion he found in its pages. "It might be a whole issue devoted to the story of Robert Emmet's effort to seize Dublin Castle in 1803, and of his capture, trial, and execution, with long quotations from his stirring speech on the scaffold," Brophy recalled in the 1960s. "Or I might read the story of the United Irishmen of 1798, the failure of the French troops to arrive in support of the rebellion, the capture of Wolfe Tone, and his suicide."[40]

Harry Bridges, born in Melbourne, Australia, in 1901, came from a more socially and ideologically mixed family background than Brophy. His father, Alfred Ernest Bridges, was a Protestant, a successful entrepreneur, and an enthusiastic supporter of the British Empire. His mother, Julia Dorgan Bridges, and her two sisters, Ellen and Beatrice, were of Irish background. They were not only devout Catholics but also dedicated Irish nationalists. After the Easter Rising, Julia Bridges vocally supported the Irish-born Archbishop Daniel Mannix's anticonscription campaign, and her teenage son absorbed her admiration for this charismatic "Australian Sinn Féiner." Though later events in Bridges's life also shaped his left-wing labor activism, these earlier experiences of Irish nationalism and anti-imperialism were extremely significant.[41]

For no figure was the connection between Irish nationalism and labor activism closer than for the New York Transport Workers Union (TWU) leader Mike Quill. Born in County Kerry in 1905, Quill grew up in a strongly republican family, reared on stories of Tone, Emmet (the youngster would weep when his father recited Emmet's speech from the dock to him), Parnell, and, especially, Michael Davitt and the Land League. "Years later I understood that the Land League was actually a trade union of Irish tenants," he told his wife, Shirley, in the 1960s. As a teenager, Quill joined the Fianna Eireann, the nationalist youth organization founded by the republican activist Countess Markievicz, and he later fought with the IRA in both the independence struggle and the Civil War. Like many other anti-Treatyites who foresaw a bleak economic and political future in the Free State, he emigrated to the United States, settling in New York where he eventually found work with the Interborough Rapid Transit Company, which ran the city's subways. He joined the anti-Treaty Clan na Gael along with a number of other Irish societies, and when layoffs and pay cuts in the early 1930s triggered discontent among New York transit workers, Quill quickly emerged as the key union organizer, working closely with the Communist Party activists who initiated the union drive, while effectively reaching out to the many Irish transit workers he knew from the Clan and other Irish organizations. The Transport Workers Union was founded in April 1934 and the following December Quill was elected president, bringing the union into the CIO in 1937. Heading a union with 30,000 members and with a series of successfully negotiated union contracts behind him, Quill became an important political figure in New York and was elected to the New York City Council from the Bronx in November 1937. Though (like Harry Bridges on the West Coast) Quill consistently denied being a member of the Communist Party, he remained ideologically close to the party into the postwar years, once proclaiming that he would "rather be called a Red by the rats than a rat by the Reds."[42]

Irish American labor leaders could be found on both sides of the fight over communism that tore the CIO apart after the war and led to the expulsion of nine allegedly "Communist-dominated" unions in 1948. Bridges, at one time the West Coast head of the CIO, was expelled that year, along with his union. Quill moved in a different direction, breaking with the communists in 1948 and (working closely with CIO president Philip Murray and New York mayor William O'Dwyer) defeating an opposing group of TWU officials who fought to retain their communist connections. Quill went on to become a CIO national vice president in 1950, though he soon moved to the left again, criticizing Joe McCarthy's anti-communist crusade and calling for the founding of an American labor party.

A more representative Irish American labor leader than either Bridges or Quill was Murray himself, who supported Harry Truman's foreign and domestic policies and helped engineer the 1955 merger with the American Federation of Labor. Also representative was the leader of the new AFL-CIO, a third-generation Irish American named George Meany, who combined a kind of working-class Keyneseanism with a vigorous Cold War anti-communism that he championed well into the years of the Vietnam War, making the labor federation a byword for political conformity in an era of dramatic social change. Meany's childhood had shaped him in myriad ways, not only his father's union activism and his parents' Catholicism but also the Irish nationalist movement that swept over his Bronx neighborhood just as he was reaching adulthood in the early 1920s. "The lessons I learned in the Bronx and the lessons I learned as the son of Irish forebears have stayed with me through the years," Meany said in 1976. "The yearning for freedom—the insistence on human dignity—are forever enshrined as part of the Irish character." The implications Meany drew from the Irish nationalist tradition were very different from those of Bridges or Quill, illustrating the tradition's central (if protean) role in the American labor movement.[43]

If an early exposure to Irish nationalism had shaped some of the country's most important labor leaders, it also played a role in the formation of that quintessential figure of twentieth-century Irish American life, the big city politician. Though World War I–era Irish nationalists never managed to interest New York's young reform-minded mayor, John Purroy Mitchel, in the cause to which his grandfather, the Young Ireland exile John Mitchel, had devoted much of his life, William O'Dwyer, who was mayor of the city from 1945 to 1950, was a different matter altogether. A native of County Mayo, O'Dwyer had emigrated to the United States in 1910. He participated in a wide range of Irish (including Irish nationalist) organizations and did a stint in the 1920s as the promoter of the Free State's national Gaelic football team's annual tours of the United States, work that endeared him to many of the city's Irish American population. Meanwhile, one of the most famous of all such Irish American politicians, Thomas P. ("Tip") O'Neill, who would end his career as the Speaker of the US House of Representatives, grew up in a heavily Irish section of North Cambridge, Massachusetts, "where the old timers still spoke Gaelic." Though only a small child at the time of Terence MacSwiney's 1920 hunger strike, O'Neill still remembered it vividly sixty-five years later, probably because he was taking lessons in Gaelic and Irish step dancing from MacSwiney's sister-in-law at the time. "And each year on Easter Sunday, men in our neighborhood would go from door to door, collecting money for the Irish Republican Army," he recalled in his 1987 autobiography, adding somewhat defensively that "in those days, of course, the IRA was a very different organization from what it is today; back then, it simply stood for the united freedom of Ireland."[44]

World War II and the Postwar Years

Whatever residual power Irish American nationalism might have possessed in the labor or political arenas could not stop the long and steady decline of actually existing Irish nationalist organizations, which proceeded through World War II and into the postwar years. Such organizations were hurt badly not only by rumors of IRA-Nazi dealings, but much more significantly by Éire's decision to remain neutral during the war (or "Emergency," as the citizens of that nation euphemistically called it). Unlike Northern Ireland, which naturally participated in the war as an integral part of the British Empire (though British leaders avoided the introduction of military conscription in the Catholic, and still bitterly nationalist, working-class neighborhoods of Belfast and Derry), Éire took a very different course. With the British navy no longer in its ports and de Valera's 1937 constitution publicly announcing Éire's complete national sovereignty, neutrality became the most explicit statement of (southern) Irish independence imaginable. After all, of all the sovereign rights a nation state might possess, the right to make or not make war is surely the most fundamental. Neutrality became, for many, the very apotheosis of independence.

In practice, Éire's neutrality worked in favor of the Allies; 50,000 Irishmen traveled to Britain to sign up for military service unobstructed by the Fianna Fáil government, which provided clandestine intelligence support to the Allies as well. Allied aircrews that crash-landed in Éire were transported to Britain, while German crews were interned, and when Belfast was bombed in 1941, the government sent fire engines to assist. On the other hand, de Valera could sometimes carry the symbolism of neutrality to extremes. On May 2, 1945, the day that Irish papers carried the news of Adolf Hitler's suicide in a Berlin bunker, he made a personal visit to Eduard Hempel, the head of the German legation in Dublin, "to express his condolences." This particular gesture, which was not replicated by the leaders of other neutral democracies like Switzerland or Sweden and which came just months after the discoveries of Nazi death camps by Allied troops, set off a wave of angry criticism around the world, especially in the United States. "Moral myopia" was the not atypical verdict of the *Washington Post*.[45]

De Valera's Irish American supporters did the best they could with the difficult cards they had been dealt. As the war in Europe began, some did rally to help Éire preserve its neutrality, work that the taoiseach encouraged through his assistance in forming a new organization called the American Friends of Irish Neutrality (AFIN) in November 1940. But the first meeting of the group, held in New York on November 24, illustrated the kinds of strange bedfellows that organizing for neutrality at this point in American history was bound to produce: responding to the meeting's call were not only Irish American nation-alists, but also German American Bundists, members of Father Coughlin's proto-fascist Christian Front, assorted anti-Semites, and out-and-out supporters of Nazi Germany. The left-wing Paul O'Dwyer (the mayor's younger brother) tried to control the ensuing mayhem from the chair, but when he called on a Catholic priest in a desperate effort to calm things down, the clergyman added to the combustion by ignoring the issue of Irish sovereignty altogether in order to hurl assorted insults at Britain and Jews. That his lengthy diatribe triggered sustained applause from the floor only made matters worse.[46]

Gallup polls from this period, not surprisingly, showed significant support among non-immigrant Irish Americans (even those whose parents were Irish-born) for US war preparedness, making the AFIN's already uphill battle even more difficult. Given this, it is not surprising that the three main leaders of the AFIN were immigrants, all of them coming from the most traditionally republi-can areas of the island: Counties Kerry (Mike McGlynn), Cork (Séan Keating), and Mayo (O'Dwyer). The "American" part of the American Friends of Irish Neutrality's name should not be taken literally. Nor is it surprising that Pearl Harbor and the subsequent entry of the United States into the war ended any political future the body might have had: on December 12, 1941, less than a week after the attack, the executive committee of the AFIN decided to dissolve the organization.[47]

But the damage had already been done. Over and over, from the mid-nineteenth century onward, Irish American nationalists had argued that an inde-pendent Ireland would be a trustworthy friend and ally to the United States. But in what many saw as America's greatest hour of need, Éire had stayed away. And then there was de Valera's visit to the German minister in Ireland, the response to which revealed just how isolated from the mainstream of American life many Irish American nationalists had become. Though most Irish Americans undoubt-edly agreed with Washington, DC, resident Patrick Murphy, who wrote in a let-ter to the *Post* that "Irish-Americans, and Irishmen everywhere, will deplore De Valera's action," important leaders of what remained of the Irish nationalist movement in the United States launched a venomous counterattack on labor leader Mike Quill when he criticized de Valera for the visit. Quill, a committed anti-fascist, was admittedly intemperate in his comments, denouncing the tao-iseach for betraying the "desire for freedom and justice" exemplified by the lives of patriots from Wolfe Tone and Robert Emmet to James Connolly and Terence MacSwiney when he "plodded his way to the Nazi legation in Dublin City and there publicly shed tears over the reported death of Adolf Hitler." Though other factors were at play, including Quill's connections to the Communist Party and some long-brewing personal animosities among New York's Irish republicans, the response to Quill from the main leaders of Irish nationalism in the city was overwhelming: he was condemned by the United Irish Counties Association, the Gaelic Athletic Association, the Old IRA Association, the Bronx Irish American Citizens Committee, the Association of Catholic Trade Unionists, and the Wolfe Tone Council of the AARIR. "No English enemy of de Valera ever stooped so low," charged the Association of Catholic Trade Unionists, with the AARIR adding that Quill's remarks were "vicious and cowardly." Such organizations demonstrated a tin ear, to say the least, when they denounced Quill for comments that most Americans (and most Irish Americans) would have rushed to endorse.[48]

The harm done to Irish American nationalism by the IRA's British bombing campaign and Éire's decision to remain neutral during the war was accentuated by three important demographic trends that picked up speed in the postwar years. First, emigration from Ireland to the United States continued to fall, a trend that had begun with the onset of the Great Depression. The near total collapse of the American job market in the 1930s brought immigration from Ireland to the United States to a virtual halt and the perils of an Atlantic crossing during World War II (in contrast to a much safer migration to Britain, where thousands of new wartime jobs awaited) only served to solidify the pattern. When emigration to the United States began to revive again at the end of the war, it was at a significantly lower level. Britain, not the United States, was the primary destination for Irish emigrants in the postwar period. An era of Irish emigration had come to an end. And Irish American nationalism, which had depended on the "new blood" provided by exiles or politicized immigrants from its very beginnings in the 1790s, would apparently no longer be able to do so.[49]

Second, Irish America continued to improve its material conditions, a trend connected to the general prosperity and opportunity of the long postwar economic expansion. Statistics are not available for the third generation or beyond, but by 1950, 24 percent of even Irish-born men already held white-collar jobs (the professions, managers, clerks, and salesmen), while nearly 42 percent of second-generation men could be found in such occupations. Professional jobs, especially as accountants, clergymen, and lawyers, were particularly important in the occupational profile of second-generation men, while second-generation women were heavily represented in law, teaching, engineering, and clerical work. Irish immigrants—and particularly their children and grandchildren—were slowly moving up America's occupational ladder. This was not a story of "rags to riches" by any means, and even the second generation remained mainly working-class in the early 1950s, but the trend was clear enough. For Irish American nationalists, who, from the days of the Famine onward, had tapped into the economic hardships and deprivation experienced by Irish immigrants—even as they usually eschewed more radical economic ideologies—the handwriting on the wall was there. American prosperity was a powerful balm for Irish America's "fanatic heart."[50]

Third, postwar federal policies that encouraged highway construction, home ownership, and affordable mortgage financing for white Americans opened up the entirely new vista of suburbanization for many Irish Americans, especially in the second generation and beyond. The concentration of most recent Irish immigrants in America's urban areas persisted and New York City remained the largest single Irish city in the country, as it had been for many decades. But for the later generations—the children, grandchildren, and great-grandchildren of immigrants—the new suburbs beckoned. As they left the concentrated Irish neighborhoods of large cities or industrial mill towns, they also left behind the dense web of ethnic and religious institutions that had nurtured both Irish nationalism and its rich memories of its own history of struggle. Tom Hayden, a third-generation Irish American and leader of the American New Left, who was born in Detroit in 1939 but grew up in suburban Royal Oak, Michigan, would later describe his childhood as "growing up unconscious" in relation to the history of Irish nationalism. Though he had been told that he had been named after a famous Irishman, young Thomas Emmet Hayden had no idea who that Irishman was.[51]

Small groups of Irish American activists, representing both constitutional and revolutionary traditions, continued to labor on into the postwar era. A group calling itself the American League for an Undivided Ireland, formed in New York in March 1947, lobbied Congress over the question of partition and worked "to awaken American public opinion as to the justice of Ireland's right to complete freedom." The League's efforts were given a boost by de Valera's speaking tour of the United States the following year, part of Fianna Fáil's international anti-partition campaign that also took its leader to Britain, Australia, New Zealand, and India. But though de Valera was greeted with a huge parade in New York and enthusiastic crowds in Boston, Chicago, Detroit, Los Angeles, San Francisco, and Philadelphia, the tour was a political failure, with the British Dominions Office reporting that it "had little effect in influencing general United States opinion on the partition question." Irish politics, the departing British ambassador to the United States observed, had "seem to have ceased to be an issue of the moment to the mass of Americans."[52]

The failure of de Valera's anti-partition campaign was one of the factors leading to a period of renewed armed struggle in Northern Ireland. Clan na Gael members in New York tried to give public support to the IRA during "Operation Harvest," its disastrous border campaign, which lasted from 1956 to 1962—unsurprisingly since the campaign's central military strategist was a returned emigrant and one-time Clan member, Séan Cronin. Other New Yorkers participated in clandestine efforts to ship arms to the organization in those years, holding out-of-door meetings at sites like Thomas Addis Emmet's memorial at St. Paul's churchyard in lower Manhattan and Matilda Tone's gravesite in Brooklyn's

Green-Wood Cemetery to avoid federal surveillance. In Easter Week 1961, the Clan, in conjunction with an organization called the IRA Veterans of America, Inc., issued what its authors must have viewed as an inspiring statement to the youth of Ireland, a kind of passing of the torch from these elderly Irish Americans and Irish political exiles: "Young Irishmen: You are the standard-bearers of the Flag of the Irish Republic."[53]

But the time when such rhetoric could bring crowds to their feet had long since passed. Operation Harvest sputtered to an end in February 1962, with the IRA complaining about the lack of support in Northern Ireland. Austin Currie, a young Northern Irish Catholic and nationalist, was not alone in believing that "it was the end of them for all time as a force in politics!" A similar situation existed in America. In November 1963, IRA leader Cathal Goulding traveled to Philadelphia to attend the Clan na Gael convention, but the organization that he encountered was a shadow of its former self, weak in members, funds, and energy. When Irish taoiseach Seán Lemass visited Philadelphia that year, only five Clan supporters turned out to protest his visit, and a protest at United Nations headquarters in New York the following year brought out only fifteen. In the early 1960s, the FBI cut back on its surveillance of the organization, refer-ring in its memoranda to its "lack of activity."[54]

Few serious students of American life would have disagreed with the sociolo-gist Daniel Patrick Moynihan, when he offered his sweeping verdict on the state of Irish American nationalism in 1963: "Its dogmas no longer dominate; its divi-sions no longer interest; its institutions no longer direct the patterns of life." The Irish nationalist movement in the United States, so important to both Ireland and America for so many decades, had finally come to the end of the line.[55]

Or so it seemed.

The American Connection, 1966–1998

Less than a decade after Moynihan penned his obituary for Irish American nationalism, the landscape had changed dramatically. By 1972, a reinvigorated Irish republican movement was attracting hundreds of American supporters and collecting thousands of dollars for the organization that had inherited the mantle of physical force Irish nationalism, the Provisional Irish Republican Army (PIRA). Opposing republicanism at every turn was a transformed and dynamic constitutional nationalist movement (among whose supporters would soon be found Moynihan himself) that was working to bring American policy and public opinion behind the evolving political strategy of the Irish government. Even small groups of left-wing Irish American activists appeared on the scene, drawing inspiration both from the Irish socialist republican tradition personified by James Connolly and from the New Left and African American freedom struggle. The different wings of this reinvigorated Irish American nationalism had their ups and downs over the last three decades of the twentieth century, but taken together, they played a central role in shaping what was the perhaps most astonishing development of this entire history: the sustained and concerted effort, at the highest levels of the US government, to help bring Ireland to a lasting peace.[1]

The Emergence of the Troubles

How could such a remarkable change have occurred in the fortunes of Irish American nationalism, which had seemed all but dead in 1966? The key was the outbreak of the so-called Troubles in Northern Ireland, though "troubles" is an inadequate term for what actually occurred. Between 1966 and the end of 1998, the Northern Irish conflict took the lives of more than 3,600 people, in a region of fewer than 1.5 million. Car bombings, political assassinations, and sectarian killings made Northern Ireland infamous in these years, as did the armed

robberies, knee-capping, and other forms of intimidation practiced by both loyalist and republican paramilitary groups. The British army and Northern Irish
security forces, too, acted in ways that gave the British government a grisly reputation among human rights advocates: the internment without trial of suspected
paramilitaries between 1971 and 1975; the 1972 killing of fourteen unarmed
civilian demonstrators by troops from a British parachute regiment; the use of
torture, no-jury courts, and paid informers to obtain quick convictions of suspected paramilitaries; and cases of collaboration between British security forces
and loyalist assassination squads in the murder of republican sympathizers.
These were not "troubles" but a full-fledged civil war.[2]

This war emerged, paradoxically, from the ashes of what had initially been
a nonviolent civil rights movement (modeled partly on the African American
civil rights movement) that had struggled to transform the deep structural
inequalities that existed in Northern Ireland in the 1960s, especially in the areas
of jobs, housing, and the franchise. It is important not to overstate the parallels between the experiences of the Catholic minority in Northern Ireland and
African Americans in the Jim Crow South: Northern Ireland's Unionist majority never resorted to a "lynch law," nor did it disenfranchise Catholics with the
brutal efficiency of political elites in states like Alabama or Mississippi. There
was, however, something more than just individualized anti-Catholic prejudice
at work in Northern Ireland that made parallels between the two "closed societies" seem reasonable.[3]

Economic inequality between Protestants and Catholics, far from accidental,
was woven into the fabric of Northern Irish society. Catholics, who resided in
greater numbers in the western counties of the region, were adversely affected
by the location of most industries in the east (especially in and around Belfast),
which was considerably more Protestant and Unionist than the west. Every time
the Stormont government made a decision about where to locate new industries
or economic activities, it had the possibility of either modifying or reinforcing
this pattern, but it consistently favored the east. Between 1949 and 1963, areas
with Catholic majorities received only about three-quarters of the amount of
new employment awards enjoyed by Protestant areas. A direct consequence of
such decisions was not just the persistence of regional inequality but a growing
disparity in employment between the more industrialized (and Protestant) eastern part of Northern Ireland and the less developed (and Catholic) west.[4]

Beyond regional inequality, there was an observable and deeply entrenched
pattern of direct discrimination in the private sector, especially when it came to
better paying skilled jobs. Statistics for 1972, for example, indicated that almost
one-third of Catholic men were unskilled, and taken as a group, Catholic men
were twice as likely to be unskilled as Protestant men. Though low-paid industrial jobs were available for Catholic women in cities like Derry, unemployment

was generally much more acute among Catholics than among Protestants. Even after the reform of employment laws in the 1970s and 1980s, substantial differences remained.[5]

Since this private sector discrimination had long been systematically encouraged by the Unionist regime that controlled Northern Ireland (Basil Brooke, Northern Ireland's prime minister from 1943 to 1963, had once famously made a direct appeal to "those people who are Loyalists not to employ Roman Catholics, 99 per cent of whom are disloyal"), it is not surprising that anti-Catholic discrimination was deeply entrenched in the public sector as well. Catholics were almost totally excluded from the security services, such as the Royal Ulster Constabulary (RUC) (where they never represented more than 10 percent of the uniformed personnel) and entirely excluded from the all-Protestant part-time police force, the B-Specials. The civil service employed few Catholics, especially at the higher levels (only one Catholic permanent secretary could be found in the civil service in the late 1950s), and local councils (if they were Unionist controlled, which they usually were) sometimes excluded Catholics from municipal jobs altogether. As late as the mid-1960s, the Derry municipal government employed 177 workers, of whom only 32 were Catholic. A 1969 investigation into the causes of the outbreak of violence the previous year conducted by a Scottish judge, Lord John Cameron, for the Northern Irish government itself, cited example after example where Unionist-controlled councils used their power to hire in ways that benefited Protestants and harmed Catholics. "This would appear to be a very clear case of sectarian and political discrimination," the Cameron report concluded.[6]

Discrimination was equally apparent in the area of housing. To be sure, both Catholic and Protestant working-class communities had long suffered poor housing conditions, partly because local councils were generally reluctant to build any kind of public housing. Only 50,000 new houses were built between the two world wars, for example.

But in the years after the end of World War II, discrimination actually increased, as competition arose between Catholics and Protestants for new public housing, which was allocated by mainly Unionist-controlled local councils. There was a clear willingness by these councils to allow Catholics to continue to reside in older slum dwellings, so despite being the poorer sector of the population, Catholics were less likely to be rehoused. A good deal of arbitrariness in housing allocation was reflected in the decisions of local councils, but beneath this arbitrariness, the primary aim of local councils often appeared to be the preservation of residential segregation.[7]

As with the jobs situation, evidence for housing discrimination was not hard to come by. Of the more than 1,000 public housing units constructed in County Fermanagh between 1945 and 1967, for example, approximately 82 percent were allocated to Protestants, even though Catholics represented a majority of the population. In Dungannon, a medium-sized town in County Tyrone with a Catholic majority, every one of the nearly 200 new houses built in 1965 was allocated to a Protestant. Particularly galling was the allocation of homes to rehouse single Protestants, at the expense of Catholic families. In June 1968, the Dungannon Rural District Council decided to bypass a Catholic family that had been waiting for a number of years in favor of a single, nineteen-year-old Protestant woman, who was also the secretary of a local Unionist politician; this case led to widespread outrage and triggered protests including that of Austin Currie, a Nationalist member of the Stormont assembly, who physically occupied the house until he was removed by the police. According to the Cameron report, the incident expressed "in concentrated form . . . the objections felt by many non-Unionists to the prevailing system of housing allocations." Again, slum conditions and dilapidated housing affected both communities, but discrimination worked to make it much more likely that Protestants could escape such conditions over time.[8]

Egregious as was the situation in jobs and housing, the most overt examples of discrimination were found in the area of electoral practices. In part, this discrimination was built into the very fabric of the Northern Irish state, since a Protestant and Unionist majority had been deliberately created when Northern Ireland's boundaries were drawn, and it could not be overturned through normal democratic means. But at least under the conditions of Britain's 1920 Government of Ireland Act, elections in Northern Ireland were supposed to be conducted using a system of proportional representation, designed to give some kind of political voice to the nationalist minority. As early as 1922, however, the Unionist government had abolished proportional representation in local elections in favor of a "first-past-the-post" system; seven years later, that system was put into place for the Northern Irish Parliament as well, virtually guaranteeing the perpetuation of single-party Unionist control.[9]

Voting qualifications at the local level were also based on financial criteria, which worked to systematically disenfranchise many poorer Catholics. Since only ratepayers and their spouses could vote, many Catholics had no right to vote in local elections at all. On top of this, Catholics were also disadvantaged by the existence of what were called "business franchises," under which businesses could hold up to six extra votes, cast by people that the business owners nominated. Since Protestants more frequently owned businesses than Catholics, this also systematically favored them. The level of Catholic disenfranchisement at the local level could be seen in the contrasting size of the overall electorate for local and Stormont and British parliamentary elections. While the total number of voters for the Stormont or Westminster constituencies throughout the period was about 900,000, for local elections it was only about 600,000.

On top of everything else was the practice that the residents of Northern Ireland called "gerrymandering," the manipulation of electoral boundaries to effectively reinforce Unionist electoral dominance, especially at the local level. Local district boundaries were devised to ensure Unionist council majorities, even in mainly nationalist areas. Most notorious was the example of Derry, where for years a Unionist-dominated local council governed a city with a substantial Catholic majority. Towns like Dungannon and Omagh also had solid Catholic majorities—and Unionist-controlled local councils. By the early 1960s, in fact, Unionists controlled 85 percent of Northern Ireland's local councils, even though the Unionists amounted to just two-thirds of the voting population.

For Catholics, the situation seemed utterly hopeless. The few Catholic members of the Stormont assembly, mainly members of the ineffectual Nationalist Party, complained, but there seemed little that could actually be done. Deserted by Irish nationalists in the Republic, as well as most British politicians, who simply turned a blind eye to their situation, some of the handful of Nationalist members of the Northern Irish Parliament simply stopped showing up for sessions. Constitutional nationalism, in the form of the Nationalist Party, had proved a dead end, but so too had its historic antagonist, physical force republicanism. The Irish Republican Army made one last attempt in this vein, with the border campaign that began in 1956 and led to the deaths of eighteen people and the internment of numerous IRA volunteers. But the campaign petered out long before the IRA officially ended it, in 1962, with a statement lamenting the lack of support from the nationalist community in Northern Ireland.[10]

In such circumstances, the apparent failure of both constitutional and republican nationalism to alter the deep patterns of discrimination in Northern Ireland, those seeking change began a search for some other kind of model, a "third road." Given the long connections that existed between Irish and Indian nationalisms, it is not surprising that some looked to the strategy of nonviolent direct action that had been pioneered by Gandhi in India. In 1948, Eddie McAteer, an up-and-coming figure in the Nationalist party, proposed just such a policy of nonviolent action for Northern Irish Catholics. "Most Irish people who are active in seeking freedom used to believe that it would come to us by force of either constitutional agitation or by violence," McAteer observed. "Then the mighty spirit of the late Mahatma Gandhi pointed a third road—non-co-operation, non-violence. Maybe we could follow that road and be proud to draw inspiration from its pioneer."[11]

Little immediately came of this Irish nationalist effort to emulate the Indian independence movement. But by the early 1960s there was another, even more powerful, example of a "third road" at hand: the unfolding African American civil rights movement across the Atlantic. Inspired by its achievements in what seemed like an even more unpromising context, some Northern Irish activists began to draw rhetorical parallels between the struggles of African Americans and their own situation. In Derry's Springtown Camp, a World War II–era US Navy base that was populated by impoverished Catholic families squatting in abandoned tin huts, for example, a group of activists fighting for more equitable allocation of public housing marched in January 1963 behind a placard with the slogan, "Springtown—Derry's Little Rock," a reference to the 1957 school desegregation fight in Arkansas.[12]

Republicanism was not entirely dead, of course. In the same year that Derry housing activists paid homage to the nonviolent civil rights movement in America, other activists in Ireland were marking the bicentenary of the birth of Theobald Wolfe Tone by commemorating the man they considered, in the words of one Belfast organizer, the "father figure of Irish Republicanism." Some of those involved in the commemoration went on to organize "Wolfe Tone Societies," including a particularly active one in Belfast that strove "to foster republicanism by educating the masses in their cultural and political heritage." Though these were small groups (the Belfast society never had more than a dozen members, for example), they went on to commemorate the 200th anniversary of the birth of Ulster Presbyterian United Irishman, Henry Joy McCracken, and the centenary of the birth of James Connolly. As in previous eras in the history of Irish nationalism, memories of the past were tethered to the needs of the present.[13]

The commemoration of what was by now the most important republican event of all occurred three years later, with the fiftieth anniversary of the Easter Rising. Though 1916 commemorations also occurred in 1966 in Dublin and in such traditional centers of diasporic politics as New York and San Francisco, these turned out to be sedate affairs, hardly surprising given the decline of Irish nationalism in these locales by the mid-1960s. In Belfast, by contrast, an estimated 70,000 people watched or participated in a parade up the Falls Road on April 17, the main artery of the city's Catholic working-class community, with marchers waving Irish tricolor flags and triggering (among other unintended consequences) the creation of a new loyalist group calling itself the Ulster Volunteer Force (UVF)—the name taken from the organization that had been at the center of the fight against Home Rule back in the 1910s. Loyalists as well as nationalists, it seemed, looked to history for legitimacy. By the end of the year, this new UVF had carried out three killings, generally regarded as the first deaths of the modern Troubles.[14]

In the mid-1960s, it was neither republicans nor loyalists who were gaining momentum. It was rather the new civil rights movement. In 1964, an organization called the Campaign for Social Justice was founded, drawing on mainly middle-class Catholics in Dungannon and headed by Patricia McCluskey and her husband, Dr. Conn McCluskey, who spent many hours of their time documenting examples of discrimination, gerrymandering, and unfair housing allocation by local government and its administrative agencies. Responding to this initiative within Northern Ireland, a group of Labour Party backbenchers in the British Parliament calling themselves the Campaign for Democracy in Ulster came into being the following year, seeking to end the long parliamentary gag rule on human rights abuses in the province.[15]

There was much more still to come. Led and supported by what was Northern Ireland's first generation of Catholic university students and graduates, the first to benefit from the dramatic expansion of higher education in the United Kingdom (particularly the 1947 Education Act, which provided grants and scholarships for post-secondary education), the Northern Irish civil rights movement gradually gained confidence and embarked on new projects. In January 1967, activists representing a wide range of views, from left-wing republicans and socialists to more moderate trade unionists and professionals, organized the Northern Ireland Civil Rights Association. Carefully avoiding the traditional republican demand for an end to partition, this group instead called for the extension of all established British rights to Northern Irish Catholics; more concretely, their demands included implementation of "one man-one vote" in local elections, the abolition of the Special Powers Act (which had been central to the Northern Irish security apparatus since the 1920s), and the disbanding of the sectarian B-Specials. Significantly, their demands did not include a united Ireland.[16]

This organizational work came to fruition in 1968, a year of protest and reaction around the globe. The year brought huge anti-Vietnam war demonstrations in London in March, the assassination of Martin Luther King Jr. in Memphis in April, the May events in Paris that nearly brought down the French government, more anti-war demonstrations at the Democratic Party's Chicago convention and the Soviet invasion of Czechoslovakia (both in August), the killing of unarmed student demonstrators in Mexico City in October; an increasingly globalized media—and especially television—brought such events into the homes and into the imagination of activists and would-be activists in many locales throughout the world—including Northern Ireland, where on October 5, 1968, the civil rights movement in Derry held its first small march.[17]

Called to draw attention to grievances in the areas of jobs, housing, and electoral practices, the march was spearheaded by a band of mainly young political radicals (some of whom also identified themselves as Irish republicans), organized in a group called the Derry Housing Action Committee, with the official support of the more moderate Northern Ireland Civil Rights Association. Many Unionists vehemently opposed the march because its proposed route would take it into the heart of Protestant Derry (Unionists called it Londonderry), to the so-called Diamond, where only Protestants had historically been allowed to parade. William Craig, the hardline Unionist minister for home affairs in Northern Ireland, responded to their pressure by banning the march. A small number of activists gathered despite the ban, but they were trapped between police barricades and beaten and assaulted with fire hoses by the RUC in what is probably best described as a police riot. The whole scene was captured by a cameraman from Raidió Teilifís Éireann (RTÉ), the Irish Republic's television network, and broadcast on evening news programs throughout Ireland, Britain, Europe, and the United States. Anti-war demonstrators in Chicago had chanted two months earlier that the whole world was watching; now it was true for Northern Ireland.[18]

More protest—and much more violence—was to follow. In Belfast, another new organization called the People's Democracy, formed in October 1968 and consisting mainly of left-wing student activists at Queen's University, planned a week-long march from Belfast to Derry—one modeled explicitly on the Selma-to-Montgomery march that had helped win passage of the historic 1965 Voting Rights Act in the United States. The response from loyalists to this march was especially severe at Burntollet Bridge, near Derry, where on January 4, 1969, an organized group of 200 loyalists attacked the demonstrators with rocks, bricks, and iron bars. Things went from bad to worse in the spring of 1969 and, as summer approached, many feared that deadly violence was to come. Loyalist rioting (sometimes abetted by the RUC or the hated B-Specials) began in Belfast in the early summer, even before the start of the traditional Protestant marching season, when the Orange Order and related organizations commemorated William of Orange's 1690 victory over the Catholic James II. Though its volunteers had long seen themselves as the protectors of the nationalist community, the Irish Republican Army in the city had few members or weapons and was in no position to provide effective protection. As it turned out, only a last-minute decision of the British government to send troops onto the streets of Belfast and Derry shielded Catholics from a deadly explosion of loyalist violence. Belfast Catholics quipped later that the letters "IRA" stood for "I ran away." British troops, not the IRA, had saved the Catholic community, a fact noted with great bitterness among some IRA volunteers, especially those already unhappy with the organization's shift under Cathal Goulding's leadership away from physical force and toward a Marxist-influenced strategy of reaching out to the Protestant section of Northern Ireland's working class. In nationalist Belfast, recalled one veteran republican, "the name of the IRA was mud."[19]

A group of old–line republicans (not all of them old in years) began to plan what became a kind of coup within the organization. In December 1969 a group of Belfast republicans set up a secret organization they called the Provisional Army Council. The following month, at the annual Sinn Féin congress in Dublin, the split was exposed, with those calling themselves "Provisionals" walking out of the congress and forming a new organization, the Provisional IRA. They took the name not because they believed their organization would be temporary, but as a gesture toward the "Provisional Irish Republic" that had been declared in front of the Dublin General Post Office in 1916.[20]

The leaders of the new organization came from a range of backgrounds. Joe Cahill, who would be a central figure in forging a renewed American connection with Irish republicanism from this point until his death in 2004, had been born in Belfast in 1920 and had joined the IRA in 1938, serving seven years in prison in the 1940s for killing an RUC constable. Cahill was also interned for four years during the IRA's border campaign and after his release in 1961 he became increasingly dissatisfied with the leftward turn of his organization, recalling later his conclusion that "it was taking the wrong course, the wrong road." He was one of the handful of armed republicans fighting to defend Belfast's Catholics against loyalists in the summer of 1969, was an enthusiastic supporter of the PIRA walkout the following January, and would become a key figure in the new IRA's Army Council, its governing body. Other dissidents came from the diaspora itself. Seán Mac Stiofáin, the Provisional IRA's first chief of staff, had been born in England, with the birth name of John Stephenson. Mac Stiofáin's mother was Irish and he became active in Irish republican circles in London before he ever stepped foot in Ireland. Those born outside of Ireland, the children of the diaspora, apparently still had a role to play in Irish republican politics, as much as they had in the era of the Edinburgh-born Connolly or the New York-born de Valera. Meanwhile, the youthful Gerry Adams represented yet another variation: though inexperienced himself, he came from a much-honored Belfast republican family, with roots on both parents' sides going back to the Irish War of Independence.[21]

The new group began training and arming itself almost immediately, and by the summer of 1970 it was ready for action. In the violence and chaos associated with the loyalist marching season, the PIRA quickly made a name for itself through its armed defense of St. Matthew's Catholic Church against loyalist rioters in the Short Strand district of Belfast in June. It is unclear whether this was a spontaneous action, as IRA volunteers asserted at the time, or a carefully staged affair, designed to provide a positive public image for the organization. Either way, the "battle of St. Matthew's" went down in republican lore and attracted many new recruits to the organization. The IRA had not run away this time.[22]

The organization might have remained small, however, had it not been for three actions of British troops (and the British politicians who directed them) over the next two years. The first of these, coming just days after the St. Matthew's gun battle, was a thirty-five-hour curfew, from July 3 to July 5, imposed by British military authorities with strong Unionist support, on the lower section of the Falls Road. With house-to-house searches carried out with considerable brutality and leading to four civilian deaths, the Lower Falls curfew focused only on the Catholic community, which was suspected of harboring IRA volunteers and weapons, despite the fact that most of the street violence at this point was emanating from the Protestant working-class community. The second action, beginning on August 9, 1971, was the introduction of internment without trial for suspected paramilitary members. An old tactic employed by both Northern Irish and Irish Republic authorities, it was now directed by the British at the behest of the Northern Irish government and initially targeted only suspected IRA volunteers, not members of the loyalist paramilitary groups that were now begin to grow rapidly. The final blow was the January 1972 killing of thirteen unarmed Catholic civil rights demonstrators in Derry, who were protesting internment, by the members of a British parachute regiment. (A fourteenth demonstrator later died from his wounds.) These three events shattered much of the work of the nonviolent civil rights movement and, taken together, served almost as a recruiting poster for the IRA, which had already begun offensive operations. Northern Ireland was, by this point, far along in its descent into violence. The death toll for 1972 was nearly 500, making it the most deadly year of the conflict.[23]

Americans Respond

Across the Atlantic, Americans—and especially Irish Americans—began to respond to these events. Though few Americans had paid much attention to earlier efforts of the Northern Irish civil rights movement, the attention of US viewers was captured by the televised beating of unarmed demonstrators (some of them singing "We Shall Overcome," the anthem of the African American civil rights movement) in Derry in October 1968, and attitudes changed almost overnight. In late 1968, an American organization named the Committee for Justice in Northern Ireland appeared, organizing several chapters in New England, publishing a short-lived newspaper called *The Rising of the Moon*, and sending money to the movement in Northern Ireland that it raised at its weekly dances in the Jamaica Plain neighborhood of Boston. Meanwhile, in New York and several other cities, an organization called the Friends of the Northern Ireland Civil Rights Association emerged. Both of these groups reflected the new enthusiasm of left-wing activists, individuals not usually associated with Irish nationalism. New York lawyer Paul O'Dwyer was one such activist. An immigrant from County Mayo, O'Dwyer had been a leader in the efforts to defend Ireland's neutrality in 1940. Since then, most of his political activism had been with the left-wing National Lawyers Guild, which he headed in 1947, and in support of the movement for black equality; he worked with the National Association for the Advancement of Colored People in Jackson, Mississippi, and was a leading supporter of the Mississippi Freedom Democratic Party's challenge to the state's regular segregationist delegation at the 1964 Democratic convention. Now he leaped back into Irish affairs with passion.[24]

Small local and regional organizations soon gave way to larger national ones, the most important of which in this period was the American Congress for Irish Freedom (ACIF), which lasted until 1970. Founded by an Irish American Protestant lawyer from Buffalo named James Heaney, the ACIF established contacts with Conn and Patricia McCluskey and other activists in Northern Ireland and worked to bring attention to the civil and human rights abuses committed by the Stormont regime. While his Northern Irish civil rights contacts were generally to be found on the left end of the political spectrum, in the context of American politics, Heaney was solidly on the right. Reaching out to the Franco regime in Spain—he hoped that continuing Spanish-British tensions over Gibraltar would make that government sympathetic to the cause—Heaney was also adept at using potent anti-communist rhetoric as a weapon in his crusade. The ACIF denounced Britain not just for its role in Northern Ireland but also for "dealing with the commies" by sending medical supplies to North Vietnam. Heaney saw no contradiction between his anti-communism and his support of Catholic civil rights, maintaining that Northern Irish activists "seek a just society, not a red society."[25]

If new organizations like the ACIF seemed out of step with the generally left-wing orientation of much of the Northern Irish civil rights movement, older Irish American republican organizations appeared to be equally uncomfortable. Partly this was because the nonviolent strategy embraced by that movement seemed so foreign to their own physical force tradition. Equally troubling was the admiration that many in that movement continuously expressed for the African American freedom struggle. Derry's John Hume and other moderate civil rights leaders spoke frequently of their indebtedness to the fight against Jim Crow, and the Irish movement was beginning to adopt the American civil rights anthem, "We Shall Overcome," as its own. Other strands of the movement, represented by Michael Farrell, Bernadette Devlin, and the activists in the People's Democracy, were influenced by more radical currents in the black freedom struggle (such as the writings of Malcolm X and the model of the Student Nonviolent Coordinating Committee) and were already working to forge links with radical organizations like the Black Panther Party.[26]

The Northern Irish embrace of the black freedom struggle was deeply troubling to members of the most venerable of the Irish American republican organizations (which had just marked its centenary): the Clan na Gael. In March 1969, the Philadelphia branch of the organization agreed to carry a banner of the Northern Ireland Civil Rights Association in the city's annual St. Patrick's Parade—but only if the banner stated clearly that, as one of its members put it, "Clan na Gael was supporting civil rights in Ireland, not black civil rights in the

U.S." Northern Irish civil rights activist Austin Currie, touring the United States in the same month, found that Irish American crowds would walk out on him whenever he mentioned African American issues. The Northern Irish activists themselves had an explanation for these kinds of responses: Irish American racism. "We all knew that Irish Americans were deeply racist, or an awful lot of them were," the Derry civil rights activist Eamonn McCann recalled in an interview a quarter of a century later, "and there was something problematical about this emotional and ideological link between black American civil rights and civil rights here in Northern Ireland." Michael Farrell, the People's Democracy leader, was more blunt: "we didn't like Irish Americans because we saw them as racist bigots," he recalled.[27]

The ideological distance that separated Irish American and Northern Irish activists' political views was clearly illuminated in the tensions that accompanied Bernadette Devlin's American tour of August 1969. A well-known and highly telegenic leader in the Northern Irish movement, Devlin had been elected to the British Parliament from Belfast at the age of twenty-two and was originally welcomed by many leading politicians, much of the American media, and by Irish American organizations like the ACIF as well. But as her tour unfolded, tensions began to mount, not only triggered by her outspoken socialist beliefs (which came as a genuine surprise to many Irish Americans) but also by her efforts to reach out to African American groups ranging from Operation Bootstrap in the Watts section of Los Angeles to the Black Panthers in Chicago. Though some Irish Americans had hailed her as Ireland's "Joan of Arc" on her arrival in the United States, by the end of her tour she was being denounced as "Fidel Castro in a mini-skirt." Devlin ended her tour abruptly and angrily, borrowing money in the middle of a New Jersey dinner party in her honor and simply heading for the airport. Some months later she delegated Eamonn McCann to present a golden key to New York City, which Mayor John Lindsay had bestowed upon her during her visit, to the city's Black Panther chapter, "as a gesture of solidarity with the black liberation and revolutionary socialist movements in America." The gulf between Devlin and at least some of her Irish American hosts could not have been wider.[28]

Still, politically conservative organizations like the ACIF or the Clan na Gael did not speak for the entirety of Irish America, or even for the entirety of the Northern Irish civil rights support movement. By the late 1960s, that movement included not only old organizations like the Clan na Gael but also new groupings of young Irish Americans, many of them college students or recent graduates with roots in the New Left, such as Tom Hayden. In the fall of 1968, Hayden was awaiting trial for his role in the August anti-war Chicago demonstrations. Watching television on the evening of October 5, 1968, he experienced what he later called an "epiphany." As he saw Derry protesters "beaten into the ground, hosed with water cannons like civil rights demonstrators in our South," and "sing-ing 'We Shall Overcome,' " he suddenly felt an urge to embrace the Irish ethnic identity that his suburban parents had sought to escape. Believing that "these marchers were somehow kin to me," and that he himself could be "an American rebel not in spite of being Irish, but *because* of being Irish," Hayden was ready to embrace Northern Irish–related activism as consistent with his work for black equality and against the Vietnam War.[29]

The ranks of the Irish American New Left went far beyond a single individual. The first of several new left-wing Irish American organizations was founded in early 1969 by Brian Heron—a grandson of James Connolly no less—who was then living in the San Francisco Bay Area and had links with many local activists, including individuals working in Students for a Democratic Society, the Black Panthers, and the United Farm Workers, the Mexican American social movement then nearing the successful conclusion of its national grape boycott. In April of that year, Heron moved to New York and founded the National Association for Irish Justice (NAIJ), which, unlike the Clan na Gael or other even more mainstream Irish American organizations, was also vig-orous in its support for the black freedom movement. Growing directly out of the student radicalism that was characteristic of the later 1960s, the NAIJ claimed thirty-one chapters by the end of 1969, with particularly active groups at both Columbia University (already a New Left center) and—more surpris-ing perhaps—the Jesuit (and heavily Irish American) Fordham University in the Bronx.[30]

In addition to being caught off balance by the rapidly changing situation in Northern Ireland, especially the dramatic rise of the Provisional IRA, the NAIJ was plagued by the factional struggles then overtaking the American New Left as a whole, as supporters of the Black Panthers and the Trotskyist Socialist Workers Party vied with supporters of Students for a Democratic Society (SDS) (itself divided between rival Maoist factions) for control of the organization. The demise of the NAIJ, however, was not the end of left-wing Irish American activism. Many of the remnants of this organization eventually regrouped in two new ones. The first of these was the National Association for Irish Freedom (NAIF), which, even more than its predecessor, reached out to the African American civil rights movement, eventually counting both the Reverend Ralph Abernathy of the Southern Christian Leadership Conference and African American entertainer and activist Dick Gregory as vocal support-ers. The second was a network called the Irish Republican Clubs (IRC) of North America, which originated with loose groupings in New York, Boston, and San Francisco. The clubs eventually spread to a number of other cities, including Chicago, Philadelphia, Toronto, and Montreal. The IRC, as its name indicates, was an Irish American nationalist organization, not just a support group for the Northern Irish civil rights movement. In fact, the organization embraced the political "line" of the Official IRA (the group from which the Provisionals had split), which, after one last foray into paramilitary violence in 1972, declared a ceasefire and worked to further the cause of socialist revolution in Northern Ireland. The Irish Republican Clubs also kept a foot in the world of the North American left: they strongly supported African American civil rights, condemned the war in Vietnam, and expressed solidarity with African and Latin American liberation movements. The San Francisco Bay Area clubs, for instance, were active through nearly the end of the 1970s, engaging in activities that included everything from supporting local labor struggles to writing letters to California senators and representatives calling on them to oppose apartheid in South Africa. A strong Bay Area supporter of the IRC was the Reverend Cecil Williams, who opened the doors of his (mainly African American) Glide Memorial Church in 1975 for an IRC commemoration of Northern Ireland's Bloody Sunday.[31]

At its peak, this Irish American New Left probably embraced no more than several hundred people concentrated in just a handful of cities. In these years, the left on both sides of the Atlantic was greatly overshadowed by the rise of the old-style republican Provisional IRA and by its main American support group, the Northern Irish Aid Committee (usually referred to as Noraid), both of which the IRC opposed. It was Noraid, not the IRC, that would occupy center stage in the 1970s and through much of the following decade as well.

Republican and Constitutional
Nationalists Regroup

Noraid had been founded in 1970 by Michael Flannery, a veteran of the north Tipperary brigade of the old IRA, which he had joined in 1917 at the age of fifteen. Like many of his companions in that organization, he strongly opposed the 1921 Treaty and fought on the anti-Treaty side during the Irish Civil War. After the victory of the pro-Treaty forces, he was arrested and jailed in the Irish Free State for two years. Flannery broke with de Valera when the latter moved into mainstream Irish politics in 1927, and he emigrated to the United States in the same year. In America he immediately joined the McGarrity wing of the Clan na Gael, which worked for a renewal of the armed struggle to unify Ireland. The prospects for this seemed bleak for the next forty years, but with the renewed violence that followed the emergence of the Northern Irish civil rights movement in the late 1960s, and with the creation of the new Provisional IRA in 1970, Flannery believed he was seeing a resumption of the same struggle to which he had devoted his youth.[32]

Flannery's background does not appear to be unique among activists in Noraid, which in its early years especially was dominated by politically motivated immigrants who had come from Ireland in the 1920s ("political exiles" in an expansive definition of the term), particularly those who had fought on the losing anti-Treaty side during the Irish Civil War. Others were more recent emigrants from the Irish Republic or Northern Ireland, and, according to later interviews with veterans of the organization, there was a fairly widespread suspicion of Irish Americans among Noraid activists during the 1970s. Some of the American-born sons and daughters of such immigrants or exiles also played a part in the organization, but it would be a mistake to conclude that just because these younger people were American-born, they were fully set on an "Americanizing" path. A sense of separateness and alienation from American life, reminiscent of the Fenians or of John Devoy, characterized many of the early activists of Noraid, despite the range of their ages or place of birth.[33]

From the very the outset, Noraid was closely identified with the Provisional IRA. In fact, it had been formed following a meeting in the Republic of Ireland between Flannery and individuals who were at that moment in the process of bringing the Provisionals into being. Leaders of the group asked Flannery for help in supporting the families of the new IRA volunteers, some of whom were sure to be killed, arrested, or interned. Flannery was happy to provide this kind of assistance because he believed that one of the main reasons for the failure of the IRA's border campaign of 1956–62 had been the lack of support for the families of prisoners. His strong support for the Provisional IRA's campaign against the British presence made Noraid the most militantly republican of all the Irish American organizations taking an interest in the Northern Irish conflict. Supporting the Provisionals' campaign was the whole purpose of Noraid and, despite its leaders' constant denials, it seems likely that some of the funds it raised went directly into arming the PIRA. At least one of the Provisionals' leaders, Daithi O'Connaill, asserted in 1971 that his organization's defense of Belfast's St. Matthew's Church the previous June had been due "in no small measure, to the positive practical support" of Noraid. Noraid's fortunes, like those of its PIRA ally, soared as Northern Ireland descended into violence. With the Lower Falls curfew, the introduction of internment, and—especially—Bloody Sunday on January 30, 1972, many Americans made generous contributions to its coffers. According to US Justice Department records, in the six months following the shootings, Noraid collected $313,000, more than two-and-one-half times its take for the previous six months and perhaps its all-time high. By this time, the organization had active chapters in New York, Philadelphia, Boston, Chicago, and San Francisco.[34]

Bloody Sunday was an international disaster for the British government, generating intensely angry responses that went far beyond the small ranks of

Irish American republicans. Upon hearing the news of the killings, Bernadette Devlin stormed across the floor of the House of Commons and scratched the face of the British Home Secretary, while the government of the Irish Republic immediately recalled its ambassador to Britain. A few days later, an angry crowd in Dublin burned the British embassy to the ground. Sydney, Australia, witnessed a protest march of 5,000 people, while Gough Williams, the Australian Federal Opposition leader, denounced Britain for creating a "catastrophic" situation in Northern Ireland. In New York, large demonstrations were also held, one of them attended by the popular rock musicians John Lennon and Yoko Ono, who donated the proceeds of a protest song that Lennon quickly wrote, "The Luck of the Irish," entirely to Noraid. Immersed in the movement against the war in Vietnam (and targeted for deportation by the Nixon administration for that reason), Lennon may have subsequently provided funds directly to the IRA, though Ono has always strenuously denied this allegation. But in the wake of Bloody Sunday, even mainstream Irish American politicians with no connections to either Irish republicanism or the New Left strongly denounced the British government, sometimes even demanding an end to partition. Hugh Carey, who represented parts of Brooklyn in the US House of Representatives, called for a consumer boycott of British goods, and in late February, Senator Edward Kennedy of Massachusetts opened hearings before the Senate's Foreign Affairs Subcommittee on Europe by comparing Bloody Sunday to the 1968 My Lai massacre in Vietnam. "Just as Ulster is Britain's Vietnam," he angrily asserted, "so Bloody Sunday is Britain's My Lai."[35]

As the 1970s wore on, however, the attitude of many Irish Americans toward the Northern Irish conflict began to change. A seemingly endless series of atrocities committed by the Provisional IRA (twenty IRA bombs killed nine Belfast civilians and injured 130 in just over an hour on July 21, 1972—"Bloody Friday"—for example) led to a sharp drop in Irish American support for the armed struggle, and contributions to Noraid began falling steadily. Moreover, under the influence of Northern Ireland's new Social Democratic and Labour Party (SDLP), which by the mid-1970s was the primary expression of a reinvigorated constitutional nationalism and of the Irish government itself, mainstream Irish American politicians like Kennedy began backing off from their angrier denunciations of Britain or demands for immediate Irish unification.[36]

Little over a year after its founding in August 1970, the SDLP's first leader, Gerry Fitt (with financial backing from the Irish government), made the party's first official visit to the United States, meeting with Irish American politicians as well as with United Nations officials in an effort to bring pressure on Britain to end internment. In the wake of Bloody Sunday, the American connection became even more critical to the party, since it was at great pains to present its nonviolent electoral approach as an alternative to the PIRA's campaign of armed struggle. To advocate this approach, the SDLP's John Hume made a weeklong visit to the United States in March 1972. From this point onward, Hume was a frequent visitor to America, making political (as well as personal) connections with Kennedy and New York's Senator Daniel Patrick Moynihan, in particular, and exerting such a profound influence on the attitudes of Congress that Kennedy dubbed him "the 101st Senator from Northern Ireland."[37]

The Irish government waged a war for the hearts and minds of Irish America as well, taking a firm anti-republican position in all of its American activities. Sean Donlon, Ireland's ambassador to the United States in these years, was particularly effective in lobbying Irish American members of Congress, especially House Speaker "Tip" O'Neill, to take a modulated stance on Northern Ireland, pressuring Britain when necessary, but strongly opposing the slightest hint of physical force republicanism. Isolating those Irish Americans deemed "too green"—that is, naïvely supporting Noraid and the PIRA—was also part of the Irish government's strategy. Even figures like Paul O'Dwyer (better described as a left-leaning Irish civil rights advocate than an Irish republican) found themselves on the "undesirable" list for social events at Ireland's embassy and its New York consulate and, more important, excluded from the political conversation altogether.[38]

This ideological work in the United States, carried out by both the SDLP and the Irish government, brought its first results in a statement released on St. Patrick's Day, 1977, by a quartet of prominent Irish American politicians who would become known as the "Four Horsemen" (after the famous backfield of Notre Dame's 1924 football team): Senators Kennedy and Moynihan, Speaker O'Neill, and Hugh Carey, who had been elected governor of New York in 1974. Not surprising, given the tireless work of Hume and others on this point, the statement began by forthrightly condemning the Provisional IRA and calling on Americans to desist or avoid supporting it. But the four Democrats then called on Democratic President Jimmy Carter to take a firm stand for political reform and peace in Northern Ireland, which the president did in fact do the following August. In his own statement, Carter condemned violence, expressed support for a peaceful agreement involving the Irish government and the mainstream political parties in Northern Ireland (the Ulster Unionists and the SDLP), and promised a significant increase in US investment in Northern Ireland if such an agreement were to emerge. Though soon overshadowed by other events, Carter's statement marked an entirely new development in the US position on Irish affairs: for the first time, an American president had at least implicitly indicated that the Northern Irish situation was not simply the "domestic problem" of a long-term ally, Britain, but a legitimate concern of American foreign policy.[39]

More immediate possibilities for development along these lines, however, were shattered by three critical developments that occurred in the years from

1979 to 1981. The first was the election of Conservative Margaret Thatcher as British prime minister in 1979. Thatcher took a harder line in Northern Ireland than any of her predecessors, which had serious consequences for the prospects of a settlement to the conflict. The second was the election of Ronald Reagan to the White House in 1980. For the next twelve years of the Reagan and Bush administrations, the possibilities of an active American role in settling the conflict (the implication of Carter's 1977 statement) were almost totally foreclosed. The third event was the 1981 Northern Irish Hunger Strike, which gave physical force republicanism a massive shot in the arm while also (paradoxically) drawing Irish republicans into mainstream electoral politics.[40]

The Hunger Strike, triggered by the demand for "political status" for republican prisoners in the "H-Blocks" of Long Kesh Prison—and the absolute refusal of the Thatcher government to make this concession—eventually left ten prisoners dead while simultaneously creating yet more martyrs for a cause that, until that point, was visibly losing energy on both sides of the Atlantic. When the Hunger Strikers' leader, Bobby Sands, was elected to the British Parliament on the eve of his death, it created an international sensation, surpassing even that triggered by the hunger strike of Terence MacSwiney in 1920. In Belfast, more than 100,000 people turned out for Sands's funeral in May 1981. In the United States, Noraid and the Clan na Gael were the main beneficiaries of the largest outpouring of Irish American support for republicanism since the Irish War of Independence. Even the Ancient Order of Hibernians (AOH), the old and normally nonpolitical Irish American ethnic organization, was carried along by the tidal wave. When the AOH selected Noraid's Michael Flannery as the Grand Marshall of its 1983 New York St. Patrick's Day Parade, it was registering the extent of the shift that occurred, almost overnight. The Irish government and several prominent Irish American politicians registered their displeasure at the decision by boycotting the parade that year.[41]

The Beginnings of the Peace Process

Paradoxically, the Hunger Strike accelerated another kind of shift, within the Northern Irish republican movement itself. Already in 1980, Sinn Féin's leader, Gerry Adams, at his organization's annual Wolfe Tone commemoration, had signaled a desire to add an electoral dimension to the IRA's armed struggle. Bobby Sands's unexpected parliamentary victory on the eve of his death greatly facilitated this new direction, one summed up in the rousing speech given by Sinn Féin activist Danny Morrison three weeks after the Hunger Strike's conclusion. "Who here really believes we can win the war through the ballot box?" he asked the party's ard fheis (annual conference) attendees. "But will anyone here object if, with the ballot box in one hand and the Armalite [rifle] in the other, we take power in Ireland?"[42]

The new approach seemed to pay dividends almost immediately. In the British general election of 1983, Sinn Féin (which up until this point had been little more than the IRA's public mouthpiece), won 100,000 votes in Northern Ireland (over 40 percent of the province's Catholic vote) and elected Gerry Adams as an MP for West Belfast. In keeping with the traditional Irish republican position of abstaining from participation in British institutions, Adams did not actually take his seat. Subsequently, however, nearly sixty Sinn Féin representatives were elected to local councils throughout Northern Ireland, where they did take their seats and began to participate in local policymaking. Almost immediately, this new politics of republicanism began to create tensions and problems for the movement. The union of gun and ballot proved to be not quite as harmonious as Morrison had suggested. [43]

This could be clearly seen in the aftermath of one of the most tragic events of the Troubles. On the morning of Remembrance Sunday, November 8, 1987, an IRA bomb went off in the Fermanagh market town of Enniskillen just as large numbers of Protestant residents (many of them aging World War II veterans and their families) were beginning to assemble for an annual parade and service. Eleven civilians were killed and many more seriously injured, and the bombing (the "military" purpose of which was never clear) constituted a major setback for the republican movement. Enniskillen's recently elected Sinn Féin local councilor tried to express his condolences for the dead and injured members of his constituency, but when pressed by reporters he refused to denounce the IRA's right to engage in "legitimate" armed struggle.[44]

One senior IRA figure admitted to a journalist a few days later that Enniskillen was, in political terms, "a major setback" and predicted that "it will hurt us really badly in the Republic more than anywhere else." But in America too the effects of the Remembrance Day bombing were dramatic, partly because of the coincidence of its occurring during the US tour of an internationally popular Dublin rock band. U2 was scheduled to take the stage in Denver when its members learned of the Enniskillen bombing. In the middle of its song written to protest a British atrocity, "Sunday Bloody Sunday," U2's singer, Bono, launched into a soliloquy on the subject of Irish American attitudes toward the Northern Ireland conflict.

> I've had enough of Irish Americans, who haven't been back to their country in twenty or thirty years, come up to me and talk about the resistance, the revolution back home and the *glory* of the revolution, and the *glory* of dying for the revolution. Fuck the revolution! They don't talk about the glory of killing for the revolution. . . . Where's the

glory in bombing a Remembrance Day parade of old-age pensioners, the medals taken out and polished up for the day? Where's the glory in that? That leave them dying or crippled for life or dead under the rubble of the revolution, that the majority of the people in my country don't want. *No more!*

With the concert being filmed for *Rattle and Hum*, a documentary film about the tour that was released the following year, Bono's angry words were eventually heard by millions of rock fans, many of them young Irish Americans who were much more likely to be persuaded by him than a Kennedy or a Moynihan. Noraid, in particular, was badly damaged.[45]

By the mid-1980s, however, there was another important Irish American republican organization on the scene, one that was in some ways much more effective than Noraid. This was the Irish National Caucus (INC), a lobbying organization based in Washington. Though founded in 1974 partly at the suggestion of Noraid leaders, who wanted to counter their image as gunrunners for the IRA, the INC gradually shifted away from support for the armed struggle to a focused concentration on the issue of human rights. It achieved its first significant success when it persuaded Jimmy Carter, the Democratic nominee for president in 1976, to express a concern over British human rights violations in Northern Ireland, just six days before the election. The INC's most important leader by this time was a Northern Ireland-born Catholic priest, Father Sean McManus, who would become a central figure in Irish American nationalist circles.[46]

McManus led the fight in the 1980s and early 1990s for the implementation of the so-called MacBride Principles, one of the few clear successes of the Irish nationalist movement in America in this period. The roots of this campaign were two large developments that occurred in the 1980s, one in Northern Ireland and one in the United States. In Northern Ireland, it was the recognition on the part of many republican activists that the situation had reached a stalemate: even with no-jury courts, torture, and shoot to kill policies, the British Army could not destroy the IRA; and even with Armalites, money from America, and (beginning in the early 1980s) plastic explosives from Libya, the IRA could not drive the British out of Northern Ireland. This prompted the IRA and Sinn Féin to make a major reconsideration of their strategy and was one of the factors that prompted the latter's turn toward electoral politics.[47]

The other element that was new in the 1980s, which had a particularly large impact on Irish American activists, was the emergence of an American movement to end apartheid in South Africa. Americans—African Americans and others—had been fighting apartheid and an end to US support for the apartheid regime for a very long time, but activism moved to a new level with the Free South

Africa Movement. This movement began with the arrest of three important black political leaders (Randall Robinson, president of TransAfrica; US Congressman Walter Fauntroy; and US Civil Rights Commissioner Mary Francis Berry) after a sit-in at the South African Embassy in Washington in November 1984. This was the opening salvo of a campaign that quickly led to hundreds of sit-ins and demonstrations at South African consulates around the country, along with the arrest of hundreds of student, religious, and labor activists, as well as numerous celebrities and at least twenty-two members of Congress. Not since the civil rights heyday of the mid-1960s had African American–led protests taken center stage. The movement won a historic victory when the US Congress passed sweeping economic sanctions against the South African regime, overriding Ronald Reagan's veto, in 1986.[48]

These two developments, stalemate in Northern Ireland and a startlingly effective example of diasporic political activism in the United States, paved the way for the emergence of a new direction in Irish American nationalism, the fight for the MacBride Principles. The MacBride Principles, announced in November 1984, were named after Sean MacBride, one-time chief of staff of the old IRA, later an Irish government official, later still a founder of Amnesty International and a Nobel Peace Prize winner. They were focused on fair employment for Catholics in Northern Ireland and called on US investors in the region to pledge to increase the number of Catholics in supervisory positions and to introduce training programs for Catholic employees. In the late 1980s, with McManus at its helm, the movement literally took off, as Irish American activists from a variety of both traditionally republican and more moderate nationalist organizations threw themselves into the campaign. By 1993, thirteen states had endorsed the principles, along with a large number of municipalities that ranged in size from New York City to Santa Cruz, California. As one supporter in the Massachusetts state legislature put, "if it's good enough for South Africa, it's good enough for Northern Ireland."[49]

There were all sorts of links between the new anti-apartheid movement and the MacBride campaign. The Northern Irish principles were based loosely on the so-called Sullivan Principles, which had been propounded in the 1970s as a set of voluntary guidelines for investors in South Africa by the Reverend Leon Sullivan, the first black member of the board of directors of General Motors. By the mid-1980s, most anti-apartheid activists, including eventually even Sullivan himself, rejected this moderate and voluntary approach. They now called for total divestment in South Africa and used mass civil disobedience to directly confront the Reagan and Bush administration's policy of so-called constructive engagement. At they same time, their politics in the street were complemented by politics on Capitol Hill, as the Congressional Black Caucus worked to transform US foreign policy toward South Africa. This last point is not surprising since one of the greatest gains of the 1960s civil rights movement was the election of large numbers of black congress members—along with mayors of important cities like Chicago, Los Angeles, and Detroit, and state legislators in many states.

This was the group of politicians that the MacBride activists worked with most closely because the groups saw parallels in their respective campaigns. Just one month after the wave of anti-apartheid sit-ins started, Sean McManus was arrested outside the South African embassy in Washington, and in his speeches and writings he repeatedly drew connections between the two movements. On the anti-apartheid side, enthusiasm also ran high. Veteran African American civil rights leader the Reverend Jesse Jackson, who made altering South African policy a central part of his campaign for the presidency in 1984, was an early supporter of the MacBride Principles. So too was New York's first African American mayor David Dinkins, who narrowly defeated his Republican opponent, Rudolph Giuliani, in 1989, partly because of his close connections with Irish American activists. Dinkins and Paul O'Dwyer had been friends since the 1970s, and though Dinkins ran poorly among white Catholics overall in 1989 (receiving just 18 percent of their votes), he did significantly better among Irish Catholics, who knew him as a strong supporter of the MacBride Principles. Dinkins also publicly supported the legal efforts of Joe Doherty, an IRA volunteer, to fight extradition to Northern Ireland, a case that became, as one prominent journalist put it, "a rallying point for opposition in this country to British rule in Northern Ireland." Though Dinkins lost his bid for reelection in 1993, it was not for want of support from MacBride activists, who organized an "Irish Americans for Dinkins" group, or from the *Irish Voice*, a recent addition to the city's media scene, which gave him a ringing endorsement.[50]

The South African link was not the only relevant factor here. Some black political leaders also supported the MacBride campaign because of their belief in the value of affirmative action as a tool for combating employment discrimination— whether suffered by Northern Irish Catholics or African Americans. And on the other side of the political divide, opponents of affirmative action in the United States generally opposed the MacBride campaign as well. When San Francisco's African American mayor, Willie Brown, endorsed a boycott of Bushmills in 1996 to protest hiring practices by the Northern Irish whiskey firm that he argued discriminated against Catholics, the *Wall Street Journal* accused him of an effort to "export affirmative action to Northern Ireland." By this time, California's state legislature had already passed bills in support of the MacBride Principles, crafted mainly by Tom Hayden, the one-time leader of the New Left who was by then a California state senator. However, California's Republican governor Pete Wilson, described by the *New York Times* as "the point man in the fight to eliminate affirmative-action programs based on race and sex" across the country, had vetoed the MacBride bills in both 1991 and 1994.[51]

The Clinton Presidency

The decline of the once-significant Irish American support for the IRA's armed struggle prepared the way for other developments, which would culminate in the new pressure brought on the presidential administration of Bill Clinton in the 1990s. During the 1992 presidential campaign, a loose grouping called Irish-Americans for Clinton/Gore transformed itself into a more formal lobby, Americans for a New Irish Agenda (ANIA). Dominated neither by working-class Irish Americans nor by the once important Irish political exiles, ANIA was a coalition that drew from a much more prosperous stratum of Irish America, including lawyers, journalists, and corporate leaders. Neither left wing nor republican in its outlook, the group was very much in the tradition of constitutional nationalism, but it also worked to break the deeply established pattern of US noninvolvement in Northern Irish affairs. It demanded not a "united Ireland" but rather engagement with new peace initiatives—including direct engagement with Sinn Féin.[52]

In September 1993, a high-profile group of individuals from this organization made a trip to Northern Ireland. Niall O'Dowd, an immigrant from the Irish Republic and publisher of the relatively new but already successful New York–based weekly, the *Irish Voice*, was a key figure in the group, but also important was House Representative Bruce Morrison, a law school friend of Clinton's, who had co-chaired Irish-Americans for Clinton/Gore and was calling for immigration reform for Irish immigrants. Irish American corporate leaders were well represented by Bill Flynn and Tom Moran (respectively, the past and current CEOs of Mutual America), and by Chuck Feeney, the CEO of Atlantic Philanthropies. Very closely attuned to the political possibilities presented by this emerging group, the IRA announced a weeklong ceasefire in Northern Ireland to coincide with their visit. Drawing hope from this positive response, ANIA lobbied Bill Clinton to grant Gerry Adams a visa to attend a conference on Northern Ireland in New York City in January of the following year. Granted well before the IRA's August 1994 ceasefire, Clinton's decision ran directly counter to the advice of his own State Department and provoked an extremely angry response from John Major's conservative government in Britain. "But whether London liked it or not," as one Irish journalist later put it, the Adams visa marked "a fundamental shift in US policy which would have huge effects further down the road."[53]

ANIA could not take all the credit for this, of course: the end of the Cold War provided the overall context for the shift, allowing Clinton to take actions independent of British policy that his predecessors would have found unthinkable. But Clinton was also responding to changes in the thinking of the IRA and Sinn Féin in the early 1990s, moving in a direction that made engagement with republicanism a real possibility—even for Britain, the Republic of Ireland, and the SDLP. Shortly after John Major assumed power in November 1990, for example, the IRA had opened secret channels of communication with him. These contacts constituted an important part of the evolving peace process, even if Major disagreed with Clinton on the specific question of the Adams visa. It gradually emerged, in addition, that the SDLP's John Hume and Adams had been holding regular secret talks since the late 1980s and that Hume had been keeping Dublin fully informed on their progress.[54]

In the context of Irish American nationalism, the biggest loser was Noraid, which found itself pushed from center stage entirely in 1995 with the emergence of Friends of Sinn Féin. By this point, Sinn Féin had opened an office in Washington, headed by Rita O'Hare, a Northern Irish republican closely allied with Adams. The effort was bankrolled by an Irish American billionaire, Chuck Feeney, who was already active in ANIA; Niall O'Dowd, a key intermediary between Sinn Féin and corporate Irish America, later recalled that Feeney put up more than a million dollars "to ensure that the party was properly represented in America." In O'Dowd's view, Feeney "was helping ensure that politics, not violence took precedence in the republican movement." From this point on, Sinn Féin had full control over its own publicity and fundraising in America, developing pipelines of funding from corporate sources that would have been unimaginable in Noraid's heyday. Checks from billionaires had replaced the "Irish Aid" container in the corner bar.[55]

Not surprisingly, given the three-way contacts developing between corporate Irish America, Sinn Féin, and the Clinton White House, an economic development package became the centerpiece of the Clinton strategy, with Commerce Secretary Ron Brown joining national security advisors Anthony Lake and Nancy Soderberg to use what some foreign policy analysts call "soft power" to push the peace process forward. The IRA was more than open to being pushed, responding on August 31, 1994, with a statement that declared its commitment to "the democratic peace process" and announced that "a complete cessation of military operations" would begin at midnight, giving ordinary citizens in that region hope that the Troubles might be finally coming to an end. In the wake of the IRA's ceasefire, Clinton provided Adams with a second visa so that he could attend St. Patrick's Day celebrations in the United States and, equally important, engage in fundraising for Sinn Féin.[56]

Facing considerable suspicion from both Unionists and the Conservative government of John Major, the peace process stagnated over the summer of 1995. The British and the Unionists (led after September by David Trimble, a former law lecturer and relative newcomer to politics) demanded that the IRA fully "decommission" its weaponry before republicans could gain a seat at the negotiating table. Seeing this as more or less surrender, the IRA refused. Gerry

Adams readily admitted that "the whole issue of decommissioning of weapons obviously has to be part of finding a political settlement," but he firmly objected to "anyone trying to leap ahead on any of these issues." As British Prime Minister John Major saw it, statements like this were an example of Sinn Féin "posturing and filibustering, and avoiding genuine discussion." As Sinn Féin saw the situation, "the British government's position on the decommissioning of IRA weapons is, at best, a stalling tactic, at worst an attempt to create a situation of crisis in the peace process." The prospects for an agreement did not look good.[57]

Again, Washington—fully engaged in the peace process—tried to push things along. In November 1995, Clinton helped secure the appointment of George Mitchell, the former majority leader in the US Senate, to chair what was called the International Decommissioning Body, a high profile three-person group whose other members were a retired Canadian general, John de Chastelain, and Harri Holkeri, a former prime minister of Finland. With even greater fanfare, Bill and Hillary Clinton paid a personal visit to Northern Ireland. No sitting US president had ever visited Northern Ireland before, and amid the celebratory atmosphere in Belfast that accompanied his visit, Clinton also worked to mend fences with British and Unionist leaders. Although many commented on the president's historic handshake with Gerry Adams on the Falls Road, the most astute journalist on the scene, David McKittrick, observed that Clinton's "warmest praise was reserved for SDLP leader John Hume, who clearly has a major input into American decision making." Like Hume, McKittrick continued, Clinton "believes that the best way to deal with republicans is to draw them ever-deeper into the political net." The visit to Northern Ireland, Clinton himself later recalled, represented "two of the best days of my presidency."[58]

But even the Clinton visit and Mitchell's report, issued in January 1996, which recommended that IRA decommissioning take place in parallel with political talks, could not persuade the Major government to back off from its demand for prior decommissioning. The members of the International Decommissioning Body knew that this would be the case because the prime minister had already told them so in a private meeting. "His words had a steely candor," Mitchell later recalled. "If we recommended parallel decommissioning, he would have to reject the report." Major did just that, and on February 9, the IRA detonated a bomb at London's Canary Wharf, killing two people and bringing the peace process to a grinding halt. The IRA began a renewed military campaign that included setting off a huge bomb in the British city of Manchester and assassinating security force members in South Armagh. Meanwhile, loyalist violence surrounding Orange Order marching to Drumcree Church in Portadown gave further evidence of the obstacles on the road to peace.[59]

Yet, against all odds, some momentum was maintained. Significantly, neither Hume and the SDLP nor the Irish government broke off contacts with Sinn Féin after Canary Wharf, and even more significantly, Clinton followed their lead, despite his feeling that "the bloom [was] off the Irish rose." The final ingredient proved to be the May 1997 Labour Party landslide in Britain, ending eighteen years of Conservative political dominance. The new prime minister, Tony Blair, had put reviving the Northern Irish peace process near the top of his agenda and he was eager to work with both the Americans and the Irish government, which was led (after a Fianna Fáil-Progressive Democratic coalition victory the following month) by Bertie Ahern, well known for his pragmatism and effective negotiating skills. Responding to what were probably reassurances communicated by Ahern, Blair, and Clinton to the IRA (via Sinn Féin's Adams and Martin McGuinness)—and despite another round of loyalist rioting at Drumcree—the organization announced a new ceasefire on July 20. Talks that would include Sinn Féin—without prior IRA decommissioning—were scheduled to begin on September 15.[60]

The Varied Constituencies of Irish American Nationalism

Within a month of the new ceasefire, Gerry Adams announced plans for a tour of America. In early September, Adams and two other leaders in the party, Martin McGuinness and Caoimghín Ó Caoláin, embarked on what the *Irish Voice* called a "major U.S. blitz." The plan was for all three to appear at a series of New York events beginning on September 4, and then fan out across the nation on separate speaking tours to San Francisco, Washington, and Chicago, with the main objective being to focus Irish American attention on the upcoming talks. "Irish America has played a critical role in the search for a lasting peace with justice for Ireland," Adams proclaimed in advance of the trip. "We thank you for your support and ask you now to rally behind our Sinn Féin negotiating team."[61]

The tour proved to be an unqualified triumph. Huge crowds and well-known public figures greeted the three men everywhere they went, and the short trip added well over $300,000 to Sinn Féin's coffers. As it unfolded, the speaking tour also provided a window on the diverse constituencies of Irish republicanism in America. On Thursday, September 4, the three men appeared at the Waldorf-Astoria Hotel in Manhattan, drawing some 560 well-heeled Sinn Féin supporters for a $500-a-plate luncheon. This event, dominated by politicians, attorneys, and business executives, many of whom were taking increasingly prominent roles in the rapidly growing Friends of Sinn Féin organization, was presided over by Pat Donaghy, the Irish-born chairman and CEO of Structure Tone, one of the world's leading providers of construction services, with operations in the United Kingdom, Asia, and Ireland as well as the United States. Lunch the following day was provided by the prestigious National Committee on American Foreign Policy, chaired by the wealthy Irish American businessman Bill Flynn, with John F. Kennedy Jr. (who had recently profiled Adams in his magazine, *George*) occupying a prominent place at the gathering. A trip to City Hall followed, where Mayor Rudolph Giuliani praised Sinn Féin for its commitment "to achieving a peaceful and democratic solution" in Northern Ireland. Could the Northern Irish republicans get any closer to the center of power in New York? Perhaps. On Sunday, September 7, Adams attended Mass at St. Patrick's Cathedral, after which he held a private meeting with John Cardinal O'Connor.[62]

Wealthy Irish Americans, prominent politicians, and Catholic prelates did not constitute Sinn Féin's only American constituency. On September 5, the team that some were calling "the three tenors" appeared before a large, energetic, and distinctly working-class crowd at the Roseland Ballroom. Here, as a reporter for the *Irish Echo* put it, they demonstrated an ability to "change their line to suit their audience." More than 2,000 people, who paid just $10 for admission—the Friends of Sinn Féin had reduced the price from $20 at the last minute—were entertained by figures such as the popular raconteur Malachy McCourt and the New York–based Irish rap artist, Shanachie. Rather than talk of achieving peaceful and democratic solutions to the conflict in Northern Ireland, the crowd was treated to a video depicting violent skirmishes on streets of Derry and Belfast and to what the *Echo* called "feisty rebel songs," performed by a well-known Irish folk band called the Wolfe Tones. The crowd gave Adams and McGuinness "rapturous applause" as they took the stage to deliver what the *Echo* characterized as militant, even threatening, speeches. Adams asked the audience to honor IRA volunteers who had been killed in action during the Northern Irish conflict, and he praised the Clan na Gael and Noraid for their support of the IRA during its years of armed struggle. As Irish republicans embarked on a new course that would lead them to negotiations and to inevitable political compromise, it seemed, they found it more important than ever to refresh memories of their physical force tradition, a tradition that, they asserted, stretched all the way back to Wolfe Tone himself.

Republican rhetoric blended seamlessly with a working-class sensibility far removed from the Waldorf-Astoria event. Looking ahead to the upcoming talks, Martin McGuinness, Sinn Féin's chief negotiator, characterized them mainly in class terms. "This is a battle between the Cambridge- and Oxford-educated intelligentsia and the people of the Bogside and the Falls Road," he told the crowd, referring to the Catholic working-class neighborhoods of Derry (his home town) and Belfast. But that evening it was Adams who tied together Irish republicanism and the Irish American working-class experience most effectively. An *Irish Voice* reporter captured the moment:

"Does anybody remember Margaret Thatcher?" asked Adams, in a speech which solicited participation from the willing crowd. "Is anyone here from Tyrone?" he asked, and the whole room cheered. "Is anybody here from the Bronx?" They cheered even louder.[63]

Not all Irish republicans in the United States were pleased with Sinn Féin's willingness to negotiate, however. Even before it began, the tour met opposition from a previously unknown organization calling itself "Exiled Children in America." The group told a Belfast newspaper that they would be protesting the planned events in New York because they believed the IRA and Sinn Féin had sold out republicanism by calling their ceasefire and agreeing to participate in the upcoming all-party talks.[64]

The delegation simply ignored these protests. But as their individual speaking tours progressed, other dimensions of Sinn Féin's American activities and connections came into view. The evening of September 6 found McGuinness in San Francisco, where he participated in what the *San Francisco Chronicle* called "a Sinn Féin lovefest" at the city's Russian Center. A crowd of more than 500, mainly from San Francisco's large Irish American community, filled the hall. Also present were public figures better known in other arenas of political life. One was California state senator Tom Hayden. Hayden, who had recently authored a bill requiring California schools to "include the study of the inhumanity of the Great Irish Famine of 1845–1850" in their social studies curricula, presented McGuinness with a commendation from the California legislature.[65]

The highlight of the evening was the short speech by San Francisco's mayor, Willie Brown. A veteran of the African American urban political mobilization that had accompanied the civil rights movement of the 1960s and the first black mayor of San Francisco, Brown presented McGuinness with the key to the city and then drew a direct connection between McGuinness's efforts and those of the African American civil rights movement. "I link the struggle that you are negotiating for with the Empire with the struggle we had here for equal justice under the law," Brown told McGuinness. "The struggle which you are engaged in is a very noble one. You are exhibiting the qualities that make us proud to have you as an honorary San Franciscan."[66]

The Good Friday Agreement

The SDLP's John Hume and the Ulster Unionists' David Trimble dominated the difficult peace negotiations, which were chaired (at Clinton's suggestion) by George Mitchell and lasted through April of the following year. Despite Trimble's dislike of Irish American lobbying and his irritation with the Clinton administration over the Adams visa, he did not share the general suspicion of US politicians that was typical of older Unionists. As Clinton advisor Nancy Soderberg put it, Washington had been "knocking on the unionist door for some time and Trimble was the first one to answer." Sinn Féin and the smaller Northern Irish parties at the table had much less influence than Hume and Trimble, and much less than the "outsiders" Ahern, Blair, and Clinton. Among the more dramatic moments of the negotiations were Ahern's decision to abruptly leave his mother's funeral in Dublin to return to the talks on April 8, and Clinton's 2:30 AM and 5:00 AM telephone calls to Gerry Adams on April 10, urging him to accept a longer waiting period on the critical question of paramilitary prisoner release.[67]

The key pieces of the final agreement, announced at 5:00 PM that day—Good Friday 1998—were a "devolved" Northern Irish government, based on power-sharing between nationalists and unionists, new cross-border institutions linking Northern Ireland and the Irish Republic, sweeping reform of the RUC, early prisoner release for members of republican and loyalist paramilitary groups that were part of the agreement, and the decommissioning of all paramilitary weapons. Though this last would be a sticking point, blocking full implementation of the Good Friday Agreement for nearly a decade, the accord marked a fundamental turning point in Irish history. Although so-called dissident republican violence, beginning with the horrifying Omagh bombing of August 1998 (in which twenty-nine people were killed by an IRA breakaway group styling itself the "Real IRA") and continuing up through the present, remains part of the reality in Northern Ireland—along with ongoing loyalist violence and deep communal and sectarian tensions—the agreement brought to an end mainstream republicanism's long tradition of armed struggle. A complicated chapter of Irish—and Irish American—history that had begun with Wolfe Tone, the United Irishmen, and the 1798 rebellion had come to a close.

Epilogue

"Ireland is at Peace"

On April 30, 2008, the Irish taoiseach, Bertie Ahern, rose to address a joint meeting of the US Congress. It was an appropriate time to give such an address. Ahern was about to step down as taoiseach and he was able to do so with a sense of accomplishment. The previous year, on May 8, 2007, Sinn Féin had gone into devolved power-sharing government with the Democratic Unionist Party (DUP), headed by the aging unionist hardliner, the Reverend Ian Paisley, who became first minister of Northern Ireland. Paisley's deputy first minister was Martin McGuiness, one-time commander of the Provisional Irish Republican Army in Derry. When McGuinness took the oath of office, which included swearing his loyalty to the Police Service of Northern Ireland (the new name for the newly reformed RUC), the British diplomat Jonathan Powell later remembered, "I felt dizzy and slightly faint, as if I had just finished pushing a very large boulder uphill." Those sitting alongside him, Taoiseach Ahern and Prime Minister Tony Blair of the United Kingdom, may have felt something similar. The political breakthrough they marked that day meant that the tenth anniversary of the Good Friday Agreement could be a moment for genuine celebration, in the United States as well as in Ireland.[1]

Getting to this point had not been easy. On one side of the equation, a number of factors made unionists difficult partners in the actual implementation of the Good Friday Agreement: deep divisions over the Agreement within the Ulster Unionist Party itself (which led to David Trimble's resignation as leader in 2005), the rapid ascendance of Paisley's anti-Agreement DUP to become the biggest vote-getter in Northern Ireland by 2003, and ongoing bouts of loyalist rioting and paramilitary activity all played a part. On the republican side was a seemingly unending series of embarrassing and destabilizing incidents, including the arrest of three Sinn Féin leaders in an area of Colombia controlled by FARC (Revolutionary Armed Forces of Colombia) rebels in August 2001, the December 2004 robbery of the Northern Bank in Belfast (widely believed to be the work of the IRA), and the January 2005 killing of a republican named Robert McCartney in a Belfast bar frequented by high-level IRA and Sinn Féin members. In a somewhat different category was Sinn Féin's vocal opposition to the 2003 invasion of Iraq, which, though emerging from considered discussion within the party, temporarily burned some bridges with both Blair and his Washington ally in the "war on terror," George W. Bush. Still, the biggest obstacle of all on either the unionist or republican side was the continuing reluctance of the IRA to decommission its weapons. When that finally occurred in July 2005, with a dramatic IRA statement announcing a final "end to the armed campaign," other pieces of this complicated puzzle, including the unexpected partnership—and eventually even friendship—between Paisley and McGuinness, began to fall into place. This was the context for Ahern's dramatic words, formally addressed to the Speaker of the US House of Representatives, Nancy Pelosi: "After so many decades of conflict, I am so proud, Madam Speaker, to be the first Irish leader to inform the United States Congress: Ireland is at peace."[2]

Though he might have been the first Irish leader to bring this message, Ahern was well aware that many others had come before him. Noting that Pelosi herself had some family links to County Wicklow, he began his address by recalling that "a famous son of Wicklow, Charles Stewart Parnell, stood in this place 128 years ago, the first Irish leader to do so." After Parnell came a long line of others, many of them Irish nationalists. "In the early part of the last century, Eamon De Valera came here seeking help as Ireland struggled for her independence. In more recent times, many Irish leaders"—here Taoiseach Ahern was undoubtedly thinking about the constitutional nationalist John Hume—"have come here in the quest for peace in Northern Ireland." Ahern did not mention Wolfe or Matilda Tone, but later that day he paid homage to the Irish republican tradition that they represented by presenting the sword of Thomas Francis Meagher, the Young Ireland leader, political exile, and Union army hero, to the Congressional Friends of Ireland, which Senators Kennedy, Moynihan, and House Speaker O'Neill had founded back in 1981.

Generations of Irish nationalists had turned to the United States, Ahern asserted, "as we strove to emulate the achievements of America and vindicate the principles that inspired your founding fathers: the principles of liberty, of equality and of justice." Though obviously trying to flatter his audience at this point, there was more than a little truth in these words: certainly Tone and the other United Irishmen had deeply admired the Jeffersonian "founding fathers," if not their Federalist adversaries. There was also some truth in Ahern's subsequent homage to Martin Luther King Jr., whose "dream, born of America but heard by the whole world, inspired us through its unanswerable commitment to justice and to non-violence." Hume and some of the other constitutional nationalists in Northern Ireland had indeed considered themselves followers of King. More important, there were deep links between Irish and Irish American nationalism and the African American freedom struggle extending over many decades—though these links were far more complicated and contested than Ahern's words allowed.

But the bulk of Ahern's speech concerned the deeper ties between Ireland and the United States that stemmed from immigration. Ahern gave tribute to the many generations of Irish immigrants and Irish Americans, from the Ulster Presbyterian pioneers of the eighteenth century, through the impoverished Catholic laborers of the Famine era, to "the Irish that are now to be found in the police departments and the fire houses, in the hospitals, the schools and the universities, in the board rooms and on the construction sites, in the churches and on the sports fields of America." As long as this particular story was, however, it was now reaching its conclusion, for Ireland in the era of the "Celtic Tiger" was itself becoming, like the United States, a nation of immigrants. "The New Ireland—once a place so many left—is now a place to which so many come."

History rarely provides us with such neat endings, of course. Even as he spoke these words, Ahern was under investigation for receiving illegal payments from Irish real estate developers; four years later on the eve of his expulsion, he resigned from the Fianna Fáil party that he had once led. Meanwhile, the deep economic crisis that stemmed in part from the speculative mania of the Ahern era resulted in not only very high levels of unemployment (which reached a staggering 33 percent among those under age twenty-five in 2011) but also to Ireland's becoming—once again—a place that "many left." The subsequent supervision of Irish economic policy by the so-called troika of international lenders (the European Union, the International Monetary Fund, and the European Central Bank) raised troubling questions for some about the very meaning of the "sovereignty" that nationalists of all stripes had struggled so hard to achieve over the preceding two centuries.[3]

The effects of these new developments lie far beyond the scope of the present work. What this book has demonstrated is that Irish nationalists in America played a central part in a complicated and important transnational story that lasted over many decades and took many different forms. Irish nationalism in the United States was not the unmediated expression of some timeless, primordial Irish identity but rather an ongoing work of political invention and imagination, involving multiple generations of men and women. The labors of these men and women, many of whom were—or considered themselves to be—political exiles, shaped both Irish and American history in critically important ways.

NOTES

Abbreviations for Notes

AIA   Archives of Irish America, Bobst Library, New York University
AIHS   American Irish Historical Society, New York
BPL   Boston Public Library, Department of Rare Books and Manuscripts
COHA   Columbia University Oral History Archives, New York
HL   Hatcher Library, Special Collections, University of Michigan, Ann Arbor
LOC   Library of Congress, Manuscript Division, Washington, DC
NLI   National Library of Ireland, Dublin
NYPL   New York Public Library, Manuscripts and Archives Division
SJUA   St. John's University Archives and Special Collections, New York

Introduction

1. Tim O'Brien, "In Brooklyn, Irish Patriotism Remembered," *Irish America*, February 28, 1997, 14; *New York Daily News*, October 9, 1996. The event is documented in Tierney's evocative film, *Matilda Tone*.

2. Hart, *Young Irelander Abroad*, 62. Matilda Tone figures prominently in Elliott, *Wolfe Tone*, but for the fullest and most thoughtful treatment of her life, see Curtin, "Matilda Tone and Virtuous Republican Femininity."

3. Tone, *Life of Theobald Wolfe Tone*; Kiberd, "Republican Self-Fashioning," 16. For a full consideration of Matilda Tone's contribution to Irish nationalism, see Brundage, "Matilda Tone in America."

4. Quinn, "Review Article: Theobald Wolfe Tone and the Historians," 114–16, 126–27; Elliott, *Wolfe Tone*, 395–401; Adams, *A Farther Shore*, 12; *Irish Echo*, September 10–16, 1997.

5. Janis, *A Greater Ireland*; Davitt quoted in McCaffrey, *The Irish Catholic Diaspora in America*, 160; Holland, *The American Connection*. Following Meagher's invaluable reference work, *The Columbia Guide to Irish American History*, I refer to the members of the first generation to come to the United States as "Irish immigrants," using "Irish Americans" to refer to members of the second or later generations, born in the United States. I use the phrases "Irish America," "Irish in America," and "American Irish" to encompass both immigrants and their descendants.

6. Despite their importance, the Irish in America have received scant attention in the standard histories of Irish nationalism: Kee, *The Green Flag*; Cronin, *Irish Nationalism*; Boyce, *Nationalism in Ireland*; Garvin, *The Evolution of Irish Nationalist Politics*; and English, *Irish Freedom*. Although valuable insights are to be found in all of these works, only Kee and Cronin provide more than a passing mention of the American Irish. For a brief but stimulating overview, however, see Murphy, "The Influence of America on Irish Nationalism." There have

been encouraging recent signs that Irish historians are working to more fully integrate the history of the diaspora into their understanding of social and political developments within Ireland itself. See, for example, Delaney, "Directions in Historiography: Our Island Story?" Delaney, "Migration and Diaspora," and Whelehan, ed. *Transnational Perspectives on Modern Irish History*. In the more specialized literature on Irish nationalism, O'Day's work has been notable for its attention to transnational and diasporic issues. See O'Day, "Irish Diaspora Politics in Perspective"; O'Day, "Irish Nationalism and Anglo-American Relations"; and O'Day, "Imagined Irish Communities."

7. Dalberg-Acton, "Nationality," 146. For thoughtful assessments of long-distance nationalism, see Anderson, "Long-Distance Nationalism," and Dufoix, *Diasporas*, 92–97. Important case studies include Glick Schiller and Fouron, *Georges Woke Up Laughing*; Skrbiš, *Long-Distance Nationalism*; and Fuglerud, *Life on the Outside*. While some scholars have conceded that there are historical antecedents of contemporary long-distance nationalism, as with much of the research on contemporary transnational identities generally, the historical dimension is often thin, more a matter of lip service than of serious study. For an incisive critique, see Waldinger, "Immigrant 'Transnationalism' and the Presence of the Past." The estimate of 217 million international migrants is for the year 2010 and represents 3.1 percent of the world's population. See Kenny, *Diaspora*, 95. As to the question of when nations and nationalism first emerged in world history: though some theorists, notably Smith, have argued that the formation of nations needs to be placed in a longer historical span beginning in the Middle Ages, most contemporary scholars follow Gellner, *Nations and Nationalism*, Hobsbawm, *Nations and Nationalism since 1780*, and other so-called modernists in locating the origins of the phenomenon in the era of the French Revolution, when ideas of popular sovereignty replaced traditional dynastic loyalties and transformed passive "subjects" into self-governing "citizens." See Hutchinson, *Modern Nationalism*, 1–38, for a good summary of the debate, and Smith, *Nationalism*, 95–124, for his most recent critique of the modernist approach.

8. Anderson, *Imagined Communities*. For a concise overview of this theme, see Eley and Suny, "From the Moment of Social History to the Work of Cultural Representation," 6–9. The debate over historical revisionism in Ireland is surveyed in two useful anthologies: Brady, ed., *Interpreting Irish History*, and Boyce and O'Day, eds., *The Making of Modern Irish History*. For two radically different recent assessments, see Whelan, "The Revisionist Debate," and Gkotzaridis, *Trials of Irish History*.

9. See Miller, *Emigrants and Exiles*, and, for a concise statement of his interpretation, Miller, *Ireland and Irish America*, 7–43, esp. 13–15, 40–43. Miller's argument that the migrants' predisposition to see emigration as a form of involuntarily exile hindered their ability to succeed or prosper in industrial capitalist societies like that of the United States has been subjected to much criticism over the years, but no critic has persuasively challenged the existence of this predisposition or its salience for understanding Irish American nationalism. For a good discussion, see Kenny, "Twenty Years of Irish American Historiography." For criticism of Miller's interpretation, see, most recently, Campbell, *Ireland's New Worlds*, but for an important work that extends his argument, examining "cultures of exile" among three European immigrant groups and the relationship of immigrant nationalisms to such cultures, see Jacobson, *Special Sorrows*. For important overviews of Irish American history, all of which include treatments of Irish American nationalism, see McCaffrey, *The Irish Catholic Diaspora in America*; Kenny, *The American Irish*; and Dolan, *The Irish Americans*. For an assessment of some of the specialist literature on the topic, see Brundage, "Recent Directions in the History of Irish American Nationalism."

10. See Brown, *Irish-American Nationalism*, esp. 23–24, 46, and, for his initial statement of the thesis, Brown, "The Origins and Character of Irish-American Nationalism." Elegantly written and resonating perfectly with the assimilationist consensus of the mid-1960s, *Irish-American Nationalism* dominated the field for years. Even Foner, "Class, Ethnicity, and Radicalism in the Gilded Age," 194–95, who persuasively criticized Brown for overemphasizing Irish Americans' acquisitive drive for upward social mobility, argued that when Irish American workers joined the radical Irish Land League in the 1880s they were expressing a version of assimilation—not to middle-class American standards, but to "a strong emergent oppositional working-class culture."

11. For a contemporary study arguing that the emergence of long-distance nationalism depends on a migrant population containing a critical mass of political exiles, see Skrbiš, *Long-Distance Nationalism*. Following Iwańska, *Exiled Governments*, 3, I define the phenomenon of "political exile" expansively to include not only "the expulsion of politically undesirable individuals or groups, or the escape from the threat of death or persecution," but also "elected exile in protest against the political regime."

12. For his careful and persuasive distinction between comparative and transnational approaches to the study of the Irish worldwide, see Kenny, "Diaspora and Comparison." For the transnational approach to US immigration history more generally, see Gabaccia, "Is Everywhere Nowhere?," and Ngai, "Immigration and Ethnic History."

13. These three groups are based on those analyzed by Iwańska, *Exiled Governments*, 42–44, and Shain, *Marketing the American Creed Abroad*, 11–12. I take the term "militant minority" from Montgomery, *The Fall of the House of Labor*, 2, who used it to describe rank-and-file activists in the American labor movement.

Chapter 1

1. Tone to Thomas Russell, September 1, 1795, Tone, "Autobiography (1792, 1795–6)," in Tone, *Writings*, 2:11, 16, 338–39.

2. Tone, "Autobiography (1763–92)," in Tone, *Writings*, 2:279, 283. For an excellent short introduction to Tone's life and thought, see Bartlett, *Theobald Wolfe Tone*. The fullest biography is Elliott, *Wolfe Tone*. For an incisive assessment of the research on Tone, see Quinn, "Tone and the Historians."

3. Jackson, *Ireland*, 7–8. Valuable interpretations of late eighteenth-century Ireland can be found in Dickson, *New Foundations*; Connolly, *Divided Kingdom*; and McBride, *Eighteenth-Century Ireland*. Until 1780, a sacramental test for borough seats had also restricted the number of Presbyterians in the Irish Parliament. The exceptional American state was New Jersey, where propertied unmarried women could legally vote from 1776 until their explicit disenfranchisement in 1807.

4. See Bartlett, *The Fall and Rise of the Irish Nation*, 17–29, 82–145. For a recent analysis of the penal code, emphasizing at least an element of religious motivation behind its construction, see McBride, *Eighteenth-Century Ireland*, 194–214.

5. Elliot, *Wolfe Tone*, 17. For the political and cultural significance of the Volunteers, see Mac Suibhne, "Whiskey, Potatoes and Paddies," and Higgins, *A Nation of Politicians*. For an insightful analysis of Tone's romantic military enthusiasms, see Curtin, "The Belfast Uniform."

6. Grattan's speech to the Irish Parliament, April 16, 1782, as reported in the *Morning Herald* (London), April 29, 1782, quoted in McDowell, *Grattan*, 56–57.

7. See Dickson, *New Foundations*, 171–86, for a concise discussion of the post-1782 political situation.

8. George Tandy to James Napper Tandy, October 19, 1784, quoted in Bartlett, *The Fall and Rise of the Irish Nation*, 113; Tone, "Reasons Why the Question of Parliamentary Reform Has Always Failed in the Irish Legislature [1793]," in Tone, *Writings*, 1:488.

9. "Declaration of the Rights of Man and the Citizen," in Hunt, ed., *The French Revolution and Human Rights*, 77–79. For the importance of the term "nation" in the French revolutionary lexicon, see Hunt, *Politics, Culture, and Class*, 21. For the role of the French Revolution in the emergence of nationalism in Ireland, see Elliott, "Ireland," 71–72, 78–81, and McBride, "The Nation in the Age of Revolution," 251–55, 265–66. See also Bew, *Ireland*, 1–48, who places the impact of the French Revolution at the center of his interpretation of Irish history in the 1790s.

10. Grattan's speech to the Irish Parliament, July 2, 1790, as reported in the *Dublin Chronicle*, July 3, 1790, quoted in Quinn, *Soul on Fire*, 7. See also McDowell, *Grattan*, 81–82, for a discussion of Grattan's deep commitment to maintaining "a close and permanent connection" between Britain and Ireland.

11. Tone, "Spanish War: An Enquiry How Far Ireland Is Bound, of Right, To Embark in the Impending Contest on the Side of Great Britain," in Tone, *Writings*, 1:50–61.

12. Elliot, *Tone*, 89; Sir Henry Cavendish, quoted in Bartlett, *Theobald Wolfe Tone*, 22; Tone to Thomas Russell, July 9, 1791, and Tone to the editor of *Faulkner's Dublin Journal*, July 11, 1793, in Tone, *Writings*, 1:104, 455–56 (emphasis in the original). Although some historians have interpreted Tone's July 1793 letter as a sign that he was backing away from separatism, Quinn, "Tone and the Historians," 124, shows clearly that it reveals the opposite.

13. Tone, "Autobiography (1763–92)," in Tone, *Writings*, 2:287; Quinn, *Soul on Fire*, 1–22.

14. Dickson, "Paine and Ireland," 138–39; Paine, "Rights of Man," in Paine, *Collected Writings*, 540; Tone, "Diary, 12–13 October 1791," in Tone, *Writings*, 1:132.

15. Equiano, *The Interesting Narrative*, 10, 25–26, 235, 357–58; Rodgers, "Equiano in Belfast," 73–75, 78–80. See also Rodgers, *Ireland, Slavery and Anti-Slavery*, for a broader study. For a controversial biography of Equiano that disputes his African birth and direct experience of the Middle Passage, see Carretta, *Equiano, the African*, but for a persuasive rebuttal, see Lovejoy, "Autobiography and Memory."

16. Tone, "Diary, 14, 17 July 1791," in Tone, *Writings*, 1:108.

17. Tone, "Autobiography (1763–92)," in Tone, *Writings*, 2:301.

18. Tone, "An Argument on the Behalf of the Catholics of Ireland," in Tone, *Writings*, 1:110–12, 116, 120.

19. Tone, "An Argument," in Tone, *Writings*, 1:125 (emphasis in the original).

20. Rodgers, "Equiano in Belfast," 77–78; Paine, "Rights of Man," 450; Paine, "African Slavery in America," March 8, 1775, quoted in Berlin, *Generations of Captivity*, 100. The slavery theme in Irish political writing of this era is a leitmotif of McBride, *Eighteenth-Century Ireland*.

21. Quinn, *Soul on Fire*, 61–62; Equiano, *Interesting Narrative*, xxvii; Rogers, "Equiano in Belfast," 76–77. See also Linebaugh and Rediker, *The Many-Headed Hydra*, 284–85, for a provocative discussion of Paine, Equiano, and Tone as related intellectual contributors to a multinational, multiethnic working-class world they call the "revolutionary Atlantic."

22. Tone, "An Argument," in Tone, *Writings*, 1:124–25.

23. Tone, "A Short Answer by a Liberty Boy [January 1792]," Tone to the editor of the *Northern Star*, July 13, 1792, and "To the Manufacturers of Dublin [March 1793]," in Tone, *Writings*, 1:162–64, 212, 419–21; Elliott, *Wolfe Tone*, 123.

24. Martha McTier to William Drennan, January 5, 1793, in Drennan and McTier, *Letters*, 1:460; Russell, journal entry, July 7, 1793, in Russell, *Journals and Memoirs*, 86.

25. Tone, "An Argument," in Tone, *Writings*, 1:117–18. For the "romantic conservatism" of Tone's attitudes toward women generally and for his dismissal of politically engaged women, such as Belfast's Martha McTier or Mary Ann McCracken, see Elliott, *Wolfe Tone*, 28–29, 256. For similar attitudes among American and French republican writers and political leaders, see Kerber, *Toward an Intellectual History of Women*, 100–11, 143–44; and Hufton, *Women and the Limits of Citizenship*, 3–5, 53–88.

26. Elliott, *Wolfe Tone*, 123; Dr. Hugh MacDermot to Owen O'Conor, November 21, 1791, in Tone, *Writings*, 1:153; Bartlett, *Theobald Wolfe Tone*, 27.

27. Tone, "Diary, 12–13 October 1791," in Tone, *Writings*, 1:132; "Resolutions of United Irishmen," in Joy, *Belfast Politics*, 2. For the immediate background to the founding of the Belfast organization, see Curtin, *The United Irishmen*, 38–45.

28. Edmund Burke to Richard Burke Jr., November 2, 1792, in Burke, *Correspondence*, 283; Society of United Irishmen, *Proceedings*, 9; Curtin, *The United Irishmen*, 21. As the bicentennial of the 1798 rebellion approached, historical research on the United Irishmen and the decade of the 1790s expanded dramatically. A generous sampling of this work can be found in Bartlett et al., eds., *1798*. For two thoughtful assessments of the historiography, see Smyth, "Interpreting the 1790s," and McBride, "Reclaiming the Rebellion." For a discussion of the complexities of Edmund Burke's thought in this period, especially his passionate advocacy of Catholic emancipation as a bulwark against revolution, see Bew, *Ireland*, 14–27.

29. The Roman Catholic Delegates to Home Secretary Henry Dundas, December 20, 1792, quoted in Bartlett, *The Fall and Rise of the Irish Nation*, 152; Tone, "Account of the Proceedings of the Catholic Convention from 3 December 1792 to 9 April 1793," in Tone, *Writings*, 1:483. Bartlett, *The Fall and Rise of the Irish Nation*, 146–72, provides the fullest account of these events. In addition to granting the franchise, the 1793 reform act enabled Catholics to hold civil and military offices and to receive degrees at Dublin University. The Catholic Committee

reappeared, but only briefly, in 1795; a new organization taking the same name emerged in the first decade of the nineteenth century to continue the campaign for full Catholic emancipation.

30. O'Brien, "Spirit, Impartiality and Independence," 13, 17, 23; *Northern Star,* December 22, 1792, August 20, 1795; T. A. Emmet, "Part of an Essay towards the History of Ireland," in MacNeven, *Pieces of Irish History,* 77. Neilson estimated that every copy of the paper was actually read by at least ten people. See Curtin, *The United Irishmen,* 202–27; Thuente, *The Harp Re-strung,* 89–169; and McBride, *Eighteenth-Century Ireland,* 381–87, for discussions of the critical role of print culture in popular politicization during the 1790s.

31. Curtin, *The United Irishmen* 24–26; United Irishmen, *Proceedings,* 27; Smyth, *The Men of No Property,* 165; Russell, journal entry, July 9, 1793, in Russell, *Journals,* 83. For the best discussion of these issues, see Quinn, "The United Irishmen and Social Reform."

32. Drennan to Martha McTier, July 14, 1794, in Drennan and McTier, *Letters,* 2:82. For repression in England, see Thompson, *The Making of the English Working Class,* 19–20; Goodwin, *The Friends of Liberty,* 268–358; and Wells, *Insurrection,* 44–63. For Ireland, see Curtin, *The United Irishmen,* 52–55.

33. Tone, "Diary, 15–19 September 1792," and William Todd Jones to Tone, July 10, 1793, in Tone, *Writings,* 1:283, 451–52. Tone and Russell had first discussed the possibility of emigration to America even earlier, in September 1792.

34. See Curtin, "The Transformation of the United Irishmen," 468–76, and Curtin, *The United Irishmen,* 59–61, 90–116, for the details of this reorganization. See also Smyth, *The Men of No Property,* 98; Elliott, *Partners in Revolution,* 67–68; Quinn, "The United Irishmen and Social Reform," 192–93.

35. Tone, "Autobiography (1792, 1795–6)," in Tone, *Writings,* 2:333.

36. Tone to Thomas Russell, September 1, 1795, in Tone, *Writings,* 2:13. Though his language was heated, Tone was not far off the mark. For an analysis of the post-revolutionary processes of "commercialization and industrialization, especially in the fast-growing eastern cities, [which] were engines for creating wealth and poverty simultaneously," see Nash, "Poverty and Politics in Early American History," 13–14. For the inequality-inducing effects (if not the actual intention, as Tone implied) of the Federalist policies on economic growth, see Kornblith and Murrin, "The Dilemmas of Ruling Elites in Revolutionary America."

37. Jefferson, 1818 preface to a collection of his manuscripts, quoted in Banning, *The Jeffersonian Persuasion,* 13. For Jeffersonian alarm at Federalist economic policy in these years, see McCoy, *The Elusive Republic;* Appleby, *Capitalism and a New Social Order;* Nelson, *Liberty and Property;* and, for a recent overview of the conflict, Wood, *Empire of Liberty,* 140–73. For a persuasive interpretation of the Democratic-Republican societies as the American expression of a larger international movement influenced by the democratic ideals of both the United Irishmen and the London Corresponding Society, see Cotlar, *Tom Paine's America,* 162, 171, 183–88.

38. Tone to Thomas Russell, September 1, October 25, 1795, in Tone, *Writings,* 2:13, 33. For a full account of Tone's American exile, emphasizing the way that it crystallized his republican outlook, see Elliott, *Wolfe Tone,* 249–67.

39. Tone to Thomas Russell, September 1, 1795, Tone, "Autobiography (1792, 1795–6)," in Tone, *Writings,* 2:13, 339. This is not to argue, as Tom Dunne has done, that Tone's American exile created his separatist beliefs, for these were already well formed by 1795. But the experience of exile certainly intensified his views. See Dunne, *Theobald Wolfe Tone,* 17, 50, and Quinn, "Tone and the Historians," 125.

40. Tone "Diary, 2–15 February 1796," Tone, "Autobiography (1792, 1795–6)," in Tone, *Writings,* 2:52–53, 340–41.

41. Tone, "Diary, 16–21, 22–25 February 1796," in Tone, *Writings,* 2:58, 70–73; Lyons, *France under the Directory,* 54, 200–201.

42. Earl of Westmoreland to William Pitt, January 4, 1793, quoted in Bartlett, Introduction, "Defenders and Defenderism," 376; Keating, *On the Defence of Ireland,* 5–6. For the Defenders' origins, see Miller, "The Armagh Troubles." In Smyth's view, the Defenders expressed a "gut Catholic nationalism" that was always in tension with the secular republicanism of the United Irish leaders. See Smyth, *The Men of No Property,* 182–83.

43. Bartlett, "Defenders and Defenderism," 374, 376–7, 386; Miller, ed., *Peep O'Day Boys and Defenders*, 1–3; McBride, *Eighteenth-Century Ireland*, 350; Elliott, *Partners in Revolution*, 42; Smyth, *The Men of No Property*, 100–125; Lord Camden to Duke of Portland, September 9, 1795, quoted in Chambers, *Rebellion in Kildare*, 37.

44. Hope, *United Irishman*, 50; Curtin, *The United Irishmen*, 4–5. See also Elliott, *Partners in Revolution*, 95–96, and Smyth, *The Men of No Property*, 118–19.

45. Hope, *United Irishman*, 56; Smyth, "Dublin's Political Underground," 135; Smyth, *The Men of No Property*, 142, 179–80; Wilson, *United Irishmen, United States*, 23.

46. Tone, "First Memorial to the French Government on the Present State of Ireland [1796]," Tone, "Diary, 12–22 March 1796," Tone, "An Address to the Peasantry of Ireland," in Tone, *Writings*, 2:67–68, 107, 348, 352. Whether knowingly or not, Tone vastly overstated the redistribution of land that had actually occurred during the French Revolution.

47. Tone, "Diary, 4–21 December 1796" in Tone, *Writings*, 2:419–20.

48. Tone, "Diary, 24 December 1796–1 January 1797," in Tone, *Writings*, 2:432.

49. For a succinct account of the military history of the 1790s—and the argument that the attempted French invasion at Bantry Bay marked a turning point in that history—see Bartlett, "Defence, Counter-Insurgency and Rebellion."

50. Curtin, *The United Irishmen*, 125; General Knox to the Marquis of Abercorn, March 21, 1797, quoted in Bartlett, "Defence, Counter-Insurgency and Rebellion," 270.

51. Camden to Portland, November 3, 1797, quoted in Bartlett, "Defence, Counter-Insurgency and Rebellion," 270. For a full discussion of the dragooning of Ulster, see Curtin, *The United Irishmen*, 67–89.

52. Thomas Knox to Edward Cooke, August 13, 1796, quoted in Bartlett, "Defence, Counter-Insurgency and Rebellion," 262. See also Whelan, *The Tree of Liberty*, 119, who argues persuasively that "the effort to create united Irishmen was rebuffed by a deliberate effort to create disunited Irishmen," though, for a cautionary note, see Connolly, *Divided Kingdom*, 472–74.

53. Stewart, *The Summer Soldiers*, 40–44; Camden to Portland, February 8, 1798, quoted in Curtin, *The United Irishmen*, 257. See also Malcomson, *John Foster*, 119–21, for Foster's role in shaping this hardline government strategy.

54. Edward Roche's proclamation, June 7, 1798, quoted in Whelan, "Reinterpreting the 1798 Rebellion in Wexford," 27–28. Whelan's essay, along with Cullen, "The United Irishmen in Wexford," is an important effort to reinterpret what has long been seen as the most sectarian face of the 1798 rebellion. For a vivid and scholarly account of the Wexford events, see Gahan, *The People's Rising*.

55. Hope, *United Irishman*, 104. For the United Irish discord and the rising in Ulster, see Curtin, *The United Irishmen*, 264–80, and, for a full account, Stewart, *Summer Soldiers*, especially 102–21, 153–55, 162. Suffering in the 1798 rebellion was particularly widespread among Catholic women, many of whom were raped and brutalized by British and Hessian soldiers. United Irish leaders, by contrast, regarded Protestant loyalist women as noncombatants and ordered their followers not to assault them, an order that was almost completely obeyed. See Beatty, Introduction, to Beatty, ed., *Protestant Women's Narratives of the Irish Rebellion*, 9–10; Whelan, "Reinterpreting the 1798 Rebellion in Wexford," 28; and McBride, *Eighteenth-Century Ireland*, 429, for discussions of this point.

56. For the participation of women in the fighting at Vinegar Hill, see Cannavan, "Revolution in Ireland, Evolution in Women's Rights," 33–35. For the details of the brief French campaign and United Irish mobilization in Mayo, see Murtagh, "General Humbert's Futile Campaign." For its lasting importance in Irish social memory, see Beiner, *Remembering the Year of the French*.

57. Tone, "Tone's Address to the Court Martial (II)," in Tone, *Writings*, 3:397; Elliott, *Wolfe Tone*, 378–82.

58. Quinn, "Tone and the Historians," 113.

59. According to Doyle, "The Irish in North America," 692, between 440,000 and 517,000 US residents in 1790 can be identified as of Irish birth or extraction, the majority of them Ulster Presbyterian in background. For the number of Americans claiming Irish ancestry at the end of the twentieth century, see Meagher, *The Columbia Guide to Irish American History*, 19–20, 155.

Chapter 2

1. Grabbe, "European Immigration to the United States,"194–97; Miller, *Emigrants and Exiles*, 169–92. For a careful discussion of the problems in interpreting immigration statistics for this period, see Miller et al., *Irish Immigrants in the Land of Canaan*, 656–78.

2. Carey, *Autobiography*, 115. Irish republican exiles in the United States have been the subject of a number of excellent studies in recent years. See, especially, Twomey, *Jacobins and Jeffersonians*; Durey, *Transatlantic Radicals and the Early American Republic*; Wilson, *United Irishmen, United States*; and Bric, *Ireland, Philadelphia and the Re-invention of America*.

3. For a stimulating assessment of the myriad effects of this global scattering of Irish radicals, see Whelan, "The Green Atlantic."

4. MacNeven, *Pieces of Irish History*, 143; William Pitt to Charles Cornwallis, August 1798, quoted in McDowell, *Ireland in the Age of Imperialism and Revolution*, 678–79; Lord Carysfort to Lord Grenville, August 15, 1798, quoted in Bartlett, "Britishness, Irishness and the Act of Union," 244. In the most detailed study of the passage of the act, Geoghegan, *The Irish Act of Union*, 2, argues that the 1798 rebellion "enabled Pitt to transform his aspiration for a union into government policy."

5. The Reverend Samuel Marsden, 1807 report to the London Missionary Society, quoted in Whitaker, *Unfinished Revolution*, 36. According to Whelan, *Fellowship of Freedom*, 99, the majority of rebels in 1798 were "young, unmarried men in their early twenties, officered by thirty-somethings."

6. Walter Corish Devereux to John Corish Derereux, April 1, 1798, in Miller et al., *Irish Immigrants in the Land of Canaan*, 42–43.

7. Quinn, *Soul on Fire*, 228–37.

8. For this version of Emmet's speech from the dock, see Geoghegan, *Robert Emmet*, 253–54, who provides the fullest treatment of his life. See Elliott, *Robert Emmet*, 104–236, for the long-term impact of the Emmet legend.

9. See Elliott, *Wolfe Tone*, 391; Elliott, *Partners in Revolution*, 323; Bartlett, "Miles Byrne," 118–20; and Bartlett, "Last Flight of the Wild Geese?" 160, 163, 169.

10. See Thompson, *The Making of the English Working Class*, 139–40, 145, 148, 166–67, 174; Elliott, "Irish Republicanism in England"; Goodwin, *The Friends of Liberty*, 416–50; Wells, *Insurrection*, 69–71; Keogh, Introduction to Coigly, *A Patriot Priest*, 14–19.

11. See Elliott, "The 'Despard Conspiracy' Reconsidered"; McFarland, *Ireland and Scotland in the Age of Revolution*, 129–79; Mitchell, *The Irish in the West of Scotland*, 64–111; Stedman Jones, *Languages of Class*, 2; and Thompson, *The Chartists*, 280, 301–2.

12. Kevin Whelan, "Introduction to Section VIII," in Bartlett et al., eds., *1798*, 597–99; O'Donnell, "'Liberty or Death,'" 607; O'Farrell, *The Irish in Australia*, 29–34. The most detailed study of the United Irishmen in Australia is Whitaker, *Unfinished Revolution*, though still valuable for its analysis of the Castle Hill rebellion is Connell, "The Convict Rebellion of 1804." For the Irish and the Australian ethos of "mateship," see Hughes, *The Fatal Shore*, 320, 352–59.

13. Elliott, *The Catholics of Ulster*, 261–66; Farrell, *Rituals and Riots*, 43–64; Drennan to McTier, April 7, 1807, in Drennan and McTier, *Letters*, 3:595; Sheil, quoted in Bartlett, *The Fall and Rise of the Irish Nation*, 304. See Whelan, "The Green Atlantic," 230–31, for a succinct analysis of this point.

14. Carey, *Autobiography*; O'Toole, *The Faithful*, 34. According to Branson, *These Fiery Frenchified Dames*, 38, Carey was convinced that he could sell 1,500 copies of Wollstonecraft's book, even though London and Boston editions were already available to American readers.

15. Weber, *On the Road to Rebellion*, 39–40; Coughlan, *Napper Tandy*, 97–109; Elliott, *Partners in Revolution*, 44–50; Rowan *Autobiography*, 210–79, 283–84; McNally to ____, September 12, 1795, quoted in Bartlett, Introduction to Higgins, *Revolutionary Dublin*, 44.

16. Tandy's words excerpted in Leonard McNally, report, July 26, 1796, quoted in Coughlan, *Napper Tandy*, 112; Rowan to Jefferson, [before] July 19, 1798, in Jefferson, *Papers*, 460–61; Mathew Carey to John Chambers, June 19, 1795, quoted in Bric, *Ireland, Philadelphia and the Re-invention of America*, 219; Rowan, *Autobiography*, 283, 323.

17. For Duane's experiences in India and London, see Phillips, "William Duane, Revolutionary Editor," 4–100, which provides the fullest treatment of his life.

18. Jefferson to William Wirt, March 30, 1811, quoted in Phillips, "William Duane and the Origins of Modern Politics," 368. For Duane's pivotal role in Republican politics in the United States, see also Wilson, *United Irishmen, United States*, 4–5; Wilentz, *The Rise of American Democracy*, 81, 90; and, especially, Pasley, *"The Tyranny of Printers,"* 176–95.

19. Rufus King to the Duke of Portland, September 13, 1798, MacNeven to Lord Cornwallis, October 11, 1798, Emmet to ____, October 11, 1798, quoted in Wilson, *United Irishmen, United States*, 2, 31; Jefferson, message to Congress, December 8, 1800, quoted in Wilentz, *The Rise of American Democracy*, 101.

20. Madden, *The United Irishmen*, 4:154; Bartlett, "Last Flight of the Wild Geese?" 166–67; Weber, *On the Road to Rebellion*, 141–66.

21. Emmet to the editor of the *American Citizen*, April 1, 10, 1807, quoted in Walsh, "Religion, Ethnicity, and History," 53. The exiles' role in the democratization of American politics is one of the leitmotifs of Wilson, *United Irishmen, United States*, and is the central theme of Kalliomäki " 'The Most God-Provoking Democrats on This Side of Hell.' " The contribution of particular émigrés, especially Duane, is also emphasized in Wilentz, *The Rise of American Democracy*. In Pasley's view, "William Duane provides the ultimate example of an editor whose presence helped transform the early American public sphere." See Pasley, *"The Tyranny of Printers,"* 176.

22. Congressman Uriah Tracy to Oliver Wolcott, August 7, 1800, and Sampson to Carey, May 31, 1831, both quoted in Wilson, *United Irishmen, United States*, 1, 146. Research on women and politics in the early republic has been growing steadily in recent years. For two important studies, see Allgor, *Parlor Politics*, and Zagarri, *Revolutionary Backlash*.

23. Sampson and Vanière, *The Catholic Question in America*, 59, 85. See Walsh, "Religion, Ethnicity, and History," 53–61, for a full discussion of this important case.

24. Sampson's argument in *People v. Moore* [1824], quoted in Walsh, "Religion, Ethnicity, and History," 62. For the background to the Greenwich Village riot and for other examples of rioting between Irish Catholics and Orangemen in New York in this era, see Gilje, *The Road to Mobocracy*, 133–38. Though it lies beyond the scope of this book, it is worth noting that scholars of the Orange Order have recently begun to frame its history in transnational terms. See, for example, MacRaild, "The Orange Atlantic."

25. See Light, *Rome and the New Republic*, 6, 52–54, 56–57, 72–73; Wilson, "The United Irishmen and the Re-invention of Irish America," 635; and Wilson, *United Irishmen, United States*, 3, 53–54.

26. Wilson, *United Irishmen, United States*, 6. For the importance of Carey's economic ideas, see Peskin, *Manufacturing Revolution*, 65–71, 216–18. For Duane's role as a workers' advocate, see Schultz, *The Republic of Labor*, 150–64, 181–91.

27. Sampson, *Trial of the Journeymen Cordwainers*, 31. The case is one of the most studied in American labor history, but few scholars seem to be aware of the bonds of experience and ideology that linked prosecuting and defense attorneys. For an exception, see Wilentz, *Chants Democratic*, 97, who notes a shared ideology between the two that he characterizes as "exiled Irish Jacobin and Jeffersonian."

28. Driscol, in *American Patriot*, November 13, 1802, quoted in Wilson, *United Irishmen, United States*, 135–36; Brown, "United Irishmen in the American South," 87, 99–100; Campbell, in *Natchez Mississippi Republican*, March 16, 1819, quoted in Gleeson, *The Irish in the South*, 123.

29. Warden, *Statistical, Political, and Historical Account of the United States* [1819], quoted in Wilson, *United Irishmen, United States*, 135; Rowan, *Autobiography*, 291. For New York's 1799 gradual abolition law and the activities of the New York Manumission Society, see Gellman, *Emancipating New York*.

30. *Shamrock*, December 29, 1810; Gibbons, "Republicanism and Radical Memory," 228–29; "Essays, by an Irishman [Thomas O'Connor], 1839," AIHS, O'Connor Papers; Nash and Soderlund, *Freedom by Degrees*, 136; Taylor, *The Civil War of 1812*, 327–28; Carey, "Emancipation of the Slaves in the United States," in *Miscellaneous Essays*, 222–23. For an analysis of Carey's evolving views on slavery from the 1819 Missouri Crisis to the Nullification Crisis of 1832–33, see Shankman, "Neither Infinite Wretchedness nor Positive Good," 247–50, 259–63.

31. Wilson, "The United Irishmen and the Re-invention of Irish America," 640.

32. "Declaration and Constitution of the American Society of United Irishmen, August 8, 1797," reprinted in Cobbett, *Porcupine's Works*, 202, 205. See also Whelan, "The Green Atlantic," 227–28, and Bric, *Ireland, Philadelphia and the Re-invention of America*, 225–31.

33. Musgrave, *Memoirs of the Different Rebellions in Ireland*, 851. For the ideological importance of the exiles' historical writings on 1798, see Burke, "Piecing Together a Shattered Past," and Whelan, *The Tree of Liberty*, 167, who refers to these and other later works as a collective project of "reclaiming the rebellion." For a full analysis of Musgrave's "ultra-Protestant" account, see Kelly, *Sir Richard Musgrave*.

34. Gibney, *The Shadow of a Year*, 96–103; Elliott, *Robert Emmet*, 159–60.

35. In what follows, I have drawn freely on my article, "Matilda Tone in America."

36. Curtin, "Matilda Tone and Virtuous Republican Femininity," 34–35, 39; Martha McTier to William Drennan, undated [1797], April 2, 1801, and February 19, 1802, in Drennan and McTier, *Letters*, 2: 293, 693, 3: 11; Elliott, *Wolfe Tone*, 389–91.

37. See St. Mark, "Matilda and William Tone in New York and Washington."

38. McDowell and Woods, General Introduction to Tone, *Writings*, 1: xxiii–xxiv; Elliott, *Wolfe Tone*, 395–96.

39. William T. W. Tone, "Preface" [1826], in Tone, *Life*, 4. Though the title page of the work named only William Tone as editor, Curtin, "Matilda Tone and Virtuous Republican Femininity," 37, concludes that Matilda was "the uncredited collaborator in this edition of Tone's memoirs." Elliott, *Wolfe Tone*, xvi, goes further, asserting that it was Matilda, not William, "who decided the tone and format" of the book that became "arguably one of the most influential writings in the history of Irish nationalism." For details on the various excisions in the work, see Curtin, "Matilda Tone and Virtuous Republican Femininity," 36, 37, 39, 44; Elliott, *Wolfe Tone*, 70–71, 256, 330; and Quinn, "Tone and the Historians," 121–22. For the critical importance of imaginative ideological labor in nationalist movements, see Eley and Suny, "From the Moment of Social History to the Work of Cultural Representation," 8.

40. The most thorough account of these events is O'Ferrall, *Catholic Emancipation*, but see also MacDonagh, *The Hereditary Bondsman*, 161–81, 205–80.

41. William Drennan to O'Connell, January 30, 1819, in O'Connell, *Correspondence*, 2: 195–96; Chief Secretary for Ireland Henry Goulburn, February 10, 1825, quoted in MacDonagh, *The Hereditary Bondsman*, 215; "Speech of William Sampson," quoted in Wilson, *United Irishmen, United States*, 168. See also Moriarty, "The Irish American Response to Catholic Emancipation," 366; Manning, *The Revolt of French Canada*, xiv; and Brown, "United Irishmen in the American South," 102.

42. Funchion, "Friends of Ireland," 116; Richard Sheil, February 1829 speech, quoted in Moriarty, "The Irish American Response to Catholic Emancipation," 361; MacDonagh, *The Hereditary Bondsman*, 244–45; Wyse, *Historical Sketch of the Catholic Association*, 1: 310–11, 320.

43. *Democratic Press*, May 14, 1829, and John Binns, *Recollections of the Life of John Binns* [1854], quoted in Wilson, *United Irishmen, United States*, 168.

44. Rowan, *Autobiography*, 472; Wilson, *United Irishmen, United States*, 168; Sampson's 1827 address to the New York Bar, in "Thomas Addis Emmet," 130.

45. For MacNeven's address, see "Emmet Monument" (1833), reprinted in Emmet [1828–1919; Emmet's grandson], *Memoir of Thomas Addis and Robert Emmet*. Sampson himself captured this point by ending his address to the New York Bar with the already familiar words of Emmet's martyred brother, "which may yet but be too applicable: 'Let no man write my epitaph till my country is free.'" See "Thomas Addis Emmet," 131.

Chapter 3

1. Thomas O'Connor, untitled and undated [1829] fragment of manuscript on Catholic Emancipation, AIHS, O'Connor Papers.

2. See MacDonagh, *The Hereditary Bondsman*, 92–93, 102–3, and MacDonagh, *The Emancipist*, 74–75, 119–22.

3. *Freeman's Journal* (Dublin), October 9, 1840, quoted in Nowlan, *The Politics of Repeal*, 6; O'Connell to W. J. O'Neill Daunt, September 9, 1842, in O'Connell, *Correspondence*, 7: 173; Boyce, *Nationalism in Ireland*, 154.

4. Nowlan, "O'Connell and Irish Nationalism," 10; O'Connell to Maurice O'Connell, January 23, 1797, O'Connell to P. V. FitzPatrick, May 10, 1839, in O'Connell, *Correspondence,* 1: 30, 6: 242. For O'Connell's youth and early experiences in France and London, see MacDonagh, *The Hereditary Bondsman,* 7–70. Despite his flirtation with Paineite deism in the 1790s, he had returned fully to the beliefs and practices of Catholicism by 1809 at the latest. For O'Connell's rhetorical emphasis on the moderate character of "Grattan's Parliament," the ways he "inscribed 'Loyal' on his banners with all the purposive ostentation of an Orange lodge," and for his ideas (never fully fleshed out) about the constitutional forms that an Irish-British connection might take after repeal, see MacDonagh, *The Emancipist,* 80–87.

5. Francis Higgins to Edward Cooke, March 7, 1798, in Higgins, *Revolutionary Dublin,* 227; O'Connell to Mary O'Connell, August 28, 1803, in O'Connell, *Correspondence,* 1: 99. See also Woods, "Was O'Connell a United Irishman?" 183; MacDonagh, *The Hereditary Bondsman,* 54–56, 62–64, 94, 168–71; MacDonagh, *The Emancipist,* 37–38.

6. Joseph Hayes to O'Connell, August 14, 1840, in O'Connell, *Correspondence,* 6: 352; MacDonagh, *The Emancipist,* 220. For an insightful analysis of the political and religious symbols of the monster meetings, see Owens, "Nationalism without Words."

7. See Nowlan, *The Politics of Repeal,* 54–57.

8. Mooney, *Nine Years in America,* 118.

9. For migration statistics for this era, which must be treated with a great deal of caution, see Fitzpatrick, "Emigration," 565, and Doyle, "The Irish in North America," 682–83. Miller, *Emigrants and Exiles,* 193–240, provides a detailed and nuanced account of the forces shaping pre-Famine emigration from Ireland. Kenny, *The American Irish,* 45–56, and Meagher, *The Columbia Guide to Irish American History,* 52–58, provide concise synopses of these trends.

10. Foster, *Modern Ireland,* 318, argues persuasively that 1815, rather than one of the Famine years, was actually the "watershed year" in the social and economic history of nineteenth-century Ireland, setting in motion many of the demographic and economic changes usually associated with the Famine.

11. For agrarian protest in the 1820s, see Donnelly, *Captain Rock,* 3–25.

12. Doyle, "The Irish in North America," 695–96.

13. Mooney, *Nine Years in America,* 118. My discussion of the emerging Irish American middle class here draws on the findings of a number of detailed local studies: Mitchell, *The Paddy Camps,* 7, 40–41, 47–48, 52–55; Marston, "Public Rituals and Community Power," 258–59; Powers, *"Invisible Immigrants,"* 240–85; Montgomery, "The Shuttle and the Cross," 412–13, 416–19; Feldberg, *The Turbulent Era,* 62–64; Light, *Rome and the New Republic,* 275–79, 382–84; and Gilje, "The Development of an Irish American Community in New York City," 71–72.

14. O'Toole, *The Faithful,* 100–101; McGreevy, *Catholicism and American Freedom,* 14; Kenny, *The American Irish,* 75; Doyle, "The Irish in North America," 713–14.

15. *New York Evening Post,* November 1, 1834. For Mike Walsh, see Wilentz, *Chants Democratic,* 326–35. For the decline of the United Irish influence in New York and its replacement by "ethnic politics, class politics, and machine politics," see Walsh, "Religion, Ethnicity, and History," 64–68.

16. Doyle, "The Irish in North America," 716; Feldberg, *The Turbulent Era,* 9–32; Montgomery, "The Shuttle and the Cross," 422–39. See also Knobel, *Paddy and the Republic,* and Emmons, *Beyond the America Pale,* 44–75, for insightful discussions of anti-Irish Catholic nativism in this period.

17. Grattan, *Civilized America,* 2: 44–45; Handlin, *Boston's Immigrants,* 152, 162; Potter, *To the Golden Door,* 388–89. Although historians have long recognized the importance of support for repeal among Irish Americans, only with the publication of Murphy, *American Slavery, Irish Freedom* did we get a history of the American wing of the movement equal to its significance. For insightful brief assessments by previous historians, however, see Miller, *Emigrants and Exiles,* 277–79; Doyle, "The Irish in North America," 720–23; and Funchion, "Repeal Associations."

18. *Boston Pilot,* February 28, 1841. See also Mitchell, *The Paddy Camps,* 7, 73–74, 167, 182; Handlin, *Boston's Immigrants,* 247; Clark, *The Irish in Philadelphia,* 18–19; and Doyle, "The Irish in North America," 720. My discussion of the growth of the American repeal network

here and in the following few paragraphs draws heavily on Murphy, *American Slavery, Irish Freedom*, 54–72.

19. O'Connell quoted in Madden, *The United Irishmen*, 3:178–79; Thomas O'Connor, undated handwritten notes, AIHS, O'Connor Papers; Funchion, "Repeal Associations," 237.

20. Clark, *The Irish in Philadelphia*, 18–19.

21. Potter, *To the Golden Door*, 396–98; *Proceedings of the National Repeal Convention*, 5. According to Light, "The Role of Irish-American Organisations," 127–28, 59 percent of the Philadelphia Repeal Association's members held white-collar occupations, 32 percent were skilled workers, and just 9 percent were laborers. A full 42 percent of its members owned property.

22. *New York Freeman's Journal*, September 4, October 2, 1841, quoted in Murphy, *American Slavery, Irish Freedom*, 64; *Proceedings of the National Repeal Convention*, 20–21, 24.

23. Quinn, "The Rise and Fall of Repeal," 69; *Public Ledger* (Philadelphia), October 7, 26, 1843, and *Boston Pilot*, June 24, 1843, quoted in Murphy, *American Slavery, Irish Freedom*, 64–65.

24. O'Connell journal entry, January 3, 1796, quoted in MacDonagh, *The Hereditary Bondsman*, 42; *Freeman's Journal*, April 5, 1842, quoted in Murphy, *American Slavery, Irish Freedom*, 65; O'Dowd, "O'Connell and the Lady Patriots." For the remarkable proliferation and diversity of women-run organizations in American cities by the early 1840s, see, in particular, Boylan, *The Origins of Women's Activism*. As O'Dowd has shown, however, "actively" observing meetings could be a way for Irish women to exert political influence and was a tradition of elite women's activism in Ireland going back to the era of the Volunteers. See O'Dowd, "The Women in the Gallery."

25. Gleeson, *The Irish in the South*, 68; James Faye to Thomas Steele, September 14, 1841, and *Freeman's Journal*, September 17, 1841, quoted in Murphy, *American Slavery, Irish Freedom*, 61–62; Quinn, "The Rise and Fall of Repeal," 54; *Proceedings of the National Repeal Convention*, 34, 36.

26. *Cincinnati Catholic Telegraph*, May 21, 1842; Potter, *To the Golden Door*, 390–92.

27. *Wrongs and Rights of Ireland*, 1; Snay, *Horace Greeley and the Politics of Reform*, 95–98; Williams, *Horace Greeley*, 139–40; John Tyler, quoted in Duffy, *Young Ireland*, 318–19.

28. *New York Herald*, June 9, 10, 1843, quoted in Murphy, *American Slavery, Irish Freedom*, 152; *Proceedings of the National Repeal Convention*, 7; Quinn, "The Rise and Fall of Repeal," 64–65; Wilentz, *The Rise of American Democracy*, 164–65, 533.

29. Remarks by Francis W. Pickens, February 13, 1841, *Congressional Globe*, quoted in Crapol, *John Tyler*, 72–73, 92–93; Josiah Abbott, in *Lowell Courier*, March 21, 1843, quoted in Mitchell, *The Paddy Camps*, 73. For a persuasive analysis of the importance of Anglophobia within America's political and foreign policy elite in this decade and how it encouraged sympathy for repeal, see Sim, *A Union Forever*, 11–38.

30. Howe, *The Political Culture of the American Whigs*, 27, 77; Snay, *Horace Greeley and the Politics of Reform*, 96–98; Seward, *An Oration on the Death of O'Connell*, 47.

31. See Potter, *To the Golden Door*, 401–3, for a description of this discussion.

32. Guy, *Edmund Bailey O'Callaghan*, 1, 4, 6–8, 14–15, 20, 24–25, 35; Manning, *The Revolt of French Canada*, 204–5; Grace, *The Irish in Quebec*, 128, 193–94; Wilson, *The Irish in Canada*, 15; Doyle, "The Irish in North America," 721.

33. *Public Ledger*, June 3, 1843, quoted in Clark, *The Irish in Philadelphia*, 18–19. On the weaknesses of repeal relative to later nationalist movements, see Miller, *Emigrants and Exiles*, 278–79.

34. McCaffrey, *O'Connell and the Repeal Year*, 72; Wilson, *The Irish in Canada*, 15; Clarke, *Piety and Nationalism*, 155–56.

35. See Fitzpatrick, *Oceans of Consolation*, 6–9, and O'Farrell, *The Irish in Australia*, 203–4.

36. McCaffrey, *O'Connell and the Repeal Year*, 72; Crowe, "The Reminiscences of a Chartist Tailor" [1902], quoted in Thompson, *Outsiders*, 103.

37. MacDonagh, *The Emancipist*, 94–95; O'Connor, *Letters to O'Connell*, 20; Thompson, *The Chartists*, 94–101.

38. Lee, "The Social and Economic Ideas of O'Connell," 78; MacDonagh, *The Emancipist*, 184; Davis, *The Young Ireland Movement*, 189–90. British historians are divided on this last issue. For an influential argument that Irish immigrants in Britain had little contact with Chartism

before 1848, see Treble, "O'Connor, O'Connell and the Attitudes of Irish Immigrants Towards Chartism." For a persuasive rebuttal, see Thompson, _Outsiders_, 103–28.

39. The following discussion is indebted to the analysis of Murphy, _American Slavery, Irish Freedom_, but it should be noted that the literature on this topic is large. Osofsky, "Abolitionists, Irish Immigrants," first drew attention to the relationship between abolition and the American repeal movement, but more recent work by Roediger, Ignatiev, and others has presented the American repeal movement's rejection of abolition as an integral part of a process by which oppressed Irish Catholic working-class immigrants "became white." Putting aside the question of whether the larger argument is persuasive or whether, as several critics have noted, Irish working-class immigrants who could become citizens under the 1790 naturalization law should be seen as "white on arrival," the argument actually has little relevance to the American repeal movement, which was not (at least after its Boston beginnings) a movement dominated by working-class immigrants. Rather, as Murphy conclusively demonstrates, the movement was a cross-class and cross-confessional one and was led by the emerging Irish American middle class. See Murphy, _American Slavery, Irish Freedom_, esp. 15–17, 57–58. For key contributions to the wider debate, see Roediger, _The Wages of Whiteness_, 133–63, Ignatiev, _How the Irish Became White_, 6–31; Kenny, _The American Irish_, 61–71; Kolchin, "Whiteness Studies"; Arnesen et al., "Scholarly Controversy: Whiteness and the Historians' Imagination"; and Nelson, _Irish Nationalists and the Making of the Irish Race_, 57–85. Pertinent also is the important study of Italian immigrants by Guglielmo, _White on Arrival_.

40. Charlton, "The State of Ireland in the 1820s," 321–23, 327, 338–39; MacDonagh, _The Emancipist_, 54; Riach, "O'Connell and Anti-Slavery," 3–25; Murphy, _American Slavery, Irish Freedom_, 29–35; Osofsky, "Abolitionists, Irish Immigrants," 890. The fullest account of O'Connell's anti-slavery career is now Kinealy, _O'Connell and the Anti-Slavery Movement_.

41. _Liberator_ (Boston), January 26, 1833, quoted in Osofsky, "Abolitionists, Irish Immigrants," 890–92; "From Some Philadelphia Citizens" to O'Connell, February 2, 1838, in O'Connell, _Correspondence_, 6: 129–30; McDaniel, _The Problem of Democracy_, 43–45, 167–68. The historical literature on abolitionism after 1830 is immense; for a helpful survey, see Stewart, _Holy Warriors_.

42. James Canning Fuller, 1840, quoted in Bric, "Debating Slavery and Empire," 70; Riach, "O'Connell and Anti-Slavery," 6, 8; Murphy, _American Slavery, Irish Freedom_, 36–41; Maynard, "The World's Anti-Slavery Convention," 452, 459–61, 463, 465.

43. _Freeman's Journal_ (Dublin), May 29, 1841, quoted in Murphy, _American Slavery, Irish Freedom_, 49–50. For Remond, see also Ripley, Introduction, _The Black Abolitionist Papers_, 7–8, 17–18, and, for Douglass's 1845 lecture tour of Ireland, Chaffin, _Giant's Causeway_, 35–106.

44. O'Connell, _O'Connell upon American Slavery_, 37–38; _Liberator_, February 4, 1842, quoted in Murphy, _American Slavery, Irish Freedom_, 50–52.

45. O'Connell, _O'Connell upon American Slavery_, 40–41; Murphy, _American Slavery, Irish Freedom_, 52–53.

46. _Boston Pilot_, February 5, March 19, 1842, quoted in Murphy, _American Slavery, Irish Freedom_, 84; Hughes, _Complete Works_, 1: 153. For American Catholic teachings on slavery and Hughes's opinions on it, see McGreevy, _Catholicism and American Freedom_, 43–67; Wallace, _Catholics, Slaveholders, and American Evangelicalism_, 118–19; and Sharrow, "John Hughes and a Catholic Response to Slavery."

47. See Murphy, _American Slavery, Irish Freedom_, 85–88, for an analysis of the discussion.

48. See Murphy, _American Slavery, Irish Freedom_, 88–97.

49. Murphy, _American Slavery, Irish Freedom_, 121–22. See also Murphy, "The Influence of America on Irish Nationalism," 110.

50. Gleeson, _The Irish in the South_, 131; _Public Ledger_, July 6, 1843, quoted in Murphy, _American Slavery, Irish Freedom_, 129.

51. _National Anti-Slavery Standard_ (New York), July 13, August 10, 1843, quoted in Murphy, _American Slavery, Irish Freedom_, 126–28. Vermont had abolished slavery in 1777, the first state in the new nation to do so.

52. See Quinn, "The Rise and Fall of Repeal," 66–68, for the conflict in Philadelphia.

53. In addition to Murphy's work, my discussion here draws on Riach, "O'Connell and Anti-Slavery," 6–7, 11; Kenny, *The American Irish*, 61–71; and Osofsky, "Abolitionists, Irish Immigrants."

54. Murphy, "O'Connell and the 'American Eagle,'" 6. The following discussion draws on this important article and on Murphy, *American Slavery, Irish Freedom*, 192–215. Few previous scholars gave much attention to this speech, assuming that it was Irish American opposition to abolition that killed the American repeal movement. Murphy, however, demonstrates conclusively that the American repeal network survived O'Connell's anti-slavery stance but not his support of British foreign policy objectives as these came into conflict with policy of the United States.

55. See Anderson and Clayton, *Dominion of War*, 276; Wilentz, *The Rise of American Democracy*, 577–78, 580–81; O'Connell, speech to the Loyal National Repeal Association, March 30, 1845, *Nation* (Dublin), April 5, 1845, quoted in Murphy, "O'Connell and the 'American Eagle,'" 5.

56. John F. H. Claiborne to James K. Polk, May 17, 1845, in Polk, *Correspondence*, 382; *Boston Pilot*, May 17, 31, 1845, quoted in Murphy, "O'Connell and the 'American Eagle,'" 12, 17.

57. Davis, *The Young Ireland Movement*, 1, 13–14. Davis's book remains the most thorough account of Young Ireland.

58. Davis, *The Young Ireland Movement*, 34–35, 231; O'Connell in conversation with W. J. O'Neill Daunt, 1833, quoted in MacDonagh, *The Hereditary Bondsman*, 11–12. It can be argued, in fact, that the strong emphasis on literary nationalism—in English—actually hastened the decline of Ireland's old Gaelic ballad culture. For an analysis of what he terms the "racial language of Celts and Saxons" that was so important to the history of Young Ireland, see McMahon, *The Global Dimensions of Irish Identity*, 16–32.

59. Davis, *The Young Ireland Movement*, 34–35.

60. Davis, *The Young Ireland Movement*, 40, 42, 95–99.

61. Meagher, *Meagher of the Sword*, 36. See Davis, *The Young Ireland Movement*, 99–104, for a full description of the debate.

62. Riach, "O'Connell and Anti-Slavery," 17, 19–20, 22–23; Davis, *The Young Ireland Movement*, 141; Doheny, *The Felon's Track*, 25; *Nation*, January 13, 1844, quoted in O'Connell, "O'Connell, Young Ireland, and Negro Slavery," 206; *Nation*, April 12, 1845, quoted in Murphy, *American Slavery, Irish Freedom*, 208. See also Delahanty, "'A Noble Empire in the West.'" By way of context, it should be noted that the other main Irish repeal newspapers (not just the *Nation*) were also distancing themselves from O'Connell's anti-slavery position.

63. Elliott, *Wolfe Tone*, 396–99; Quinn, "Tone and the Historians," 114.

64. Davis, *The Young Ireland Movement*, 15; Whelan, *The Tree of Liberty*, 167–68; Woods, "R. R. Madden," 497–501.

65. Rodgers, "Richard Robert Madden," 119–25; Riach, "O'Connell and Anti-Slavery," 6; Murphy, *American Slavery, Irish Freedom*, 40, 46. O'Connell's efforts to change Irish American attitudes toward slavery may have been influenced by a speech that Madden made in February 1840, urging the Irish people and clergy to work to alter Irish American views on the question.

66. Meagher, *Meagher of the Sword*, 89; Davis, *The Young Ireland Movement*, 34–35.

67. Davis, *The Young Ireland Movement*, 124–25; Mitchel, quoted in Belchem, "Nationalism, Republicanism and Exile," 108–9. Not surprisingly, Young Ireland was no more open to women's participation than the larger Repeal Association had been. The *Nation* did open its pages to some highly talented women poets, particularly Jane Francesca Elgee (whose fame would later be surpassed by that of her son, Oscar Wilde). But at the founding of the Irish Confederation, the possibility of women's membership was never discussed. Michael Joseph Barry reflected the dominant view in the organization when he called on Irish women to use their "gentle influence" to bolster their husbands' and sons' "steady resolution." See Davis, *The Young Ireland Movement*, 80, 84–85, 120.

68. Boyce, *Nationalism in Ireland*, 170–71.

69. Mitchel quoted in Boyce, *Nationalism in Ireland*, 172–73; Davis, *The Young Ireland Movement*, 145–46.

70. See Boyce, *Nationalism in Ireland*, 173–75, for a full discussion.

71. Hart, *Young Irelander Abroad*, 2; Duffy, *Four Years of Irish History*, 609.
72. John F. Crampton, diplomatic dispatch, April 2, 1848, quoted in Belchem, "Nationalism, Republicanism and Exile," 114. For the enthusiasm with which a broad cross-section of Americans greeted the 1848 revolutions, see Roberts, *Distant Revolutions*, 42–62.
73. Press clippings in "Irish Republican Union" file, British Foreign Office Papers, quoted in Belchem, "Nationalism, Republicanism and Exile," 114; *Boston Pilot*, May 13, 1848.
74. *Boston Pilot*, May 27, 1848; *New York Herald*, May 10, 1848.
75. *New York Herald*, June 6, 1848. For Greeley's support for the new turn, see Snay, *Horace Greeley and the Politics of Reform*, 97–98, and Williams, *Horace Greeley*, 141.
76. *Boston Pilot*, May 27, June 24, July 1, 1848; Kinealy, *Repeal and Revolution*, 164.
77. Potter, *To the Golden Door*, 506; Belchem, "Nationalism, Republicanism and Exile," 117; *Boston Pilot*, August 12, 19, 1848.
78. Kinealy, *Repeal and Revolution*, 211–17; Crampton, diplomatic dispatch, October 9, 1848, quoted in Belchem, "Nationalism, Republicanism and Exile," 118–19.
79. Hart, *Young Irelander Abroad*, 61–62, 85.

Chapter 4

1. Hughes to Society for Propagation of the Faith, Paris, June 26, 1849, quoted in Dolan, *The Immigrant Church*, 33. See also Ó Gráda, *Black '47 and Beyond*, 114–15, and, for a full history of the neighborhood, Anbinder, *Five Points*.
2. The significance of the Famine for Irish America, of course, went far beyond its impact on Irish American nationalism. For a comprehensive study of its long-term social and cultural consequences, see Kelly, *Ireland's Great Famine in Irish-American History*.
3. "In so far as such things can be dated, the Irish revolution started with the founding of the IRB in 1858," noted Garvin in his seminal 1987 work, *Irish Nationalist Revolutionaries in Ireland*, 5, and most scholars today would agree. As with many other moments in the history of Irish nationalism, however, the historiography of Fenianism has been a battlefield between nationalist, revisionist, and various post-revisionist interpretations. See, for example, Newsinger's critique of revisionist work on the IRB, "Fenianism Revisited," along with the response by Comerford, "Comprehending the Fenians." Important book-length studies include Moody, ed., *The Fenian Movement*; Comerford, *The Fenians in Context*; Newsinger, *Fenianism in Mid-Victorian Britain*; Rafferty, *Church, State, and the Fenian Threat*; McGee, *The IRB*; and, though it focuses mainly on a later period, Kelly, *The Fenian Ideal and Irish Nationalism*. For assessments of recent trends in the historiography, see Kelly, "Faith in Fraternity," and McGarry and McConnel, Introduction, *The Black Hand of Republicanism*, xi–xxii.
4. Though less heated than the historiographical debate in Ireland, research on Fenianism in the United States has also been characterized by markedly different interpretive approaches since D'Arcy published his pioneering work, *The Fenian Movement in the United States*, more than sixty years ago. While Brown, *Irish-American Nationalism*, proposed that even physical force nationalists like the Fenians could be seen as exhibiting a powerful drive for acceptance and respectability ("in the Lace Curtain Irishman the rebel found fulfillment," he memorably observed [p. 46]), Miller, *Emigrants and Exiles*, argued that the Fenians both reflected and exacerbated a deep sense of alienation from American society that characterized Irish immigrants generally in the era of the Famine. Two historians trained by Miller have written the most thorough account of the Brotherhood's American history. See Steward and McGovern, *The Fenians*.
5. The historical literature on the Famine has been growing rapidly since the 1990s. For an authoritative summation of current research, see Crowley et al., eds., *Atlas of the Great Irish Famine*. My discussion draws heavily on this work, as well as on Donnelly's concise overview, *The Great Irish Potato Famine*.
6. Estimating the Famine's death toll has been a contentious issue for Irish historians. Though some revisionist historians in the 1970s and 1980s proposed a much lower figure (less than 500,000), the figure of a million or more is now once again widely accepted. See Donnelly, *The Great Irish Potato Famine*, 169–71.

7. For a full discussion of Peel's relief policies, see Gray, *Famine, Land and Politics*, 95–141, and for a concise overview, Gray, "British Relief Measures." Gray makes the point that while the continuing export of food from Ireland undoubtedly worsened the situation, retaining high-cost food products in Ireland, as O'Connell proposed, would not have done much for the rural poor in the absence of an effective distribution system. See also the concluding assessment of British famine policies in Kinealy, *This Great Calamity*, 349–59.

8. Maguire, *The Irish in America*, 607; Gray, "British Relief Measures," 83–84. Historians disagree on the number of people evicted during the Famine. For the estimate of 500,000 persons either formally or informally evicted, see Donnelly, *The Great Irish Potato Famine*, 157.

9. Charles Trevelyan, *The Irish Crisis* [1848], quoted in Donnelly, *The Great Irish Potato Famine*, 20; John Mitchel in the *Irish Citizen*, February 22, 29, April 24, 1868, quoted in Quinn, *John Mitchel*, 79. Though Mitchel's importance to both Irish and Irish American history has long been acknowledged, his racist and pro-slavery views, along with what Foster, *Modern Ireland*, 316, calls his "almost psychotic Anglophobia," have made him an extremely unattractive figure and have probably discouraged modern historians and biographers from assessing his career. This is beginning to change, however. For an excellent brief examination of Mitchel's life and thought, see Quinn, *John Mitchel*. For a full-scale recent biography, particularly attuned to his influence among the American Irish, see McGovern, *John Mitchel*.

10. D'Arcy, *The Fenian Movement in the United States*, 3.

11. Mitchel, *Jail Journal*, 1. See also Quinn, "John Mitchel and the Rejection of the Nineteenth Century," and Lynch, "Defining Irish Nationalist Anti-Imperialism." For a penetrating analysis of the pro-slavery propagandist George Fitzhugh, another devotee of Carlyle who shared much of Mitchel's worldview, see Genovese, *The World the Slaveholders Made*, 115–244.

12. Mitchel, *The Last Conquest of Ireland (Perhaps)*, 219.

13. Thomas D'Arcy McGee, in the *Nation*, April 24, July 21, 1847, quoted in Wilson, *Thomas D'Arcy McGee*, 1: 156–57; O'Leary, *Recollections of Fenians and Fenianism*, 1:42–43; *The Citizen*, March 11, 1854. For a penetrating discussion of Mitchel's ability to articulate the views of those who considered themselves his fellow exiles, see Miller, *Emigrants and Exiles*, 338–40.

14. Charles Gavan Duffy, MP, retiring address to his New Ross constituents, 1855, quoted in Pigott, *Personal Recollections*, 53; O'Leary, *Recollections of Fenians and Fenianism*, 1: 57; Bagenal, *The American Irish*, 109–10. For the 1849 conspiracy and its significance, see Ramón, *A Provisional Dictator*, 53–57, and Kinealy, *Repeal and Revolution*, 224–25.

15. See Riall, *Garibaldi*, 106–15; Roberts, *Distant Revolutions*, 146–67; and for the German '48ers, Levine, *The Spirit of 1848*.

16. Mitchel, *Jail Journal*, 205; Roberts, *Distant Revolutions*, 150; McGovern, *John Mitchel*, 111–14; *New-York Daily Times*, October 31, 1851. Irish American support for Kossuth soon waned, however, not only because of the Catholic Church's position, but because his advocacy of an Anglo-American alliance to liberate Hungary led him to reject calls for Irish independence. See Komlos, *Kossuth in America*, 147–48.

17. For these early republican efforts in the 1850s, see Funchion, "Emmet Monument Association," 101–5.

18. D'Arcy, *The Fenian Movement in the United States*, 5; Comerford, *The Fenians in Context*, 34. For persuasive documentation of the widespread Irish enthusiasm for Britain's war against Russia, see Murphy, *Ireland and the Crimean War*, 3–17, 186–96, 206–12.

19. Doheny, *The Felon's Track*; D'Arcy, *The Fenian Movement in the United States*, 6; Comerford, *The Fenians in Context*, 38.

20. Denieffe, *A Personal Narrative*, x, 1–3; Funchion, "Emmet Monument Association," 102; John F. Crampton to William L. Marcy, October 13, 1855, quoted in Royle, *Crimea*, 386–87; D'Arcy, *The Fenian Movement in the United States*, 6–7.

21. D'Arcy, *The Fenian Movement in the United States*, 8–9; Sim, *A Union Forever*, 74. Sim speculates that the name "Irish Emigrant Aid Society" alluded to the free soil Massachusetts Emigrant Aid Society, which sent anti-slavery advocates to Kansas territory in the 1850s.

22. Denieffe, *A Personal Narrative*, 3, 7–11; Comerford, "Churchmen, Tenants, and Independent Opposition," 413–14. According to his own account, Denieffe's initial recruits included a printer, a draper, a nail maker, a master chimneysweep, an iron manufacturer, a bookkeeper, and the proprietor of a lumberyard.

23. Kee, *The Green Flag*, 299–302; Comerford, *The Fenians in Context*, 41–42; O'Leary, *Recollections of Fenians and Fenianism*, 1: 87.

24. Bayly, "Ireland, India and the Empire," 387–88, argues that for the "radicals in Ireland and America who were soon to become known as 'Fenians,'" an important shift had occurred by the time of the Great Rebellion: "Assumed racial difference began to be supplanted by a sense of common grievance under the yoke of imperialism." See also Bayly, *The Birth of the Modern World*, 151–54. For Stephens, the most important figure in this emerging transatlantic movement, see Ryan's classic biography, *The Fenian Chief*, and the excellent recent study by Ramón, *A Provisional Dictator*.

25. For Stephens's political outlook in this period, see Ramón, *A Provisional Dictator*, 29–30; and McGee, *The IRB*, 15–20.

26. James Stephens to Michael Doheny, January 1, 1858, reprinted in Denieffe, *A Personal Narrative*, 159–60.

27. Denieffe, *A Personal Narrative*, 25–27, 58; D'Arcy, *The Fenian Movement in the United States*, 13–15.

28. Keating, *The History of Ireland*, 7, 343, 345. In his annotations of this work, O'Mahony portrayed "Fenian history" as a golden age when the rule of native kings was characterized by deep obligations to their warrior subjects. See also O'Leary, *Recollections of Fenians and Fenianism*, 1: 123; and Meagher, *The Columbia Guide to Irish American History*, 250. Townshend, *Political Violence in Ireland*, 25, argues that by using these vague names, members of the IRB in Ireland were consciously trying to convey its "natural" place in Irish life.

29. The best treatment of these developments remains Hobsbawm's chapter on "the world unified," in *The Age of Capital*, 48–71. For a more recent discussion, see Stearns's assessment of "the 1850s as a turning point," in his *Globalization in World History*, 90–123. Comerford, *The Fenians in Context*, 8–9, also draws attention to these developments but without exploring their implications for what might be called the internationalization of Fenianism. For a recent investigation of Irish nationalism in this period as a transnational phenomenon, owing much to the growth of the popular press, see McMahon, *The Global Dimensions of Irish Identity*.

30. *New York Times*, September 16, 1861. See also Bisceglia, "The Fenian Funeral of Terence Bellew McManus"; Brophy, "Rivalry between Irish Associations in San Francisco"; and Kelly, *The Shamrock and the Lily*, 134–37.

31. Denieffe, *A Personal Narrative*, 64; James Stephens, oration, delivered November 4, 1861, reprinted in O'Leary, *Recollections of Fenians and Fenianism*, 1: 165–67. See also Lee, *The Modernisation of Irish Society*, 55, and Beiner, "Fenianism and the Martyrdom-Terrorism Nexus," 200–201.

32. Crapol, *John Tyler*, 269–70; Schneirov, *Labor and Urban Politics*, 28. Like the Famine, the Civil War's importance in the history of Irish America went far beyond its relationship to Irish nationalism, and it has been the focus of several excellent recent studies. See Ural, *The Harp and the Eagle*; Samito, *Becoming American under Fire*; Gleeson, *The Green and the Gray*; and for an up-to-date overview, Shiels, *The Irish in the American Civil War*.

33. Ural, *The Harp and the Eagle*, 31–33, 42–81; Jentz and Schneirov, "Chicago's Fenian Fair," 6; Gleeson, *The Green and the Gray*, 195. John Mitchel, not surprisingly, became a vocal supporter of the Confederacy and, in fact, lost two of his sons as soldiers under the Confederate flag. But Mitchel had become disillusioned with the Fenians as early as 1862. After the war, he was employed as a Fenian agent in Paris but he quit after a few months and by 1867 had become a vocal critic of the Brotherhood.

34. Rutherford, *The Secret History of the Fenian Conspiracy*, 2:4, 29.

35. See Jentz and Schneirov, "Chicago's Fenian Fair." The best study of the labor movement in this period remains Montgomery, *Beyond Equality*.

36. Jentz and Schnierov, "Chicago's Fenian Fair," 16–17; *New York Times*, August 24, 1865; Novak, "Ellen O'Leary," 62–68; Steward and McGovern, *The Fenians*, 75, 78, 100–103; Joyce, "'Ireland's Trained and Marshalled Manhood,'" 70–72, 76–80. For this last point, see Curtin, "'A Nation of Abortive Men,'" 44–45.

37. Ural, *The Harp and Eagle*; Meagher, *The Columbia Guide to Irish American History*, 250. The number of IRB members in Ireland at its 1865 peak is difficult to ascertain, but Comerford's

careful estimate of something over 50,000 is probably the best one. See Comerford, *The Fenians in Context*, 124–25.

38. For an assessment of Roberts, who would go on to a career in American politics, see Ramón, *A Provisional Dictator*, 198–99. See also Miller, *Emigrants and Exiles*, 336–44, for a helpful discussion of the complexities of Irish American nationalist leadership in these years.

39. For the most thorough account of the Fenian attacks on Canada, see Senior, *The Last Invasion of Canada*.

40. Sweeny's proclamation, quoted in Snay, *Fenians, Freedmen, and Southern Whites*, 1. For O'Neill, see Samito, *Becoming American under Fire*, 184, 186–87.

41. For a lively account of the 1867 rising, see Kee, *The Green Flag*, 330–40.

42. Maguire, *The Irish in America*, 607.

43. Hamilton Fish, unpublished diary, entry for May 30, 1870, quoted in D'Arcy, *The Fenian Movement in the United States*, 359. See also Brown, *Irish-American Nationalism*, 30.

44. British Naturalisation Act, 1870, quoted in Sim, *A Union Forever*, 99. Sim, 97–127, provides the fullest discussion of this issue, but see also Snay, *Fenians, Freedmen, and Southern Whites*, 162–63; Salyer, "Crossing Borders"; and, for the larger context, Green, "Expatriation, Expatriates, and Expats."

45. Senior, *The Last Invasion of Canada*, 173–86.

46. Brown, *Irish-American Nationalism*, 64–65.

47. Meagher, *The Columbia Guide to Irish American History*, 240; Brown, *Irish-American Nationalism*, 65–66.

48. Meagher, *The Columbia Guide to Irish American History*, 240; Devoy, *Recollections of an Irish Rebel*, 399–400; Brown, *Irish-American Nationalism*, 66–74. For the *Catalpa* rescue and its legacy, see Fennell, "History into Myth."

49. Amos, *The Fenians in Australia*, 46–48, 52, 66–67, 196–99. See also O'Farrell, "The Irish in Australia and New Zealand," 674, 680; "The Proposed Revolutionary Directory," Dr. William Carroll to (probably) Patrick Mahon, June 12, 1876, and Carroll to John Devoy, July 26, 1876, in Devoy, *Devoy's Post Bag*, 1: 130, 181, 184, 198–99.

50. "Memoirs of T. C. Luby," quoted in Fitzpatrick, "'A Peculiar Tramping People,'" 654–55; Newsinger, *Fenianism in Mid-Victorian Britain*, 47–53.

51. See Toner, "The 'Green Ghost,'" for a persuasive analysis of the trajectory of the Canadian Fenians.

52. Brown, *Irish American Nationalism*, 66; Walkowitz, *Worker City, Company Town*, 160–61, 169; Phelan, *Grand Master Workman*, 20–21, 41, 49–50.

53. O'Leary, *Recollections of Fenians and Fenianism*, 2:239; Bull, *Land, Politics and Nationalism*, 40–42; James Stephens, Reminiscences [1882], quoted in Kee, *The Green Flag*, 303; "Proclamation of an Irish Republic, 1867," in O'Day and Stevenson, eds., *Irish Historical Documents*, 76–77.

54. Ó Gráda, "Fenianism and Socialism"; Newsinger, *Fenianism in Mid-Victorian Britain*, 29–32, 68–72; Hobsbawm, *The Age of Capital*, 98–100; Montgomery, *Beyond Equality*, 127–34, 271–75.

Chapter 5

1. J. M. Dalzell to John Sherman, July 29, 1877, quoted in Foner, *Reconstruction*, 586, who also (pp. 583–86) provides a brief description of the 1877 railroad strike, the first nationwide strike in American history.

2. For Devoy's version of these events, see Devoy, *The Land of Eire*, 40–44. The historiography of this key moment in the history of Irish nationalism begins with Moody, "The New Departure in Irish Politics." For subsequent work, see Brown, *Irish-American Nationalism*, 85–98; Foner, "Class, Ethnicity, and Radicalism," 154–55; Moody, *Davitt and Irish Revolution*, 250–70; Golway, *Irish Rebel*, 103–13; and Janis, *A Greater Ireland*, 8–11, 23–27. For a good introduction to Davitt's life and thought, see King, *Michael Davitt*. The term "Home Rule" grew in popularity after Isaac Butt's 1870 formation of the Home Government Association, which ran candidates for Parliament pledged to winning limited self-government for Ireland.

3. Important studies of the Land War include Clark, *Social Origins of the Land War*, and for County Mayo, where it began, Jordan, *Land and Popular Politics in Ireland*. Despite the efforts of its leaders, agrarian violence, some of it associated with a mythical "Captain Moonlight," increased sharply over the years of the Land War and included beatings, the maiming of animals, and, in a few cases, murder.

4. Healy, *Letters and Leaders*, 1: 83. See also Janis, *A Greater Ireland*, 17–18, 29–46; O'Day, *Charles Stewart Parnell*, 57–60; McCartney, "Parnell and the American Connection," 46–55; and Foner, "Class, Ethnicity, and Radicalism," 155–56. British MPs did not receive any kind of annual salary until 1911.

5. *Irish World*, March 6, 1880; Jackson, *Home Rule*, 2–3, 41. For Parnell's Cincinnati speech and his later claim that he had been misquoted, see O'Day, *Charles Stewart Parnell*, 59–60, and Janis, *A Greater Ireland*, 35–36.

6. For a concise overview of these developments, see Montgomery, "Labor Movement," 526–28, who observes that "Irish-American communities and the American labor movement came of age together during the last quarter of the nineteenth century." See also Kenny, *The American Irish*, 131–58, for an authoritative portrait of Irish America in the last part of the nineteenth century.

7. Kenny, *The American Irish*, 149. See also Doyle, "The Regional Bibliography of Irish America," and, for the integration of wealthy Irish Catholics into New York City's elite, Beckert, *The Monied Metropolis*, 266–67.

8. Davitt, *Speech in Defence of the Land League*, 105; Brown, *Irish-American Nationalism*, 103–4; Foner, "Class, Ethnicity, and Radicalism," 156; Janis, *A Greater Ireland*, 122.

9. See Moody, "The New Departure in Irish Politics"; Moody, *Davitt and Irish Revolution*, xv–xvii, 221–327; Boyce, *Nationalism in Ireland*, 205–11; Brown, *Irish-American Nationalism*, 85–98; Foner, "Class, Ethnicity, and Radicalism," 154–58.

10. *Irish World*, January 8, 1881; Brown, *Irish-American Nationalism*, 108; Foner, "Class, Ethnicity, and Radicalism," 158–60, 168–77; Gordon, "Studies in Irish and Irish-American Thought and Behavior," 431–38; Gibson, *The Attitudes of the New York Irish*, 273–75, 303–8.

11. *New York Herald*, February 24, 1848. For New York's Tenant League, see Blackmar, *Manhattan for Rent*, 246–48.

12. George, *Progress and Poverty*, 10–11, 312–13; Marley, *Michael Davitt*, 43–44; O'Donnell, "'Though Not an Irishman,'" 407–410. O'Donnell argues that Irish Americans accounted for most of the early sales of *Progress and Poverty* and paved the way for its eventual popularity. See O'Donnell, *Henry George and the Crisis of Inequality*, for a full elaboration of the argument.

13. Joseph Buchanan, editorial, *Denver Labor Enquirer*, December 15, 1883. See also Brundage, *The Making of Western Labor Radicalism*, 45–47; Miller, *Emigrants and Exiles*, 545–47; Walsh, "'A Fanatic Heart,'" 196–97.

14. For a more complete portrait of Murray, see Brundage, *The Making of Western Labor Radicalism*, 49–51.

15. MacCarthy, *Political Portraits*, 201; *Denver Labor Enquirer*, December 15, 1883.

16. Gibson, *The Attitudes of the New York Irish*, 326–27; Foner, "Class, Ethnicity, and Radicalism," 177–79; Gordon, "The Labor Boycott in New York City," 194–98; Erie, *Rainbow's End*, 50.

17. *New York Freeman's Journal*, July 15, 1882, quoted in McGreevy, *Catholicism and American Freedom*, 133. See also Foner, "Class, Ethnicity, and Radicalism," 187–89, 193, and Curran, "The McGlynn Affair," 185–86.

18. Sheehy-Skeffington, *Michael Davitt*, 114–16; Meagher, *Inventing Irish America*, 183–86; Brundage, *The Making of Western Labor Radicalism*, 43–44. For the most thorough treatment of the American Ladies Land League, see Janis, "Petticoat Revolutionaries."

19. Michael Davitt, diary entry, July 29, 1880, quoted in Marley, *Michael Davitt*, 45; Côté, *Fanny and Anna Parnell*, 183–86; Lee, *The Modernisation of Irish Society*, 93–94.

20. *Denver Labor Enquirer*, August 11, 1883; Curran, "The McGlynn Affair," 191–92; Speek, *The Singletax and the Labor Movement*, 101–4.

21. *Irish World*, January 5, 1884; Rodechko, *Patrick Ford*, 166–68; Bagenal, *The American Irish*, 65–67. Thomas Flynn, for example, a McGlynn supporter and father of the twentieth-century

radical activist, Elizabeth Gurley Flynn, left the church after McGlynn's excommunication. See Flynn, *The Rebel Girl*, 42–43.

22. Rodechko, "An Irish-American Journalist and Catholicism," 524–25; Rodechko, *Patrick Ford*, 28–35.

23. Foner, "Class, Ethnicity, and Radicalism," 150, 181–83; McKivigan, *Forgotten Firebrand*, 159–61; Fortune, editorial, *New York Freeman*, May 28,1887, quoted in Alexander, *An Army of Lions*, 10–11; Frederick Douglass, lecture, Washington, DC, October 22, 1883, quoted in Chaffin, *Giant's Causeway*, 193–94.

24. *Irish World*, January 15, 1881.

25. Devoy, quoted in Moody, "The New Departure in Irish Politics," 321; *Irish World*, July 29, August 19, 1876, June 2, 1877, April 2, 1881. For Ford's central role in promoting the cause of Indian nationalism among Irish nationalists, see Brasted, "Indian Nationalist Development," 47–48. See Slotkin, *The Fatal Environment*, 475–76, 583, for a discussion of the *Irish World*'s harsh criticisms of US Indian policy and for the importance of its "colonization column."

26. Gibbons, *Transformations in Irish Culture*, 13–14; Rodechko, "An Irish-American Journalist and Catholicism" 527; Rodechko, *Patrick Ford*, iii–v. In light of this evidence, Roediger's view that Irish Americans in the nineteenth century were unable to see "their struggles as bound up with those of colonized and colored people around the world" and that "they came to see their struggles as against such people" requires qualification. See Roediger, *The Wages of Whiteness*, 136–37.

27. *Irish World*, October 16, 1880; Shumsky, *The Evolution of Political Protest*, 160–6l; Roney, *Frank Roney*, 274, 361; Saxton, *The Indispensable Enemy*, 121–27. The question of a specifically Irish dimension to San Francisco's Workingmen's Party has been a point of disagreement among historians. While Burchell argues that the party was "primarily a movement of the disadvantaged" that was "only incidentally" Irish or Catholic, Shumsky emphasizes its heavily Irish immigrant membership and traces its use of violent crowd action, directed against both the rich and powerful and the city's Chinese population, to patterns of crowd violence found in rural Ireland. See Burchell, *The San Francisco Irish*, 153, and Shumsky, *The Evolution of Political Protest*, 132–34, 154–55.

28. Henry George, "The Chinese in California," *New York Tribune*, May 1, 1869, reprinted in George, *Collected Journalistic Writings*, 1: 157–72; *Irish World*, April 15, 1882. Although Gyory, *Closing the Gate*, 246, argues that the *Irish World*'s support for Chinese exclusion was lukewarm and motivated more by opposition to imported contract labor than to racism, the same cannot be said of Henry George. For the integral role that anti-Chinese racism played in George's thought, see Saxton, *The Indispensable Enemy*, 92–103, and Thomas, *Alternative America*, 61–63.

29. Montgomery, *The Fall of the House of Labor*, 79, 85; Painter, "Black Workers from Reconstruction to the Depression," 65–66.

30. *Irish World*, October 8, December 17, 1881; Davis, *Irish Issues in New Zealand Politics*, 100–101; Doorley, *Irish-American Diaspora Nationalism*, 168; Lyons, *John Dillon*, 104.

31. Clarke, *Piety and Nationalism*, 226–27; Kealey and Palmer, *Dreaming of What Might Be*, 313–16.

32. Davitt, *The Fall of Feudalism in Ireland*, 449; Moody, *Davitt and Irish Revolution*, 461, 480–81, 525; Foner, "Class, Ethnicity, and Radicalism."

33. *Freeman's Journal*, June 9, 1882, quoted in Marley, *Michael Davitt*, 61.

34. Moody, *Davitt and Irish Revolution*, 544–45.

35. Foner, "Class, Ethnicity, and Radicalism," 189–92; Brown, *Irish-American Nationalism*, 153–77. For a full treatment of this transnational bombing campaign, see Whelehan, *The Dynamiters*.

36. For the Redmond brothers' mission to Australia, New Zealand, and the United States, see Meleady, *Redmond*, 66–84.

37. Foner, "Class, Ethnicity, and Radicalism," 196–98.

38. Thomas, *Alternative America*, 175–81, 220–27; Gibson, *The Attitudes of the New York Irish*, 396–98; Foner, "Class, Ethnicity, and Radicalism," 184–86, 198; Curran, "The McGlynn Affair," 186–88; Brundage, *The Making of Western Labor Radicalism*, 125–26.

Chapter 6

1. Baron Brabourne in *Blackwood's Magazine*, January 1891, quoted in Callanan, *The Parnell Split*, 9; *The Times*, November 18, 1890.

2. T. M. Healy, speech to Irish Parliamentary Party meeting, November 20, 1890, quoted in Callanan, *The Parnell Split*, 11. Callanan provides the fullest account of these events.

3. *National Press* (Dublin), March 11, 1891, quoted in Callanan, *The Parnell Split*, 111.

4. *National Press*, March 11, 1891, quoted in Callanan, *The Parnell Split*, 111–12; *The Times*, March 11, 1891.

5. Important studies of Irish nationalism in the period from the fall of Parnell to the Easter Rising include Maume, *The Long Gestation*; Pašeta, *Irish Nationalist Women*; and, for a broader portrait of what he calls "the revolutionary generation," Foster, *Vivid Faces*. For Irish American nationalism in this period and in the revolutionary years from 1916 to 1921, see especially Ward, *Ireland and Anglo-American Relations*, and Carroll, *American Opinion and the Irish Question*.

6. Emmet, *Incidents of My Life*, 278, 281; Lyons, *The Irish Parliamentary Party*, 202, 213; O'Connor, *Memoirs of an Old Parliamentarian*, 2:195–97.

7. Speech by Dr. William B. Wallace, May 7, 1891, quoted in Emmet, *Incidents of My Life*, 281–82.

8. Emmet, *Incidents of My Life*, 285–86; Meagher, *Inventing Irish America*, 203; Dennis Flaherty to Thomas Emmet, June 11, 1893, quoted in Sammon, "The History of the Irish National Federation of America," 15.

9. Sammon, "The History of the Irish National Federation of America," 11; Beckert, *The Monied Metropolis*, 54, 267; Murphy and Mannion, *The History of the Friendly Sons of Saint Patrick*, 348; Meagher, *Inventing Irish America*, 203; Emmet, *Incidents of My Life*, 288, 301.

10. Carroll, *American Opinion and the Irish Question*, 7; Sammon, "History of the Irish National Federation of America," 18–19; Emmet, *Incidents of My Life*, 281–89; Boyce, *Nationalism in Ireland*, 259–62; Garvin, *The Evolution of Irish Nationalist Politics*, 94–98; McCarthy to J. F. X. O'Brien, December 14, 1894, quoted in O'Day, "Imagined Irish Communities," 400.

11. Bridget Fay, witness statement to the Irish Bureau of Military History, Dublin, quoted in Pašeta, *Irish Nationalist Women*, 25. See also McMahon, *Grand Opportunity*, 87–88, who provides the most thorough study of the Gaelic League. For the Gaelic Athletic Association, see Mandel, *The Gaelic Athletic Association and Irish Nationalist Politics*, and Cronin, *Sport and Nationalism in Ireland*.

12. *An Gaodhal*, April 1897, quoted in Ní Bhroiméil, *Building Irish Identity in America*, 50; Doorley, "Judge Daniel Cohalan," 118–19; Clan na Gael circular, quoted in Carroll, *American Opinion and the Irish Question*, 9.

13. Accounts of this intra-Fenian rivalry can be found in Ó Broin, *Revolutionary Underground*, 60–83, and Kelly, *The Fenian Ideal and Irish Nationalism*, 99–108. For the Cronin murder, see O'Brien, *Blood Runs Green*.

14. Foster, *Modern Ireland*, 432; Carroll, *American Opinion and the Irish Question*, 7–8; Ward, *Ireland and Anglo-American Relations*, 12–21.

15. Lee, *Ireland*, 15; Rodechko, *Patrick Ford*, 168–82.

16. Quinn to William Butler Yeats, July 13, 1906, in Quinn, *Letters to Yeats*, 78. For Quinn, see also Reid, *The Man from New York*.

17. My discussion of the Irish Home Rulers here follows the analysis of Hutchinson, *The Dynamics of Cultural Nationalism*, 152. For the parallel views in the United States, see UILA, *Proceedings of the Second National Convention*, 48.

18. Bourke Cockran to Moreton Frewen, May 19, 1914, NYPL, Cockran Papers; Carroll, *American Opinion and the Irish Question*, 23–24.

19. John Redmond to Bourke Cockran, November 21, 1901; John D. Crimmins to Bourke Cockran, November 21, 1901; William Redmond to Bourke Cockran, March 1901, NYPL, Cockran Papers.

20. Miller, *Emigrants and Exiles*, 541–48; Clark *Erin's Heirs*, 157–70; Patrick J. Brophy to Joseph Devlin, July 18, 1905, quoted in Emmons, *The Butte Irish*, 325–26.

21. Leinenweber, "Socialists in the Streets," 152–71. See also Dubofsky, *When Workers Organize*, and, for an authoritative overview of American labor in the progressive era, Brody, *Workers in Industrial America*, 3–47.

22. Laslett, *Labor and the Left*, 54–97, 241–86; Leinenweber, "Socialists in the Streets," 152–53; Emmons, *The Butte Irish*, 103, 265.

23. See Morgan, *James Connolly*, for a particularly useful biography among many.

24. Reeve and Reeve, *James Connolly and the United States*, 27–28; COHA, William O'Dwyer interview, 81–85. For a nuanced analysis of patterns of Irish American labor activism in this era, and for the Irish influence on more recent immigrant workers, see Barrett, *The Irish Way*, 105–55.

25. Rodechko, *Patrick Ford*, 108–17; Bedford, *Socialism and the Workers in Massachusetts*, 190; Quinn to Ezra Pound, January 12, 1917, quoted in Reid, *The Man from New York*, 285; Carroll, *American Opinion and the Irish Question*, 40.

26. Adams, *Age of Industrial Violence*, 115–16; Huthmacher, "Charles Evans Hughes and Charles Francis Murphy"; Brody, *Workers in Industrial America*, 21–32.

27. UILA, *Proceedings of the Second National Convention*, 47–48, 50–51, 80–82.

28. Maume, *The Long Gestation*, 65. See also Murphy, *The Women's Suffrage Movement*, and Ward, *Hanna Sheehy Skeffington*. As Pašeta, *Irish Nationalist Women*, 19–23, shows, however, many women in Ireland did take active roles in the Gaelic League, which paved the way for their further political and cultural activism in the early twentieth century.

29. Murphy, *The Women's Suffrage Movement*, 172–78; Carroll, *American Opinion and the Irish Question*, 16; *New York Times*, May 5, 1912; Bourke Cockran to Moreton Frewen, March 25, 1914, NYPL, Cockran Papers.

30. Circular issued to members of the Clan na Gael, October 10, 1900, AIHS, Cohalan Papers.

31. Devoy to Editor of the *Freeman's Journal* (Dublin), December 11, 1878, reprinted in Bagenal, *The Irish Agitator*, 131; Ward, *Ireland and Anglo-American Relations*, 9; Doorley, "Judge Daniel Cohalan," 113–15.

32. Devoy, *Recollections of an Irish Rebel*, 392–96, 416–22; Ward, *Ireland and Anglo-American Relations*, 8–10, 24–29; Carroll, *American Opinion and the Irish Question*, 6–9, 26–36.

33. Mary J. O'Donovan Rossa to John Devoy, Autumn 1915, in Devoy, *Devoy's Post Bag*, 2:482–83. See also Garvin, *Nationalist Revolutionaries in Ireland*, 176–77, for the provocative argument that "revolutionary nationalism in Ireland was, and is, radical in style and means, but not in ends."

34. Circular issued to members of the Clan na Gael, October 10, 1900, AIHS, Cohalan Papers; Ward, *Unmanageable Revolutionaries*, 88–107; Pašeta, *Irish Nationalist Women*, 140–41, 158–59.

35. Dr. Gertrude B. Kelly to Bourke Cockran, October 2, 1914, NYPL, Cockran Papers; Diner, *Erin's Daughters in America*, 25; Carroll, *American Opinion and the Irish Question*, 267.

36. See Garvin, *Nationalist Revolutionaries*, 50–51.

37. Adams, *Age of Industrial Violence*, 115–18.

38. See Gilley, "The Catholic Church and Revolution," for a good discussion.

39. See Jensen, *Passage from India*, 19–20, 189, 241–43, and Silvestri, *Ireland and India*, 13–45.

40. See Young, *Postcolonialism*, 2, for a persuasive analysis of Casement's politics as "a form of national internationalism." See also O'Callaghan, "'With the Eyes of Another Race,'" for a nuanced discussion of the "complicated and dialectical" relationship between Casement's "mounting anti-imperialism and his increasingly self-conscious nationalism."

41. Carroll, *American Opinion and the Irish Question*, 35.

42. Bonar Law, quoted in Ward, *The Easter Rising*, 96, which also provides a concise overview of the constitutional crisis of 1912–14, 95–103.

43. *Irish World*, August 22, 1914; Redmond, speech to the House of Commons, September 16, 1914, quoted in McConnel, *The Irish Parliamentary Party*, 300.

44. Dr. Gertrude B. Kelly to Bourke Cockran, October 2, 1914, NYPL, Cockran Papers. For a similar point, see Pašeta, *Irish Nationalist Women*, 22–23, who persuasively argues for the "elasticity" of domestic discourses for Irish women in the early twentieth century.

45. Bourke Cockran to Moreton Frewen, July 30, 1915, and Anthony M. Brogan to Bourke Cockran, January 6, 1915, NYPL, Cockran Papers; Joseph Edward Cuddy, *Irish-Americans and National Isolationism*, 44–47; Buckley, *The New York Irish*; Carroll, "America and Irish Political Independence," 274.

46. Carroll, *American Opinion and the Irish Question*, 51.

47. See MacAtasney, *Tom Clarke*, 2–106; Carroll, *American Opinion and the Irish Question*, 30–31; and Moran, *Patrick Pearse*, 140–44. For a concise analysis of the role that Irish American republicans played in the Easter Rising, see Carroll, "America and the 1916 Rising."

48. Carroll, *American Opinion and the Irish Question*, 49–50. Among Casement's possessions in Brixton prison, where he awaited his execution in August 1916, was a copy of Tone's *Life*. See Quinn, "Tone and the Historians," 115; John Quinn, quoted in Kevin Whelan, "Introduction to Section VII," in Bartlett et al., eds., *1798*, 533–34. See also Bartlett, "Last Flight of the Wild Geese?" 161, who argues that Casement's efforts to form an Irish Brigade were a throwback to Napoleon's Irish Brigade in the era of the United Irishmen.

Chapter 7

1. For authoritative accounts of the Easter Rising, see Townshend, *Easter 1916*, and McGarry, *The Rising*.

2. "Proclamation of the Irish Republic, issued 24 April 1916," in O'Day and Stevenson, eds., *Irish Historical Documents*, 160–61.

3. There are many accounts of the events taking place from 1916 to the Anglo-Irish Treaty of 1921. For two recent treatments, see Hopkinson, *The Irish War for Independence*, and Townshend, *The Republic*. See also Fitzpatrick, *The Two Irelands*, 3–114.

4. On the Black and Tans, and their differences with the more disciplined (and often Catholic) Royal Irish Constabulary, see Hart, *The I.R.A. and Its Enemies*, 4–8.

5. See Kee, *The Green Flag*, 682, 696–97. The most thorough treatment of MacSwiney's hunger strike is Costello, *Enduring the Most*, 157–216.

6. Joseph P. Quinn to Members of the AARIR, June 7, 1922, HL, Finerty Papers. For the most thorough treatment of Irish American nationalism in these years, see Carroll, *American Opinion and the Irish Question*, 55–176. See also Ward, *Ireland and Anglo-American Relations*, 101–268; Doorley, *Irish-American Diaspora Nationalism*, 36–137; Cuddy, *Irish-Americans and National Isolationism*, 105–235; and Buckley, *The New York Irish*, 62–390.

7. Doorley, *Irish-American Diaspora Nationalism*, 36–42.

8. *New York Times*, May 15, 1916; Carroll, *American Opinion and the Irish Question*, 68–69.

9. See Brody, *Workers in Industrial America*, 39–46, and Montgomery, *The Fall of the House of Labor*, 358–59.

10. Kazin, *Barons of Labor*, 239–40; McKillen, *Chicago Labor and a Democratic Diplomacy*, 50.

11. E. M. House and Sir William Wiseman, Memorandum on "Relations between the United States and Great Britain," March 8, 1917, and Secretary of State Robert Lansing, telegram to Ambassador Walter Hines Page, April 10, 1917, both quoted in Carroll, *American Opinion and the Irish Question*, 90.

12. See Carroll, *American Opinion and the Irish Question*, 102–6; Kazin, *Barons of Labor*, 240–43; McKillen, *Chicago Labor and a Democratic Diplomacy*, 78–79.

13. This is the main point advanced by Carroll, whose *American Opinion and the Irish Question* is the fullest examination of the IPL. See also Nelson, *Irish Nationalists and the Making of the Irish Race*, 16, 222–36.

14. My discussion of the IPL is based on press clippings, correspondence, handbills, and selected issues of the *Bulletin of the Irish Progressive League*, all in NLI, Golden Papers.

15. Helen Golden to Welsh, September 19, 1920, NLI, Golden Papers; *Bulletin of the IPL*, no. 4, September 1919, 4–5.

16. Carroll, *American Opinion and the Irish Question*, 106–7, 239–40; Hanna Sheehy-Skeffington to Peter Golden, March 20, 1918, NLI, Golden Papers. For Sheehy-Skeffington's activities in America in 1917–18, see Levenson and Natterstad, *Hanna Sheehy-Skeffington*, 101–10, and Ward, *Hanna Sheehy Skeffington*, 184–210.

17. *New York Times*, February 17, 1934; Kelly to Bourke Cockran, October 2, 1914, NYPL, Cockran Papers; *New York Call*, December 3, 21, 1917; Larkin, *James Larkin*, 229; Carroll, *American Opinion and the Irish Question*, 48, 67, 239–40.

18. Carroll, *American Opinion and the Irish Question*, 128–31; Doorley, *Irish-American Diaspora Nationalism*, 92–95; MacMillan, *Paris 1919*, 11.

19. See MacMillan, *Paris 1919*, 10–15, for the ambiguities of the concept of self-determination and for Wilson's views on the Irish question.

20. Carroll, "America and Irish Political Independence," 282–83. The traditional view of an isolationist US foreign policy has come under revision lately, with recent work highlighting the role of business and other nongovernmental actors in vastly expanding America's international presence in the 1920s and 1930s. Still, the unwillingness of the American government to confront the growing dangers posed by German and Japanese military expansion was real enough and remains an important feature of these decades.

21. Doyle, "Striking for Ireland," 360–62; *New York Times*, April 3, 1920.

22. Doorley, *Irish-American Diaspora Nationalism*, 168–69; O'Farrell, *The Irish in Australia*, 254, 270.

23. For the most thorough discussion of the strike, see Doyle, "Striking for Ireland." See also Nelson, *Irish Nationalists and the Making of the Irish Race*, 235–38.

24. *New York Times*, August 28, 1920; *New York Tribune*, August 28, 1920; Helen Golden to Edmond Butler, n.d., NLI, Golden Papers.

25. United States, *Historical Statistics of the United States*, pt. 1, 105, 117; Freeman, *In Transit*, 30–35; Barnes, *The Longshoremen*, 4–12.

26. For a good discussion of "new" Irish immigrants in this era, see Emmons, *The Butte Irish*, 340–97, and, for the significance of the exile motif among them, Miller, *Emigrants and Exiles*, 548–51.

27. Barnes, *The Longshoremen*, 8–9; Spero and Harris, *The Black Worker*, 198–201; *New York Times*, August 17, September 3, 1920. New York's black population climbed from fewer than 92,000 in 1910 to over 152,000 in 1920.

28. See "Signs for Colored Pickets" and "Negro Longshoremen" folders, NLI, Golden Papers.

29. "Report by Special Agent P-138," September 20, 1920, in Hill, ed., *The Marcus Garvey Papers*, 3:12–13; "Negro Longshoremen" folder, NLI, Golden Papers.

30. See Hill, General Introduction to *The Marcus Garvey Papers*, 1:lxx–lxxviii. Hill stresses Garvey's admiration for MacSwiney. In early September 1920, Garvey sent a telegram to the Lord Mayor's confessor reading "Convey to McSwiney [*sic*] sympathy of 400,000,000 Negroes." A year later he expressed his belief that "the death of McSwiney [*sic*] did more for the freedom of Ireland today than probably anything they did for 500 years prior to his death." See *The Marcus Garvey Papers*, 1:lxxvi. Garvey was not alone in his admiration for Irish nationalism. Just as black radicals seeking socialist change identified primarily with the Bolshevik revolution, proponents of a black nationalism assigned primacy to the Irish revolution.

31. *New York Times*, September 11, 1920.

32. "Decision of Colored Longshoremen engaged in the breaking of the Irish Patriotic strike, 13 September 1920," NLI, Golden Papers.

33. "Report by Special Agent P-138," September 20, 1920, in Hill, ed., *The Marcus Garvey Papers*, 3:12–13; "Decision of Colored Longshoremen," NLI, Golden Papers.

34. "Decision of Colored Longshoremen," NLI, Golden Papers.

35. Murray, "Ethnic Identities and Diasporic Sensibilities," 102–7; Larkin, *James Larkin*, 221–23; Emmons, *The Butte Irish*, 355–83.

36. Dye, *As Equals and as Sisters*, 34–35, 127–28; McKillen, *Chicago Labor and a Democratic Diplomacy*, 179–80; *New York Times*, December 3, 1920.

37. *New York Times*, August 12, 1920.

38. De Valera, quoted in Carroll, "America and Irish Political Independence," 284, who also provides a concise analysis of the nature of the Cohalan-de Valera split.

39. Carroll, *American Opinion and the Irish Question*, 159–60.

40. Sarbaugh, "American Recognition and Eamon de Valera," 133–34.

41. Harding to Judge Morgan J. O'Brien, March 26, 1921, quoted in Carroll, *American Opinion and the Irish Question*, 167.

Chapter 8

1. Golden, "A Prayer for Ireland [1922]," quoted in Herlihy, *Peter Golden*, 66.

2. For an overview, see Beaumont, "Gender, Citizenship and the State," 96–97. For an outstanding synthesis of Irish social history in the post–Civil War period, see Ferriter, *The Transformation of Ireland*, 280–357.

3. Herlihy, *Peter Golden*, 69–72.

4. For a good analysis, see Kissane, *The Politics of the Irish Civil War*.

5. Both supporters and opponents of the treaty assumed that a six-county Northern Ireland, perhaps reduced even further in size by the future Boundary Commission, would not be viable. As it turned out, this was a deeply mistaken assumption.

6. Michael Collins, speech to the Dáil, quoted in Hart, *Mick*, 334; Mary MacSwiney, speech to the Dáil, Irish Free State, *Debate on the Treaty*, December 17, 1921. See also Hopkinson, *Green against Green*, 37; Regan, *The Irish Counter-Revolution*, 41; and Knirck, *Women of the Dáil*, 72–101.

7. Hart, *Mick*, 395–99. British officials had declared that they would consider the Treaty broken if no action was taken against the Irregulars and a small garrison of British troops in Dublin was readying for attack.

8. My discussion here follows Laffan, *The Resurrection of Ireland*, 346–85, as well as Reagan, *The Irish Counter-Revolution*, and Kissane, *The Politics of the Irish Civil War*. But for a vigorously argued alternative interpretation of the founding of the Free State as the "the birth of Irish democracy," see Garvin, *1922*. For the importance of economic issues in Fianna Fáil's 1932 electoral victory, see Lee, *Ireland*, 168–74.

9. For varying estimates of numbers of deaths in the Irish Civil War, see Fitzpatrick, *The Two Irelands*, 134, who puts the figure at somewhere over 1,000, and Hopkinson, "Civil War and Aftermath," 54, who estimates that 4,000 were killed. The Civil War has received nothing like the kind of sustained historical attention of the preceding War of Independence. See Hopkinson, *Green against Green*, for an authoritative scholarly account. For Collins's short-lived military dictatorship, drawing on the secret Irish Republican Brotherhood, see Regan, "Michael Collins, General Commanding-in-Chief."

10. Hopkinson, "Irish Americans and the Anglo-Irish Treaty," 133; *Irish Press*, July 23, 1921.

11. Devoy, telegram to de Valera, August 1921, quoted in Tansill, *America and the Fight for Irish Freedom*, 420–21; *Gaelic American*, December 10, 17, 1921; *New York Times*, December 8, 1921; Hopkinson, "Irish Americans and the Anglo-Irish Treaty," 136–37.

12. *New York Times*, December 8, 1921, and *Gaelic American*, December 10, 1921, both quoted in Doorley, *Irish-American Diaspora Nationalism*, 142–43; *Gaelic American*, March 17, August 18, 1923, and Peter Golden, diary entry, October 1925, quoted in Hanley, "Irish Republicans in Interwar New York," paragraph 5. As Knirck shows in *Women of the Dáil*, 129–68, misogynist statements like these were typical of Ireland's pro-Treatyites' response to women republicans, characterizing them as unbalanced and emotional and dismissing opposition to the Treaty as the work of the "women and Childers party," a reference to the republican activist Erskine Childers. The anti-Semitism was Devoy's own particular contribution to the debate.

13. B. D. McKernon to M. Collins, February 13, 1922, *Bronx Home News*, December 15, 1921, and Mary MacSwiney to An Uachtaran, March 30, 1925, quoted in Hanley, "Irish Republicans in Interwar New York," paragraph 3. For the editorial comment in American newspapers, see Hopkinson, "Irish Americans and the Anglo-Irish Treaty," 133–35.

14. *Freeman's Journal*, January 5, 12, 1922, quoted in Campbell, *Ireland's New Worlds*, 182; *Catholic Register*, December 15, 1921, and *Catholic Record*, December 24, 1921, both quoted in McEvoy, "Canadian Catholic Press Reaction to the Irish Crisis," 137; *Saskatoon Daily Star*, January 17, 1922, quoted in Elliott, *Robert Emmet*, 210. See also Toner, "Fanatic Heart of the North," 47, who notes that most Canadian Irish men and women "accepted the Anglo-Irish Treaty as enough to satisfy their ambitions for Ireland."

15. Joseph Connelly, unpublished memoirs, quoted in Hopkinson, "Irish Americans and the Anglo-Irish Treaty," 136; Frank Walsh to Stephen O'Mara, March 17, 1922, quoted in Carroll, *American Opinion and the Irish Question*, 181; *Gaelic American*, February 3, 1923, quoted in Hanley, "Irish Republicans in Interwar New York," paragraph 5.

16. Charles Edward Russell to Sir William Joynson-Hicks, June 7, 1925, LOC, Russell Papers.

17. *Cincinnati Times-Star*, May 28, 1926, enclosed in J. J. Castellini to Russell, May 29, 1926, LOC, Russell Papers.

18. Chester Alan Arthur III to a Miss Swinbourne, July 23, 1922, LOC, Arthur Papers.

19. "Pinkey" Skinner to Arthur, November 27, 1922; Arthur to President of the International Red Cross, November 21, 1922; Arthur to Miss Swinbourne, January 10, 1923; and (for the respect that Arthur was accorded among leaders of the AARIR) Michael Kelly to Arthur, March 22, 1923, LOC, Arthur Papers.

20. Mary S. O'Kane to Austin Ford, February 1922; John O'Kane to Muriel MacSwiney, n.d.; John F. Kelly to Anatole Vanier, n.d., BPL, MacSwiney Club Papers. For a recent study of the nationalist activities of Kelly, the leading figure in the Club until his death in October 1922, see Chapman, "'How to Smash the British Empire.'"

21. Jack Middleton to John M. Flynn, August 22, 1922; Peter Walsh to Flynn, September 3, 1922; D. D. Bassett to Flynn, September 4, 1922; John F. Kelly to John O'Kane, December 12, 1922; Margaret A. Scanlon to Margaret Murray, September 8, 1922, BPL, MacSwiney Club Papers. With the demise of Joseph McGarrity's *Irish Press* in May 1922, the *Irish World*, edited by Patrick Ford's nephew, Austin J. Ford, was the only major Irish American paper to oppose the Treaty. Robert Briscoe would go on to have a long political career in Ireland, becoming the first Jewish lord mayor of Dublin in 1956.

22. For a persuasive analysis of this fundamental gulf in the history of twentieth-century Irish nationalism, see Reagan, "Southern Irish Nationalism." See also Foster, "'Colliding Cultures,'" 52–55.

23. See Garvin, *1922*.

24. *Irish Times*, September 9, 1922, quoted in Bew, *Ireland*, 445; Daly, *Industrial Development and Irish National Identity*, 4–7, 14–15; Murphy, *Ireland in the Twentieth Century*, 64–65.

25. See Brown, *Ireland*, 35–67, and Ferriter, *The Transformation of Ireland*, 325–31.

26. See Regan, "Southern Irish Nationalism."

27. Cohalan, "America's Advice to Ireland," 213; *Gaelic American*, August 29, 1925; Doorley, *Irish-American Diaspora Nationalism*, 151–52; McCarthy, "The Friends of Irish Freedom and the Irish Free State," 124.

28. *Gaelic American*, April 28, 1923; Doorley, *Irish-American Diaspora Nationalism*, 152–54, 200.

29. *Gaelic American*, July 26, 1924; *The Times,* October 1, 1928; Golway, *Irish Rebel*, 306–7, 318–19.

30. Funchion, "Clan na Gael," 89–90; Hanley, "Irish Republicans in Interwar New York," paragraph 6.

31. *Chicago Daily Tribune*, March 16, 1931; Daly, "Nationalism, Sentiment, and Economics," 263. Cosgrave gave his first address several years before King George V began making annual Christmas radio broadcasts to the British Empire. The annual St. Patrick's address to the Irish diaspora continues to this day, though it is now delivered by the president rather than the prime minister, and conveyed online instead of through the airwaves.

32. Éamon de Valera to Mary MacSwiney, August 7, 1923, quoted in Boyce, *Nationalism in Ireland*, 343; Mary MacSwiney to Russell, April 12, 1926, LOC, Russell Papers.

33. Mary MacSwiney to Charles Edward Russell, April 12 and 25, 1926, LOC, Russell Papers; Hanley, "Irish Republicans in Interwar New York," paragraph 2.

34. Éamon de Valera to Russell, December 19, 1929, LOC, Russell Papers; O'Brien, *De Valera, Fianna Fáil and the Irish Press*. For the fundraising efforts in one particularly important state, see Sarbaugh, "Éamon de Valéra and the *Irish Press* in California."

35. Boyce, *Nationalism in Ireland*, 340. The fullest study of the organization in this period is Hanley, *The IRA*.

36. Cronin, *The McGarrity Papers*, 151–74; Bardon, *A History of Ulster*, 538–39. For a full discussion of the deep structures of anti-Catholic discrimination in Northern Ireland, see Chapter 9, this volume.

37. Hanley, "Irish Republicans in Interwar New York," paragraphs 7–8.

38. The literature on the CIO as an Americanizing institution among immigrants is vast. See Göbel, "Becoming American," for a good overview.

39. Montgomery, "Labor Movement," 530; Walter P. Reuther and James B. Carey, "Foreword" to Brophy, *A Miner's Life*, v.

40. Schatz, "Phillip Murray and the Subordination of the Industrial Unions," 235–36, 246; Brophy, *A Miner's Life*, 3, 7, 10, 31, 78. For the impact of Catholic social thought on labor in this era, see Schatz, "American Labor and the Catholic Church."

41. Cherny, "The Making of a Labor Radical," 363–66. Another influence on Bridges was that of his favorite uncle, Henry Renton Bridges, who had become a bitter critic of British imperialism after his service in the South African War.

42. Quill, *Mike Quill, Himself*, 13–14; *New York Times*, September 23, 1938, quoted in Freeman, *In Transit*, 137.

43. Freeman, *In Transit*, 267–85; Zieger, "George Meany," 324–26; Meany, quoted in Robinson, *George Meany*, 31–32.

44. O'Neill, *Man of the House*, 7–9.

45. Coogan, *Eamon de Valera*, 609–10; Dwyer, *Strained Relations*, 166; *Washington Post*, May 5, 1945. For a full discussion of this incident, see Keogh, "De Valera, Hitler and the Visit of Condolence." But for a discussion of the actual workings of what some have called Éire's "friendly neutrality," see Keogh, *Twentieth-Century Ireland*, 120–24.

46. See Dwyer, "American Friends of Irish Neutrality," 35–36.

47. Not coincidentally, however, the public faces of the AFIN, Fordham University Professor James J. O'Brien, who was elected president, and a former Hearst reporter named Wesley Hammar, who was hired as public relations officer, were both American-born.

48. See Hanly, "'No English Enemy . . . Ever Stooped so Low,'" 246–48, for a full analysis.

49. See Lee, "Interpreting Irish America," 36, and Lee, "Emigration: 1922–1998."

50. Blessing, "The Irish in America," 467.

51. Kenny, *The American Irish*, 226–67; Hayden, *Irish on the Inside*, 10, 30–31, 69–70.

52. "Platform and Resolutions of the Irish Race Convention, New York, November 22–23, 1947," SJUA, American League for an Undivided Ireland Records; *New York Times*, March 14, 1948; telegram from Commonwealth Relations Office to UK High Commissioner in India, June 2, 1948, quoted in O'Malley, *Ireland, India and Empire*, 159; Lord Innverchapel to Aneurin Bevan, April 16, 1948, quoted in Kelly, "A Policy of Futility," paragraph 9.

53. O'Donnell, "The IRA and America during the 'Border Campaign'"; Anderson, *Joe Cahill*, 133–34; *Irish Republican Bulletin*, Easter 1961, in NLI, Tighe Papers. "Yankee" Séan Cronin, as some IRA volunteers called him, would later become the first Washington correspondent for the *Irish Times* and would author numerous books, including the scholarly history, *Irish Nationalism*.

54. Currie, *All Hell Will Break Loose*, 34; Hanley and Millar, *The Lost Revolution*, 48–49.

55. Glazer and Moynihan, *Beyond the Melting Pot*, 253. Moynihan was using words originally penned by Alfred North Whitehead in 1935 to describe Protestantism.

Chapter 9

1. Important works on Irish American nationalism in this period include Holland, *The American Connection*; Wilson, *Irish America and the Ulster Conflict*; and Thompson, *American Policy and Northern Ireland*.

2. For statistics on deaths attributable to the conflict, see McKittrick et al., *Lost Lives*, 1551–67. For an effort to produce a full audit of the various human, civil liberties, economic, and other costs of the conflict through the early 1990s, see O'Leary and McGarry, *The Politics of Antagonism*, 8–53.

3. For an extended and systematic comparison of patterns of discrimination and protest in Northern Ireland and the American South, see Wright, *Northern Ireland*. The term "closed society" was frequently used to describe the state of Mississippi in the era of the civil rights movement. My own discussion of patterns of inequality in Northern Ireland draws mainly on O'Leary and McGarry, *The Politics of Antagonism*, 106–52; Tonge, *Northern Ireland*, 19–34; and McKittrick and McVea, *Making Sense of the Troubles*, 1–29.

4. See the concise discussion of industrial location and discrimination in Wilson, *Ulster*, 98–106.

5. According to one authoritative study, among Catholic and Protestant men sharing the same set of personal characteristics (i.e., skilled but without formal qualifications, between twenty-five and forty-four years of age, and with two children), the rate of unemployment for Catholics was double that for Protestants. See Smith and Chambers, *Inequality in Northern Ireland*, 152–234, for a full analysis.

6. Basil Brooke, address to the Derry Unionist Association, March 20, 1934, quoted in O'Leary and McGarry, *The Politics of Antagonism*, 129; Cameron Commission, *Disturbances in Northern Ireland*, 56, 60. Darby, *Conflict in Northern Ireland*, 78, summed up the scholarly

consensus in the mid-1970s with his assertion of the existence of "a consistent and irrefutable pattern of deliberate discrimination against Catholics."

7. Tonge, *Northern Ireland*, 23.

8. Farrell, *Northern Ireland*, 87–89; Cameron Commission, *Disturbances in Northern Ireland*, 21.

9. See Tonge, *Northern Ireland*, 20–22, for a concise discussion of the various forms of electoral discrimination.

10. The sense of hopelessness is effectively conveyed in McCann, *War and an Irish Town*, 9–29. For the IRA's border campaign, see Hanley and Millar, *The Lost Revolution*, 1–21.

11. McAteer "Irish Action" [1948], in Campbell and McAteer, *Irish Action*, 52. See also Prince and Warner, *Belfast and Derry in Revolt*, 17–19, for a discussion.

12. *Derry Journal*, January 31, 1963, quoted in Prince and Warner, *Belfast and Derry in Revolt*, 15.

13. Heatley, "The Beginning," 10; English, *Armed Struggle*, 85–91.

14. See Higgins, *Transforming 1916*, 1–2, 86–88, 198–99; O'Callaghan, " 'From Casement Park to Toomebridge,' " 93–94, 105, 109–10; McKittrick et al., *Lost Lives*, 23–29.

15. Purdie, *Politics in the Streets*, 82–120.

16. Purdie, *Politics in the Streets*, 121–58. For an insider's account, see also Northern Ireland Civil Rights Association, *"We Shall Overcome."*

17. For a lively account of 1968 as a global phenomenon, see Kurlansky, *1968*. Television was becoming increasingly significant in Northern Ireland in this period and, in the words of a leading scholar, "proved transformative, challenging a conservative society and ultimately undermining the status quo." BBC Northern Ireland began broadcasting in 1955 and reached almost everywhere in Northern Ireland by the early 1960s. See Savage, *A Loss of Innocence?* 318–82 (quote on p. 318).

18. Much has been written about the events of this day. For the classic firsthand account, see McCann, *War and an Irish Town*, 27–50. See also Purdie, *Politics in the Streets*, 159–97; Ó Dochartaigh, *From Civil Rights to Armalites*, 19–34; and Prince and Warner, *Belfast and Derry in Revolt*, 85–95, who call October 5, 1968, "the day the troubles began."

19. Cahill, interviewed by Anderson, 2000–2002, quoted in Anderson, *Joe Cahill*, 176.

20. English, *Armed Struggle*, 104–8, provides a concise narrative of the split.

21. Cahill, interviewed by Anderson, 2000–2002, quoted in Anderson, *Joe Cahill*, 153; English, *Armed Struggle*, 109–12.

22. For a plausible, if not conclusive, argument that the battle at St. Matthew's was less "a heroic defense of a threatened minority" than a carefully pre-planned and "stage-managed" Provisional IRA effort to discredit the security forces and strengthen its own credibility, see Prince and Warner, *Belfast and Derry in Revolt*, 252. For the still most common view, see Taylor, *Behind the Mask*, 94–97.

23. For a brief discussion of these events, see Elliott, *The Catholics of Ulster*, 419–22. Her overall assessment of British policy over these two years ("a vicious circle—misguided security decisions feeding the IRA machine") is one widely shared by scholars.

24. Wilson, *Irish America and the Ulster Conflict*, 23; O'Dwyer, *Counsel for the Defense*, 116–18, 133–36, 142–43, 211–25. For a good overview of initial Irish American responses in this period, see Ó Dochartaigh, " 'Sure It's Hard to Keep Up with the Splits Here.' "

25. Wilson, *Irish America and the Ulster Conflict*, 27–28, 31.

26. See Dooley, *Black and Green*, 53–55, for a good discussion.

27. Bernard, *Daughter of Derry*, 65; Dooley, interviews with McCann and Farrell, July 1996, quoted in Dooley, *Black and Green*, 78.

28. *New York Times*, March 3, 1970; Davidson, "Bernadette Devlin," 78, 86–87; McAliskey, "A Peasant in the Halls of the Great," 87. The best description of Devlin's tour can be found in Wilson, *Irish America and the Ulster Conflict*, 31–40.

29. Hayden, *Irish on the Inside*, 4, 100–101.

30. Wilson, *Irish America and the Ulster Conflict*, 30–31; Hanley and Millar, *The Lost Revolution*, 115.

31. See Senator Alan Cranston to Ms. Anne Devlin [*sic*], April 23, 1979, and program for "Bloody Sunday: A Commemoration" [January 25, 1975], AIA, Daughton Collection.

32. For an influential analysis of Noraid's history, see Holland, *The American Connection*, 27–62. A more recent and scholarly analysis can be found in Hanley, "The Politics of Noraid."

33. For this point, see especially Hanley, "The Politics of Noraid," 3. Clark, *Irish Blood*, offers a somewhat different perspective on Noraid, drawing attention to the role of the American born.

34. *Irish Echo*, April 24, 1971, quoted in Hanley, "The Politics of Noraid," 2; Holland, *The American Connection*, 35; Thompson, *American Policy and Northern Ireland*, 32.

35. McKittrick and McVea, *Making Sense of the Troubles*, 88–90; Wiener, *Gimme Some Truth*, 198–202; *The Times*, February 7, 1972; Thompson, *American Policy and Northern Ireland*, 37–39; Senator Edward Kennedy, opening statement to the US Senate Foreign Affairs Subcommittee on Europe, February 28, 1972, quoted in Wilson, *Irish America and the Ulster Conflict*, 64–65.

36. McKittrick et al., *Lost Lives*, 229–31. Formed in the heat of the civil rights struggle in August 1970 and originally describing itself as a "radical socialist party" that would prioritize social and economic activism above the call for a united Ireland, constitutional nationalism had replaced socialism as the SDLP's main commitment by the time of the so-called Sunningdale power-sharing experiment in 1974. Though left-wing currents remained in the party, the resignation of the Belfast working-class activist Gerry Fitt as SDLP leader in 1979 finalized its transformation into a mainly Derry-based nationalist party. For a good analysis, see Campbell, "New Nationalism?"

37. Farren, *The SDLP*, 46–47, 54–55; Edward M. Kennedy, Foreword to Hume, *A New Ireland*, 7.

38. Thompson, *American Policy and Northern Ireland*, 84, 104–7; O'Dowd, "The Awakening," 65.

39. Holland, *The American Connection*, 127–28.

40. One important exception to the general picture of Thatcher's intransigence and American disengagement in this period was the 1985 Anglo-Irish Agreement, an international treaty between Britain and the Republic of Ireland that gave formal recognition to what became known as the "Irish dimension" to the conflict. Thatcher's motivations revolved mainly around improving cooperation with Irish security forces against the IRA and bolstering the political strength of constitutional nationalists in both the Republic and Northern Ireland against Sinn Féin. But the Anglo-Irish Agreement also saw significant involvement from the Reagan administration and House Speaker O'Neill, who brought considerable pressure to bear on the Thatcher government, setting a precedent for Clinton's more active role. For analysis, see Arthur, *Special Relationships*, 116–59, and Lynch, *Turf War*, 21, who argues that White House diplomacy in 1985 was a "dry run" for the diplomacy that led to the 1998 Good Friday agreement.

41. Hennessey, *Hunger Strike*, 214–15, 340; Kenny, "American-Irish Nationalism," 299.

42. Adams, *A Farther Shore*, 12; McKittrick and McVea, *Making Sense of the Troubles*, 171–72.

43. See McKittrick and McVea, *Making Sense of the Troubles*, 183–89, for a concise discussion of Sinn Féin's rise.

44. See McDaniel, *Enniskillen*, for a harrowing account of this incident.

45. U2, *Rattle and Hum* [1988], quoted in Bardon, *A History of Ulster*, 777. Bardon observes that Bono's words "may have done more to discourage Irish-American financial support for the Provisional IRA than all the politicians' appeals put together." See also McDaniel, *Enniskillen*, 180–81.

46. McNamara, *The MacBride Principles*, 14–15; Wilson, *Irish America and the Ulster Conflict*, 99–105; Holland, *The American Connection*, 117–18, 121; McManus, *My American Struggle for Justice*, 106–18.

47. This is the generally accepted interpretation of Sinn Féin's electoral turn and of the Northern Irish peace process more generally. See, for example, McKittrick and McVea, *Making Sense of the Troubles*, 195–214.

48. The best discussion of these events is Nesbitt, *Race for Sanctions*. See also Shain, *Marketing the American Creed Abroad*, 84, who argues that this victory marked "one of the most effective diasporic efforts to alter world politics in recent years."

49. Massachusetts State Senator Joseph B. Walsh, *Boston Globe*, March 23, 1983, quoted in McNamara, *The MacBride Principles*, 13. My discussion is based largely on McNamara's thorough monograph, as well as on files for "MacBride Principles: California Campaign," AIA, Daughton Collection.

50. Linda Greenhouse, "Supreme Court Ruling Clears Way for Deportation of an I.R.A. Man," *New York Times*, January 16, 1992; Thompson, *Double Trouble*, 190–91; McNickle, *The Power of the Mayor*, 291, 327; Dinkins, *A Mayor's Life*, 83–84. O'Dwyer, whom Dinkins called

"Uncle Paul," had helped him get a position as New York City Clerk in 1974. For the Doherty case and other high-profile extradition battles in this period, see Holland, *The American Connection*, 152–95.

51. *Wall Street Journal*, September 25, 1996; McNamara, *The MacBride Principles*, 62–63, 82–83, 110; *New York Times*, August 8, 1995; *Irish Echo*, February 16, 1999. A new MacBride bill, crafted by the state senator from San Francisco, John Burton, was finally signed into law by Democratic governor Gray Davis in 1999.

52. See Clinton, *My Life*, 401, for a description of the role of this group in the 1992 campaign and for Clinton's assertion that he "had been interested in the Irish issue since 'the Troubles' began in 1968." For ANIA, see Arthur, *Special Relationships*, 153; Dumbrell, "'Hope and History,'" 216; Guelke, "Northern Ireland and the International System," 136; and Cochrane, "Irish-America, the End of the IRA's Armed Struggle," 220–21.

53. Clinton, *My Life*, 578–81; De Bréadún, *The Far Side of Revenge*, 11.

54. Dumbrell, "'Hope and History,'" 220. The end of the Cold War also allowed Britain to take steps that would have been unimaginable earlier, such as the 1993 Downing Street Declaration, which stated that the British government no longer had a strategic interest in retaining Northern Ireland within the United Kingdom.

55. O'Dowd, quoted in Cochrane, "Irish-America, the End of the IRA's Armed Struggle," 221–22; Hanley, "The Politics of Noraid," 15.

56. For a discussion of the concept of "soft power," see Cochrane, "Irish-America, the End of the IRA's Armed Struggle," 216–17.

57. McKittrick and McVea, *Making Sense of the Troubles*, 238; Major, *John Major*, 476; Sinn Féin submission to British government, January 16, 1995, quoted in Gerry Adams, "Sinn Féin's Influence Can Stretch to IRA Arms Issue," *Irish Voice*, January 25, 1995.

58. McKittrick, *The Nervous Peace*, 159; Clinton, *My Life*, 686.

59. Mitchell, *Making Peace*, 31.

60. Clinton, *My Life*, 700; McKittrick, *Through the Minefield*, 83.

61. *Irish Voice*, August 26, 1997.

62. *Irish Voice*, September 10, 1997.

63. *Irish Voice*, September 10, 1997; *Irish Echo*, September 10, 1997.

64. *Irish Voice*, August 27, 1997.

65. *San Francisco Chronicle*, September 10, 1997; *Irish Herald*, October 1997.

66. *San Francisco Chronicle*, September 10, 1997.

67. Godson, interview with Nancy Soderberg, April 26, 1999, quoted in Godson, *Himself Alone*, 185, which provides the fullest analysis of Trimble's relationship with Washington; Mallie and McKittrick, *Endgame in Ireland*, 231, 241; Clinton, *My Life*, 784–85.

Epilogue

1. Powell, *Great Hatred, Little Room*, 1.

2. "Speech by Bertie Ahern to US Congress."

3. For an overview of the difficulties continuing to face what some Irish commentators have called the "lost generation," see *Irish Times*, August 16, 2015.

BIBLIOGRAPHY

Published Primary Sources

Adams, Gerry. *A Farther Shore: Ireland's Long Road to Peace*. New York: Random House, 2003.

Bagenal, Philip. H. *The American Irish and Their Influence on Irish Politics*. Boston: Roberts, 1882.

Bagenal, Philip. H. *The Irish Agitator in Parliament and on the Platform*. Dublin: Hodges, Foster, and Figgis, 1880.

Barnes, Charles B. *The Longshoremen*. New York: Russell Sage, 1915.

Bartlett, Thomas, ed. "Select Documents: Defenders and Defenderism in 1795." *Irish Historical Studies* 24, no. 95 (May 1985): 373–94.

Burke, Edmund. *The Correspondence of Edmund Burke*. Vol. 7, *January 1792–August 1794*. Edited by P. J. Marshall and John A. Woods. Chicago: University of Chicago Press, 1968.

Beatty, John D., ed. *Protestant Women's Narratives of the Irish Rebellion of 1798*. Dublin: Four Courts, 2001.

Brophy, John. *A Miner's Life*. Edited by John O. P. Hall. Madison: University of Wisconsin Press, 1964.

Cameron Commission. *Disturbances in Northern Ireland: Report of the Commission Appointed by the Governor of Northern Ireland*. Belfast: HMSO, 1969.

Campbell, T. J., and Eddie McAteer. *Irish Action: Nationalist Politics in Northern Ireland in the Stormont Period, as Expressed by Nationalist Leaders*. Belfast: Athol, 1979.

Carey, Mathew. *Autobiography*. Brooklyn, NY: Schwaab, 1942.

Carey, Mathew. *Miscellaneous Essays*. Philadelphia: Carey and Hart, 1830.

Clinton, Bill. *My Life*. New York: Knopf, 2004.

Cobbett, William. *Porcupine's Works: Containing Various Writings and Selections, Exhibiting a Faithful Picture of the United States of America*. London: Cobbett and Morgan, 1801.

Cohalan, Daniel F. "America's Advice to Ireland." In *The Voice of Ireland*, edited by William G. Fitz-Gerald, 212–14. Dublin: Heywood, 1924.

Coigly, James. *A Patriot Priest: The Life of Father James Coigly, 1761–1798*. Edited by Dáire Keogh. Cork: Cork University Press, 1998.

Currie, Austin. *All Hell Will Break Loose*. Dublin: O'Brien, 2004.

Dalberg-Acton, John. "Nationality." In *Essays in the Liberal Interpretation of History*, edited by William H. McNeill, 131–59. Chicago: University of Chicago Press, 1967.

Davidson, Sara. "Bernadette Devlin: An Irish Revolutionary in Irish America." *Harper's Magazine*, January 1, 1970.

Davitt, Michael. *The Fall of Feudalism in Ireland; Or, The Story of the Land League Revolution*. London: Harper, 1904.

Davitt, Michael. *Speech Delivered by Michael Davitt in Defence of the Land League*. London: Kegan Paul, 1890.

Denieffe, Joseph. *A Personal Narrative of the Irish Revolutionary Brotherhood*. Reprint ed. Shannon: Irish University Press, 1969.

Devoy, John. *Devoy's Post Bag, 1871–1928*. Edited by William O'Brien and Desmond Ryan. 2 vols. Dublin: Fallon, 1948.

Devoy, John. *The Land of Eire*. New York: Patterson and Neilson, 1882.

Devoy, John. *Recollections of an Irish Rebel*. Reprint ed. Shannon: Irish University Press, 1969.

Dinkins, David N., with Peter Knobler. *A Mayor's Life: Governing New York's Gorgeous Mosaic*. New York: PublicAffairs, 2013.

Doheny, Michael. *The Felon's Track*. Dublin: Gill, 1951.

Drennan, William, and Martha Drennan McTier. *The Drennan-McTier Letters*. Edited by Jean Agnew. 3 vols. Dublin: Women's History Project in association with the Irish Manuscripts Commission, 1998–1999.

Duffy, Charles Gavan. *Four Years of Irish History, 1845–1849*. London: Cassell, Petter, Galpin, 1883.

Duffy, Charles Gavan. *Young Ireland: A Fragment of Irish History, 1840–1845*. London: Cassell, Petter, Galpin, 1880.

Emmet, Thomas Addis. *Incidents of My Life*. New York: Putnam, 1911.

Emmet, Thomas Addis. *Memoir of Thomas Addis and Robert Emmet with Their Ancestors and Immediate Family*. New York: Emmet, 1915.

Equiano, Olaudah. *The Interesting Narrative and Other Writings*. Edited by Vincent Carretta. Rev. ed. New York: Penguin, 2003.

Flynn, Elizabeth Gurley. *The Rebel Girl: An Autobiography, My First Life (1906–1926)*. Reprint ed. New York: International Publishers, 1973.

George, Henry. *Collected Journalistic Writings*. Edited by Kenneth C. Wenzer. 4 vols. Armonk, NY: Sharpe, 2003.

George, Henry. *Progress and Poverty*. New York: Modern Library, 1929.

Grattan, Thomas Colley. *Civilized America*. 2 vols. New York: Johnson Reprint Corporation, 1969.

Hart, Charles. *Young Irelander Abroad: The Diary of Charles Hart*. Edited by Brendan Ó Cathaoir. Cork: Cork University Press, 2003.

Hayden, Tom. *Irish on the Inside: In Search of the Soul of Irish America*. London: Verso, 2001.

Healy, T. M. *Letters and Leaders of My Day*. 2 vols. New York: Stokes, 1929.

Heatley, Fred. "The Beginning 1964–Feb. 1968." *Fortnight*, March 22, 1974.

Higgins, Francis. *Revolutionary Dublin, 1795–1801: The Letters of Francis Higgins to Dublin Castle*. Edited by Thomas Bartlett. Dublin: Four Courts, 2004.

Hill, Robert A., ed. *The Marcus Garvey and Universal Negro Improvement Association Papers*. 10 vols. Berkeley: University of California Press, 1983–2006.

Hope, James. *United Irishman: The Autobiography of James Hope*. Edited by John Newsinger. London: Merlin, 2001.

Hughes, John Joseph. *Complete Works of the Most Reverend John Hughes*. 2 vols. New York: Catholic Publication House, 1864.

Hume, John. *A New Ireland: Politics, Peace, and Reconciliation*. Boulder, CO: Roberts Rinehart, 1996.

Hunt, Lynn, ed. and trans. *The French Revolution and Human Rights: A Brief Documentary History*. Boston: Bedford, 1996.

Irish Free State. *Debate on the Treaty between Great Britain and Ireland Signed in London on the 6th December, 1921*. Dublin: Talbot, 1922.

Jefferson, Thomas. *The Papers of Thomas Jefferson*. Vol. 30, *1 January 1798 to 31 January 1799*. Edited by Barbara B. Oberg. Princeton, NJ: Princeton University Press, 2003.

Joy, Henry. *Belfast Politics, Or a Collection of the Debates, Resolutions, and Other Proceedings of that Town in the Years 1792 to 1793*. Belfast: Joy, 1794.

Keating, Geoffrey. *The History of Ireland, From the Earliest Period to the English Invasion*. New York: Kirker, 1866.

Keating, Henry S. *On the Defence of Ireland*. Dublin: Byrne, 1795.

McAliskey, Bernadette (Devlin). "A Peasant in the Halls of the Great." In *Twenty Years On*, edited by Michael Farrell, 75–88. Dingle, Ireland: Brandon, 1988.

McCann, Eamonn. *War and an Irish Town.* Updated ed. London: Pluto, 1980.

MacCarthy, James. *Political Portraits by Fitz-Mac.* Colorado Springs, CO: Gazette, 1888.

McDaniel, Denzil. *Enniskillen: The Remembrance Day Sunday Bombing.* Niwot, CO: Irish American Book Company, 1997.

McKittrick, David. *The Nervous Peace.* Belfast: Blackstaff, 1996.

McKittrick, David. *Through the Minefield.* Belfast: Blackstaff, 1999.

McManus, Seán. *My American Struggle for Justice in Northern Ireland.* Cork: Collins, 2011.

MacNeven, William James. *Pieces of Irish History.* New York: Dornin, 1807.

Madden, R. R. *The United Irishmen: Their Lives and Times.* 4 vols. 2nd ed. Dublin: Duffy, 1858–60.

Maguire, John Francis. *The Irish in America.* New York: Sadlier, 1868.

Major, John R. *John Major: The Autobiography.* New York: HarperCollins, 1999.

Meagher, Thomas Francis. *Meagher of the Sword: Speeches of Thomas Francis Meagher in Ireland, 1846–1848.* Edited by Arthur Griffith. Dublin: Gill, 1916.

Miller, David W., ed. *Peep o'day Boys and Defenders: Selected Documents on the Disturbances in County Armagh, 1784–1796.* Belfast: Public Record Office of Northern Ireland, 1990.

Mitchel, John. *Jail Journal.* Reprint ed. Dublin: University Press of Ireland, 1982.

Mitchel, John. *The Last Conquest of Ireland (Perhaps).* Glasgow: Cameron and Ferguson, 1876.

Mitchell, George J. *Making Peace.* Updated ed. Berkeley: University of California Press, 2000.

Mooney, Thomas. *Nine Years in America.* Dublin: McGlashan, 1850.

Musgrave, Richard. *Memoirs of the Different Rebellions in Ireland.* Edited by Steven W. Myers and Delores E. McKnight. 4th ed. Fort Wayne, IN: Round Tower, 1995.

Northern Ireland Civil Rights Association. *"We Shall Overcome": The History of the Struggle for Civil Rights in Northern Ireland, 1968–1978.* Belfast: Northern Ireland Civil Rights Association, 1979.

O'Connell, Daniel. *The Correspondence of Daniel O'Connell.* Edited by Maurice R. O'Connell. 8 vols. Dublin: Irish University Press, 1972–80.

O'Connell, Daniel. *Daniel O'Connell upon American Slavery: With Other Irish Testimonies.* New York: American Anti-Slavery Society, 1860.

O'Connor, Feargus. *A Series of Letters from Feargus O'Connor to Daniel O'Connell.* Reprint ed. New York: Garland, 1986

O'Connor, T. P. *Memoirs of an Old Parliamentarian.* 2 vols. London: Benn, 1929.

O'Day, Alan, and John Stevenson, eds. *Irish Historical Documents since 1800.* Dublin: Gill and Macmillan, 1992.

O'Dwyer, Paul, *Counsel for the Defense: The Autobiography of Paul O'Dwyer.* New York: Simon and Schuster, 1979.

O'Leary, John. *Recollections of Fenians and Fenianism.* 2 vols. Reprint ed. New York: Barnes and Noble, 1969.

O'Neill, Tip, with William Novak. *Man of the House: The Life and Political Memoirs of Speaker Tip O'Neill.* New York: Random House, 1987.

Paine, Thomas. *Collected Writings.* Edited by Eric Foner. New York: Library of America, 1995.

Pigott, Richard. *Personal Recollections of an Irish National Journalist.* 2nd ed. Dublin: Hodges, Figgis, 1883.

Powell, Jonathan. *Great Hatred, Little Room: Making Peace in Northern Ireland.* London: Bodley Head, 2008.

Polk, James K. *Correspondence of James K. Polk.* Vol 9, *January–June 1845.* Edited by Wayne Cutler. Nashville, TN: Vanderbilt University Press, 1996.

Quill, Shirley. *Mike Quill, Himself: A Memoir.* Greenwich, CT: Devin-Adair, 1985.

Quinn, John. *The Letters of John Quinn to William Butler Yeats.* Edited by Alan Himber. Ann Arbor: UMI Research Press, 1983.

Ripley, C. Peter, ed. *The Black Abolitionist Papers.* Vol. 1, *The British Isles, 1830–1865.* Chapel Hill: University of North Carolina Press, 1985.

Report of the Proceedings of the National Repeal Convention of the Friends of Ireland in the United States of America. Philadelphia: Fithian, 1842.

Roney, Frank. *Frank Roney, Irish Rebel and California Labor Leader: An Autobiography*. Edited by Ira B. Cross. Reprint ed. New York: AMS, 1977.

Rowan, Archibald Hamilton. *The Autobiography of Archibald Hamilton Rowan*. Edited by William H. Drummond. Reprint ed. Shannon: Irish University Press, 1972.

Russell, Thomas. *Journals and Memoirs of Thomas Russell, 1791–5*. Edited by C. J. Woods. Dublin: Irish Academic Press, 1991.

Rutherford, John. *The Secret History of the Fenian Conspiracy: Its Origin, Objects and Ramifications*. 2 vols. London: Kegan Paul, 1877.

Sampson, William. *Memoirs of William Sampson*. 2nd ed. Leesburg, VA: Caldwell, 1817.

Sampson, William. *Trial of the Journeymen Cordwainers of the City of New-York*. New York: Riley, 1810.

Sampson, William, and J. Vanière. *The Catholic Question in America: Whether a Roman Catholic Clergyman Be in Any Case Compellable to Disclose the Secrets of Auricular Confession*. New York: Gillespy, 1813.

Seward, William Henry. *An Oration on the Death of Daniel O'Connell: Delivered at Castle Garden, New York, September 22, 1847*. Auburn, NY: Derby, 1847.

Society of United Irishmen of Dublin. *Proceedings of the Society of United Irishmen, of Dublin*. Dublin: Society of United Irishmen of Dublin, 1793.

Sheehy-Skeffington, Francis. *Michael Davitt, Revolutionary, Agitator and Labour Leader*. London: Unwin, 1908.

"Speech by Bertie Ahern to US Congress." *Ireland-Irish Information Website*, http://www.ireland-information.com/articles/bertieahernspeechtouscongress.htm, consulted December 22, 2014.

Spero, Sterling D., and Abram Lincoln Harris. *The Black Worker: The Negro and the Labor Movement*. Reprint ed. New York: Atheneum, 1968.

"Thomas Addis Emmet." *City-Hall Reporter and New-York Law Magazine*, December 1, 1833.

Tone, Theobald Wolfe. *Life of Theobald Wolfe Tone*. Compiled and arranged by William Theobald Wolfe Tone. Edited by Thomas Bartlett. Dublin: Lilliput, 1998.

Tone, Theobald Wolfe. *The Writings of Theobald Wolfe Tone, 1763–98*. Edited by T. W. Moody, R. B. McDowell, and C. J. Woods. 3 vols. Oxford: Clarendon, 1998–2007.

United Irish League of America. *Proceedings of the Second National Convention of the United Irish League of America, New York City, August 30 and 31, 1904*. New York: United Irish League of America, 1904.

Wrongs and Rights of Ireland, Depicted by Distinguished Americans. 2nd ed. Albany, NY: Jones, 1844.

Wyse, Thomas, Sir. *Historical Sketch of the Late Catholic Association of Ireland*. 2 vols. London: Colburn, 1829.

Newspapers and Periodicals

Boston Pilot
Bulletin of the Irish Progressive League
Chicago Daily News
Cincinnati Catholic Telegraph
The Citizen (New York)
Denver Labor Enquirer
Gaelic American (New York)
Irish America (New York)
Irish Echo (New York)
Irish Herald (San Francisco)
Irish Press (Philadelphia)
Irish Times (Dublin)
Irish Voice (New York)

Irish World (New York)
New York Call
New York Daily News
New York Evening Post
New York Herald
New York Times
New York Tribune
Northern Star (Belfast)
San Francisco Chronicle
Shamrock (New York)
The Times (London)
Wall Street Journal
Washington Post

Manuscript Collections

American Irish Historical Society, New York
    Daniel F. Cohalan Papers
    Thomas O'Connor Papers
Archives of Irish America, Bobst Library, New York University
    Patrick Daughton Papers
Boston Public Library, Department of Rare Books and Manuscripts
    MacSwiney Club Papers
Columbia University Oral History Archives, New York
    William O'Dwyer interview transcript
Hatcher Library, Special Collections, University of Michigan, Ann Arbor
    John F. Finerty Papers
Library of Congress, Manuscript Division, Washington, DC
    Arthur Family Papers
    Charles Edward Russell Papers
National Library of Ireland, Dublin
    Peter Golden Papers
    Gerard Tighe Papers
New York Public Library, Manuscripts and Archives Division
    William Bourke Cockran Papers
St. John's University Archives and Special Collections, New York
    American League for an Undivided Ireland Records

Secondary Works

Adams, Graham. *Age of Industrial Violence, 1910–15: The Activities and Findings of the United States Commission on Industrial Relations.* New York: Columbia University Press, 1966.
Alexander, Shawn Leigh. *An Army of Lions: The Civil Rights Struggle before the NAACP.* Philadelphia: University of Pennsylvania Press, 2012.
Allgor, Catherine. *Parlor Politics: In Which the Ladies of Washington Help Build a City and a Government.* Charlottesville: University Press of Virginia, 2000.
Amos, Keith. *The Fenians in Australia, 1865–1880.* Kensington, Australia: New South Wales University Press, 1988.
Anbinder, Tyler. *Five Points: The 19th-Century New York City Neighborhood That Invented Tap Dance, Stole Elections, and Became the World's Most Notorious Slum.* New York: Free Press, 2001.
Anderson, Benedict. *Imagined Communities: Reflections on the Origin and Spread of Nationalism.* Rev. ed. London: Verso, 2006.
Anderson, Benedict. "Long-Distance Nationalism." Chapter 3 in *The Spectre of Comparisons: Nationalism, Southeast Asia, and the World.* London: Verso, 1998.

Anderson, Brendan. *Joe Cahill: A Life in the IRA*. Dublin: O'Brien, 2002.

Anderson, Fred, and Andrew Clayton. *Dominion of War: Empire and Liberty in North America, 1500–2000*. New York: Viking, 2005.

Appleby, Joyce. *Capitalism and a New Social Order: The Republican Vision of the 1790s*. New York: New York University Press, 1984.

Arnesen, Eric, et al. "Scholarly Controversy: Whiteness and the Historians' Imagination." *International Labor and Working-Class History* 60 (Fall 2001): 1–92.

Arthur, Paul. *Special Relationships: Britain, Ireland and the Northern Ireland Problem*. Belfast: Blackstaff, 2000.

Banning, Lance. *The Jeffersonian Persuasion: Evolution of a Party Ideology*. Ithaca, NY: Cornell University Press, 1978.

Bardon, Jonathan. *A History of Ulster*. Updated ed. Belfast: Blackstaff, 2001.

Barrett, James R. *The Irish Way: Becoming American in the Multiethnic City*. New York: Penguin, 2012.

Bartlett, Thomas. "Britishness, Irishness and the Act of Union." In *Acts of Union: The Causes, Context and Consequences of the Act of Union*, edited by Dáire Keogh and Kevin Whelan, 243–58. Dublin: Four Courts, 2001.

Bartlett, Thomas. "Defence, Counter-Insurgency and Rebellion: Ireland, 1793–1803." In *A Military History of Ireland*, edited by Thomas Bartlett and Keith Jeffery, 247–93. Cambridge: Cambridge University Press, 1996.

Bartlett, Thomas. *The Fall and Rise of the Irish Nation: The Catholic Question, 1690–1830*. Savage, MD: Barnes and Noble, 1992.

Bartlett, Thomas. *Ireland: A History*. Cambridge: Cambridge University Press, 2010.

Bartlett, Thomas. "Last Flight of the Wild Geese? Bonaparte's Irish Legion, 1803–15." In *Irish Communities in Early-Modern Europe*, edited by Thomas O'Connor and Mary Ann Lyons, 160–71. Dublin: Four Courts, 2006.

Bartlett, Thomas. "Miles Byrne: United Irishman, Irish Exile and *Beau Sabreur*." In *The Mighty Wave: The 1798 Rebellion in Wexford*, edited by Dáire Keogh and Nicholas Furlong, 118–38. Dublin: Four Courts, 1996.

Bartlett, Thomas. *Theobald Wolfe Tone*. Dundalk, Ireland: Dundalgan, 1997.

Bartlett, Thomas, David Dickson, Dáire Keogh, and Kevin Whelan, eds. *1798: A Bicentenary Perspective*. Dublin: Four Courts, 2003.

Bayly, C. A. *The Birth of the Modern World, 1780–1914*. Oxford: Blackwell, 2004.

Bayly, C. A. "Ireland, India and the Empire: 1780–1914." *Transactions of the Royal Historical Society*, 6th series, 10 (2000): 377–97.

Beaumont, Caitríona. "Gender, Citizenship and the State in Ireland, 1922–1990." In *Ireland in Proximity: History, Gender, Space*, edited by Scott Brewster, Virginia Crossman, Fiona Becket, and David Alderson, 94–108. London: Routledge, 1999.

Beckert, Sven. *The Monied Metropolis: New York City and the Consolidation of the American Bourgeoisie, 1850–1896*. Cambridge: Cambridge University Press, 2001.

Bedford, Henry F. *Socialism and the Workers in Massachusetts, 1886–1912*. Amherst: University of Massachusetts Press, 1966.

Beiner, Guy. "Fenianism and the Martyrdom-Terrorism Nexus in Ireland before Independence." In *Martyrdom and Terrorism: Pre-Modern to Contemporary Perspectives*, edited by Dominic Janes and Alex Houen, 199–220. New York: Oxford University Press, 2014.

Beiner, Guy. *Remembering the Year of the French: Irish Folk History and Social Memory*. Madison: University of Wisconsin Press, 2007.

Belchem, John. "Nationalism, Republicanism and Exile: Irish Emigrants and the Revolutions of 1848." *Past & Present* 146 (February 1995): 103–35.

Berlin, Ira. *Generations of Captivity: A History of African-American Slaves*. Cambridge, MA: Belknap Press of Harvard University Press, 2003.

Bernard, Margie. *Daughter of Derry: The Story of Brigid Sheils Makowski*. London: Pluto, 1989.

Bew, Paul. *Enigma: A New Life of Charles Stewart Parnell*. Dublin: Gill and Macmillan, 2011.

Bew, Paul. *Ideology and the Irish Question: Ulster Unionism and Irish Nationalism, 1912–1916.* Oxford: Clarendon, 1994.

Bew, Paul. *Ireland: The Politics of Enmity, 1789–2006.* Oxford: Oxford University Press, 2007.

Bisceglia, Louis. "The Fenian Funeral of Terence Bellew McManus." *Éire-Ireland* 14, no. 3 (Spring 1979): 45–64.

Blackmar, Elizabeth. *Manhattan for Rent, 1785–1850.* Ithaca, NY: Cornell University Press, 1989.

Blessing, Patrick J. "The Irish in America." In *The Encyclopedia of the Irish in America.* Edited by Michael Glazier, 453–70. Notre Dame, IN: University of Notre Dame Press, 1999.

Boyce, D. George. *Nationalism in Ireland.* 3rd ed. London: Routledge, 1995.

Boyce, D. George, and Alan O'Day, eds. *The Making of Modern Irish History: Revisionism and the Revisionist Controversy.* London: Routledge, 1996.

Boylan, Anne M. *The Origins of Women's Activism: New York and Boston, 1797–1840.* Chapel Hill: University of North Carolina Press, 2002.

Brady, Ciaran, ed. *Interpreting Irish History: The Debate on Historical Revisionism, 1938–1994.* Dublin: Irish Academic Press, 1994.

Branson, Susan. *These Fiery Frenchified Dames: Women and Political Culture in Early National Philadelphia.* Philadelphia: University of Pennsylvania Press, 2001.

Brasted, Howard. "Indian Nationalist Development and the Influence of Irish Home Rule, 1870–1886." *Modern Asian Studies* 14, no. 1 (1980): 37–63.

Bric, Maurice J. "Debating Slavery and Empire: The United States, Britain and the World's Anti-Slavery Convention of 1840." In *A Global History of Anti-Slavery Politics in the Nineteenth Century*, edited by William Mulligan and Maurice J. Bric, 59–77. New York: Palgrave Macmillan, 2013.

Bric, Maurice J. *Ireland, Philadelphia and the Re-invention of America, 1760–1800.* Dublin: Four Courts, 2008.

Brody, David. *Workers in Industrial America: Essays on the 20th Century Struggle.* 2nd ed. New York: Oxford University Press, 1993.

Brophy, Thomas J. "Rivalry between Irish Associations in San Francisco over the Second Funeral of Terence Bellew McManus." In *Associational Culture in Ireland and Abroad*, edited by Jennifer Kelly and R. V. Comerford, 67–84. Dublin: Irish Academic Press, 2010.

Brown, Katharine L. "United Irishmen in the American South: A Re-evaluation." In *Ulster Presbyterians in the Atlantic World: Religion, Politics and Identity*, ed. David A. Wilson and Mark G. Spencer, 87–103. Dublin: Four Courts, 2006.

Brown, Terence. *Ireland: A Social and Cultural History, 1922–2002.* 2nd ed. London: Harper Perennial, 2004.

Brown, Thomas N. *Irish-American Nationalism, 1870–1890.* Philadelphia: Lippincott, 1966.

Brown, Thomas N. "The Origins and Character of Irish-American Nationalism." *Review of Politics* 18, no. 3 (July 1956): 327–58.

Brundage, David. "'In Time of Peace, Prepare for War': Key Themes in the Social Thought of New York's Irish Nationalists, 1890–1916." In *The New York Irish*, edited by Ronald H. Bayor and Timothy J. Meagher, 321–34. Baltimore: Johns Hopkins University Press, 1996.

Brundage, David. *The Making of Western Labor Radicalism: Denver's Organized Workers, 1878–1905.* Urbana: University of Illinois Press, 1994.

Brundage, David. "Matilda Tone in America: Exile, Gender, and Memory in the Making of Irish Republican Nationalism." *New Hibernia Review* 14, no. 1 (Spring 2010): 96–111.

Brundage, David. "Recent Directions in the History of Irish American Nationalism." *Journal of American Ethnic History* 28, no. 4 (Summer 2009): 82–89.

Buckley, John Patrick. *The New York Irish: Their View of American Foreign Policy, 1914–1921.* New York: Arno, 1976.

Bull, Philip. *Land, Politics and Nationalism: A Study of the Irish Land Question.* Dublin: Gill and Macmillan, 1996.

Burchell, R. A. *The San Francisco Irish, 1848–1880.* Berkeley: University of California Press, 1980.

Burke, Martin. "Piecing Together a Shattered Past: The Historical Writings of the United Irish Exiles in America." In *The United Irishmen: Republicanism, Radicalism and Rebellion*, ed. David Dickson, Dáire Keogh, and Kevin Whelan, 297–306. Dublin: Lilliput, 1993.

Callanan, Frank. *The Parnell Split, 1890–91*. Cork: Cork University Press, 1992.

Campbell, Malcolm. *Ireland's New Worlds: Immigrants, Politics, and Society in the United States and Australia, 1815–1922*. Madison: University of Wisconsin Press, 2008.

Campbell, Sarah. "New Nationalism? The S.D.L.P. and the Creation of a Socialist and Labour Party in Northern Ireland, 1969–75." *Irish Historical Studies* 38, no. 151 (May 2013): 422–38.

Cannavan, Jan. "Revolution in Ireland, Evolution in Women's Rights: Irish Women in 1798 and 1848." In *Irish Women and Nationalism: Soldiers, New Women and Wicked Hags*, edited by Louise Ryan and Margaret Ward, 30–44. Dublin: Irish Academic Press, 2004.

Carretta, Vincent. *Equiano, the African: Biography of a Self-Made Man*. Athens: University of Georgia Press, 2005.

Carroll, Francis M. "America and Irish Political Independence, 1910–33." In *The Irish in America: Emigration, Assimilation, and Impact*, edited by P. J. Drudy, 271–93. Cambridge: Cambridge University Press, 1985.

Carroll, Francis M. "America and the 1916 Rising." In *1916: The Long Revolution*, edited by Gabriel Doherty and Dermot Keogh, 121–40. Cork: Mercier, 2007.

Carroll, Francis M. *American Opinion and the Irish Question, 1910–23: A Study in Opinion and Policy*. New York: St. Martin's Press, 1978.

Chaffin, Tom. *Giant's Causeway: Frederick Douglass's Irish Odyssey and the Making of an American Visionary*. Charlottesville: University of Virginia Press, 2014.

Chambers, Liam. *Rebellion in Kildare, 1790–1803*. Dublin: Four Courts, 1998.

Chapman, Michael E. "'How to Smash the British Empire': John Forrest Kelly's *Irish World* and the Boycott of 1920–21." *Éire-Ireland* 43, nos. 3–4 (Fall–Winter 2008): 217–52.

Charlton, Kenneth. "The State of Ireland in the 1820s: James Cropper's Plan."*Irish Historical Studies* 17, no. 67 (March 1971): 320–39.

Cherny, Robert W. "The Making of a Labor Radical: Harry Bridges, 1901–1934." *Pacific Historical Review* 64, No. 3 (August 1995): 363–88.

Clark, Dennis. *Erin's Heirs: Irish Bonds of Community*. Lexington: University Press of Kentucky, 1991.

Clark, Dennis. *Irish Blood: Northern Ireland and the American Conscience*. Port Washington, NY: Kennikat, 1977.

Clark, Dennis. *The Irish in Philadelphia: Ten Generations of Urban Experience*. Philadelphia: Temple University Press, 1973.

Clark, Samuel. *Social Origins of the Irish Land War*. Princeton, NJ: Princeton University Press, 1979.

Clarke, Brian P. *Piety and Nationalism: Lay Voluntary Associations and the Creation of an Irish-Catholic Community in Toronto, 1850–1895*. Montreal: McGill-Queens University Press, 1993.

Cochrane, Feargal. "Irish-America, the End of the IRA's Armed Struggle and the Utility of 'Soft Power.'" *Journal of Peace Research* 44, no. 2 (March 2007): 215–31.

Comerford, R. V. "Churchmen, Tenants, and Independent Opposition, 1850–56." In *A New History of Ireland*. Vol. 5, *Ireland under the Union I, 1801–1870*, edited by W. E. Vaughan, 396–414. Oxford: Clarendon, 1989.

Comerford, R. V. "Comprehending the Fenians." *Saothar* 17 (1992): 52–56.

Comerford, R. V. *The Fenians in Context: Irish Politics and Society, 1848–82*. Dublin: Wolfhound, 1985.

Coogan, Tim Pat. *Eamon de Valera: The Man Who Was Ireland*. New York: HarperCollins, 1995.

Côté, Jane McL. *Fanny and Anna Parnell: Ireland's Patriot Sisters*. New York: St. Martin's Press, 1991.

Connell, R. W. "The Convict Rebellion of 1804." *Melbourne Historical Journal* 5 (1965): 27–37.

Connolly, S. J. *Divided Kingdom: Ireland, 1630–1800*. Oxford: Oxford University Press, 2008.

Costello, Francis J. *Enduring the Most: The Life and Death of Terence MacSwiney*. Dingle, Ireland: Brandon, 1995.

Cotlar, Seth. *Tom Paine's America: The Rise and Fall of Transatlantic Radicalism in the Early Republic*. Charlottesville: University of Virginia Press, 2011.

Coughlan, Rupert J. *Napper Tandy*. Dublin: Anvil, 1976.

Crapol, Edward P. *John Tyler: The Accidental President*. Chapel Hill: University of North Carolina Press, 2006.

Cronin, Mike. *Sport and Nationalism in Ireland: Gaelic Games, Soccer and Irish Identity since 1884*. Dublin: Four Courts, 1999.

Cronin, Sean. *Irish Nationalism: A History of Its Roots and Ideology*. Dublin: Academy Press, 1980.

Cronin, Sean. *The McGarrity Papers: Revelations of the Irish Revolutionary Movement in Ireland and America, 1900–1940*. Tralee, Ireland: Anvil, 1972.

Crowley, John, William J. Smyth, and Mike Murphy, eds. *Atlas of the Great Irish Famine*. New York: New York University Press, 2012.

Cuddy, Joseph Edward. *Irish-Americans and National Isolationism, 1914–1920*. New York: Arno, 1976.

Cullen, L. M. "The United Irishmen in Wexford." In *The Mighty Wave: The 1798 Rebellion in Wexford*, edited by Dáire Keogh and Nicholas Furlong, 48–64. Dublin: Four Courts, 1996.

Curran, Robert Emmett. "The McGlynn Affair and the Shaping of the New Conservatism in American Catholicism, 1886–1894." *Catholic Historical Review* 66, no. 2 (April 1980): 184–204.

Curtin, Nancy J. "The Belfast Uniform: Theobald Wolfe Tone." *Éire-Ireland* 20, no. 2 (Summer 1985): 40–69.

Curtin, Nancy J. "Matilda Tone and Virtuous Republican Femininity." In *The Women of 1798*, edited by Dáire Keogh and Nicholas Furlong, 26–46. Dublin: Four Courts, 1998.

Curtin, Nancy J. "'A Nation of Abortive Men': Gendered Citizenship and Early Irish Republicanism." In *Reclaiming Gender: Transgressive Identities in Modern Ireland*, ed. Marilyn Cohen and Nancy J. Curtin, 33–52. New York: St. Martin's Press, 1999.

Curtin, Nancy J. "The Transformation of the Society of United Irishmen into a Mass-Based Revolutionary Organisation, 1794–6." *Irish Historical Studies* 24, no. 96 (November 1985): 463–92.

Curtin, Nancy J. *The United Irishmen: Popular Politics in Ulster and Dublin, 1791–1798*. New York: Oxford University Press, 1994.

Daly, Mary E. *Industrial Development and Irish National Identity, 1922–1939*. Syracuse, NY: Syracuse University Press, 1992.

Daly, Mary E. "Nationalism, Sentiment, and Economics: Relations between Ireland and Irish America in the Postwar Years." In *New Directions in Irish-American History*, edited by Kevin Kenny, 263–79. Madison: University of Wisconsin Press, 2003.

Darby, John. *Conflict in Northern Ireland: The Development of a Polarised Community*. Dublin: Gill and Macmillan, 1976.

D'Arcy, William. *The Fenian Movement in the United States: 1858–1886*. Washington, DC: Catholic University of America Press, 1947.

Davis, Richard P. *Irish Issues in New Zealand Politics, 1868–1922*. Dunedin, NZ: University of Otago Press, 1974.

Davis, Richard P. *The Young Ireland Movement*. Dublin: Gill and Macmillan, 1987.

De Bréadún, Deaglán. *The Far Side of Revenge: Making Peace in Northern Ireland*. Cork: Collins, 2001.

Delahanty Ian. "'A Noble Empire in the West': Young Ireland, the United States and Slavery." *Britain and the World* 6, no. 2 (September 2013): 171–91.

Delaney, Enda. "Directions in Historiography: Our Island Story? Towards a Transnational History of Late Modern Ireland." *Irish Historical Studies* 37, no. 148 (November 2011): 599–621.

Delaney, Enda. "Migration and Diaspora." In *The Oxford Handbook of Modern Irish History*, edited by Alvin Jackson, 126–47. New York: Oxford University Press, 2014.

Dickson, David. *New Foundations: Ireland 1660–1800*. 2nd ed. Dublin: Irish Academic Press, 2000.

Dickson, David. "Paine and Ireland." In *The United Irishmen: Republicanism, Radicalism and Rebellion*, edited by David Dickson, Dáire Keogh, and Kevin Whelan, 135–50. Dublin: Lilliput, 1993.

Diner, Hasia R. *Erin's Daughters in America: Irish Immigrant Women in the Nineteenth Century*. Baltimore: Johns Hopkins University Press, 1983.

Dolan, Jay P. *The Immigrant Church: New York's Irish and German Catholics, 1815–1865*. Baltimore: Johns Hopkins University Press, 1975.

Dolan, Jay P. *The Irish Americans: A History*. New York: Bloomsbury, 2008.

Donnelly, James S. Jr. *The Great Irish Potato Famine*. Phoenix Mill, UK: Sutton, 2001.

Donnelly, James S. Jr. *Captain Rock: The Irish Agrarian Rebellion of 1821–1824*. Madison: University of Wisconsin Press, 2009.

Dooley, Brian. *Black and Green: The Fight for Civil Rights in Northern Ireland and Black America*. London: Pluto, 1998.

Doorley, Michael. *Irish-American Diaspora Nationalism: The Friends of Irish Freedom, 1916–1935*. Dublin: Four Courts, 2005.

Doorley, Michael. "Judge Daniel Cohalan: A Nationalist Crusader against British Influence in American Life." *New Hibernia Review* 19, no. 2 (Summer 2015): 113–29.

Doyle, David Noel. "The Irish in North America, 1776–1845." In *A New History of Ireland*. Vol. 5, *Ireland under the Union I, 1801–1870*, edited by W. E. Vaughan, 682–725. Oxford: Clarendon, 1989.

Doyle, David Noel. "The Regional Bibliography of Irish America, 1800–1930." *Irish Historical Studies* 23, no. 91 (May 1983): 254–83.

Doyle, Joe. "Striking for Ireland on the New York Docks." In *The New York Irish*, edited by Ronald H. Bayor and Timothy J. Meagher, 357–73. Baltimore: Johns Hopkins University Press, 1996.

Dubofsky, Melvyn. *When Workers Organize: New York City in the Progressive Era*. Amherst: University of Massachusetts Press, 1968.

Dufoix, Stéphane. *Diasporas*. Translated by William Rodarmor. Berkeley: University of California Press, 2008.

Dumbrell, John. "'Hope and History': The US and Peace in Northern Ireland." In *A Farewell to Arms? Beyond the Good Friday Agreement*, edited by Michael Cox, Adrian Guelke, and Fiona Smith, 214–22. Manchester, UK: Manchester University Press, 2000.

Dunne, Tom. *Theobald Wolfe Tone, Colonial Outsider: An Analysis of His Political Philosophy*. Cork: Tower, 1982.

Durey, Michael. *Transatlantic Radicals and the Early American Republic*. Lawrence: University Press of Kansas, 1997.

Dwyer, T. Ryle. "American Friends of Irish Neutrality." In *Irish American Voluntary Organizations*, edited by Michael F. Funchion, 34–48. Westport, CT: Greenwood, 1983.

Dwyer, T. Ryle. *Strained Relations: Ireland at Peace and the USA at War 1941–45*. Dublin: Gill and Macmillan, 1988.

Dye, Nancy Schrom. *As Equals and as Sisters: Feminism, the Labor Movement, and the Women's Trade Union League of New York*. Columbia: University of Missouri Press, 1980.

Eley, Geoff, and Ronald Grigor Suny. "From the Moment of Social History to the Work of Cultural Representation." In *Becoming National: A Reader*, edited by Geoff Eley and Ronald Grigor Suny, 3–37. New York: Oxford University Press, 1996.

Elliott, Marianne. *The Catholics of Ulster: A History*. New York: Basic Books, 2001.

Elliott, Marianne. "The 'Despard Conspiracy' Reconsidered." *Past and Present* 75 (May 1977): 46–61.

Elliott, Marianne. "Ireland." In *Nationalism in the Age of the French Revolution*, edited by Otto Dunn and John Dinwiddy, 71–86. London: Hambledon, 1988.

Elliott, Marianne. "Irish Republicanism in England: The First Phase, 1797–99." In *Penal Era and Golden Age: Essays in Irish History, 1690–1800*, edited by Thomas Bartlett and D. W. Hayton, 204–23. Belfast: Ulster Historical Foundation, 1979.

Elliott, Marianne. *Partners in Revolution: The United Irishmen and France.* New Haven, CT: Yale University Press, 1982.

Elliott, Marianne. *Robert Emmet: The Making of a Legend.* London: Profile, 2003.

Elliott, Marianne. *Wolfe Tone.* 2nd ed. Liverpool: Liverpool University Press, 2012.

Emmons, David M. *Beyond the American Pale: Irish Outlanders and the American West, 1845–1910.* Norman: University of Oklahoma Press, 2010.

Emmons, David M. *The Butte Irish: Class and Ethnicity in an American Mining Town, 1875–1925.* Urbana: University of Illinois Press, 1989.

English, Richard. *Armed Struggle: The History of the IRA.* New York: Oxford University Press, 2003.

English, Richard. *Irish Freedom: The History of Nationalism in Ireland.* London: Macmillan, 2006.

Erie, Steven P. *Rainbow's End: Irish-Americans and the Dilemmas of Urban Machine Politics, 1840–1985.* Berkeley: University of California Press, 1988.

Farrell, Michael. *Northern Ireland: The Orange State.* 2nd rev. ed. London: Pluto, 1980.

Farrell, Sean. *Rituals and Riots: Sectarian Violence and Political Culture in Ulster, 1784–1886.* Lexington: University Press of Kentucky, 2000.

Farren, Seán. *The SDLP: The Struggle for Agreement in Northern Ireland, 1970–2000.* Dublin: Four Courts, 2010.

Feldberg, Michael. *The Turbulent Era: Riot and Disorder in Jacksonian America.* New York: Oxford University Press, 1980.

Fennell, Philip A. "History into Myth: The *Catalpa's* Long Voyage." *New Hibernia Review* 9, no. 1 (Spring 2005): 77–94.

Ferriter, Diarmaid. *The Transformation of Ireland.* Woodstock, NY: Overlook, 2005.

Fitzpatrick, David. "Emigration, 1801–70." In *A New History of Ireland.* Vol. 5, *Ireland under the Union I, 1801–1870,* edited by W. E. Vaughan, 562–616. Oxford: Clarendon, 1989.

Fitzpatrick, David. *Oceans of Consolation: Personal Accounts of Irish Migration to Australia.* Ithaca, NY: Cornell University Press, 1994.

Fitzpatrick, David. "'A Peculiar Tramping People': The Irish in Britain, 1801–70." In *A New History of Ireland,* Vol. 5, *Ireland under the Union I, 1801–1870,* edited by W. E. Vaughan, 623–60. Oxford: Clarendon, 1989.

Fitzpatrick, David. *The Two Irelands, 1912–1939.* New York: Oxford University Press, 1998.

Foner, Eric. "Class, Ethnicity, and Radicalism in the Gilded Age: The Land League and Irish-America." Chapter 8 in *Politics and Ideology in the Age of the Civil War.* New York: Oxford University Press, 1980.

Foner, Eric. *Reconstruction: America's Unfinished Revolution, 1863–1877.* New York: Harper and Row, 1988.

Foster, R. F. "'Colliding Cultures': Leland Lyons and the Reinterpretation of Irish History." Chapter 3 in *The Irish Story: Telling Tales and Making It Up in Ireland.* New York: Oxford University Press, 2002.

Foster, R. F. *Modern Ireland, 1600–1972.* New York: Penguin, 1988.

Foster, R. F. *Vivid Faces: The Revolutionary Generation in Ireland, 1890–1923.* New York: Norton, 2015.

Freeman, Joshua B. *In Transit: The Transport Workers Union in New York City, 1933–1966.* New York: Oxford University Press, 1989.

Fuglerud, Øivind. *Life on the Outside: The Tamil Diaspora and Long-Distance Nationalism.* London: Pluto, 1999.

Funchion, Michael F. "Clan na Gael." In *Irish American Voluntary Organizations,* edited by Michael F. Funchion, 74–93. Westport, CT: Greenwood, 1983.

Funchion, Michael F. "Emmet Monument Association." In *Irish American Voluntary Organizations,* edited by Michael F. Funchion, 102–4. Westport, CT: Greenwood, 1983.

Funchion, Michael F. "Friends of Ireland [for Catholic Emancipation]." In *Irish American Voluntary Organizations,* edited by Michael F. Funchion, 114–19. Westport, CT: Greenwood, 1983.

Funchion, Michael F. "Repeal Associations." In *Irish American Voluntary Organizations,* edited by Michael F. Funchion, 236–41. Westport, CT: Greenwood, 1983.

Gabaccia, Donna R. "Is Everywhere Nowhere? Nomads, Nations, and the Immigrant Paradigm of United States History." *Journal of American History* 86, no. 3 (December 1999): 1115–34.

Gahan, Daniel. *The People's Rising: Wexford, 1798.* Dublin: Gill and Macmillan, 1995.

Garvin, Tom. *The Evolution of Irish Nationalist Politics.* Rev. ed. Dublin: Gill and Macmillan, 2005.

Garvin, Tom. *Nationalist Revolutionaries in Ireland, 1858–1928.* 1st paperback ed. Dublin: Gill and Macmillan, 2005.

Garvin, Tom. *1922: The Birth of Irish Democracy.* Dublin: Gill and Macmillan, 1996.

Gellman, David N. *Emancipating New York: The Politics of Slavery and Freedom, 1777–1827.* Baton Rouge: Louisiana State University Press, 2006.

Gellner, Ernest. *Nations and Nationalism.* 2nd ed. Ithaca, NY: Cornell University Press, 2008.

Genovese, Eugene D. *The World the Slaveholders Made: Two Essays in Interpretation.* New York: Pantheon, 1969.

Geoghegan, Patrick M. *The Irish Act of Union: A Study in High Politics, 1798–1801.* New York: St. Martin's Press, 1999.

Geoghegan, Patrick M. *Robert Emmet: A Life.* Montreal: McGill-Queen's University Press, 2002.

Gibbons, Luke. "Republicanism and Radical Memory: The O'Conors, O'Carolan and the United Irishmen." In *Revolution, Counter-Revolution and Union: Ireland in the 1790s*, edited by Jim Smyth, 211–37. Cambridge: Cambridge University Press, 2000.

Gibbons, Luke. *Transformations in Irish Culture.* Notre Dame, IN: University of Notre Dame Press, 1996.

Gibney, John. *The Shadow of a Year: The 1641 Rebellion in Irish History and Memory.* Madison: University of Wisconsin Press, 2013.

Gibson, Florence E. *The Attitudes of the New York Irish toward State and National Affairs, 1848–1892.* New York: Columbia University Press, 1951.

Gilje, Paul A. "The Development of an Irish American Community in New York City before the Great Migration." In *The New York Irish*, edited by Ronald H. Bayor and Timothy J. Meagher, 70–83. Baltimore: Johns Hopkins University Press, 1996.

Gilje, Paul A. *The Road to Mobocracy: Popular Disorder in New York City, 1763–1834.* Chapel Hill: University of North Carolina Press, 1987.

Gilley, Sheridan. "The Catholic Church and Revolution." In *The Revolution in Ireland, 1879–1923*, edited by D. G. Boyce, 157–72. Houndmills, UK: Macmillan Education, 1988.

Gkotzaridis, Evi. *Trials of Irish History: Genesis and Evolution of a Reappraisal, 1938–2000.* London: Routledge, 2006.

Glazer, Nathan, and Daniel P. Moynihan. *Beyond the Melting Pot: The Negroes, Puerto Ricans, Jews, Italians, and Irish of New York City.* 2nd ed. Cambridge, MA: MIT Press, 1970.

Gleeson, David T. *The Green and the Gray: The Irish in the Confederate States of America.* Chapel Hill: University of North Carolina Press, 2013.

Gleeson, David T. *The Irish in the South, 1815–1877.* Chapel Hill: University of North Carolina Press, 2001.

Glick Schiller, Nina, and Georges Eugene Fouron. *Georges Woke Up Laughing: Long-Distance Nationalism and the Search for Home.* Durham, NC: Duke University Press, 2001.

Göbel, Thomas. "Becoming American: Ethnic Workers and the Rise of the CIO." *Labor History* 29, no. 2 (Spring 1988): 173–98.

Golway, Terry. *Irish Rebel: John Devoy and America's Fight for Ireland's Freedom.* New York: St. Martin's Press, 1998.

Goodwin, Albert. *The Friends of Liberty: The English Democratic Movement in the Age of the French Revolution.* London: Hutchinson, 1979.

Godson, Dean. *Himself Alone: David Trimble and the Ordeal of Unionism.* London: HarperCollins, 2004.

Gordon, Michael A. "The Labor Boycott in New York City, 1880–1886." *Labor History* 16, no. 2 (Spring 1975): 184–229.

Gordon, Michael A. "Studies in Irish and Irish-American Thought and Behavior in Gilded Age New York City." PhD diss., University of Rochester, 1977.

Grabbe, Hans-Jürgen. "European Immigration to the United States in the Early National Period, 1783–1820." *Proceedings of the American Philosophical Society* 133, no. 2 (June 1989): 190–214.

Grace, Robert J. *The Irish in Quebec: An Introduction to the Historiography.* Quebec: Institut Québécois de Recherche sur la Culture, 1997.

Gray, Peter. "British Relief Measures." In *Atlas of the Great Irish Famine*, edited by John Crowley, William J. Smyth, and Mike Murphy, 75–86. New York: New York University Press, 2012.

Gray, Peter. *Famine, Land and Politics: British Government and Irish Society, 1843–50.* Dublin: Irish Academic Press, 1999.

Green, Nancy L. "Expatriation, Expatriates, and Expats: The American Transformation of a Concept." *American Historical Review* 114, no. 2 (April 2009): 307–28.

Guelke, Adrian. "Northern Ireland and the International System." In *Ireland on the World Stage*, edited by William Crotty and David Schmitt, 127–39. London: Pearson, 2002.

Guglielmo, Thomas A. *White on Arrival: Italians, Race, Color, and Power in Chicago, 1890–1945.* New York: Oxford University Press, 2003.

Guy, Francis Shaw. *Edmund Bailey O'Callaghan: A Study in American Historiography (1797–1880).* Reprint ed. New York: AMS, 1974.

Gyory, Andrew. *Closing the Gate: Race, Politics, and the Chinese Exclusion Act.* Chapel Hill: University of North Carolina Press, 1998.

Handlin, Oscar. *Boston's Immigrants, 1790–1880: A Study in Acculturation.* Rev. and enl. ed. New York: Atheneum, 1969.

Hanley, Brian. *The IRA, 1926–1936.* Dublin: Four Courts, 2002.

Hanley, Brian. "Irish Republicans in Interwar New York." *IJASonline* 1 (June 2009), http://www.ijasonline.com/BRIAN-HANLEY.html, consulted February 4, 2010.

Hanley, Brian. "'No English Enemy . . . Ever Stooped so Low': Mike Quill, de Valera's Visit to the German Legation, and Irish-American Attitudes during World War II." *Radharc* 5–7 (2004–6): 245–64.

Hanley, Brian. "The Politics of Noraid." *Irish Political Studies* 19, no. 1 (Summer 2004): 1–17.

Hanley, Brian, and Scott Millar. *The Lost Revolution: The Story of the Official IRA and the Workers' Party.* Dublin: Penguin Ireland, 2009.

Hart, Peter. *The I.R.A. and Its Enemies: Violence and Community in Cork, 1916–1923.* Oxford: Clarendon, 1998.

Hart, Peter. *Mick: The Real Michael Collins.* New York: Viking, 2005.

Hennessey, Thomas. *Hunger Strike: Margaret Thatcher's Battle with the IRA, 1980–1981.* Sallins, Ireland: Irish Academic Press, 2014.

Herlihy, Jim. *Peter Golden: The Voice of Ireland.* Cork: Peter Golden Commemoration Committee, 1994.

Higgins, Padhraig. *A Nation of Politicians: Gender, Patriotism, and Political Culture in Late Eighteenth-Century Ireland.* Madison: University of Wisconsin Press, 2010.

Higgins, Roisín. *Transforming 1916: Meaning, Memory and the Fiftieth Anniversary of the Easter Rising.* Cork: Cork University Press, 2012.

Hobsbawm, E. J. *The Age of Capital, 1848–1975.* New York: Scribner, 1975.

Hobsbawm, E. J. *Nations and Nationalism since 1780: Programme, Myth, Reality.* 2nd ed. Cambridge: Cambridge University Press, 1992.

Holland, Jack. *The American Connection: U.S. Guns, Money, and Influence in Northern Ireland.* 2nd ed. Boulder, CO: Roberts Rinehart, 1999.

Hopkinson, Michael. "Civil War and Aftermath, 1922–4." In *A New History of Ireland.* Vol.7, *Ireland, 1921–1984*, edited by J. R. Hill, 31–61. Oxford: Oxford University Press, 2003.

Hopkinson, Michael. *Green against Green: The Irish Civil War.* Dublin: Gill and Macmillan, 1988.

Hopkinson, Michael. "Irish Americans and the Anglo-Irish Treaty of 1921." In *Essays Presented to Michael Roberts*, edited by John Bossy and Peter Jupp, 133–45. Belfast: Blackstaff, 1976.

Hopkinson, Michael. *The Irish War for Independence.* Dublin: Gill and Macmillan, 2002.

Howe, Daniel Walker. *The Political Culture of the American Whigs*. Chicago: University of Chicago Press, 1979.

Hutchinson, John. *The Dynamics of Cultural Nationalism: The Gaelic Revival and the Creation of the Irish Nation State*. London: Allen and Unwin, 1987.

Hutchinson, John. *Modern Nationalism*. London: Fontana, 1994.

Hufton, Olwen H. *Women and the Limits of Citizenship in the French Revolution*. Toronto: University of Toronto Press, 1992.

Hughes, Robert. *The Fatal Shore*. New York: Knopf, 1987.

Hunt, Lynn. *Politics, Culture, and Class in the French Revolution*. Berkeley: University of California Press, 1984.

Huthmacher, J. Joseph. "Charles Evans Hughes and Charles Francis Murphy: The Metamorphosis of Progressivism." *New York History* 46, no. 1 (January 1965): 25–40.

Ignatiev, Noel. *How the Irish Became White*. New York: Routledge, 1995.

Iwańska, Alicja. *Exiled Governments: Spanish and Polish: An Essay in Political Sociology*. Cambridge, MA: Schenkman, 1981.

Jackson, Alvin. *Home Rule: An Irish History, 1800–2000*. New York: Oxford University Press, 2004.

Jackson, Alvin. *Ireland, 1798–1998: War, Peace and Beyond*. 2nd ed. Chichester, UK: Wiley, 2010.

Jackson, Alvin, ed. *The Oxford Handbook of Modern Irish History*. New York: Oxford University Press, 2014.

Jacobson, Matthew Frye. *Special Sorrows: The Diasporic Imagination of Irish, Polish, and Jewish Immigrants in the United States*. Cambridge, MA: Harvard University Press, 1995.

Janis, Ely M. *A Greater Ireland: The Land League and Transatlantic Nationalism in Gilded Age America*. Madison: University of Wisconsin Press, 2015.

Janis, Ely M. "Petticoat Revolutionaries: Gender, Ethnic Nationalism, and the Irish Ladies' Land League in the United States." *Journal of American Ethnic History* 27, no. 2 (Winter 2008): 5–27.

Jensen, Joan M. *Passage from India: Asian Indian Immigrants in North America*. New Haven, CT: Yale University Press, 1988.

Jentz, John B., and Richard Schneirov. "Chicago's Fenian Fair: A Window into the Civil War as a Popular Awakening." *Labor's Heritage* 6, no. 3 (Winter 1995): 4–19.

Jordan, Donald E. *Land and Popular Politics in Ireland: County Mayo from the Plantation to the Land War*. Cambridge: Cambridge University Press, 1994.

Joyce, Toby. "'Ireland's Trained and Marshalled Manhood': The Fenians in the Mid-1860s." In *Gender Perspectives in Nineteenth-Century Ireland: Public and Private Spheres*, edited by Margaret Kelleher and James H. Murphy, 70–80. Dublin: Irish Academic Press, 1997.

Kalliomäki, Aki. "'The Most God-Provoking Democrats on This Side of Hell': The United Irishmen in the United States." PhD diss., University of California, Santa Cruz, 2005.

Kazin, Michael. *Barons of Labor: The San Francisco Building Trades and Union Power in the Progressive Era*. Urbana: University of Illinois Press, 1987.

Kealey, Gregory S., and Bryan D. Palmer. *Dreaming of What Might Be: The Knights of Labor in Ontario, 1880–1900*. Cambridge: Cambridge University Press, 1982.

Kee, Robert. *The Green Flag: A History of Irish Nationalism*. London: Weidenfeld and Nicolson, 1972.

Kelly, James. *Sir Richard Musgrave, 1746–1818: Ultra-Protestant Ideologue*. Dublin: Four Courts, 2009.

Kelly, Mary C. *Ireland's Great Famine in Irish-American History: Enshrining a Fateful Memory*. Lanham, MD: Rowman and Littlefield, 2014.

Kelly, Mary C. *The Shamrock and the Lily: The New York Irish and the Creation of a Transatlantic Identity, 1845–1921*. New York: Lang, 2005.

Kelly, M. J. *The Fenian Ideal and Irish Nationalism, 1882–1916*. Woodbridge, UK: Boydell, 2006.

Kelly, M. J. "Review Article: Faith in Fraternity: New Perspectives on the Irish Republican Brotherhood." *Irish Historical Studies* 35, no. 139 (May 2007): 380–84.

Kelly, Stephen. "A Policy of Futility: Eamon de Valera's Anti-Partition Campaign, 1948–1951." *Études Irlandaises*, no. 36-2 (2011), http://etudesirlandaises.revues.org/2348, consulted December 22, 2014.

Kenny, Kevin. *The American Irish: A History*. Harlow, UK: Longman, 2000.

Kenny, Kevin. "American-Irish Nationalism." In *Making the Irish American: History and Heritage of the Irish in the United States*, edited by J. J. Lee and Marion R. Casey, 289–301. New York: New York University Press, 2006.

Kenny, Kevin. *Diaspora: A Very Short Introduction*. New York: Oxford University Press, 2013.

Kenny, Kevin. "Diaspora and Comparison: The Global Irish as a Case Study." *Journal of American History* 90, no. 1 (June 2003): 134–62.

Kenny, Kevin. "Twenty Years of Irish American Historiography." *Journal of American Ethnic History* 28, no. 4 (Summer 2009): 67–75.

Keogh, Dermot. "De Valera, Hitler and the Visit of Condolence, May 1945." *History Ireland* 5, no. 3 (Autumn 1997): 58–61.

Keogh, Dermot. *Twentieth-Century Ireland: Nation and State*. New York: St. Martin's Press, 1995.

Kerber, Linda K. *Toward an Intellectual History of Women: Essays*. Chapel Hill: University of North Carolina Press, 1997.

Kiberd, Declan. "Republican Self-Fashioning: The Journal of Wolfe Tone." In *Ireland Abroad: Politics and Professions in the Nineteenth Century*, edited by Oonagh Walsh, 16–35. Dublin: Four Courts, 2003.

Kinealy, Christine. *Daniel O'Connell and the Anti-Slavery Movement: "The Saddest People the Sun Sees."* London: Pickering and Chatto, 2011.

Kinealy, Christine. *This Great Calamity: The Irish Famine, 1845–52*. Dublin: Gill and Macmillan, 1994.

Kinealy, Christine. *Repeal and Revolution: 1848 in Ireland*. Manchester, UK: Manchester University Press, 2009.

King, Carla. *Michael Davitt*. Dublin: University College Dublin Press, 2009.

Kissane, Bill. *The Politics of the Irish Civil War*. Oxford: Oxford University Press, 2005.

Knirck, Jason. *Women of the Dáil: Gender, Republicanism and the Anglo-Irish Treaty*. Dublin: Irish Academic Press, 2006.

Knobel, Dale T. *Paddy and the Republic: Ethnicity and Nationality in Antebellum America*. Middletown, CT: Wesleyan University Press, 1986.

Kolchin, Peter. "Whiteness Studies: The New History of Race in America." *Journal of American History* 89, no. 1 (June 2002): 154–73.

Komlos, John H. *Louis Kossuth in America, 1851–1852*. Buffalo, NY: East European Institute, 1973.

Kornblith, Gary J., and John M. Murrin. "The Dilemmas of Ruling Elites in Revolutionary America." In *Ruling America: A History of Wealth and Power in a Democracy*, edited by Steve Fraser and Gary Gerstle, 27–63. Cambridge, MA: Harvard University Press, 2008.

Kurlansky, Mark. *1968: The Year that Rocked the World*. New York: Ballantine, 2004.

Laffan, Michael. *The Resurrection of Ireland: The Sinn Féin Party, 1916–1923*. Cambridge: Cambridge University Press, 1999.

Larkin, Emmet. *James Larkin, 1876–1947: Irish Labour Leader*. London: Routledge and Kegan Paul, 1965.

Laslett, John H. M. *Labor and the Left: A Study of Socialist and Radical Influences in the American Labor Movement, 1881–1924*. New York: Basic Books, 1970.

Lee, J. J. "Emigration: 1922–1998." In *The Encyclopedia of the Irish in America*, edited by Michael Glazier, 263–66. Notre Dame, IN: University of Notre Dame Press, 1999.

Lee, J. J. "Introduction: Interpreting Irish America." In *Making the Irish American: History and Heritage of the Irish in the United States*, edited by J. J. Lee and Marion R. Casey, 1–60. New York: New York University Press, 2006.

Lee, J. J. *Ireland, 1912–1985: Politics and Society*. Cambridge: Cambridge University Press, 1989.

Lee, J. J. *The Modernisation of Irish Society, 1848–1918*. Dublin: Gill and Macmillan, 1973.

Lee, J. J. "The Social and Economic Ideas of O'Connell." In *Daniel O'Connell: Portrait of a Radical*, edited by Kevin B. Nowlan and Maurice R. O'Connell, 70–86. Belfast: Appletree, 1984.

Leinenweber, Charles. "Socialists in the Streets: The New York City Socialist Party in Working Class Neighborhoods, 1908–1918." *Science & Society* 41, no. 2 (Summer 1977): 152–71.

Levenson, Leah, and Jerry H. Natterstad. *Hanna Sheehy-Skeffington: Irish Feminist*. Syracuse, NY: Syracuse University Press, 1986.

Levine, Bruce C. *The Spirit of 1848: German Immigrants, Labor Conflict, and the Coming of the Civil War*. Urbana: University of Illinois Press, 1992.

Light, Dale B. "The Role of Irish-American Organisations in Assimilation and Community Formation." In *The Irish in America: Emigration, Assimilation, and Impact*, edited by P. J. Drudy, 113–41. Cambridge: Cambridge University Press, 1985.

Light, Dale B. *Rome and the New Republic: Conflict and Community in Philadelphia Catholicism between the Revolution and the Civil War*. Notre Dame, IN: University of Notre Dame Press, 1996.

Linebaugh, Peter, and Marcus Rediker. *The Many-Headed Hydra: Sailors, Slaves, Commoners, and the Hidden History of the Revolutionary Atlantic*. Boston: Beacon, 2000.

Lovejoy, Paul E. "Autobiography and Memory: Gustavus Vassa, Alias Olaudah Equiano, the African." *Slavery & Abolition* 27, no. 3 (December 2006): 317–47.

Lynch, Niamh. "Defining Irish Nationalist Anti-Imperialism: Thomas Davis and John Mitchel." *Éire-Ireland* 42, nos. 1–2 (Spring–Summer 2007): 82–107.

Lynch, Timothy J. *Turf War: The Clinton Administration and Northern Ireland*. Aldershot, UK: Ashgate, 2004.

Lyons, F. S. L. *The Irish Parliamentary Party, 1890–1910*. London: Faber and Faber, 1951.

Lyons, F. S. L. *John Dillon: A Biography*. Chicago: University of Chicago Press, 1968.

Lyons, Martyn. *France under the Directory*. Cambridge: Cambridge University Press, 1975.

MacAtasney, Gerard. *Tom Clarke: Life, Liberty, Revolution*. Dublin: Irish Academic Press, 2013.

McBride, Ian. *Eighteenth-Century Ireland: The Isle of Slaves*. Dublin: Gill and Macmillan, 2009.

McBride, Ian. "The Nation in the Age of Revolution." In *Power and the Nation in European History*, edited by Len Scales and Oliver Zimmer, 248–71. Cambridge: Cambridge University Press, 2005.

McBride, Ian. "Review Article: Reclaiming the Rebellion: 1798 in 1998." *Irish Historical Studies* 31, no. 123 (May 1999): 395–410.

McCaffrey, Lawrence J. *Daniel O'Connell and the Repeal Year*. Lexington: University of Kentucky Press, 1966.

McCaffrey, Lawrence J. *The Irish Catholic Diaspora in America*. Rev. ed. Washington, DC: Catholic University Press of America, 1997.

McCarthy, John P. "The Friends of Irish Freedom and the Founding of the Irish Free State." *Recorder* 6, no. 2 (Fall 1993): 116–28.

McCartney, Donal. "Parnell and the American Connection." In *The Ivy Leaf: The Parnells Remembered*, edited by Donal McCartney and Pauric Travers, 38–55. Dublin: University College Dublin Press, 2006.

McConnel, James. *The Irish Parliamentary Party and the Third Home Rule Crisis*. Dublin: Four Courts, 2013.

McCoy, Drew R. *The Elusive Republic: Political Economy in Jeffersonian America*. Chapel Hill: University of North Carolina Press, 1980.

McDaniel, W. Caleb. *The Problem of Democracy in the Age of Slavery: Garrisonian Abolitionists and Transatlantic Reform*. Baton Rouge: Louisiana State University Press, 2013.

McDowell, R. B. *Grattan: A Life*. Dublin: Lilliput, 2001.

McDowell, R. B. *Ireland in the Age of Imperialism and Revolution, 1760–1801*. New York: Oxford University Press, 1979.

McEvoy, Frederick J. "Canadian Catholic Press Reaction to the Irish Crisis, 1916–1921." In *Irish Nationalism in Canada*, edited by David A. Wilson, 121–39. Montreal: McGill-Queen's University Press, 2009.

McKittrick, David, Seamus Kelters, Brian Feeney, and Chris Thornton. *Lost Lives: The Stories of the Men, Women and Children Who Died as a Result of the Northern Ireland Troubles*. Updated ed. Edinburgh: Mainstream, 2007.

McKittrick, David, and David McVea. *Making Sense of the Troubles: The Story of the Conflict in Northern Ireland*. Revised and updated ed. London: Viking, 2012.

McKivigan. John. *Forgotten Firebrand: James Redpath and the Making of Nineteenth-Century America*. Ithaca, NY: Cornell University Press, 2008.

MacDonagh, Oliver. *The Emancipist: Daniel O'Connell, 1830–47*. London: Weidenfeld and Nicolson, 1989.

MacDonagh, Oliver. *The Hereditary Bondsman: Daniel O'Connell, 1775–1829*. London: Weidenfeld and Nicolson, 1988.

McFarland, E. W. *Ireland and Scotland in the Age of Revolution: Planting the Green Bough*. Edinburgh: Edinburgh University Press, 1994.

McGarry, Fearghal. *The Rising: Ireland—Easter 1916*. Oxford: Oxford University Press, 2010.

McGarry, Fearghal, and James McConnel, eds. *The Black Hand of Republicanism: Fenianism in Modern Ireland*. Dublin: Irish Academic Press, 2009.

McGee, Owen. *The IRB: The Irish Republican Brotherhood, from the Land League to Sinn Féin*. Dublin: Four Courts, 2005.

McGovern, Bryan P. *John Mitchel: Irish Nationalist, Southern Secessionist*. Knoxville: University of Tennessee Press, 2009.

McGreevy, John T. *Catholicism and American Freedom: A History*. New York: Norton, 2003.

McGurrin, James. *Bourke Cockran: A Free Lance in American Politics*. New York: Scribner's, 1948.

McKillen, Elizabeth. *Chicago Labor and the Quest for a Democratic Diplomacy, 1914–1924*. Ithaca, NY: Cornell University Press, 1995.

McMahon, Cian T. *The Global Dimensions of Irish Identity: Race, Nation, and the Popular Press, 1840–1880*. Chapel Hill: University of North Carolina Press, 2015.

McMahon, Timothy G. *Grand Opportunity: The Gaelic Revival and Irish Society, 1893–1910*. Syracuse, NY: Syracuse University Press, 2008.

MacMillan, Margaret. *Paris 1919: Six Months That Changed the World*. New York: Random House, 2002.

McNamara, Kevin. *The MacBride Principles: Irish America Strikes Back*. Liverpool: Liverpool University Press, 2009.

McNickle, Chris. *The Power of the Mayor: David Dinkins, 1990–1993*. New Brunswick, NJ: Transaction, 2013.

MacRaild, Donald M. "The Orange Atlantic." In *The Irish in the Atlantic World*, edited by David T. Gleeson, 307–26. Columbia: University of South Carolina Press, 2010.

Mac Suibhne, Breandán. "Whiskey, Potatoes and Paddies: Volunteering and the Construction of the Irish Nation in Northwest Ulster, 1778–1782." In *Crowds in Ireland, c. 1720–1920*, edited by Peter Jupp and Eoin Magennis, 45–82. New York: St. Martin's Press, 2000.

Malcomson, A. P. W. *John Foster (1740–1828): The Politics of Improvement and Prosperity*. Dublin: Four Courts, 2011.

Mallie, Eamonn, and David McKittrick. *Endgame in Ireland*. London: Hodder and Stoughton, 2001.

Mandle, W. F. *The Gaelic Athletic Association and Irish Nationalist Politics, 1884–1924*. Dublin: Gill and Macmillan, 1987.

Manning, Helen Taft. *The Revolt of French Canada, 1800–1835: A Chapter of the History of the British Commonwealth*. New York: St. Martin's Press, 1962.

Marley, Laurence. *Michael Davitt: Freelance Radical and Frondeur*. Dublin: Four Courts, 2007.

Marston, Sallie A. "Public Rituals and Community Power: St. Patrick's Day Parades in Lowell, Massachusetts, 1841–1874." *Political Geography Quarterly* 8, no. 3 (July 1989): 255–69.

Maume, Patrick. *The Long Gestation: Irish Nationalist Life, 1891–1918*. New York: St. Martin's Press, 2000.

Maynard, Douglas H. "The World's Anti-Slavery Convention of 1840." *Mississippi Valley Historical Review* 47, no. 3 (December 1960): 452–71.

Meagher, Timothy J. *The Columbia Guide to Irish American History*. New York: Columbia University Press, 2005.

Meagher, Timothy J. *Inventing Irish America: Generation, Class, and Ethnic Identity in a New England City, 1880–1928*. Notre Dame, IN: University of Notre Dame Press, 2001.

Meleady, Dermot. *Redmond: The Parnellite*. Cork: Cork University Press, 2008.

Miller, David W. "The Armagh Troubles, 1784–95." In *Irish Peasants: Violence and Political Unrest, 1780–1914*, edited by Samuel Clark and James S. Donnelly, 155–91. Madison: University of Wisconsin Press, 1983.

Miller, Kerby A. *Emigrants and Exiles: Ireland the Irish Exodus to North America*. New York: Oxford University Press, 1985.

Miller, Kerby A. *Ireland and Irish America: Culture, Class, and Transatlantic Migration*. Dublin: Field Day, 2008.

Miller, Kerby A., Arnold Schrier, Bruce D. Bolling, and David N. Doyle. *Irish Immigrants in the Land of Canaan: Letters and Memoirs from Colonial and Revolutionary America, 1675–1815*. New York: Oxford University Press, 2003.

Mitchell, Brian C. *The Paddy Camps: The Irish of Lowell, 1821–61*. Urbana: University of Illinois, 1988.

Mitchell, Martin J. *The Irish in the West of Scotland, 1797–1848: Trade Unions, Strikes and Political Movements*. Edinburgh: Donald, 1998.

Montgomery, David. *Beyond Equality: Labor and the Radical Republicans, 1862–1872*. New York: Knopf, 1967.

Montgomery, David. *The Fall of the House of Labor: The Workplace, the State, and American Labor Activism, 1865–1925*. New York: Cambridge University Press, 1987.

Montgomery, David. "Labor Movement." In *The Encyclopedia of the Irish in America*, edited by Michael Glazier, 525–31. Notre Dame, IN: University of Notre Dame Press, 1999.

Montgomery, David. "The Shuttle and the Cross: Weavers and Artisans in the Kensington Riots of 1844." *Journal of Social History* 5, no. 4 (Summer 1972): 411–46.

Moody, T. W. *Davitt and Irish Revolution, 1846–82*. Oxford: Clarendon, 1981.

Moody, T. W., ed. *The Fenian Movement*. Cork: Mercier, 1968.

Moody, T. W. "The New Departure in Irish Politics, 1878–9." In *Essays in British and Irish History in Honour of James Eadre Todd*, edited by H. A. Cronne, T. W. Moody, and D. B. Quinn, 303–33. London: Muller, 1949.

Moran, Seán Farrell. *Patrick Pearse and the Politics of Redemption: The Mind of the Easter Rising, 1916*. Washington, DC: Catholic University of America Press, 1994.

Morgan, Austen. *James Connolly: A Political Biography*. Manchester, UK: Manchester University Press, 1988.

Moriarty, Thomas F. "The Irish American Response to Catholic Emancipation." *Catholic Historical Review* 66, no. 3 (July 1980): 353–73.

Morley, Vincent. *Irish Opinion and the American Revolution, 1760–1783*. Cambridge: Cambridge University Press, 2002.

Murphy, Angela. *American Slavery, Irish Freedom: Abolition, Immigrant Citizenship, and the Transatlantic Movement for Irish Repeal*. Baton Rouge: Louisiana State University Press, 2010.

Murphy, Angela. "Daniel O'Connell and the 'American Eagle' in 1845: Slavery, Diplomacy, Nativism, and the Collapse of America's First Irish Nationalist Movement." *Journal of American Ethnic History* 26, no. 2 (Winter 2007): 3–26.

Murphy, Cliona. *The Women's Suffrage Movement and Irish Society in the Early Twentieth Century*. New York: Harvester Wheatsheaf, 1989.

Murphy, David. *Ireland and the Crimean War*. Dublin: Four Courts, 2002.

Murphy, John A. "The Influence of America on Irish Nationalism." In *America and Ireland, 1776–1976: The American Identity and the Irish Connection*, edited by David Noel Doyle and Owen Dudley Edwards, 105–15. Westport, CT: Greenwood, 1980.

Murphy, John. *Ireland in the Twentieth Century*. Dublin: Gill and Macmillan, 1975.

Murphy, Richard C., and Lawrence J. Mannion. *The History of the Society of the Friendly Sons of Saint Patrick in the City of New York, 1784 to 1955*. New York: Dillon, 1962.

Murray, Damien. "Ethnic Identities and Diasporic Sensibilities: Transnational Irish American Nationalism in Boston after World War I." *Éire-Ireland* 46, nos. 3–4 (Fall–Winter 2011): 102–31.

Murtagh, Harman. "General Humbert's Futile Campaign." In *1798: A Bicentenary Perspective*, edited by Thomas Bartlett, David Dickson, Dáire Keogh, and Kevin Whelan, 174–87. Dublin: Four Courts, 2003.

Nash, Gary B. "Poverty and Politics in Early American History." In *Down and Out in Early America*, edited by Billy G. Smith, 1–37. University Park: Pennsylvania State University Press, 2004.

Nash, Gary B., and Jean R. Soderlund. *Freedom by Degrees: Emancipation in Pennsylvania and Its Aftermath*. New York: Oxford University Press, 1991.

Nelson, Bruce. *Irish Nationalists and the Making of the Irish Race*. Princeton, NJ: Princeton University Press, 2012.

Nelson, John R. *Liberty and Property: Political Economy and Policymaking in the New Nation, 1789–1812*. Baltimore: Johns Hopkins University Press, 1987.

Nesbitt, Francis Njubi. *Race for Sanctions: African Americans against Apartheid, 1946–1994*. Bloomington: Indiana University Press, 2004.

Newsinger, John. *Fenianism in Mid-Victorian Britain*. London: Pluto, 1994.

Newsinger, John. "Fenianism Revisited: Pastime or Revolutionary Movement?" *Saothar* 17 (1992): 46–52.

Ní Bhroiméil, Úna. *Building Irish Identity in America, 1870–1915: The Gaelic Revival*. Dublin: Four Courts, 2003.

Nowlan, Kevin B. "O'Connell and Irish Nationalism." In *Daniel O'Connell: Portrait of a Radical*, edited by Kevin B. Nowlan and Maurice R. O'Connell, 9–18. Belfast: Appletree, 1984.

Nowlan, Kevin B. *The Politics of Repeal: A Study in the Relations between Great Britain and Ireland, 1841–50*. London: Routledge and Kegan Paul, 1965.

Novak, Rose. "Ellen O'Leary: A Bold Fenian Poet." *Éire-Ireland* 43, nos. 3–4 (Fall–Winter 2008): 59–84.

Ngai, Mae M. "Immigration and Ethnic History." In *American History Now*, edited by Eric Foner and Lisa McGirr, 358–75. Philadelphia: Temple University Press, 2011.

O'Brien, Gillian. *Blood Runs Green: The Murder That Transfixed Gilded Age Chicago*. Chicago: University of Chicago Press, 2015.

O'Brien, Gillian. "Spirit, Impartiality and Independence: The *Northern Star*, 1792–97." *Eighteenth-Century Ireland* 13 (1998): 7–23.

O'Brien, Mark. *De Valera, Fianna Fáil and the Irish Press*. Dublin: Irish Academic Press, 2001.

Ó Broin, Leon. *Revolutionary Underground: The Story of the Irish Republican Brotherhood, 1858–1924*. Dublin: Gill and Macmillan, 1976.

O'Callaghan, Margaret. "'From Casement Park to Toomebridge': The Commemoration of the Easter Rising in Northern Ireland in 1966." In *1916 in 1966: Commemorating the Easter Rising*, edited by Mary E. Daly and Margaret O'Callaghan, 86–147. Dublin: Royal Irish Academy, 2007.

O'Callaghan, Margaret. "'With the Eyes of Another Race, of People Once Hunted Themselves': Casement, Colonialism and a Remembered Past." In *Ireland in Transition, 1867–1921*, edited by D. George Boyce and Alan O'Day, 159–75. London: Routledge, 2004.

O'Connell, Maurice R. "O'Connell, Young Ireland, and Negro Slavery: An Exercise in Romantic Nationalism." *Thought: A Review of Culture and Idea* 64, no. 253 (June 1989): 130–36.

O'Day, Alan. *Charles Stewart Parnell*. Dundalk, Ireland: University College Dublin Press, 2012.

O'Day, Alan. "Imagined Irish Communities: Networks of Social Communication of the Irish Diaspora in the United States and Britain in the Late Nineteenth and Early Twentieth Centuries." *Immigrants & Minorities* 23, nos. 2–3 (July–November 2005): 399–424.

O'Day, Alan. "Irish Diaspora Politics in Perspective: The United Irish Leagues of Great Britain and America, 1900–14." In *The Great Famine and Beyond: Irish Migrants in Britain in the*

Nineteenth and Twentieth Centuries, edited by Donald M. MacRaild, 214–39. Dublin: Irish Academic Press, 2000.

O'Day, Alan. "Irish Nationalism and Anglo-American Relations in the Later Nineteenth and Early Twentieth Centuries." In *Anglo-American Attitudes: From Revolution to Partnership*, edited by Fred M. Leventhal and Roland Quinault, 168–94. Aldershot, UK: Ashgate, 2000.

Ó Dochartaigh, Niall. *From Civil Rights to Armalites: Derry and the Birth of the Irish Troubles.* Cork: Cork University Press, 1997.

Ó Dochartaigh, Niall. "'Sure It's Hard to Keep Up with the Splits Here': Irish-American Responses to the Outbreak of Conflict in Northern Ireland, 1968–1974." *Irish Political Studies* 10, no. 1 (1995): 138–60.

O'Donnell, Edward T. *Henry George and the Crisis of Inequality: Progress and Poverty in the Gilded Age.* New York: Columbia University Press, 2015.

O'Donnell, Edward T. "'Though Not an Irishman': Henry George and the American Irish." *American Journal of Economics and Sociology* 56, no. 4 (October 1997): 407–19.

O'Donnell, Ruán. "The IRA and America during the 'Border Campaign' (1956–62)." Paper presented at the annual meeting of the American Conference for Irish Studies, New York, April 2007.

O'Donnell, Ruán. "'Liberty or Death': The United Irishmen in New South Wales, 1800–4." In *1798: A Bicentenary Perspective*, edited by Thomas Bartlett, David Dickson, Dáire Keogh, and Kevin Whelan, 607–19. Dublin: Four Courts, 2003.

O'Dowd, Mary. "O'Connell and the Lady Patriots: Women and O'Connellite Politics, 1824–1850." In *Politics and Political Culture in Britain and Ireland, 1750–1850: Essays in Tribute to Peter Jupp*, edited by Allan Blackstock and Eoin Magennis, 283–304. Belfast: Ulster Historical Foundation, 2007.

O'Dowd, Mary. "The Women in the Gallery: Women and Politics in Late Eighteenth-Century Ireland." In *From the United Irishmen to Twentieth Century Unionism: A Festschrift for A. T. Q. Stewart*, edited by Sabine Wichert, 35–47. Dublin: Four Courts, 2004.

O'Dowd, Niall. "The Awakening: Irish-America's Key Role in the Irish Peace Process." In *The Long Road to Peace in Northern Ireland: Peace Lectures from the Institute of Irish Studies at Liverpool University*, edited by Marianne Elliott, 64–74. Liverpool: Liverpool University Press, 2002.

O'Farrell, Patrick. *The Irish in Australia, 1788 to the Present.* 3rd ed. Notre Dame, IN: Notre Dame University Press, 2001.

O'Farrell, Patrick. "The Irish in Australia and New Zealand, 1791–1870." In *A New History of Ireland.* Vol. 5, *Ireland under the Union I, 1801–1870*, edited by W. E. Vaughan, 661–81. Oxford: Clarendon, 1989.

O'Ferrall, Fergus. *Catholic Emancipation: Daniel O'Connell and the Birth of Irish Democracy, 1820–1830.* Dublin: Gill and Macmillan, 1985.

Ó Gráda, Cormac. *Black '47 and Beyond: The Great Irish Famine in History, Economy, and Memory.* Princeton, NJ: Princeton University Press, 1999.

Ó Gráda, Cormac. "Fenianism and Socialism: The Career of Joseph Patrick McDonnell." *Saothar* 1 (1975): 31–41.

O'Leary, Brendan, and John McGarry. *The Politics of Antagonism: Understanding Northern Ireland.* 2nd ed. London: Athlone, 1996.

O'Malley, Kate. *Ireland, India and Empire: Indo-Irish Radical Connections, 1919–64.* Manchester, UK: Manchester University Press, 2008.

Osofsky, Gilbert. "Abolitionists, Irish Immigrants and the Dilemmas of Romantic Nationalism." *American Historical Review* 80, no. 4 (October 1975): 889–912.

O'Toole, James M. *The Faithful: A History of Catholics in America.* Cambridge, MA: Belknap Press of Harvard University Press, 2008.

Owens, Gary. "Nationalism without Words: Symbolism and Ritual Behavior in the Repeal 'Monster Meetings' of 1843–45." In *Irish Popular Culture, 1650–1850*, edited by J. S. Donnelly Jr. and Kerby A. Miller, 242–69. Dublin: Irish Academic Press, 1998.

Painter, Nell Irvin. "Black Workers from Reconstruction to the Depression." In *Working for Democracy: American Workers from the Revolution to the Present*, edited by Paul Buhle and Alan Dawley, 63–72. Urbana: University of Illinois Press, 1985.

Pašeta, Senia. *Irish Nationalist Women, 1900–1918*. New York: Cambridge University Press, 2013.

Pasley, Jeffrey L. *"The Tyranny of Printers": Newspaper Politics in the Early American Republic*. Charlottesville: University Press of Virginia, 2001.

Peskin, Lawrence A. *Manufacturing Revolution: The Intellectual Origins of Early American Industry*. Baltimore: Johns Hopkins University Press, 2003.

Phelan, Craig. *Grand Master Workman: Terence Powderly and the Knights of Labor*. Westport, CT: Greenwood, 2000.

Phillips, Kim T. "William Duane, Philadelphia's Democratic Republicans, and the Origins of Modern Politics." *Pennsylvania Magazine of History and Biography* 101, no. 33 (July 1977): 365–87.

Phillips, Kim T. "William Duane, Revolutionary Editor." PhD diss., University of California, Berkeley, 1968.

Potter, George W. *To the Golden Door: The Story of the Irish in Ireland and America*. Boston: Little, Brown, 1960.

Powers, Vincent Edward. *"Invisible Immigrants": The Pre-Famine Irish Community in Worcester, Massachusetts, from 1826 to 1860*. New York: Garland, 1989.

Prince, Simon, and Geoffrey Warner. *Belfast and Derry in Revolt: A New History of the Start of the Troubles*. Dublin: Irish Academic Press, 2011.

Purdie, Bob. *Politics in the Streets: The Origins of the Civil Rights Movement in Northern Ireland*. Belfast: Blackstaff, 1990.

Quinn, James. *John Mitchel*. Dublin: University College Dublin Press, 2008.

Quinn, James. "John Mitchel and the Rejection of the Nineteenth Century." *Eire-Ireland* 38, nos. 3–4 (Fall–Winter 2003): 90–108.

Quinn, James. "Review Article: Theobald Wolfe Tone and the Historians." *Irish Historical Studies* 32, no. 125 (May 2000): 113–28.

Quinn, James. *Soul on Fire: A Life of Thomas Russell*. Dublin: Irish Academic Press, 2002.

Quinn, James. "The United Irishmen and Social Reform." *Irish Historical Studies* 31, no. 122 (November 1998): 188–201.

Quinn, John F. "The Rise and Fall of Repeal: Slavery and Irish Nationalism in Antebellum Philadelphia." *Pennsylvania Magazine of History and Biography* 130, no. 1 (January 2006): 45–78.

Rafferty, Oliver P. *The Church, the State and the Fenian Threat, 1861–75*. New York: St. Martin's Press, 1999.

Ramón, Marta. *A Provisional Dictator: James Stephens and the Fenian Movement*. Dublin: University College Dublin Press, 2007.

Reeve, Carl, and Ann Barton Reeve. *James Connolly and the United States: The Road to the 1916 Irish Rebellion*. Atlantic Highlands, NJ: Humanities, 1978.

Regan, John M. *The Irish Counter-Revolution, 1921–1936: Treatyite Politics and Settlement in Independent Ireland*. Dublin: Gill and Macmillan, 1999.

Regan, John M. "Michael Collins, General Commanding-in-Chief, as a Historiographical Problem." *History* 92, no. 307 (July 2007): 318–46.

Regan, John M. "Southern Irish Nationalism as a Historical Problem." *Historical Journal* 50, no. 1 (March 2007): 197–223.

Reid, B. L. *The Man from New York: John Quinn and His Friends*. New York: Oxford University Press, 1968.

Riach, Douglas C. "Daniel O'Connell and American Anti-Slavery." *Irish Historical Studies* 20, no. 77 (March 1976): 3–25.

Riall, Lucy. *Garibaldi: Invention of a Hero*. New Haven, CT: Yale University Press, 2007.

Roberts, Timothy Mason. *Distant Revolutions: 1848 and the Challenge to American Exceptionalism*. Charlottesville: University of Virginia Press, 2009.

Robinson, Archie. *George Meany and His Times: A Biography*. New York: Simon and Schuster, 1981.

Robinson, Thomas P. "The Life of Thomas Addis Emmet." PhD diss., New York University, 1955.

Rodechko, James P. "An Irish-American Journalist and Catholicism: Patrick Ford of the *Irish World*." *Church History* 39, no. 4 (December 1970): 524–40.

Rodechko, James P. *Patrick Ford and His Search for America: A Case Study of Irish-American Journalism, 1870–1913*. New York: Arno, 1976.

Rodgers, Nini. "Equiano in Belfast: A Study of the Anti-Slavery Ethos in a Northern Town." *Slavery & Abolition* 18, no. 2 (August 1997): 73–89.

Rodgers, Nini. *Ireland, Slavery and Anti-Slavery: 1612–1865*. New York: Palgrave Macmillan, 2007.

Rodgers, Nini. "Richard Robert Madden: An Anti-Slavery Activist in the Americas." In *Ireland Abroad: Politics and Professions in the Nineteenth Century*, edited by Oonagh Walsh, 119–31. Dublin: Four Courts, 2003.

Roediger, David R. *The Wages of Whiteness: Race and the Making of the American Working Class*. London: Verso, 1991.

Royle, Trevor. *Crimea: The Great Crimean War, 1854–1856*. New York: St. Martin's Press, 2000.

Ryan, Desmond. *The Fenian Chief: A Biography of James Stephens*. Coral Gables, FL: University of Miami Press, 1967.

Salyer, Lucy. "Crossing Borders: Fenians and the Expatriation Crisis of the 1860s." Paper presented at the annual meeting of the Law and Society Association, Montreal, May 2008.

Samito, Christian G. *Becoming American under Fire: Irish Americans, African Americans, and the Politics of Citizenship during the Civil War Era*. Ithaca, NY: Cornell University Press, 2009.

Sammon, Peter J. "The History of the Irish National Federation of America." MA thesis, Catholic University of America, 1951.

Sarbaugh, Timothy J. "American Recognition and Eamon de Valera: The Heyday of Irish Republicanism in California, 1920–1922." *Southern California Quarterly* 69, no. 2 (Summer 1987): 133–50.

Sarbaugh, Timothy J. "Éamon de Valéra and the *Irish Press* in California, 1928–1931." *Éire-Ireland* 20, no. 4 (Winter 1985): 15–22.

Savage, Robert J. *A Loss of Innocence? Television and Irish Society, 1960–72*. Manchester, UK: Manchester University Press, 2010.

Saxton, Alexander. *The Indispensable Enemy: Labor and the Anti-Chinese Movement in California*. Berkeley: University of California Press, 1971.

Schatz, Ronald W. "American Labor and the Catholic Church, 1919–1950." *International Labor and Working Class History* 20 (Fall 1981): 46–53.

Schatz, Ronald W. "Phillip Murray and the Subordination of the Industrial Unions to the United States Government." In *Labor Leaders in America*, edited by Melvyn Dubofsky and Warren van Tine, 234–57. Urbana: University of Illinois Press, 1987.

Schneirov, Richard. *Labor and Urban Politics: Class Conflict and the Origins of Modern Liberalism in Chicago, 1864–97*. Urbana: University of Illinois Press, 1998.

Schultz, Ronald. *The Republic of Labor: Philadelphia Artisans and the Politics of Class, 1720–1830*. New York: Oxford University Press, 1993.

Senior, Hereward. *The Last Invasion of Canada: The Fenian Raids, 1866–1870*. Toronto: Dundurn, 1991.

Shain, Yossi. *Marketing the American Creed Abroad: Diasporas in the U.S. and Their Homelands*. New York: Cambridge University Press, 1999.

Shankman, Andrew. "Neither Infinite Wretchedness nor Positive Good: Mathew Carey and Henry Clay on Political Economy and Slavery during the Long 1820s." In *Contesting Slavery: The Politics of Bondage and Freedom in the New American Nation*, edited by John Craig Hammond and Matthew Mason, 247–66. Charlottesville: University of Virginia Press, 2011.

Sharrow, Walter G. "John Hughes and a Catholic Response to Slavery in Antebellum America." *Journal of Negro History* 57, no. 3 (July 1972): 254–69.

Shiels, Damian. *The Irish in the American Civil War*. Dublin: History Press Ireland, 2013.

Shumsky, Neil L. *The Evolution of Political Protest and the Workingmen's Party of California.* Columbus: Ohio State University Press, 1991.

Silvestri, Michael. *Ireland and India: Nationalism, Empire and Memory.* Basingstoke, UK: Palgrave Macmillan, 2009.

Sim, David. *A Union Forever: The Irish Question and U.S. Foreign Relations in the Victorian Age.* Ithaca, NY: Cornell University Press, 2013.

Skrbîs, Zlatko. *Long-Distance Nationalism: Diasporas, Homelands and Identities.* Aldershot, UK: Ashgate, 1999.

Slotkin, Richard. *The Fatal Environment: The Myth of the Frontier in the Age of Industrialization, 1800–1890.* Norman: University of Oklahoma Press, 1998.

Smith, Anthony D. *Nationalism:Theory, Ideology, History.* 2nd ed. Cambridge: Polity, 2010.

Smith, David J., and Gerald Chambers. *Inequality in Northern Ireland.* Oxford: Clarendon, 1991.

Smyth, James. "Dublin's Political Underground in the 1790s." In *Parliament, Politics, and People: Essays in Eighteenth-Century Irish History,* edited by Gerard O'Brien, 129–48. Dublin: Irish Academic Press, 1989.

Smyth, James. "Interpreting the 1790s." *History Ireland* 6, no. 2 (Summer 1998): 54–58.

Smyth, James. *The Men of No Property: Irish Radicals and Popular Politics in the Late Eighteenth Century.* New York: St. Martin's Press, 1992.

Snay, Mitchell. *Fenians, Freedmen, and Southern Whites: Race and Nationality in the Era of Reconstruction.* Baton Rouge: Louisiana State University Press, 2007.

Snay, Mitchell. *Horace Greeley and the Politics of Reform in Nineteenth-Century America.* Lanham, MD: Rowman and Littlefield, 2011.

Speek, Peter A. *The Singletax and the Labor Movement.* Madison: University of Wisconsin Press, 1917.

St. Mark, J. J. "Matilda and William Tone in New York and Washington after 1798." *Éire-Ireland* 22, no. 4 (Winter 1987): 4–10.

Stearns, Peter N. *Globalization in World History.* New York: Routledge, 2010.

Stedman Jones, Gareth. *Languages of Class: Studies in English Working Class History, 1932–1982.* Cambridge: Cambridge University Press, 1983.

Steward, Patrick, and Bryan P. McGovern. *The Fenians: Irish Rebellion in the North Atlantic World, 1858–1876.* Knoxville: University of Tennessee Press, 2013.

Stewart, A. T. Q. *The Summer Soldiers: The 1798 Rebellion in Antrim and Down.* Belfast: Blackstaff, 1995.

Stewart, James Brewer. *Holy Warriors: The Abolitionists and American Slavery.* Rev. ed. New York: Hill and Wang, 1996.

Tansill, Charles Callan. *America and the Fight for Irish Freedom, 1866–1922: An Old Story Based upon New Data.* New York: Devin-Adair, 1957.

Taylor, Alan. *The Civil War of 1812: American Citizens, British Subject, Irish Rebels, and Indian Allies.* New York: Knopf, 2010.

Taylor, Peter. *Behind the Mask: The IRA and Sinn Fein.* New York: TV Books, 1999.

Thomas, John L. *Alternative America: Henry George, Edward Bellamy, Henry Demarest Lloyd and the Adversary Tradition.* Cambridge, MA: Belknap Press of Harvard University Press, 1983.

Thompson, Dorothy. *The Chartists: Popular Politics in the Industrial Revolution.* New York: Pantheon, 1984.

Thompson, Dorothy. *Outsiders: Class, Gender, and Nation.* London: Verso, 1993.

Thompson, E. P. *The Making of the English Working Class.* New York: Vintage, 1966.

Thompson, J. Phillip. *Double Trouble: Black Mayors, Black Communities, and the Call for a Deep Democracy.* New York: Oxford University Press, 2006.

Thompson, Joseph E. *American Policy and Northern Ireland: A Saga of Peacebuilding.* Westport, CT: Praeger, 2001.

Thuente, Mary Helen. *The Harp Re-strung: The United Irishmen and the Rise of Irish Literary Nationalism.* Syracuse, NY: Syracuse University Press, 1994.

Tierney, Moira, director. *Matilda Tone.* 16mm film. 2005.

Toner, Peter. "Fanatic Heart of the North." In *Irish Nationalism in Canada*, edited by David A. Wilson, 34–51. Montreal: McGill-Queen's University Press, 2009.

Toner, Peter. "The 'Green Ghost': Canada's Fenians and the Raids." *Éire-Ireland* 16, no. 4 (Winter 1981): 27–47.

Tonge, Jonathan. *Northern Ireland: Conflict and Change*. 2nd ed. Harlow, UK: Longman, 2002.

Townshend, Charles. *Easter 1916: The Irish Rebellion*. London: Allen Lane, 2005.

Townshend, Charles. *Political Violence in Ireland: Government and Resistance since 1848*. New York: Oxford University Press, 1983.

Townshend, Charles. *The Republic: The Fight for Irish Independence, 1918–1923*. London: Allen Lane, 2013.

Treble, J. H. "O'Connor, O'Connell and the Attitudes of Irish Immigrants Towards Chartism in the North of England, 1838–48." In *The Victorians and Social Protest: A Symposium*, edited by John Butt and I. F. Clarke, 33–70. Hamden, CT: Archon, 1973.

Twomey, Richard J. *Jacobins and Jeffersonians: Anglo-American Radicalism in the United States, 1790–1820*. New York: Garland, 1989.

United States. *Historical Statistics of the United States, Colonial Times to 1970*. Washington: US Dept. of Commerce, Bureau of the Census, 1975.

Ural, Susannah J. *The Harp and the Eagle: Irish-American Volunteers and the Union Army, 1861–1865*. New York: New York University Press, 2006.

Waldinger, Roger. "Immigrant 'Transnationalism' and the Presence of the Past." In *From Arrival to Incorporation: Migrants to the U.S. in a Global Era*, edited by Elliott R. Barkan, Hasia Diner, and Alan M. Kraut, 267–85. New York: New York University Press, 2008.

Walkowitz, Daniel J. *Worker City, Company Town: Iron and Cotton-Worker Protest in Troy and Cohoes, New York, 1855–84*. Urbana: University of Illinois Press, 1978.

Wallace, W. Jason. *Catholics, Slaveholders, and the Dilemma of American Evangelicalism, 1835–1860*. Notre Dame, IN: University of Notre Dame Press, 2010.

Walsh, Victor A. "'A Fanatic Heart': The Cause of Irish-American Nationalism in Pittsburgh during the Gilded Age." *Journal of Social History* 15, no. 2 (Winter 1981): 187–204.

Walsh, Walter J. "Religion, Ethnicity, and History: Clues to the Cultural Construction of Law." In *The New York Irish*, edited by Ronald H. Bayor and Timothy J. Meagher, 48–69. Baltimore: Johns Hopkins University Press, 1996.

Ward, Alan J. *The Easter Rising: Revolution and Irish Nationalism*. 2nd ed. Wheeling, IL: Harlan Davidson, 2003.

Ward, Alan J. *Ireland and Anglo-American Relations, 1899–1921*. London: Weidenfeld and Nicolson, 1969.

Ward, Margaret. *Hanna Sheehy Skeffington: A Life*. Dublin: Attic, 1997.

Ward, Margaret. *Unmanageable Revolutionaries: Women and Irish Nationalism*. Reprint ed. London: Pluto, 1995.

Weber, Paul. *On the Road to Rebellion: The United Irishmen and Hamburg, 1796–1803*. Dublin: Four Courts, 1997.

Wells, Roger. *Insurrection: The British Experience, 1795–1803*. Gloucester, UK: Sutton, 1983.

Whelan, Kevin. *Fellowship of Freedom: The United Irishmen and 1798*. Cork: Cork University Press, 1998.

Whelan, Kevin. "The Green Atlantic: Radical Reciprocities between Ireland and America in the Long Eighteenth Century." In *A New Imperial History: Culture, Identity, and Modernity in Britain and the Empire, 1660–1840*, edited by Kathleen Wilson, 216–38. Cambridge: Cambridge University Press, 2004.

Whelan, Kevin. "Reinterpreting the 1798 Rebellion in County Wexford." In *The Mighty Wave: The 1798 Rebellion in Wexford*, edited by Dáire Keogh and Nicholas Furlong, 9–36. Dublin: Four Courts, 1996.

Whelan, Kevin. "The Revisionist Debate in Ireland." *boundary 2* 31, no. 1 (Spring 2004): 179–205.

Whelan, Kevin. *The Tree of Liberty: Radicalism, Catholicism and the Construction of Irish Identity, 1760–1830*. Notre Dame, IN: University of Notre Dame Press, 1996.

Whelehan, Niall. *The Dynamiters: Irish Nationalism and Political Violence in the Wider World, 1867–1900.* Cambridge: Cambridge University Press, 2012.

Whelehan, Niall, ed. *Transnational Perspectives on Modern Irish History.* New York: Routledge, 2015.

Whitaker, Anne-Maree. *Unfinished Revolution: United Irishmen in New South Wales, 1800–1810.* Sydney: Crossing Press, 1994.

Whyte, John Henry. *Interpreting Northern Ireland.* Oxford: Clarendon, 1990.

Wiener, Jon. *Gimme Some Truth: The John Lennon FBI Files.* Berkeley: University of California Press, 1999.

Wilentz, Sean. *Chants Democratic: New York City and the Rise of the American Working Class, 1788–1850.* New York: Oxford University Press, 1984.

Wilentz, Sean. *The Rise of American Democracy: Jefferson to Lincoln.* New York: Norton, 2005.

Wilson, Andrew J. *Irish America and the Ulster Conflict, 1968–1995.* Washington, DC: Catholic University of America Press, 1995.

Wilson, David A. *The Irish in Canada.* Ottawa: Canadian Historical Association, 1989.

Wilson, David A. *Thomas D'Arcy McGee.* 2 vols. Montréal: McGill-Queen's University Press, 2008–11.

Wilson, David A. "The United Irishmen and the Re-invention of Irish America." In *1798: A Bicentenary Perspective,* edited by Thomas Bartlett, David Dickson, Dáire Keogh, and Kevin Whelan, 634–41. Dublin: Four Courts, 2003.

Wilson, David A. *United Irishmen, United States: Immigrant Radicals in the Early Republic.* Ithaca, NY: Cornell University Press, 1998.

Wilson, Tom. *Ulster: Conflict and Consent.* Oxford, UK: Blackwell, 1989.

Williams, Robert C. *Horace Greeley: Champion of American Freedom.* New York: New York University Press, 2006.

Wood, Gordon S. *Empire of Liberty: A History of the Early Republic, 1789–1815.* New York: Oxford University Press, 2009.

Woods, C. J. "Historical Revision: Was O'Connell a United Irishman?" *Irish Historical Studies* 35, No. 138 (November 2006): 173–83.

Woods, C. J. "R. R. Madden, Historian of the United Irishmen." In *1798: A Bicentenary Perspective,* edited by Thomas Bartlett, David Dickson, Dáire Keogh, and Kevin Whelan, 497–511. Dublin: Four Courts, 2003.

Wright, Frank. *Northern Ireland: A Comparative Analysis.* Dublin: Gill and Macmillan, 1987.

Young, Robert J. C. *Postcolonialism: An Historical Introduction.* Oxford: Blackwell, 2001.

Zagarri, Rosemarie. *Revolutionary Backlash: Women and Politics in the Early American Republic.* Philadelphia: University of Pennsylvania Press, 2007.

Zieger, Robert H. "George Meany: Labor's Organization Man." In *Labor Leaders in America,* edited by Melvyn Dubofsky and Warren van Tine, 324–49. Urbana: University of Illinois Press, 1987.

INDEX

AARIR. *See* American Association for the Recognition of the Irish Republic
abolition movement, 235n21
  African Americans in, 72–73, 76
  in Britain, 13–14, 70, 82
  Fenians and, 101
  Ford's work for, 119–21
  Garrison's work in, 70–72, 73, 75, 120
  in Ireland, 72
  newspapers and media on, 70–71, 233n62
  O'Connell's work in, 70–72, 74–77, 81, 233n54, 233n62, 233n65
  repeal movement with, 71, 72, 73–77, 81, 232n39, 233n54
  Young Ireland's stand on, 81
ACIF. *See* American Congress for Irish Freedom
Act of Union, 35, 50. *See also* repeal movement
Acton, Lord, 1, 4, 7
Adams, Gerry, 2, 206, 207, 211–17
Adams, John, 41
AFIN. *See* American Friends of Irish Neutrality
AFL. *See* American Federation of Labor
Africa, 141–42, 208–9, 210
African American longshoremen, 157–59
African Americans, 46, 120, 122. *See also* abolition movement; racial discrimination
  apartheid protests by, 208–9, 210
  civil rights movement for, 189, 193–94, 199–201, 209–10, 216, 246n3
  discrimination parallels of Catholics and, 190, 194
  protest and support for Irish causes from, 157–59, 243n30
agrarian reform and revolution, 58, 83, 94, 109. *See also* Home Rule movement; Land League; Land War
  Davitt's work on, 111–12, 118–19, 140
  New Departure on, 112–18, 123–26
  poverty with land monopoly and, 115–16

US labor movement and, 116, 117
Ahern, Bertie, 214, 217, 218, 219–20
American Association for the Recognition of the Irish Republic (AARIR), 150, 161–62, 168–69, 177–78, 186
American Civil War, 101–2
American Congress for Irish Freedom (ACIF), 199, 200
"American Eagle" speech, 78–79, 81
American Federation of Labor (AFL), 126, 151, 183
American Friends of Irish Neutrality (AFIN), 184–85, 246n47
American Provisional Committee for Ireland, 85–86
American Revolution, 10, 15, 80
Americans for a New Irish Agenda (ANIA), 211–12
American Women Pickets, 156–57, 158, 159–60
Anglo-Irish Treaty. *See also* Free State government; Northern Ireland
  Boundary Commission of, 165, 174, 175, 244n5
  Clan's division on, 176, 179–80, 182
  details of, 165–66
  division in IRA on, 166–68
  Irish American division over, 168–69, 171, 172, 175–78, 245n21
  non-Irish opposition to, 170–71
  protest and demonstrations of, 172
Anglo-Irish War. *See* Irish War of Independence
Anglophobia, 66, 231n29, 235n9
ANIA. *See* Americans for a New Irish Agenda
anti-colonialism, 40, 121–22, 140–41, 160–61, 239n26
anti-imperialism, 153–54, 160–61, 170, 181, 245n41
anti-Semitism, 168, 172, 185, 244n12
anti-slavery societies, 70, 71, 72, 75, 81, 82